JOSS WHEDON

GEEK KING OF THE UNIVERSE

A BIOGRAPHY

BY AMY PASCALE

FOREWORD BY NATHAN FILLION

Aurum
Press

First published in Great Britain
2014 by Aurum Press Ltd
74—77 White Lion Street
Islington
London N1 9PF
www.aurumpress.co.uk

A catalogue record for this book is
available from the British Library.

ISBN 978 1 84513 719 9

1 3 5 7 9 10 8 6 4 2
2014 2016 2018 2017 2015

Interior design: PerfecType, Nashville, TN
Printed and bound by CPI Group (UK) Ltd, Croydon, CR0 4YY

To Bronzers everywhere

"Bottom line is, even if you see 'em coming, you're not ready for the big moments. No one asks for their life to change, not really. But it does. So what are we, helpless? Puppets? No. The big moments are gonna come. You can't help that. It's what you do afterwards that counts. That's when you find out who you are."

—Whistler, "Becoming, Part 1"

// CONTENTS //

Foreword by Nathan Fillion vii

Introduction 1

1 A Family of Storytellers **9**

2 "Being British" in the Land of Shakespeare (and Giles)....... **23**

3 Crash Course in Television **37**

4 The Blonde in the Alley Fights Back **51**

5 The World Upends **57**

6 To Infinity and Beyond: *Toy Story* and *Alien: Resurrection*... **69**

7 *Buffy:* Resurrection **87**

8 *Buffy* Premieres **103**

9 The Bronze **115**

10 The *Buffy* Way **121**

11 Front-Page News.. **135**

12 Growing Up: *Angel*.. **145**

13 A New Challenge: Silence..................................... **157**

14 Shakespeare Fanboy... **165**

15 Buffy Goes Back to High School **173**

16 Once More, with Feeling...................................... **181**

17 We Aim to Misbehave: *Firefly*............................... **199**

18 Curse Your Sudden but Inevitable Cancellation **211**

19 End of (*Buffy's*) Days **223**

20 An Astonishing Return to His Roots **231**

21 Not Fade Away **237**

22 Grant Me the Serenity **247**

23 Election 2004 .... **251**

24 I Wrote My Thesis on You **257**

25 *Serenity* Lands **261**

26 Strong Female Characters **265**

27 A New Way of Storytelling **279**

28 WGA Writers' Strike **285**

29 Doctor Horrible, I Presume **297**

30 *Dollhouse* **311**

31 *The Cabin in the Woods* **319**

32 Fanboy Dreams Come True: *The Avengers* **329**

33 *Buffy* Lives, Again? **341**

34 Avengers Assemble **345**

35 Something Personal: *Much Ado About Nothing* **357**

36 The Year of Joss Whedon **371**

37 The Year of Joss Whedon, Again (Really) **381**

Acknowledgments **388**

Notes **391**

Bibliography **416**

Index **430**

// FOREWORD //

My generation, we were kind of raised on the super-cool, "I can handle anything" with a gun in his hand hero. Any situation you throw at him, he can handle it—with catchphrases. It was very cool.

But Joss Whedon's version of a hero doesn't always win. He loses more than he wins, and when he wins, the victories are tiny, but he takes 'em. "That's a victory! I call that a victory!" It's a tiny victory—he takes it, and that's what he walks away with. And that's something I can actually relate to.

That's something that people can relate to—because that's actually life. I don't know a lot of people who win more than they lose. Life is kind of a losing proposition as you go. It's not all winning lotteries every day. It's a lot of "What do I do with this problem? Now how do I handle this?" I think people can relate easier to someone who isn't prepared to handle every single situation, and everything comes out roses and their way, and all they've got to do is be cool. We don't have that in real life.

A friend of mine once told me that what he finds so satisfying about Joss Whedon is his way of telling stories. As a society, we are incredibly story literate: We know story. This is the hero; this is the villain. This is the denouement; this is where the twist comes; this is where the learning experience is; this is where the turn is. We know story.

He said, "Joss Whedon will give you a story twist. But instead of twisting it to the story tradition that we know, he twists it and says, 'That's what happens in stories. This is what happens in real life. This is how real life went.'"

I described Joss to a friend as we were on our way over to his house for a party. And she's heard me tell stories over the years about this fellow. We went to his house, we had a great time, and on the way home, she said, "You know, I got to say, from your description of the kind of guy this guy is, and from all the stories you've told me—I expected him to be six two, chiseled jaw, long, wavy golden hair and bright blue eyes and gleaming teeth, and just chesty and . . ." The guy, she said, "when you describe him, he's so heroic."

And yeah, he is. He's heroic like that.

NATHAN FILLION

// INTRODUCTION //

In June 2011, Joss Whedon stepped onto the set of *The Avengers*. He was just over a month into shooting on Marvel's highly anticipated, high-profile comic book movie, with a $220 million budget and a plethora of A-list talent who came to the table with their own high expectations, and it would have been fair to wonder whether he was up for the task. This wasn't Joss's first time directing, but his only other feature film was 2005's *Serenity*, a big-screen continuation of his short-lived sci-fi western series *Firefly*. *Serenity*'s budget was $39 million, and it pulled in just $25.5 million at the US box office and barely broke even worldwide.

Joss certainly had the geek cred for his *other* role on the project, as the screenwriter behind *The Avengers*' script. A lifelong Marvel Comics fan-boy who'd attended his first comic convention while still in grade school, he had a deep understanding of the superhero universe in which the film was set. He'd had his own run writing comic books—and of course, he was the acclaimed writer/producer behind such cult television hits as *Buffy the Vampire Slayer*. His TV work had given him experience handling a large ensemble cast like that of *The Avengers*, and he'd directed nearly forty television episodes.

But in television, if you make a mistake, there's always next week. That isn't the case with a blockbuster movie featuring some of the world's most beloved superheroes. So no one would have faulted Joss if he'd been panicked or overwhelmed by the project—or if, on the umpteenth grimy day of shooting, when everything had been covered in ash from daily explosions, he'd been a little bit short or impatient with me, his interviewer.

Instead, as I wished him well, Joss stopped me. "There is a tiny story that I want to tell you," he said.

"My wife is from Barnstable [Massachusetts], and we went with our friends to the Barnstable County Fair one night. We got on this ride that spins—you go up high to the side in a circle, and then you go the other way. The guy at the controls can switch directions and mess around. It's not for kids.

"Near me was this ten-year-old girl with her older friend, and she was clearly not ready and terrified. I wanted so badly to help, but there wasn't anything that I could do. 'Hey, there's a creepy old man talking to me.' That's weird.

"So I was sitting there watching her, and I felt so bad, because she's got that face. I know that face—I wear it most days when I go to work. Everyone was like, 'Whee, having fun!' and she's gripping [her seat] with this death grip. And then gradually she starts to let go a little bit, starts to swing into it. By the end, she has completely mastered it; she is screaming 'Whee!' and she has her hands up—she's completely comfortable. And I just . . . my head just exploded.

"I just watched someone get stronger. Just watched that girl get stronger, and I was like, that's the purest moment of my life. That's the real deal. That is everything I ever want with what I'm doing, but to have somebody do it for themselves would be better. It was pretty extraordinary.

"That's my story. That's the story of my life. . . .

"And now I must go and blow shit up."

///////////

That's the story I have come back to time and time again while writing Joss Whedon's biography. It's the story that came to mind nearly a year later, when I found myself on a bus, sitting next to a man who, twenty years earlier, had broken into my house. I'd woken up to find him sitting at the end of the couch where I was sleeping, and his actions had haunted me for the two decades that followed. I sat there on the bus, overwhelmed and cycling through a flurry of emotions as I tried to decide what I should do—get up and walk away and try not to break down, or confront him and finally let it go. Even though I had friends a few seats away, I alone had to make a decision that would help define me for the next two decades.

I thought about the girl Joss had watched get stronger on her own, and I realized that this was that kind of moment for me. Then I thought about all the characters Joss had created, ones I had loved since I started watching *Buffy the Vampire Slayer* in 1998. I flashed to a moment that so clearly defined his most iconic hero: in the episode "Becoming, Part 2," Buffy battles with Angel, her vampire ex-boyfriend, who is determined to literally send the world into hell, while reveling in every moment in which he can rip the Slayer into emotional shreds in the process. He knocks the sword from her hand, towering over her on the ground, and taunts her, telling her that she has nothing left in her arsenal to win this fight—no weapons, no friends, and no hope. "Take all that away," he asks, "and what's left?" As he lunges his sword at her head, the final physical betrayal by the man she loved, Buffy grabs it between her hands and answers, simply, "Me."

Joss's stories are often centered on moments just like this. He shares a conversation that he had with Stephen Sondheim, in which they were discussing the stories each of them tells. Joss said he was always going to write about adolescent girls with superpowers. Sondheim replied, "And I will always write about yearning." "Goddammit, his answer was so much cooler than mine!" Joss says—but Sondheim's answer pushed him to break down his own tales and figure out what his driving impetus was, what he was really writing about.

"*Helplessness* was what I realized was sort of the basic thing," Joss explains. "All of these empowerment stories come from my fear and hatred of the idea of somebody who is really helpless, who is a non-being."

Joss felt helpless as a boy, a small, slight child and the youngest of three brothers. He felt helpless and invisible in his first solo trip away from his mother's comforting home and into a British boarding school, where he was the only new kid and the only American. He felt helpless in his first job at the groundbreaking feminist television series *Roseanne*, because he never felt like his voice was being heard. And so, inspired by the comic books he'd loved since he was a child, filled with superheroes both spectacular and flawed, he created a superhero of his own: Buffy Summers, the blonde girl who walks into an alley alone like the helpless victim of countless horror movies—only to walk out victorious against the monsters that tried to kill her.

But the feelings of powerlessness continued when the original film version of *Buffy the Vampire Slayer* was released. Buffy's tale was not told the way Joss had planned, and she did not become the inspiration that he had hoped. Fortunately, four years later Joss was given the chance to revive his girl hero in a new medium—television—in which he would have full control over the story. He gave the character one thing that had eluded her in the film: a group of friends who supported her emotionally and in battle. With new characters as well-drawn and well-developed as the hero, *Buffy* found success, just as its hero succeeded again and again in saving the world.

All of Joss's heroes create a family out of friends, whether it's the titular character of the *Buffy* spin-off *Angel*, whose struggle for redemption hinges on allowing others in to help after years of wallowing in self-hatred, or Captain Mal Reynolds of *Firefly*, whose ragtag crew of mercenaries choose to stay together and support one another. To Joss, this is a bond stronger than blood.

It's how he himself has thrived through those continued moments of helplessness—the swift cancellation of *Firefly*, a Writers Guild strike that shut down Hollywood. He surrounds himself with a community of creative collaborators, people he has worked with before and trusts the most to help him through every project. Their support allows him to shrug off his defeats within "the system," and embrace a sort of naïveté wherein he readily admits that he doesn't know what he's doing but does it anyway, in a way that makes him happy.

This community—this chosen family—consists not just of writers and actors but of fans as well. Especially fans. They're the ones who kept *Buffy* on the air and gave him a space to engage in smart and passionate discussions about his stories, who raised money for charity while celebrating their love for *Firefly*. The conversation started more than sixteen years ago on a bare-bones website for a low-rated cult series on a baby network, and Joss has continued it to this day, allowing his fans to share in his heartbreaks as well as his triumphs, just as they share in his characters' victories and failures, their pain and their joy. Through Joss's stories, and his own story, his fans find the inspiration to make it through their own life struggles.

Today at any comic convention, black T-shirts that proudly declare Joss Whedon Is My Master Now dot the crowds. Even more fans of all ages, races, and genders are clad in costumes from the Whedonverse: Dr. Horrible. Captain Reynolds, Jayne, and Kaylee from *Firefly*. Spike and Illyria from *Angel*. For Joss's fans, it's not enough to simply declare their love; they need to wear their adoration like a neon badge for the world to see. They also don these costumes for strength—the personal strength that comes from connecting so intensely with a character that the fans also feel more comfortable in their own skin.

//////////

After fighting back from the brink of hopelessness and saving the world in the aforementioned "Becoming, Part 2," Buffy runs away to Los Angeles, hoping to escape both her responsibilities and her grief over the loss of her beloved Angel. She wants to disappear into the masses, but ends up trapped in a demon dimension with other lost souls. The captives are beaten down by demon slave drivers until they answer the question "Who are you?" with "I'm no one."

When it's her turn to answer, she again finds the inner strength she had doubted: "I'm Buffy, the Vampire Slayer. And you are?" It's a funny moment, and Sarah Michelle Gellar plays the comedy of it perfectly. Yet the humor masks the inspirational power of that scene. In a world that wants to make you invisible, there is such strength in declaring who you are and that you are worthy of the identity you choose. Buffy owns her destiny, with all the responsibilities and challenges that she knows will come with it. She announces that she is not only the Slayer but, even more consequentially, "*Buffy*, the Vampire Slayer." It is not just her title the world needs to know; it's the person that she is.

It may seem like a small win, especially compared to heading off multiple apocalypses, but it is just as important as every battle she fights over *Buffy*'s seven seasons. And while Joss's fans might not be able to take on a giant demon snake on their graduation day like Buffy Summers, they can demand to be seen and make their own statement about who they are. Like the ten-year-old girl in Joss's story, they can find unknown strength within themselves to conquer their fears. Like Joss and all his characters, they can find friends and build a community to create something better in the world.

It's why so many people are drawn to Joss's work. Because being special is not about being a Chosen One. All of his characters, whether they're super smart or super strong or just "ordinary" people, are both troubled and capable of great heroism—as are we all. In 2014, an American television show interviewed Russians about their country's oppressive laws against the LGBT community. To explain what had inspired her decision to protest these laws, one woman quoted a line from *Angel*: "If nothing we do matters, then all that matters is what we do."

//////////

In Joss's hands, *The Avengers*, too, became a tale of restored hope and chosen family. The film's superhero team, he said, are people who "should not even be in the same room, let alone on the same team. And that, to me, is the very definition of family." Joss took the reins of one of the highest-profile blockbusters of the year and turned it into an intimate personal story. And he was rewarded with the highest box office grosses of 2012—over $1.5 billion worldwide. Joss will revisit this dysfunctional family in a 2015 sequel, and as he prepares for the film, he'll simultaneously oversee its TV spin-off *Agents of S.H.I.E.L.D*, Marvel's first US network series since *The Incredible Hulk* went off the air in 1982.

And while fans will no doubt be heartbroken if the series fails to find an audience, they can take solace in the fact that Joss Whedon's career is a testament to defeat. The defeated, like Buffy and Mal Reynolds, face every challenge and celebrate every victory along the way, even if the final battle doesn't go their way. The defeated do not fail, because they keep on fighting.

For much of his life, Joss Whedon has been struck down by defeat far more often than he climbed the winner's podium. Before he was known for creating a feminist icon or directing the third most successful blockbuster film of all time, Joss was a lonely kid who thought that if he could just crack the code, people would understand what an awesome person he was and love him for it. As *Buffy* executive producer and *Angel* cocreator David Greenwalt said, "If Joss Whedon had had one good day in high school, we wouldn't be here."

And if he hadn't landed in Los Angeles after college, broke and jobless and living with his father, he wouldn't have found a champion in the elder Whedon, who encouraged him to bypass the traditional path to Hollywood success. If he hadn't been let down by his first job, on *Roseanne*, he wouldn't have learned how the choices producers make can either unite or divide a set, or that it can be good to walk away from what you thought was your dream job. If *Buffy* the film had been a hit, there would most likely not have been *Buffy* the television series—nor Joss Whedon the director, a role he honed on the *Buffy* series after an initial terrible experience with a crew who didn't like him. If the Writers Guild strike hadn't shut down Joss's work on his Fox series *Dollhouse*, he wouldn't have had the time to discuss web series ideas with his younger brother and his fiancée, which led to *Dr. Horrible's Sing-Along Blog* and a new model for launching original creative content online.

And if all of these failures had been avoided, the world would be bereft of Joss's characters. And without them, many people might not have found touchstones of strength and guidance to help them through hard times. Without Joss and Buffy, I, personally, would not have found the fortitude and bravery to confront the man next to me on the bus—to tell him what he had done, so that I could leave that twenty-year burden with him and finally move on.

Even with an impressive résumé that includes the highest-grossing blockbuster of 2012, two beloved cult series, and significant contributions to several pop culture phenomena, Joss still loses more than he wins. But like his heroes, Joss Whedon not only counts his victories, no matter how small, but shows how his defeats can be counted as wins too.

1

A FAMILY OF STORYTELLERS

Much has been made of Joss Whedon's ability to reinvent modern storytelling. First, he upended the "blonde girl trapped in an alley" horror trope with the 1992 film *Buffy the Vampire Slayer*. Five years later, his "high school is hell" approach to the *Buffy* TV series reignited both teenage dramas and sci-fi/fantasy television. Most recently, he assembled a bunch of outsiders into *The Avengers*, or as it's been called, "the perfect comic-book movie." But he wasn't the first in his family to find success in Hollywood. He wasn't even the second.

Joseph Hill Whedon—he would name himself "Joss" in college—was the third son of Ann Lee Jeffries Whedon, a teacher and author, and Thomas Avery Whedon, a television writer who worked on *Captain Kangaroo*, *The Electric Company*, and *The Golden Girls*. His paternal grandfather, John Ogden Whedon, wrote for such classic TV series as *The Donna Reed Show*, *The Andy Griffith Show*, and *The Dick Van Dyke Show*.

In the mid-1920s, John Whedon left his hometown of New York City and headed up the East Coast to Cambridge, Massachusetts, to attend Harvard University. The school would graduate several members of the Whedon family: Burt Denison Whedon, John's father, received a bachelor of laws degree in 1903; John's brother, Roger, graduated in 1929; and John was in the class of 1927. Both John and Roger focused on writing and were named to the literary board of the famed undergraduate humor magazine the *Harvard Lampoon*. John was elected president of the *Harvard Lampoon* in 1926 and was a member of another long-lived Harvard institution: the Hasty Pudding Club.

The oldest collegiate social club in America, which counted Theodore Roosevelt, Franklin D. Roosevelt, and John F. Kennedy among its members, the group staged musicals that were completely written, composed, and produced by students. In the spring of his senior year, John Whedon was chosen to collaborate on *Gentlemen, the Queen*, the eighty-first annual production of Hasty Pudding Theatricals.

After graduation, John returned to New York and started writing and editing for several magazines, including the *Forum, Harper's Magazine, Collier's Weekly*, and the brand-new *New Yorker*, where he later served as managing editor. There he penned Comment essays, Talk of the Town vignettes about life in the city, political commentaries, features, and short stories. John also found a bride, a woman who shared his love for skillfully crafted words and performance.

Louise Carroll Angell had been deeply involved with the drama club at Pelham Memorial High School in Pelham, New York. In her junior year, she won a rave review from the local paper for her starring turn as Katherine in Shakespeare's *Taming of the Shrew*. The year prior, she directed *The Silver Lining* by Constance D'Arcy Mackay, a one-act play that is set in Victorian England and follows Frances "Fanny" Burney as she wrote *Evelina: Or the History of a Young Lady's Entrance into the World*. Burney's novel was noted for its flawed female protagonist, who determines her own path in a harsh and antagonistic world. Carroll made her own way up to Vassar, one of the all-female Seven Sisters colleges of the Northeast, where she served as the editor in chief of the school's principal student publication, *Miscellany News*, during the 1930–31 school year. On June 12, 1931, three days after her graduation, she wed John, and they settled into a Greenwich Village apartment on West Tenth Street, a few blocks from Washington Square Park.

Thomas Avery Whedon was born just over a year later, on August 3, 1932; a daughter, Julia, came four years after. John and Carroll moved their small family out of the Village and in with John's parents in the Jamaica Estates section of Queens, New York. The extended family lived together in a two-story home on Croydon Road. John and his father commuted into Manhattan—Burt to the law firm of Wing & Russell, his son to the *New Yorker*.

By 1939 John had moved into radio, writing for NBC. He worked on Rudy Vallée's variety show, as well as *The Chase and Sanborn Hour* and *Tommy Riggs and Betty Lou*, before taking a lead role writing for the popular comedy *The Great Gildersleeve* in August 1942. There, with writing partner Sam Moore, he was credited with developing more serialized storytelling for the series and expanding the supporting characters to create a "vivid, realistic image of wartime small-town America." Carroll entered the radio business as well, joining CBS in 1941 as copy chief in advertising and sales promotion. After five years with *The Great Gildersleeve*, John once again brought his writing to the stage, and his musical *Texas, Lil' Darlin* (cowritten by Moore, with lyrics by Johnny Mercer) bowed on Broadway on November 25, 1949.

Tom remembered the daily commitment his father made to his craft. "When I was a child, my father wrote at home," he said. "He locked himself in the study, and no one was allowed in there. He worked a real nine-to-five day, and he'd break out for lunch for a half-hour. I kept hearing the typewriter going all the time. The 40 years that I was an active member of the Writers Guild, everything I wrote was on a manual typewriter. That sound was important to me."

//////////

In his teens, Tom attended Phillips Exeter Academy, a then-male-only private preparatory school in New Hampshire. By the time he graduated in 1951, his father had changed his media outlet to television. John started writing for *Lux Video Theatre*, a spin-off of the radio show in which Hollywood stars performed original comedy and dramatic teleplays. But his success was hindered by the witch hunt of the US House of Representatives' Un-American Activities Committee (HUAC). Created in 1938, HUAC investigated people and organizations suspected of having links to Communism or other supposedly subversive ties. In October 1947, the committee held nine days of hearings interrogating over forty people about the alleged Communist propaganda and influence in the motion picture industry. More than three hundred individuals were blacklisted by the studios, with a particular focus on screenwriters who were seen as disseminating Soviet and Communist propaganda through their scripts.

HUAC held a second Hollywood investigation in 1951, pushing many of those under investigation to cooperate by naming others with Communist involvement. When one of them implicated a writer John had worked with on *Gildersleeve*, John himself was blacklisted as well. His agent recommended that he relocate to the West Coast full time in hopes that the blacklist wouldn't follow him. By this time, he and Carroll were living separately; they would finalize their divorce in August 1954.

John's move paid off. He spent the next decade writing in Hollywood for such series as the television version of *The Great Gildersleeve*, *Kraft Television Theatre* (for which he received an Emmy nomination), *Leave It to Beaver*, *The Donna Reed Show*, *The Andy Griffith Show*, and *The Dick Van Dyke Show*.

//////////

Tom Whedon did not move to California with his father, as he had been accepted into Harvard University's class of 1957. In Cambridge, Tom both showed off his athletic prowess on the lacrosse field and made a big impression on the Harvard stage. Like his father years earlier, he cowrote the book for the Hasty Pudding musical, 1953's *Ad Man Out*. In addition to his time with Hasty Pudding Theatricals, he expanded his range through his work in the Harvard Radcliffe Dramatic Club (HRDC).

At the time, Harvard did not admit women into its undergraduate studies program, but it was closely connected to Radcliffe, one of the Seven Sisters women's colleges. Radcliffe was considered a school of the arts; by the early 1900s, its women had established groups to put on theatrical performances of their own. Students took on every facet of production, from writing scripts and scores to building sets and directing. As Harvard often had men playing women's roles, Radcliffe women played heroic, dramatic, and romantic male roles. Until World War I, men were completely forbidden to perform in Radcliffe shows.

However, in 1955, Radcliffe's main outlet for theatrical and artistic expression, the Idler Club, was shuttered, halfway through the schooling of undergrad Lee Jeffries. An English major with a desire to be on stage, Lee wasn't deterred—she forged ahead, taking active roles in every possible performance put on by various dramatic groups at Radcliffe's brother school, Harvard, including the HRDC. She was soon cast in several musicals and plays, including *The Seagull* and *Alice in Wonderland*, the latter directed by Tom Whedon. Tom performed in those plays and other HRDC productions as well; he and Lee even appeared opposite each other in the club's first musical outing, *Great to Be Back!*, scoring two of the few accolades for the performance in the Harvard school paper's review of the production: "Lee Jeffries and Thomas Whedon were the stalwarts of the cast. . . . Miss Jeffries was the only reason for including a tired sequence about planned amusement at the beach, and Whedon met every demand of the evening good-humoredly and ably."

The pairing continued offstage. "My mother . . . was extremely intelligent and witty," Joss said. "I think that's what attracted her and my father in the first place." In May 1959, Lee and Tom were married in her home state of Kentucky. Her father, James Harvey Jeffries, a Jewel Tea salesman and another Harvard grad, was living in Louisville with his second wife, Margaret. Her mother, Anna Lee Hill Jeffries, had died in August 1954, five years before her daughter married.

The Whedons had already relocated from Cambridge to New York City, where Lee was on the administrative staff at Finch College. Finch was a girls' finishing school that had gotten its accreditation as a baccalaureate liberal arts college seven years before Lee joined the staff. It was founded in 1900 by Jessica Garretson Finch (later Cosgrave), a women's rights activist who campaigned for suffrage; feeling that her undergraduate studies at Barnard left her without any practical skills, she was determined to establish a secondary school that would give women a well-rounded education and also prepare them to enter the working world. Lee also had a professional life in the theater. She worked at the American Academy of Dramatic Arts and took her skills as a musical comedy singer off-Broadway in *Oklahoma!*, *Finian's Rainbow*, *Bus Stop*, and *Riders to the Sea*.

Years earlier, Tom had told his father that he had no intention of becoming a writer, because it was too hard. John had responded, "You're gonna be a writer." Sure enough, Tom kept his Harvard-honed theatrical skills sharp, penning musicals such as *All Kinds of Giants* and *Money* that eventually found runs off-Broadway.

The couple had an apartment in an "Italian Renaissance-palazzo-style building" on West End Avenue on the Upper West Side of Manhattan. A year after they wed, in May 1960, son Samuel arrived; Matthew Thomas was born in February 1962. That same year, Tom started writing for the children's show *Captain Kangaroo*.

It was difficult working with the temperamental Bob Keeshan, who played the titular captain, and soon Tom realized how that stress seeped into his family life. Just as he had listened to his father typing away when he was a young boy, his oldest son, Sam, mimicked his father's daily habits. "We were living in a Westside apartment with a long hall. . . . I came out one day, and my son was marching up and down the hall, saying 'Shit, fuck, shit, fuck,'" Tom said. "He had been listening to his father write."

Perhaps it was no surprise when Tom left the series after three years, moving on in 1964 to develop a TV pilot with writing partner Jon Stone and Jim Henson for a series in which Henson's puppets would retell the Cinderella story from their point of view. (The project would not be picked up, but Henson later redeveloped the idea into the 1969 television special *Hey Cinderella!*)

//////////

Joseph Hill Whedon was born on June 23, 1964, on Midsummer's Eve—a date that was probably notable to Lee, a Shakespeare lover who staged readings with friends and family after Thanksgiving dinners. The youngest of the three boys, Joss often felt that he was much smaller and more vulnerable than everyone else. "Was I the weak person who got pounded on? Oh, totally! I was little and cute. I was actually mistaken for a girl very often, because I had lovely, flowing red hair," Joss says. "Let us take a moment to remember my lovely, flowing red hair!"

Whether it was his delicate features or delicate sensibilities, Joss was often intimidated by the world around him. "Something that I've felt very much as a child was a fear of patriarchy and anybody bigger than me, like my brothers or my father," he says. He considered his brothers "charming, but merciless" and his father "an incredibly dear man" who was "not necessarily great with kids."

Joss's relationship with his father found common ground in a surprising source: the words and music of Stephen Sondheim. His musicals scored the story of the Whedon home and were a way for Tom to connect with his son. "Some fathers can't really talk to their sons, but they can throw a baseball," Joss said. "We'd throw on all the Sondheim albums."

Joss had a far less tenuous relationship with his mother, in whom he found an "extremely outspoken, strong and loving" exemplar. "She was very smart, uncompromising, cool as hell," Joss recalled. "You had to prove yourself—not that she wouldn't come through if you didn't, but she expected you to hold your own." Lee was also a strong role model for many of the children who came through her classroom at Riverdale Country School, a private primary/secondary school in an affluent section of the Bronx where she began teaching history when Joss was four. Her son was enrolled in the school himself beginning in the first grade.

Lee's feminist leanings started to come through early in her tenure at Riverdale. Though the institution's upper grades were divided into a school for boys and a school for girls, and she'd been hired to teach at the latter, she was a member of the department that started holding the first academic classes that mixed students from the girls' school and the boys' school. In addition to teaching American and European history, she also developed courses on feminism and women in literature, and her other classes ranged from British Authors to Heroes and Anti-Heroes to Socialist and Communist Thought. With another teacher, she created a social studies course in which students studied educational theory, visited schools, and for their final exam, designed their own ideal schools.

Drama was another of Lee's great loves that she brought to her career at Riverdale. She created opportunities for students and teachers to work together onstage as well as in the classroom, directing joint student-faculty productions of plays by Brecht, Tennessee Williams, and others and even performing in several plays herself over the years, including Sondheim's *A Little Night Music*. She directed all-student casts as well, and the student production of Jane Martin's *Talking With* was so successful that she managed to arrange a public showcase production at Symphony Space in Manhattan.

Lee's model of strength and nurturance was a source of comfort for young Joss, who called upon her example to shield his own vulnerability. Joss began to take an interest in female characters, and to be excited by stories in which the girl was "let into the club." He also retreated frequently into his imagination, creating his own stories for his toys and regaling his mother with little strange tales.

////////////

By 1970, Tom Whedon was writing for *The Dick Cavett Show*, ABC's late-night alternative to NBC's *The Tonight Show Starring Johnny Carson*. Joss's home was often filled with his father's fellow comedy writers, along with other friends of his parents who were actors, artists, and teachers. Later that year, Tom left late night after being "lured back" to children's television. Tom's former writing partner Jon Stone had continued to work with Jim Henson following the failure of their Cinderella project, and he had gone on to become one of the original producers of Henson's *Sesame Street*. Now Stone was working with the Children's Television Workshop to develop a new educational series for PBS geared toward older children. *The Electric Company* would be less about Muppets and more about sketch comedy. (Bill Cosby, Rita Moreno, and Morgan Freeman would be early stars of the series.) Tom joined the project as head writer.

Electric Company writers poured into the Whedons' Upper West Side apartment to continue working on the show's development after business hours. They would arrive starting in the early evening and might stay all night, their writing and planning often fueled by alcohol. "There were always eight or ten or fifteen of us exchanging views and jokes and ideas, and sipping vodka and laughing till all hours," said Jon Stone.

Young Joss loved it. He soaked up the energy and creative spirit of his parents and their friends, often enlisting them as his audience. "While I really enjoyed all of the funny things my dad was working on, it was really just being *around* someone who was that funny. And all of his friends were comedy writers. So the house was constantly filled with these very sweet, erudite, intelligent guys just trying to crack jokes," he said. "It just had a great air to it, and what you wanted to do is go into that room and make those guys laugh."

It was with great excitement that Joss discovered that he *could* make people laugh. "There were times when I didn't feel as though I was getting attention I deserved, and I learned that if you said something funny, people would stop and listen," he said.

//////////

The Electric Company, with Tom at the helm, premiered on October 25, 1971. At Riverdale, Lee played a strong role in the movement that led to the merging of the boys' and girls' schools into one coed institution in 1972. Perhaps the stress of two enormous undertakings was too much for their marriage to handle. Around this time, they made an amicable agreement to separate.

Joss worked through his feelings by referencing the works of Stephen Sondheim. By the age of nine, he knew all of Sondheim's *Follies*, a musical that examines two unhappy marriages against the backdrop of a showgirl reunion right before their former theater is demolished. One number from *Follies* in particular stood out for young Joss. "The Road You Didn't Take" is sung by Benjamin Stone, an incredibly successful but cold and detached man, who looks back at his life and sees it filled with lost opportunities:

> You take one road
> You try one door
> There isn't time for any more
> One's life consists of either/or

The character finds himself pondering where the door he didn't choose might have taken him, and acknowledging that he'll never know. "The notion that every choice you make means that other possibilities are eliminated forever—as a kid, I found that terrifying," Joss recalled. "As an adult, I still find it scary."

Sondheim's work echoed his personal experiences, he explained. "Sondheim wasn't someone you would go to if you wanted to be told that everything was perfect. Neither were my parents, for that matter—all concerned were greatly relieved when they got divorced." The Whedons finalized their split in 1973.

///////////

By 1974, the kid who had cut his comedy chops by making seasoned comedy writers laugh was honing his skills daily with his Riverdale schoolmates. "He was always the funniest kid in the world. A witty kind of funny—I wouldn't ever call him the class clown," remembers Chris Boal, Joss's best friend at Riverdale. Despite Joss's declarations of being unpopular at school, Boal insists that "girls really liked him, because he was funny—not too many ten-year-olds can pull that off."

The boys met when Boal transferred into the school. He and Joss got into a dispute over a chair, which quickly escalated into a fight. As punishment, their teacher made them sit together at a separate table, and as quickly as their fight had begun, so did their friendship. "We didn't like sports, we didn't like Led Zeppelin. We were unusual, we were little geeks," says Boal, now a playwright. "That was a time when geeky kids were not particularly cool."

In Chris, Joss finally found a proper cohort. While his brothers were only two and four years older, they towered over Joss. To the younger boys, Sam and Matt seemed like tough, cool lacrosse players, and they were very popular in school. Sam was like a superhero to them, and a bit of a guardian for Joss—kids wouldn't mess with him as much because Sam was his older brother. Matt took on the typical middle-brother role of picking on the youngest and his friends (a role Joss and Boal later took on to tease Boal's younger brother).

The two developed the all-consuming friendship that young boys often do. They were inseparable—Boal's mother thought of Joss as a son—and inconsolable at times when their plans were overruled by parents. "One time where we were supposed to hang out on the weekend and we couldn't," Boal laughs, "we were crying on the phone." The boys had sleepovers during which they'd have crazy dance parties, with special preference given to Elton John's "Crocodile Rock," and later lie in bed and make up stories about being superheroes, saving the girls that they liked from the guys in the class who were "awful, jocky, and terrible."

Joss and Boal also realized they were passionate about many of the same things, including movies and comic books. Joss's own introduction to the illustrated world of superheroes had come from the serendipitous decision that *The Electric Company* do a recurring live-action Spider-Man segment called Spidey Super Stories. The sketches aired from 1974 to 1977 and spawned their own line of comics in the Marvel universe.

In preparation for the Spidey Stories series, Tom brought home a collection of Marvel comic books for research, and he shared them with Joss. "I was like nine, and I'm like, What's all this? What's all this that will now obsess me for the rest of my life?" Joss said. "So in a weird way, *The Electric Company* was my gateway and Spider-Man was the guy." Before long, Joss was attending his first Marvel comic convention, where he bought *Howard the Duck* #1 and, full of geeker joy, got Marvel god Stan Lee's autograph.

//////////

Both of Joss's parents remarried within a few years. Tom wed Pamela Merriam Webber, a script supervisor on *The Electric Company*. By 1975, Tom and Pam had moved across the country to Pacific Palisades in Los Angeles, where there were far more opportunities for television writers. A son, Jed Tucker, arrived in July and another, Zachary Webber, would come four years later in August 1979. Joss's older brothers also made the move to the West Coast, but Joss chose to stay in New York with his mother.

Lee married Stephen Jerold Stearns, a history professor, which brought Joss a stepsister, Lisa. In their Manhattan apartment, Lee and Stephen fostered a flourishing academic atmosphere. Lee's Shakespeare performances became more common, as the couple invited people over for elaborate meals, expecting everyone who was there to take a role in the play being performed that night. Joss became quite familiar with Shakespeare being read in a very casual, welcoming setting.

Lee, Stephen, and Joss spent their summers on a commune-like farm in the Catskill Mountains of upstate New York. In sharp contrast to the intensity of the city in the 1970s, they lived in a creaky old house, with a big, rustic kitchen, a water pump, and a lot of acreage. The hallways were painted with fake bookshelves that featured funny made-up titles. They shared the space with other families and couples, as well as several of Lee's students. "We kicked it full '70s," Joss remembers. "We had an ex-con living in the barn; we had poetry readings with harp accompaniment. We had a potting wheel—I can make an ashtray that doesn't fall down."

His time at the farm wasn't all hippie peaceful. Everyone had to obey the "quiet time" rule, in which no one was allowed to make a noise between breakfast and lunch. Lee spent that time writing, while Joss spun tales in his head, "walking up and down [the] driveway creating giant science-fiction universes and various elaborate vengeance schemes upon [my] brothers."

Back in Manhattan, Lee and Stephen eschewed the television set for regular film viewings. Long before the days of personal VHS players, they set up a small projector in their home to screen classic films, sparking a lifelong love of film in young Joss. Their one exception to the no-TV atmosphere was British television series on PBS. Even during the summer, they'd rush back from the farm on Sunday nights to watch the latest offerings from *Masterpiece Theatre*, *Monty Python's Flying Circus*, *Ripping Yarns* (a comedy series from *Monty Python*'s Michael Palin and Terry Jones) and *Connections*, a documentary series that explored how seemingly unrelated historical events and innovations were highly essential and influential to the development of certain modern technologies.

/////////////

With such focus on academics and cultural studies, the two teachers didn't quite understand the pull that the decidedly less literary comic books had on Joss and his friends, and felt that the kids were wasting their time on the hours spent poring over these "funny books." Joss and Chris Boal would go down to the newsstand and spend their allowances on the newest comic books—a pursuit more dangerous than it may sound, as they were both mugged at various times en route. "He looks like an easy mark," Joss's wife, Kai Cole, explains. "If I was going to mug someone, I'd mug Joss. He'd probably give me all his money without a fight, because he looks nice."

Yet the first time Joss was mugged, he didn't go down easy. He was thirteen and alone, heading to the Broadway newsstand for the latest issues. As he approached, he saw five older boys and immediately intuited their intent. Hoping to take refuge at the newsstand, Joss took off running with the crew close behind him, only to find that the stand was closed.

"I duck under them with a certain degree of athletic precision and run the other way. But they catch up with me, grab me by the hair, throw me to the ground, and start kicking me around," Joss said. "We were on Broadway during rush hour. It was filled with people. They parted like the sea and walked around us. That's an impression that doesn't go away." In the end, though, the boys never got his money.

On another occasion, a man approached Joss and demanded all of his money. This time, Joss offered what he had in his pocket: thirteen cents. "You just hold onto that," the would-be mugger told him.

With real life beating them down at every turn, Joss and Boal wrote and drew new stories in which to find refuge. Their comics starred characters based on themselves: the adventures of a fencer (for Joss, who fenced in school) and his nunchaku-wielding friend (for Boal, who studied karate). The boys continued their pilgrimages to comic conventions, where they collected art from their favorite artists, fantasy / science fiction painter Frank Frazetta and hugely popular comic book artist John Buscema of *The Avengers* and *The Silver Surfer*. Joss and his friend were both incredibly excited when Buscema drew and autographed a picture of the Mighty Thor on the back of Boal's convention booklet. It was a major moment in the lives of two budding comic book artists—actually getting to talk to their idols, artists like them who had succeeded in a world they wanted to be a part of.

Marvel superheroes defined their day-to-day thoughts. In the mid-1970s, Joss and Boal closely followed a storyline in the Hulk comic books: Jarella, a green-skinned princess from another world, has fallen in love with the Hulk. She accepts him both as his human self, Bruce Banner, and in his monstrous Hulk form; this probably resonated strongly with two preteen boys aching for girls to find them appealing in all their geeky glory. But during a battle on Earth in one issue, Jarella is crushed to death. Joss was devastated. "We were super upset, because we were in love with her, too," Boal says. "It just killed us." So they did what so many *Buffy*, *Angel*, and *Firefly* fans would do decades later: they took matters into their own hands and rewrote the story, crafting scripts for their favorite superheroes. This evolved into staging elaborate scenes in their apartments, as the future director/screenwriter and playwright strung up action figures and sent them flying across the room.

The boys were avid consumers of cinema as well. They saw the 1977 blockbuster *Star Wars*, of course; when *Superman* came along in 1978, they saw it so many times they could eventually hum the entire John Williams score. The 1979 classic *Alien* made such an impact that thirty years later, Joss declared it his favorite horror movie, for the fact that it terrified him. "It was the first horror movie I'd seen where I didn't think the people in it would look out for each other," he said. "The way they related to each other frightened me as much as the Alien because usually there's a safe haven of, 'Well, we've got each others' backs.' And they didn't seem like they did."

That sense of alienation was familiar to Joss, despite his close friendship with Boal. He compared himself to superhero Luke Cage, whom he saw to be an outsider to Marvel's Fantastic Four team. "I wanted to be a part of a group. But I felt like Luke Cage. . . . Very often you'll be in a group and you'll discover that every single person in it feels like they're the one on the perimeter," he said.

"As soon as I was old enough to have a feeling about it, I felt like I was alone. No matter how much I loved my family—and I actually got along better with my family than I think most people do—I just always felt separate from everybody, and was terribly lonely all the time," Joss said. "I wasn't living a life that was particularly different from anybody else's . . . it wasn't like I didn't have friends, but . . . we, all of us, are alone in our own minds, and I was very much aware of that from the very beginning of my life. Loneliness and aloneness—which are different things—are very much, I would say, [among the] main things I focus on in my work."

Loneliness was also a common subject in the musical works of Stephen Sondheim—ironically, another interest Joss shared with Chris Boal. "We'd walk down the street, singing the entire libretto to *Sweeney Todd*," Boal says. Later, they both took part in a school production of the Sondheim-penned *West Side Story*, in which, Boal insists, Joss stole the show with the comedic number "Gee, Officer Krupke."

///////////

Musicals aside, Joss often found himself in a yearly rut with his classes. By fourteen years of age, he realized that every September when he returned to school, he'd be excited for all the new things to learn—yet within a few weeks, he had fallen behind in his schoolwork. "I gave myself this little mantra: I was like, you know, 'I'm gonna be fierce this year,'" Joss said. "I can't remember the whole mantra, but it had to do with me being a rocket ship. And it worked. . . . I'm fierce homework guy, engaged guy, doing my work, I'm a rocket ship, I'm not gonna let up. And I was working great, and then I told somebody about my rocket ship mantra, and they laughed at it. And I just stopped."

While his interest in classes waned, Joss was very aware of the interpersonal relationships of those around him. He was not as obtuse as most students about the lives of their educators; since he attended the same school where his mother taught, he knew many of his teachers personally. He knew that when the school day was over, they all continued to deal with their own families and their own lives. Later, it would bother him that so many teen-oriented movies and television shows ignored this seemingly simple piece of knowledge and treated every teacher as a joke, every parent as clueless. His frustration went on to inform the character of Rupert Giles, the stuffy British school librarian who serves as Buffy's mentor and father figure in *Buffy the Vampire Slayer*. The character would also have its roots in the next phase of Joss's life: he was about to embark on a transatlantic adventure.

"BEING BRITISH" IN THE LAND OF SHAKESPEARE (AND GILES)

In 1980, the boy who had spent most of his youth tussling with loneliness made what may seem like a strange choice: he left his friends behind and moved to England.

The dramatic change in scenery was prompted by his mother's decision to spend a half-year sabbatical in the United Kingdom. It was the middle of his sophomore year of high school, and Joss could have reunited with his father and brothers in California. But Lee didn't trust the schools in California and strongly suggested that fifteen-year-old Joss join her. To the less-than-stellar student's surprise, he was accepted into Winchester College in Hampshire, one of the highest-rated and most prestigious boarding schools in the country. Despite the fact that up until this point, Joss had never spent a significant amount of time away from his family and had never even traveled outside the United States before, he was intrigued by the chance to "be British" and experience a life he'd seen only on PBS.

Founded in 1382, Winchester is the oldest continuously run school in England, with a long line of notable graduates and visitors. The school represented a sea change for Joss and his mother, both of whom were accustomed to the fairly progressive environment of Riverdale Country School. For her part, Lee pushed aside any worries she may have had about Winchester's conservative leanings, weighing that against the excellent educational environment. For Joss, nearly everything was new and unfamiliar. He was living the life of a British boarding school student at a very traditional school where he had to attend chapel services several times a week. He knew to expect certain adjustments—sharing a room with eleven other boys, for example—but he also struggled to adapt to circumstances British television hadn't prepared him for.

"Winchester is timelessly beautiful, famously academic and a bastion of blithe cruelty," Joss said. "Everyone else was used to this; I was the only new kid. Older boys relentlessly bullied younger, and teachers (called 'dons') bullied everyone, often physically." Joss felt out of sync with his wealthy classmates there, far more than he ever had at Riverdale. "All the students, even boys younger than I, knew each other and came from the same social strata," he recalled. "On top of it all, I was of course that most dread creation, an American. It was clear to me from the start that I must take an active role in my survival."

Joss decided to establish himself as the weird kid, even pushing boundaries of what he himself considered weird before "anyone had time to get their mock on." He posted a nonsensical notice outside his assigned cubicle that made it clear that ridiculing him would "not only be weak and redundant, but might actually please me in some unseemly way." His classmates read his declaration and walked away either laughing or puzzled, and he felt a little safer, comforted by his ability to defuse potential taunting with his own wit.

In H. Bramston's boarding house—more commonly known as Trant's—he studied his housemates, trying to crack the code to popularity. He spent some days at Winchester wondering if anyone knew he existed. "I was lonely," he said. "I wish that I could have made some moves on a girl at some point in my high school career. . . . Intellectually, it was a staggering gift to be able to be around that much intelligence." But "socially, every boy that comes out of Winchester was completely pathetic."

His ungainliness is on blatant display in the 1980 Trant's house photo. Joss stands in the back row, eyes pointed downward and almost lost behind the mop of curly red hair that mushrooms from his head. The awkward fifteen-year-old makes no attempt to interact with the rest of the boys, nor to connect with the camera capturing them.

Years earlier, Joss had been able to earn accolades and get the attention he felt was due from established comedy writers. But surrounded by boys of his own age, he couldn't make any headway. He would later say that he felt many at Winchester were bothered by everything he wore or said, and that they tried to quash his creativity and his personality. These feelings would eventually inspire a number of *Buffy*'s early plotlines, including the episode "Out of Mind, Out of Sight," in which a high schooler is so completely ignored by everyone around her that she literally turns invisible.

Joss, however, took a different route, further embracing the role of the outsider. "I was very dark and miserable, this hideous little homunculus, who managed to annoy everyone," he said. "I mean everyone—because I made a list." He went "extracurricular" with his ideas, writing stories and drawing comic books and sending them back home to Chris Boal, who added more to the tales and returned them. The comics were mostly about characters nobody took seriously, who knew something nobody else did. They were Joss's way of declaring, "I'm alone out here, but there's something in me that people don't see. . . . I have a secret that nobody else has, and therefore I'm exalted, and the fact that nobody pays attention to me or thinks I'm cool or will dance with me *makes me better*."

//////////

Originally, the plan was for Joss to enroll in Winchester for half a year, as long as Lee's sabbatical. The school asked him to stay on, however, so he decided to continue his enrollment and graduate. His feelings of loneliness hadn't completely dissipated, but he appreciated the opportunity he had to study classic literature and great drama. And despite feeling mocked for being American, he had made unexpected inroads with his housemates.

One night after the boys had settled into the beds of their "ice-cold room," they all started reciting a piece from a *Monty Python* episode. While he may not have understood all of Winchester's customs, *Monty Python* was something that Joss knew well. "When there was a lull, I unthinkingly chimed in with the next line. I was answered with unfiltered silence, and then one of the older boys called out from the corner, 'OK. He's in.' He literally said that. Like a cheesy movie: 'He's in,'" Joss said. "And I, in whatever limited capacity I have to be, was. Speaking their language startled them as much as making up my own had."

The importance of language was nothing new to Joss. In a home filled with storytellers, he had learned early how empowering it was to make someone laugh. But earlier audiences had been family and friends, people who were predisposed to be open to him. Now he was suddenly accepted by a far more hostile audience. He learned that he could connect with them, too, and get his ideas across just by finding the right way to talk to them.

No longer the shunned outcast he would still often consider himself to be, Joss found friends for all sorts of endeavors. One time, he and his friends were caught sneaking out at night to stage an impromptu reading of Oscar Wilde's *The Importance of Being Earnest*.

Joss also spent weekends in town at the cinema. Unsurprisingly, he had several epiphanies while in the theater seats. While watching Stanley Kubrick's *The Shining*, he was moved not so much by the story as by the craft of the scene in which young Danny Torrance rides his Big Wheel through the hallways of the Overlook Hotel. A single Steadicam shot follows Danny for just over thirty seconds, and it was in that moment that Joss realized "somebody makes these [films], somebody directed that," he explained. "It just opened up everything—that was a big moment for me."

During another solo trip to London, he experienced the kind of epiphany that generally comes in the early acts of his beloved superhero tales, the kind that resets long-held beliefs and sends the hero down a new path. Of course, as this is Joss's tale, it's only fitting that this big moment also came courtesy of a movie.

In fall 1980, he was on a one-week break from school and renting a small room in the city by himself. One day, he went to see a special-edition rerelease of Steven Spielberg's 1977 classic *Close Encounters of the Third Kind*. He was instantly moved by the story of an ordinary man who sees an extraterrestrial being, and by the idea that in the end, the man would board an alien ship for a journey through outer space, even though everyone he knew would be dead by the time he returned. The movie brought Joss to a realization about the "reality of being human"—and the accompanying limitations.

"[I] came out of the theater with an understanding of the concept of existence and time and life and humanity that I could not contain. I couldn't stop moving," he said. The sixteen-year-old went back to his room, still overwhelmed mentally and physically. "I was just going back and forth going, 'Oh my God, oh my God, oh my God, oh my God, oh my God, oh my God, oh my God.'"

For the rest of the week, he kept going back to see the film, even watching it three times in a single sitting until the ushers kicked him out. He was doing more than just rewatching a movie that he loved; he was developing a comforting ritual to deal with what he called the "extraordinary epiphany of the nature and reality and magnitude and ecstasy of pure, meaningless existence." His return trips "became sort of a way to codify my joy and my terror and my misery at this extraordinary change that my brain had undergone, this sort of becoming of a grown-up," he said.

When he returned to Winchester, Joss tried to explain his experience to a friend, who gave him a copy of Jean-Paul Sartre's *Nausea*. The 1938 novel follows the journal entries of Antoine Roquentin, who searches for meaning in all the things that fill his life as he attempts to finish a research project. Ultimately, Roquentin realizes that life and freedom are meaningless unless a person makes commitments to give them meaning.

The book struck a chord. "Oh! Other people have gone through this!" he realized. The boy who often felt emotionally apart from those around him now had a movement that he could connect with. "Basically, [*Close Encounters*] had made me an existentialist." Since that intense week, he hasn't been able to revisit the film. "It's just too important an experience in my life."

///////////

Arguably, however, the film's impact loomed over the remainder of his time at Winchester. By 1981, Joss had become a "full-tilt" Deadhead, making the hour-long trek into London several times to see the Grateful Dead perform. He never followed the band from place to place as many committed fans would, but by his count he would ultimately see the group at least fifteen times. "I saw them in the front row twice in London—you got in the front row by running," Joss says. "When I started going by myself, everyone would be, like, trying to sneak to the front. I was like, 'Well I've done that,' so I'd go to the back of the theater so that I could just sit and just basically concentrate on hearing every instrument separately at the same time. Which is not easy to do."

Not an easy task, indeed, but it was made easier by the standard Deadhead accompaniments of marijuana and LSD. Joss regularly indulged in the drugs for what he calls "mind-expanding partying." "I'm a big fan of anything that forces you to see things differently. Most people go through their lives without ever even trying," Joss explains. "It's the idea of being taken out of your own narrative, of your own expectations, and it's the only truly pure thing that we can experience—becoming something less than the axis of the universe. That's beautiful, that's important. And that's part of how that all works."

Joss's heady pursuits seem to have affected his schoolwork as well. His housemaster, Dick Massen, wrote in his report at the end of Joss's stay that at first, things went well: Joss worked hard and played a full part in the busy life of the school. But perhaps due to his change in outlook, Joss became "difficult to teach" and reluctant to do any work.

Outside the classroom, Joss was still finding success. He was a member of the Winchester fencing team and wielded his saber to help the school defeat its "old enemy" Eton College, earning accolades from the school newspaper in December 1981 for the "American, and sometimes rather dubious, tactics" he used to clinch the win. He took part in several of Trant's house's student revues, and for one, he penned a sketch that retold the biblical story of Joseph and Mary—one of the first examples of him balancing his personal atheism with a respect for the tenets of a religion that others hold dear. As reimagined by Joss, Joseph is quite concerned about his intended—and virgin—wife's pregnancy. So concerned, in fact, that he hires an American detective (Joss) to learn more about Mary and what she's been up to. Understandably, housemaster Massen was worried about the sketch's potential to offend—especially given its ending, in which Joss stood up and declared, "And if you believe that, you'll believe anything."

"It could have been absolutely ghastly," Massen's wife, Jane, says. "But it was done with such good taste, it was absolutely spellbinding and wonderful."

Even Joss's schoolwork had one bright spot. His love of Shakespeare blossomed at Winchester, and he poured himself into studies for his A-level exam in English, devoting months to studying *Hamlet*, *King Lear*, and *Othello*. While his score on the A-levels would have little bearing on his academic career in the United States, he relished the idea of studying a text so deeply and being tested on a "grown-up understanding" of what he'd learned.

"We'd have class for an hour and twenty minutes . . . and then there'd be three more hours until dinner, and we'd just . . . stay and keep talking," he said. "Some of [the students] were doing it because they were desperate to get good grades, they wanted to get into Oxford or Cambridge. One of them mentioned to me, 'You know, Joss, you're not taking the A levels, you don't have to stay.' 'Dude, where else would I be?' It was amazing. Four hours at a stretch, great scholars and a great teacher completely prying open the text of *Hamlet*. I mean, what more fun can there be? . . . Spoken like a man who never had sex in high school."

(Not that he didn't want to have sex. Joss channeled some of his desires into his first-ever screenplay. There were no superhero adventures in his romantic comedy, which he remembered as a thinly veiled wish-fulfillment tale about a "clearly surrogate [Joss] as a grown-up and Goldie Hawn." He remembers that "I always had such a big crush on her—it was insane," adding that he'd returned to the cinema repeatedly to watch her in 1978's *Foul Play*.)

Except for his English studies, though, Joss had little interest in any of his classes. His teachers were very disappointed and frustrated with his downhill trajectory, noting Joss's talents but worrying over his newfound sloth. One felt that at such a young age, the boy was "a person of a great deal of originality"; another said that anyone with his abilities should have "romped home" (meaning he should have found much success at Winchester, with fun and ease). In his final house report, housemaster Massen wrote that the lapse in Joss's working ability was a mystery, and then went on to wonder if Joss was struggling simply because he was a puzzled adolescent.

The student himself couldn't provide much of an explanation; Joss tried to chalk it up to an "identity crisis." But by this time he was confident that his future was in the performing arts—and that this path didn't require a dogged pursuit of academics. His housemaster and teachers, naturally, disagreed. Massen expressed concern for Joss, still "Joe" at the time: "We would say here that this attitude is unfortunate, because the performing arts are an inconsistent mistress, and Joe a volatile human being. A liaison could be short-lived and abortive, leaving him with little but the memory of his ambitions. Somehow, we think, [someone] should persuade him that a good academic foundation is a very useful thing for him to have." Still, he ended his final house report on Joss with a prophetic statement: "This boy could go far as an actor, writer, cartoonist. This talent has no passing illusion."

Despite his poor grades, Joss still graduated from Winchester in 1982. He ended his tenure with a standout performance as four different characters in *Better Days*, a musical revue honored by being selected as the inaugural performance at the school's Queen Elizabeth II Theatre. Queen Elizabeth herself was in attendance for the performance, which was part of Winchester's six hundredth anniversary that July.

//////////

Joss returned to America to pursue higher education. He scouted several schools, undecided whether he was going to focus on theater or film. Wesleyan University in Middletown, Connecticut, caught his attention. Friends of his parents had taught there, and he had liked the town during his regular visits in his youth. Out of all the colleges he visited, Wesleyan was the one that felt right. Although it was among the most selective schools in the country, he took a leap of faith and went all in, applying to no other schools.

It was a risky choice, coming from Winchester with "no grades . . . [and] a lot of reports that said, 'He seems to be intelligent, but I wouldn't say he applies himself terribly much.' It's not like anybody was begging for me," he explained. "I was clearly a ne'er-do-well." Something must have stood out, however, as Joss was accepted into the class of 1987.

At Wesleyan, Joss developed a social life that he was finally happy with. He found himself an actual, real-life girlfriend, he made friends, and he played Dungeons & Dragons like any proper geek in the early 1980s. He was accepted into the coed Eclectic Society, the school's oldest fraternity, which is known for its "artsy" members and weekend parties featuring an impressive roster of indie bands. (Eclectic was the inspiration for the Pit, the raucous party house at the suffocatingly politically correct Port Chester University in the 1994 film *PCU*. Wesleyan class of 1990 students Adam Leff and Zak Penn based their script on their experiences at the university.) At last, Joss felt that he was accepted and valued for his creativity. He made an emotional break from the life he'd led earlier by choosing a new name. No longer "Joe Whedon," he christened himself "Joss."

//////////

Joss had not thought much about the struggle for women's equality while surrounded by hundreds of boys at a traditional British boarding school, but at Wesleyan he was suddenly confronted with the fact that the fight was far from over. "It was only when I got to college that I realized that the rest of the world didn't run the way my world was run," Joss said.

Until then, his mother had shaped his worldview tremendously. "She was an extraordinary inspiration—a radical feminist, a history teacher and just one hell of a woman. What she did was provide a role model of someone who is completely in control of her life." By this point she had even produced, almost single-handedly, a full-day feminism symposium at her school that featured guest speeches and workshops with prominent feminists such as Gloria Steinem, Cynthia Enloe, and Katha Pollitt. Lee's symposium had led to the establishment of Riverdale's Gender Issues Committee, which met frequently to keep on top of ongoing problems in the relations between the sexes. Through watching his mother, Joss had assumed that the equality issue had been "solved."

Now he was shocked and offended to see that what he had expected, especially at a private liberal arts college like Wesleyan, was not what he was faced with. He wanted to help change the political landscape for women, but he was concerned about how he could engage with gender issues without coming across as self-serving. "I was very aware that my interest in gender studies and my feminist bent went hand in hand with the sort of greasy Eurotrash '*I looooove wee-men!*' [attitude]," he says. He was working through the duality of "an almost unseemly fascination with these women and at the same time a desire to empower and protect them so they could in return empower and protect me."

This meshed with the development of Joss's voice as a writer, which he describes as that of a "literary transvestite." He was no longer just interested in female characters; he actually needed to use them as his avatars. His excitement at a young age at seeing a girl character "let into the club" had grown into a desire to tell her story himself, because it was the story he himself wanted to live: "Somebody who appears to be or is weak becoming stronger. But in almost every case, that person is female."

Joss couldn't deny his connection to the other side of the gender divide either. He took classes in feminism at Wesleyan, and in their discussions, he felt that he had an advantage over most of the girls in discussing male-female relationships because "I have seen the enemy," Joss declares, "and he's in my brain!" As a male, he explains, "I understand the murderous gaze, and I understand objectification."

Joss would come to understand that this position—respecting, admiring, and identifying with women while acknowledging the objectifying influence of the male gaze—helped him create female characters that worked and connected with an audience. "You can't write from a political agenda and make stories that are in any way emotional or iconic. You have to write it from a place that's a little dark, that has to do with passion and lust and things you don't want to talk about."

//////////

When he entered his sophomore year, Joss was at a crucial point in his academic career—did he want to follow a path like his father, grandfather, and mother and pursue theater performance and directing, or would he find greater happiness in the school's film studies department? He'd added film directing to his storytelling skillset, making short films on his own, cast with his family. Joss wrote and directed a film with his little brother Jed as the star that premiered at Jed's eighth birthday party. "It was the year that *Superman [III]* came out, so he did a film called *Stupidman*," Tom recalled.

Joss set up a meeting with Professor Jeanine Basinger, the head of the film department. A leader in the field, Basinger was a trustee of the American Film Institute and would later be named to the board of directors of the National Board of Review of Motion Pictures. Under her guidance, Wesleyan's program had become one of the most respected in the country—a status that allowed Basinger and the school to set guidelines for potential film studies students that are still in force today. Students must meet with her in person before being allowed to register for her class. During these meetings, Basinger and the potential enrollee discuss movies, books, and their lives. She asks questions, trying to work out how the student thinks and what he or she likes. Students' answers about film preferences usually give Basinger a good baseline for who they are.

Right away, Basinger saw in Joss a curiosity, a liveliness of the mind. She found him to be a flexible, creative, and deep thinker. "Sometimes people are flexible but not deep; sometimes they are creative but not flexible. There's a different level of things that you discover," Basinger explains. "I saw the hard worker he was and how seriously he took it."

The respect was mutual. "I've had two great teachers in my life," Joss has declared: his mother and Basinger. "The way everyone in the film department talks about her—she's like a god," says Kai Cole, Joss's wife. "And she is. You meet her and you really regret not going to film school [at Wesleyan]."

Basinger approved Joss's enrollment, and he chose her program instead of a theatrical track. Unlike at Winchester, in his film classes he drank in everything there was to learn. "[There were] people who understand theory in terms of filmmaking and film storytelling, and film mythos and film genre, better than anybody else does," he explained. "Lectures that were so complete, so complex, so dense and so simple that I almost had trouble following them, and by the end would realize they were dealing with things that were already in me. They were already incorporated in the way I thought about story, because they are the American mythos." In Basinger's film lectures, in particular, he was super attentive, very involved, very imaginative, and creative about his work.

Joss embraced Wesleyan's approach to film studies, which focused on theory rather than production. He wrote a paper on Alfred Hitchcock's *The Birds* in which he identified four thematic elements: the Watcher, the Watched, Isolation, and the Role of the Viewer. He said of Tippi Hedren's character, Melanie Daniels, "She has to give up her superficial life to survive," and framed the horror she faces in existential terms: "Stop thinking of why the birds are attacking . . . they just are, that's all that matters." Basinger loved reading his work. "His papers seemed so natural, like they were improvisational," she says. "And yet they were crafted to perfection, because the ideas that he had were delineated at a very precise level."

However, his need to absorb film history couldn't be quenched only by his time in the classroom, or even by Basinger's extra screenings, which most Wesleyan film students attended. When spring came and his classmates would take advantage of the break from the long winter, Joss would be alone in the basement watching a double feature—and then he'd go home at 2 AM and watch whatever was on TV. He felt it was essential to watch films over and over again, taking time to dissect and truly understand what the filmmakers were trying to do. Anyone can learn where to point a camera, he said. But no one could truly be taught *how*. Before he could shoot, Joss felt it was more important to study the meaning of each move in a film—"where the simplicity is, where the complexity is."

The film students ran and selected films for the campus movie theater. Joss's choices were the westerns *The Bad and the Beautiful* (1952) and *The Furies* (1950); the film noir *Laura* (1944); and *The Scarlet Empress* (1934), which starred Marlene Dietrich as the German princess Sophia, who became the empress Catherine the Great. Basinger explained that her students felt so strongly about their film preferences that they'd sometimes come to blows, and that "while Joss is a very effective screenwriter, he is weak in the punching department."

///////////

In his later years at Wesleyan, Joss became a teaching assistant. The first class he assisted with was Language and Film, with Joe Reed. It was an introductory course, with more than two hundred students, and Joss's first TA lecture was on lighting in film scenes. Initially, things did not look good for the young man.

"I was terrified," Joss remembers. "I was terrified until about thirty seconds after I got on stage, and then you couldn't have pulled me off." He was on a high from the quintessential point of teaching: "The best part was showing a clip while I was explaining something about lighting and hearing everybody laugh because they had figured something out because they had learned something." For Joss, that was a feeling everyone should have.

Joss later became a TA for Basinger herself, and the two grew even closer. He helped select films for her film series and was allowed to grade papers and give lectures of his own. When he graded papers, Basinger took note of his succinct, pointed commentary. "When somebody didn't get it, he'd nail them," she says. "Never mean, but he could be very precise—one of his most distinct evaluations was quite simple: 'This guy's a puddle.' And he was right; he said everything there was to say." She was also impressed by his work in the classroom. "There was a melodious, meticulous perfection to his lectures," she says. "He had a rhythm, and he had the ability to create the surprise little twist at the end."

According to Basinger, Joss's lecture on the infamous Joan Crawford vehicle *Johnny Guitar* (1954) was the best she'd heard. Joss discussed the gender politics in director Nicholas Ray's view of the world and delved into which characters the audience identifies with at what time and why, who owns the space on screen, and, ultimately, whose movie it is and whom it's about. "His lectures were absolutely brilliant. They had not only the complete understanding and the ability to clarify and delineate, but also they had a kind of poetry that showed how his heart and soul really understood the medium, as well as his brain," she explains. "He wasn't just intellectually sharp about film, he was also emotionally, creatively sharp about it."

Each lecture Joss did taught him something new. With Otto Preminger's noir *Where the Sidewalk Ends*, he and his co-TA learned how to think quickly, as they were only able to screen the film simultaneously with their talk. He returned to Alfred Hitchcock's *The Birds*, and explained to the students why it's such a polarizing movie—discussing

Hitchcock's relationship with Tippi Hedren and how he saw her, essentially, as a prop in the film. "I had an old photograph of him that I'd gotten from a book, of him marking her leg with chalk to show the cameraman where he wanted the frame to end," Joss says. "That was amazing; she was like a piece of set [decoration]."

In his lecture on *Rear Window* (1954), Joss described Jimmy Stewart's character using a term familiar to *Buffy* fans. He called him the Watcher—someone who views life as a movie, who thinks that simply watching the goings-on of the couple across the way through their window can't hurt him. But it does hurt him, both physically and, more importantly, emotionally. It's a theme that Joss would revisit in the relationship between Buffy and her trainer/mentor Giles on *Buffy the Vampire Slayer*. In the first episode of the series, Buffy pushes him to take action against vampires himself. "I-I'm a Watcher," he says, stumbling over his words, explaining that he hasn't the skill, that it's not his role in life. There is both a sense of safety and a resigned sadness in his declaration. (Giles's cover job as the librarian at Buffy's high school also has roots in this period of Joss's life; while at Wesleyan, he worked the desk at the university library.)

//////////

Another hint toward Joss's breakthrough series came in his junior-year film project, which was about a girl who goes to the prom and finds out her date is a vampire. *A Night Alone* had its premiere on Sunday, May 11, 1986, at "Wesleyan Presents: The Student Films and Videos of 1986." Joss both designed the event's poster and took the black-and-white noir detective photo featured on it. For one dollar, attendees watched several 16 mm student films, including Michael Bay's *My Brother Benjamin*, which won an award. It would be one of the only times the public had the opportunity to screen Bay's or Joss's film. At Wesleyan, the students fund their own films and thus have all ownership rights to them.

To this day, Joss refuses to let anyone screen *A Night Alone*, because he feels that it was poorly made. While Wesleyan's film program was exceptional on theory and history, it was sadly lacking in production offerings. "Pretty much what I had learned in our one production class was: Don't drop the camera. It's really expensive," Joss says. "That film was a hot mess."

Basinger had a far kinder assessment of her two students' work. "They both showed great talent for undergraduates in a liberal arts college that has one brief semester in production and who made their own projects. They are both distinctive. In Michael's case, his is a Michael Bay film: It's beautifully shot and edited, it's a fluid forward movement of action, and you could put it up anywhere," she says. "Joss's was a narrative, and he had amateur actors. So you have a rougher thing, but you very definitely have an intelligent, amusing piece of work that is clearly a Joss Whedon film, with clearly a Joss Whedon character and story."

The following year, Joss made another movie that he liked much better. This one wasn't done for school credit but instead to "ward off the evil spirits" of *A Night Alone*. And again, the project hinted at his works to come: the black-and-white, silent Super 8 film was a postapocalyptic western called *Tombstone*. Joss drew inspiration this time from the George Romero zombie apocalypse movies, *The Terminator*, and the thesis of another of his Wesleyan professors, Richard Slotkin.

In *Regeneration Through Violence: The Mythology of the American Frontier, 1600–1860*, Slotkin proposed that American narratives were developed from the frontier mythologies created as European settlers pushed farther west into Native American lands. "We just replace [the Indians] with whatever's alien, whatever's other. In WWII, it's the Japanese," Joss says. "Zombies are just the latest incarnation of Indians. It's the West all over again. There's just a few of us, and we're trying to survive."

3

CRASH COURSE IN TELEVISION

After graduating from Wesleyan in 1987, Joss faced the question so many young people confront upon leaving college: what do I do now? The film studies grad decided to move to San Diego to become an independent filmmaker.

Broke, he ended up at his father's house in Los Angeles. He picked up the requisite job for a future film director—video store clerk—and later became the part-time video production teacher at Crossroads School in Santa Monica, where his younger brothers were enrolled. Through Jeanine Basinger, he connected with a Wesleyan grad who gave him a job doing research for the Life Achievement Award at the American Film Institute. These jobs did not, however, build up his bank account enough for him to be able to move out on his own.

The disappointing circumstances did have an upside: Joss got to spend time with his father, something he hadn't done much of since his parents' divorce when he was nine. That experience, of course, had strengthened Joss's relationship with his mother, yet Joss was also like his father—himself the son of a writer. And in Los Angeles the bond between father and son, now both grown men, grew deeper.

Still, Joss was determined not to be "3G TV"—a third-generation television writer, as a friend at Wesleyan teasingly insisted would be his destiny. He'd watched Tom's career fluctuate as any television writer's does, dependent on being hired for a show and then dependent on the ratings for the show and job to continue. "That freaked me out a little bit," Joss said. "As a kid, I was like, 'You know what I want when I grow up? Financial security.' Who says that? I was always super careful to save money, and just never be in a situation where I had to do something I didn't believe in in order to make money, because that would just hurt."

Even Tom admonished his son that "under no circumstances write sit-coms, because it was too hard."

But Joss needed a way to make decent money to get out of his father's house and into his own space, and hopefully fund the movies he wanted to make. Ironically, the one career path that he had rejected for its instability now seemed like his best chance for a steady paycheck. And despite Tom's own misgivings, he wanted to support his son and believed in his talent. He felt that Joss's writing would be a good fit for the sitcom he was working on at the time, *It's a Living*, which was set in a swanky restaurant atop a Los Angeles hotel and followed the lives of its waitresses. He suggested that his son come in and pitch some ideas for the show. Joss had already spent some time on the set watching production and had taken a liking to one of the two showrunners (the writer/producers in charge of the series), whom he thought was "young, hip, and cool." He decided to go for it.

"It was the most terrifying experience of my life," Joss said. "Horrible, just terror, and then it went as badly as any bad-pitched story you've ever heard of—and I did it twice. Both times, it was a nightmare. I was so scared." The experience was made worse by the *other* showrunner, who blew off every idea that Joss had and called him out for not being prepared enough, or being overrehearsed.

Joss realized years later that the response was more about the show-runner's relationship with Tom than about Joss's own ability. But that didn't make it any easier for father or son. After one of the failed pitches, Tom came home and was almost an hour into a conversation before he told his son that he didn't think Joss would get to write for *It's a Living*. "He couldn't even get up the nerve to tell me," Joss said. "My poor father. It was harder for him, I think, than it was for me."

///////////

Feeling that he had been "eviscerated by weasels," Joss didn't pursue tele-vision writing opportunities any further for the time being. He still had his job at the video store, but that didn't mean that he stopped writing. One project was a musical parody of the Oliver North hearings, to the tune of the songs from *Oliver!* North, a former US Marine Corps lieutenant colonel, came into the public spotlight in July 1987 when he testified before a joint congressional committee investigating the Iran-Contra affair, an American political scandal that exploded in the final years of the Reagan administration. North had admitted the previous year that he had been partially responsible for the sale of weapons via intermediaries to Iran, the profits of which were channeled to anti-Communist rebels in Nicaragua. "We didn't ever shoot it or anything," Joss said. "I just recorded it with my family, with my little brothers, my dad and my stepmom, and me."

Tom played the recording at parties, where a producer for a new series heard it, liked it, and asked Joss to lunch. The producer asked if Joss had any other writing samples and Joss responded that he didn't, but if he could get all the scripts from the producer's new show, *Just in Time*, he'd write one of those. Unfortunately, *Just in Time* was canceled after two episodes aired, and before Joss could finish his script.

Joss buckled down and developed several more speculative, or spec, scripts for sitcoms that were on the air at the time. Spec scripts are the all-important calling card for aspiring writers. They're generally intended not to be produced but simply to showcase a writer's voice and demonstrate how well he or she can develop a story and write to the tone of a particular series. Once a writer has polished specs for a few different shows, he sends them out to agents in hopes of connecting with someone who likes and will champion his work. Joss wrote specs for his father's show, *It's a Living*, as well as the sitcom *It's Garry Shandling's Show*.

When he showed these scripts to his father, Tom had only encouragement and praise—which was something that Joss didn't know he needed until it was offered. Tom was so supportive that he insisted that Joss skip the traditional path to becoming a television writer—serving as an assistant to a producer, writer, or agent—and hold out for a staff writer position. "I had no idea how huge that was for me until it happened," Joss said. "This guy could have crushed the life out of me if he had a mean or competitive bone in his body. He has been completely, gushingly supportive since the day I picked up a pen."

Tom even called in some favors on his son's behalf. His literary agency, Leading Artists (a precursor to United Talent Agency), was willing to have someone read his scripts. Another young upstart, Chris Harbert, had just joined Leading Artists as an agent in 1988. After graduating from Boston University, Harbert had worked his way up from the mailroom at ICM before moving to Leading Artists. When he had Joss in for a meeting during his first year on the job, he was surprised by the length of the writer's hair.

"It came down to about the middle of my back," Joss says. "Yes, I was often mistaken for a rock star. Not anyone in particular, usually just sort of vaguely people thought I might be a rock star. I was asked to sign a Simply Red album by a record store owner." Not knowing the lead singer's name (Mick Hucknall), he declined, as he didn't feel that he could inscribe it with "Signed, the guy from Simply Red."

Harbert, who was a year older than Joss, had a distinctly different style. "Very '80s, slick, like frat boy," Joss said. "I'm like, there's no way." But once the initial shock over each other's appearance wore off, Harbert signed Joss as his first client. They began a relationship that would take them through the ups and downs of Joss's whole career, from his long, curly red locks to his current buzzcut. "He's a really sweet guy," Joss said. "Turns out I'm not, but he was. That was the plot twist."

///////////

Joss spent the next year writing more comedy spec scripts. He wrote a script for *The Wonder Years*, which featured a storyline based on his own experiences of being mugged in New York City, and one for *Roseanne*. He wasn't particularly interested in writing for a sitcom, but it was the format that he was most familiar with, since both his father and grandfather had been staff on sitcoms for most of their television careers. Even with all that exposure, Joss didn't love the joke-joke-joke structure of sitcoms, which he felt wasn't as interesting as when "something creepy happened, something real" occurred in an episode.

The underlying "something real" was what excited him about the new sitcom *Roseanne*. The series, which began in 1988, was quite different from anything else on at the time. Built as a vehicle for Roseanne Barr, a stand-up comic whose routines focused on her life as a "domestic goddess," *Roseanne* told the story of a working-class family: Roseanne Conner; her husband, Dan (John Goodman); their three children, teenager Becky (Alicia Goranson), middle child Darlene (Sara Gilbert), and young D.J. (Michael Fishman); and Roseanne's sister, Jackie (Laurie Metcalf). With *Roseanne*, according to Joss, Barr "changed the landscape of American television. She should be credited for having done it."

Roseanne drew attention to the hardships facing middle-class America during the 1980s. The looming threat of unemployment came up often in storylines, and the series dealt with its effect on the Conners, who constantly struggled to make ends meet while still trying to achieve their dreams. It was a stark and honest series surrounded by prime-time dramas filled with wealthy families and their over-the-top materialism (*Dynasty, Dallas, Falcon Crest*) and sitcoms featuring well-off families who rarely fought (*The Cosby Show*). For Joss, *Roseanne* also "had a feminist agenda . . . it was real, and decent, and incredibly funny."

So when staffing season came up in April–May 1989, the time during which shows look for new writers to read, interview, and hopefully hire, Harbert sent Joss's *Roseanne* spec to the series. The usual rule is that a writer should never send a spec of a series to *that* series, since a show's own writing staff can be particularly picky if a script fails to capture some nuance of the series' tone. But apparently Joss's script was good enough to get him a meeting with executive producer Jeff Harris. Soon after, Harbert got his client an offer to work on what Joss felt was one of the most important shows on television. The producer told him to bring in his no. 2 pencil on Monday, so Joss went out and bought a hundred no. 2 pencils. "I know he meant that as a metaphor—but what if he didn't."

The novice writer was brought on staff as a story editor for the show's second season, which he quickly determined was "total chaos." The chaos had its roots in the show's first season. Barr had spent much of the early days of *Roseanne* sparring with producers Marcy Carsey and Matt Williams. They battled over writing credits, storylines, even wardrobe choices. Barr had fired most of the writers and production staff at the end of the first season, and the second season wasn't starting off much calmer.

As Joss showed up to start work on the new season, Barr gathered everyone on staff and made a speech about how the tabloids were obsessed with her and had sources among the crew feeding them details of her personal life. Joss, who had heard about the tabloid drama and the staff conflicts, anticipated a speech that would bring everybody closer: "It's us against the world, and dammit, we've got good work to do here, let's all get it done." Instead, Roseanne told the writers they had better keep their mouths shut or they would all be fired. It was a plot twist that he wasn't expecting.

"It made me realize . . . that every time somebody opens their mouth they have an opportunity to do one of two things—connect or divide. Some people inherently divide, and some people inherently connect," Joss said. "Connecting is the most important thing, and actually an easy thing to do. I try to make a connection with someone every time I talk to them, even if I'm firing them. . . . People can be treated with respect. That is one of the most important things a show runner can do, is make everybody understand that we're all involved, that we're all on the same level."

//////////

All the chaos on the *Roseanne* set actually worked in Joss's favor. He was so junior that he wasn't on Barr's radar, so he wasn't held responsible for her frustrations. He kept his job all year by keeping his head down and taking on all the writing assignments he could get.

That was unusual for a first-year writer. So unusual, in fact, that when a friend of his father asked if they had let him write a script yet, Joss told him he had already written four. "Because they just . . . they had nobody. I ended up writing six scripts that year," Joss said, although he would only be credited on four episodes. "The other staff writer I know who's done that was Marti Noxon. She did it in the second year of *Buffy*."

Joss was getting an unusual crash course in television writing, and credits were stacking up on his résumé, but he was frustrated. Producers often rewrote his scripts—to their detriment, he believed—before they got to air. They backed away from important subject matter. His first assignment, the second episode of the season, had a premise that shocked and then excited him. The episode was to take on abortion: Darlene goes to visit her aunt Jackie only to find her incredibly drunk. Jackie admits that she had an abortion and hasn't told Roseanne about it. Joss couldn't believe that the episode they were starting him off on gave him something important to say and touched on the kinds of feminist issues he most wanted to explore.

A couple days later, the executive producer called him in and told him that he'd talked to the network and they decided that Jackie would have a miscarriage instead of an abortion. There would be no feminist message about a woman's right to choose; now Jackie's breakdown would be about an uncontrollable biological event. "It's totally the same—do that," an irritated Joss recalled being told. "Welcome to my dream and my first heartbreak."

In the final version of "The Little Sister," Darlene still finds Jackie drunk at home, but now she is drowning her pain over the fact that Roseanne doesn't support her choice to become a police officer. Nary an abortion nor a miscarriage to be found in the story, although the reasoning behind Roseanne's lack of support does have some weighty emotional underpinnings: she doesn't think Jackie is incapable of being a cop but rather fears that Jackie will be killed. The episode also delivers Joss's first fight scene on television; the ending has Roseanne and Jackie wrestling, both comically and seriously, as Dan quips about making a sexy video from it all. It's a small foreshadowing of all Joss's wit-infused fight sequences to come.

//////////

Joss's frustrations were relieved for a time when he wrote the script for the episode "Brain-Dead Poets Society." Tom Arnold, another writer on the series who was famously engaged to Roseanne at the time, championed Joss's work and covertly showed his script to her. "That was the first script of mine she actually read," Joss remembers.

After reading it, Barr had lunch with Joss. "It was quite extraordinary," he said. "The good Roseanne came to lunch. She got it and she was very excited about it, and it was a really fascinating time." She asked him how he, a twenty-five-year-old man, could write a middle-aged woman with such authenticity. Joss responded, "If you met my mom you wouldn't ask."

In the episode, middle child Darlene writes a poem for her seventh-grade English class. When the thirteen-year-old tomboy is asked to read it at the school's Culture Night, however, she balks. Roseanne, who wrote poems when she was younger, is excited to finally have a connection with her daughter and doesn't understand the girl's reluctance. Darlene fights to stay home and watch a basketball game with her father but eventually loses to her mother's demands.

It was his first script that ended up on the television screen largely as he wrote it, and the episode foreshadowed the way he would address the uneasiness of growing up in *Buffy*. Another comparison can be drawn between Darlene's desperation to keep her identity very separate from her mother's and Joss's own reluctance to follow his father into a television writing career.

In the finished episode, Darlene's poem, "To Whom It Concerns," starts from a sarcastic, apathetic place ("To whom it concerns, my ma made me write this / And I'm just her kid, so how could I fight this"), but ends on a beautiful, quiet note that cuts to a thirteen-year-old girl's desire to be heard, while still scared of the visibility that would entail ("To whom it concerns, I just turned thirteen / Too short to be quarterback, too plain to be queen. / To whom it concerns, I'm not made of steel / When I get blindsided my pain is quite real"). It is one of the most memorable scenes of the entire series—but this version of the poem wasn't penned by Joss. The version in his draft was about basketball. "It was about Michael Jordan," Joss explains. "It was prose, didn't rhyme, it wasn't about her emotions; it was actually just a poem."

The young writer who fretted over unnecessary script changes had now seen his work rewritten for the better. Perhaps the simplicity of Darlene's poem in his draft was a reflection of his own youth and inexperience. The man who would later stress to his *Buffy* writers that every story must be about the emotional journey, that no episode was "just about the monster," still hadn't gained the experience to know that such a pivotal poem couldn't be "just" a poem.

//////////

By the time "Brain-Dead Poets Society" aired, it was the second half of the season. The politics on the show were still in flux, and on March 27, 1990, executive producer Jeff Harris resigned by taking out a full-page ad in *Daily Variety*. The show's remaining higher-ups became increasingly insular, and Joss felt shut out. Worse, his writing assignments dried up. "Chicken Hearts," the thirteenth episode of the twenty-four-episode season, was the last for which he received a writing credit. He had the financial security he craved—story editors on *Roseanne* made at least $3,000 a week—but the junior writer who had handed in six scripts now found himself with nothing to work on.

Instead of continuing to sit in the office and write nothing, Joss decided to focus his energy on an idea for a movie script that had been brewing for a while. It would be a revisionist take on the "girl in a dark alley" trope from so many popular horror films of the 1980s, in which a young woman—usually a blonde—makes the bad choice of venturing somewhere sketchy, where she is inevitably chased and killed by a maniac. "The idea . . . came from seeing too many blondes walking into dark alleyways and being killed," Joss said. "I wanted, just once, for her to fight back . . . and kick his ass."

The idea began as the story of "Martha the Immortal Waitress." Martha was a stand-in for himself: a person to whom no one would give much concern, but who had "more power than was imaginable." Joss tinkered with the concept during his time as a video store clerk, when he watched countless films with titles like *Assault of the Killer Bimbos*. He checked them out thinking that they were a new form of female empowerment film wrapped in some ridiculous B movie premise. Upon watching them, however, he realized that they were little more than sexploitation films with silly titles.

As a result, Joss became determined to make a movie with a similar low-budget aesthetic, along the lines of legendary director George Romero's zombie movies, but one centered on the crazy notion that the girls in the film weren't stereotypical bimbos but rather intelligent and resourceful. He would combine the standard silliness and fun of a B movie with a serious feminist agenda. His main character would be an homage to all the pretty, frivolous girls who dared to have fun and have sex—like Lynda in *Halloween* and Samantha the cheerleader in *Night of the Comet*. These were the girls who no one expected could take care of themselves, much less become a superhero who would someday save the world.

And to Joss, the perfect name for his blonde hero was also the name he took least seriously: Buffy. "There is no way you could hear the name Buffy and think, 'This is an important person,'" Joss explained. "To juxtapose that with Vampire Slayer, just felt like . . . a B movie. But a B movie that had something more going on."

But that wasn't his only reasoning for naming the project *Buffy the Vampire Slayer*. Even if the sexploitation films with silly titles continually disappointed him, he still regularly picked them up off the shelf. As did many of his customers at the video shop, thinking that the movies with the silly titles might be "jolly fun." Joss knew that *Buffy*, if it even got the chance to be made, would never be a blockbuster hit in the theaters. So he designed it to look like that silly, fun movie that someone would pull from a shelf to give it a try—only to be surprised by the fact that it was actually good.

For the rest of his contract on *Roseanne*, Joss would go to work in the show's offices and, with nothing to do, instead work on *Buffy the Vampire Slayer*. He finished an eighty-five-page draft—very short by feature film standards—just to get the story out, then went back in to flesh it out. But the side project didn't alleviate Joss's discontent with his role on the series. As much as he'd admired the show for its feminism, its humor, and its honesty, he decided he couldn't work there anymore.

"I just wanted to be able to do work for one reason and one reason only, and that was because it was work worth doing," Joss said. "[Roseanne's] not the reason I quit," he hastened to add. "At the end of the day, it was a good stepping-stone, not a good experience."

///////////

After *Roseanne*, Joss was brought onto the NBC series *Parenthood* by executive producer David Tyron King. The show was based on the characters from the 1989 Steve Martin vehicle of the same name; starring Ed Begley Jr. and future household names David Arquette and Leonardo DiCaprio, it followed three generations of the Buckman family. Unlike the straight sitcom format of *Roseanne*, *Parenthood* was a half-hour, single-camera comedy-drama, or dramedy, a popular genre at the time that included *Doogie Howser, M.D.* and *The Wonder Years*. The series lasted less than a full year and was just one of a number of failed attempts to bring movies to television that season—*Ferris Bueller*, *Working Girl*, and *Uncle Buck* were all canceled in short order as well.

"It was a very talented ensemble and talented staff," Joss says. "Ty King is an amazing writer, but there were many forces conspiring against us, people who just didn't get the show."

The politicking going on behind the scenes compounded the disappointing ratings. It wasn't as dramatic as the chaos on *Roseanne*, where Joss had already had his trial-by-fire initiation into the realities of Hollywood. But, again, he was able to step up and be an active part of the writing team, complete with a lot of all-nighters. It was his second chance to shine that didn't quite deliver a Hollywood ending. On *Roseanne*, his chance had sort of been taken away from him, so he left. On *Parenthood*, the show was canceled before he could show what he could do.

Yet the experience wasn't without its merits. Joss's major takeaway from *Parenthood* was his time spent in the writers' room. In King, Joss found the guidance he'd longed for on *Roseanne*. King was easier for him to relate to than his previous coworkers; he was relatively young for a showrunner—roughly the same age Joss would be when running *Buffy* seven years later.

At one point, the two were venting about the frustrations of the show. "This is terrible," King lamented. "This is unbelievable what they're doing. They're killing us. This is just . . . I'm so angry." Then he turned to Joss, with the biggest smile, and said, "This is so much fun."

"I never forget that," Joss says. "It's so true."

//////////

The following year, Joss didn't pick up another television show gig, but his own personal narrative took an unexpected shift when Michelle "Kai" Cole literally walked into the room. She had been driving across country with Joss's cousin en route to San Francisco. On September 6, 1991, the girls made a stop in Los Angeles, at Tom Whedon's house.

Kai and Joss both describe their meeting as something intense and immediate. "He was far across the room, and the first second that I saw him—I had one of those experiences, where he got closer," Kai remembers. "He kind of came into my face really fast, but he didn't move. It was sort of this weird, physical reaction that I had to him. It was instant, and we both had it. He says he was in lust at first sight."

That moment is captured in a photograph Joss's brother Sam snapped within half an hour of them meeting. In the picture, Joss and Kai are both looking at each other. "He's directly looking at me, smiling, and I'm sort of looking under my eye, looking over at him," she describes. "It's kind of an amazing thing to have a picture where you meet someone for the first time. And we've been together ever since."

He was twenty-seven, she was twenty-five. They'd both been working to define themselves on their own terms, each even choosing a new name that they thought fit better. They were well past the teenage awkward stage, yet their meeting was quite overwhelming for both of them. Both were very silent—unusually so, Kai explains—yet they were very aware of each other. They went out to breakfast with Sam and hardly spoke to one another. The first thing Joss said to Kai was "I like your boots." Kai couldn't find any words; she barely got out a "thanks." That didn't last for very long, though—the not-talking.

They all went out dancing that night at Arena, a gay nightclub in Los Angeles. It was his dancing skills that tipped the scales, Joss jokes, and "the fact that we were at a gay bar and I was the only man that was interested in dancing with her—the lack of competition is what got it."

They just clicked from that time, Kai says. She did continue up to San Francisco but returned quickly. "We sort of celebrate [September 6] as our anniversary. It was very instant. Joss calls it the longest one-night stand, because we actually slept together that first day."

It had been a long time since Joss had dated anyone. Unlike during his teen years, however, he had taken a conscious break from romantic entanglements, and he was certainly not looking to fall in love. But the couple was so instantly, intensely together that a couple months later, Joss took her to his mother's home in New York for Thanksgiving. Naturally, it was an intimidating experience for Kai.

"His mom was the litmus test. I know Joss did love me, but if his mom didn't really like me, I think there would have been something wrong," she explains. Luckily, there were no problems. "Joss's mom was so easy. A lovely person who made a lot of sense."

Next, Kai had to pass the test with the other important female figure in Joss's life: "I felt the same way with Jeanine, that it was really important that she like me." It's a tradition that Jeanine Basinger's students take their potential long-term partners to meet her, and not one that she or they take lightly: One boy once took his soon-to-be fiancée to meet her. She was appalled to learn that the girlfriend did not like the classic Hitchcock movie *Vertigo*. Basinger questioned the student about it afterward. The couple broke up two weeks later.

So the stakes were high when Joss took her to his mentor's home, but it turned out that Kai had no reason to worry. "My husband and I were both here, and my husband fell in love with her immediately," Basinger says. "We both knew instantly she was the right one. She's a wonderful person and a very strong, intelligent, and talented woman in her own right. She's the kind of woman you know is right for Joss—a very good wife, a very good mother, but she's a full, equal partner. If Joss went to Borneo for two years, I would be happy to visit with Kai."

There were two key moments early in the relationship that solidified the connection between Joss and Kai. The first came when she read the movie script for *Buffy the Vampire Slayer*. They had been together for a while at that point, but she had yet to read any of his work. She knew she loved him but was worried that if she didn't like the way he wrote, it would affect their relationship. One night, Kai finally decided it was time, so she snuck off with a copy. She opened up to the middle of the script, rationalizing that if she didn't like it, it would be because she hadn't started it from the beginning.

To her great joy, however, she loved it—even from the middle. Kai flipped back and read the entire thing from the beginning, then rushed into his office and threw herself on Joss with enormous relief.

Around the same time, Joss saw Kai working on a dress that he particularly hated. He tentatively asked if she had sewn it, to which Kai responded, "Oh, God no. I'm trying to fix it!" Again, relief was felt.

"It was very important," Joss says. "Someone's aesthetics and art are who they are," and if you don't like it, "you can't go through life pretending that you think that's all very well."

THE BLONDE IN THE ALLEY FIGHTS BACK

A high school cheerleader named Buffy Summers has just learned that she is the Chosen One. This makes her special, she's been told, but it will take a while before anyone else believes it—hell, it will take a while before even she believes it.

Joss had been working on Buffy's story for years, since before he was even a professional writer. He'd finished the screenplay as a frustrated story editor on *Roseanne*. His fledgling agent shopped it around Hollywood, until finally it was optioned by Sandollar, a production company founded by Sandy Gallin and the legendary Dolly Parton.

In 1991, Sandollar executives Howard Rosenman and Gail Berman approached Kuzui Enterprises, in the hopes that the Tokyo-based distribution company would partner with them to produce the film and perhaps bring in some Japanese investors. The company was headed by producer Kaz Kuzui and his wife, director Fran Rubel Kuzui, whose first feature was 1988's *Tokyo Pop*. The film, which she also cowrote, tells the story of a young American woman who travels to Japan and falls into a new relationship while dealing with the clash of cultures. Fran had been looking for a new project, and within five pages, she knew *Buffy* was it.

The director responded to the script's competing notions of destiny and making one's own path, and how they related to growing up. In Joss's tale, the vapid and popular Buffy's life changes when she's approached by a (somewhat creepy) older gentleman named Merrick Jamison-Smythe. Merrick informs her that she is the latest in a long line of Vampire Slayers and he is her Watcher, who holds the sacred responsibility of guiding and training her. Buffy initially refuses to believe him, especially when

51

the ideas of "slaying" and "training" interfere with her social life. Finally, she accepts her fate as the Chosen One—even if it means she'll come to an early death fighting the undead and their vampire king, Lothos, who's primed to take down yet another Slayer. "When we're kids, [we] know we're part of *something*, and the process of being an adult is finding the something you're a part of," Fran said. "This is the story about a girl—and it's very important that it's a girl—finding out how powerful she really is."

The Kuzuis agreed to produce the film—on the condition that Fran would direct. As the director, she would have creative control over the project, and she talked with Joss about her ideas for revising the script. In addition to a female sidekick for the lead vampire and a more like-able Buffy, she wanted to make the film more of a commentary on pop culture—not unlike the way *Tokyo Pop* had explored Japanese culture through an American's eyes. "The original script of 'Buffy' was pretty simple," Kuzui said. "She was a cheerleader who killed vampires. There were no martial arts and she was a very passive, uninspired girl." Fran suggested two more iconic Asian influences to Joss: Sailor Moon, the animated schoolgirl whom she felt was very empowered, and the martial arts films of Hong Kong director John Woo. "[Joss] loved the idea," she recalled, "so we set out to rewrite the script."

Fran and Kaz then submitted the revised screenplay to 20th Century Fox to see if the studio would be interested in backing the film. It landed on the desk of script reader Jorge Saralegui. Script readers are studio gatekeepers of sorts—they read all the scripts that come in and, for each, write up a brief synopsis with a breakdown of good and bad points and suggest whether a studio should pass on it or buy it. Saralegui recommended that Fox buy *Buffy*, for its strong vampire themes and how deftly the lead character transitions from a shallow cheerleader into a warrior prepared to face her destiny. But what really blew him away was the stylized way in which the characters spoke. "That theatrical, neo-surf speak," Saralegui explains. "At that point, I actually hadn't seen that anywhere else."

Just three weeks after Joss turned in the revised draft, 20th Century Fox bought the film, retaining worldwide distribution rights and giving it a budget of $9 million. Fox wanted the movie and wanted it fast, to capitalize on the impending vampire movie trend. Francis Ford Coppola's big-budget *Dracula* was due in November 1992, filled with A-list stars Anthony Hopkins, Gary Oldman, Winona Ryder, and Keanu Reeves.

Horror director John Landis would release *Innocent Blood* the previous September, and Anne Rice's bestselling book *Interview with the Vampire* seemed to finally be headed to production after over a decade in development. And there was still room for a more youth-oriented variation on the theme; Hollywood hadn't had a big teen vampire hit since 1987's *The Lost Boys* with Kiefer Sutherland.

Casting began quickly so that the film could premiere in the summer of 1992. Kristy Swanson (*Knots Landing, Hot Shots!*) signed on for the titular role, and Donald Sutherland, Kiefer's father, took on the role of Buffy's mentor and trainer, Merrick. *Beverly Hills, 90210* heartthrob Luke Perry was her love interest / boy in need of rescue, Pike. As for the villains, Rutger Hauer, Rice's original choice for the lead in *Interview with the Vampire*, would play Lothos, while Joan Chen of *Twin Peaks* signed on as his sidekick Amilyn.

But the female sidkick Joss had added at the director's request would not make it to the screen as written. Just as filming was about to begin, Chen left the project due to a financial dispute. To replace her, producers turned to a male actor: Paul Reubens, best known for playing the child-like Pee-wee Herman. Reubens had been arrested in July 1991 for indecent exposure in an adult movie theater; the resulting media backlash caused him to retreat from the public eye. After reading Joss's script, Reubens's biggest concern was over the physical appearance of his character in his first movie after the arrest. He wanted Amilyn to look as far from Pee-wee Herman as he could get—in fact, he wanted the character to look like he did in his mug shot. The offer came in and the role of Amilyn was his; no audition was needed, and he could look how he wanted. The only stipulation was that he was not allowed to announce his involvement, and although *Variety* leaked it anyway, the news was not nearly as widely disseminated as it would have been in a more plugged-in era.

Reubens, Luke Perry, and Joss were in agreement early on about the direction the film should take. All three were very specific in their desire to make a really dark, scary movie that surprised people with a strong female protagonist and a lot of jokes. Perry was looking forward to the role reversal. "Buffy's the one who's always having to save him, which is a nice change from the way these movies usually work. If Buffy can be seen as a hero, then I suppose Pike is the damsel in distress."

///////////

Joss was on set through most of principal photography, which began in Los Angeles on February 20, 1992. Shooting mostly took place at night, which took a toll on both cast and crew—but he was more frustrated by the fact that Fran Kuzui had a distinctly different take on the script they'd revised together. Instead of the edgy B-horror movie Joss, Reubens, and Perry had in mind, Kuzui wanted to play up the comedy to the point of camp. She said that *Buffy* "isn't a vampire movie, but a pop culture comedy about what people *think* about vampires." That interpretation was a far cry from the dark tale of an empowered blonde girl who goes into a dark alley and kicks some ass. Joss had spent so much time crafting a story with a distinct purpose, but now that someone else was in charge, that purpose would go unfulfilled.

However, he also felt that as the director, Kuzui should have the final say in creating the film. "Fran Kuzui came in when nobody else wanted the film, said, 'We're going to put this together,'" Joss said. "Without [the Kuzuis], there would be no film. . . . I didn't agree with the way the movie was going, but I also kept my mouth shut because you respect the director. . . . You respect the person above you, and you make suggestions and you do your best. . . . But you don't ever disrupt the chain of command. You have to have faith in the person who's running it or things will fall apart."

"Kristy Swanson [said], 'Please, tell me how to do this. Tell me what you want,'" Joss recalled. "I literally said, 'I can't.' Because I have always treated film and television like the army, and I'm very strict about it. It was not my place. It was the director's movie. At that point I was there to try and help the director realize her vision, and that's all."

It was Donald Sutherland who ultimately drove Joss from the set. Joss felt that Kuzui allowed Sutherland to take control on set, even to rewrite his own dialogue at times with no concern for the plot. "He had a very bad attitude. He was incredibly rude to the director, he was rude to everyone around him," Joss said. "He's a great actor . . . but the thing is, he acts well enough that you didn't notice, with his little rewrites, and his little ideas about what his character should do, that he was actually destroying the movie. . . . So I got out of there. I had to run away."

Seeing how upset he was by Sutherland's actions, a friend asked Joss why he couldn't just suck it up and let all the changes go. Joss felt that was an unacceptable reaction, both for what it would say about the integrity of the story and how it would affect his writing going forward. "You can't sit down at your desk and go, 'Meh, it doesn't matter what I write, because they're going to change it, or they're going to fuck it up,'" he says. "You have to sit down and go, 'This will be perfect and pure and delightful, and realized exactly as written.'"

Interestingly, Sutherland was frustated by the course the film was taking the same way that Joss was. According to Kaz Kuzui, both Sutherland and Hauer disliked how the tone was changing from the script they'd read. "They thought the movie was very serious and became insecure," he said. "They tried to make their roles more complex, more emotional." Perhaps if Joss had sat down to talk with them, he'd have realized that they were all closer on the same page than he had thought.

//////////

The experience was not without its saving graces. One of the few redeeming aspects was working with Paul Reubens. According to Joss, Paul was his beacon of hope, the person who made him feel, "OK, that made me feel a little bit better about the movie, even for like thirty seconds."

At one point, Reubens approached Joss about potentially changing one of Amilyn's lines, concerned that the change would affect other elements of the script. Joss was ecstatic that his work was being considered so closely. "I didn't know that you people existed!" he told Reubens. "Oddly enough, I'd mostly just worked with movie stars. I hadn't met most of them, but I had worked with people who could just do whatever they wanted. And to have somebody say, 'Um, no, I get that there's a bigger picture than me' was kind of a new experience for me."

But by the time they were filming Amilyn's death scene, it was clear that this respectful attitude wouldn't rule the day. Unlike how it was written in the script, the scene would be a melodramatic, overtly comedic bit of improv in which the character spends twenty minutes dying. Joss had pretty much clocked out by this point, but Reubens was still worried about how the writer would feel. He knew that Joss wanted the film to be dark and felt that his long and funny death scene may have been a misstep.

For Joss, however, that scene redeemed, if only a little, the way he felt about Fran Kuzui's interpretation. "Paul's adjustment was about spinning on a dime and just being so goddamn funny: 'This is what I'm in, and I've giving myself up to it,'" he explains.

//////////

Production wrapped in April, and 20th Century Fox was so convinced that the film would be a box office success that it moved the release date up to July. The studio developed a surprisingly big marketing campaign for such a low-budget film, including many billboard and newspaper ads across the country. The actors, however, didn't all seem to be on the same page about how to publicize the film. In the same *Entertainment Weekly* article, Swanson described *Buffy the Vampire Slayer* as "a comedy, but also a satire about values in America," while Luke Perry said that "this is not going to be a critically acclaimed movie, but I still like it. If you're looking to find the meaning of life, don't watch our movie. If you're looking to have a good time, this is the best place to be."

Joss knew that the final film would not be representative of the dark and comedic action-horror film of empowerment that he had scripted, and he had time to prepare for the release a few months down the road. However, he had no warning of the next, far more devastating event in his life.

5

THE WORLD UPENDS

By 1992, Lee Stearns had spent nearly half her life teaching at Riverdale Country School. Two years earlier, the White House Commission on Presidential Scholars honored her as an outstanding teacher, yet people had held her in high esteem long before she received the prestigious title. Lee constantly pushed her students to think about their personal effect on the world around them, both on a global scale—she helped establish New York City's first high school chapter of the human rights organization Amnesty International—and in much smaller, more personal terms, as in the afternoon teas she cohosted for senior girls, which focused on the issues particular to the lives of female students at Riverdale.

Lee often took both her children's friends and her students into her personal life. On one of her earliest sabbaticals, instead of heading off and leaving all things work-related at home, she and husband Stephen had taken four students along with them to travel through Europe. (She also developed plans for a never-realized sojourn from Britain to the Middle East through Rome via the old Roman roads.) Over time, her home became a sanctuary for several students and faculty colleagues who needed a place to live. Joss's best friend Chris Boal lived with Lee and Stephen for a time after he left college. And a few were lucky enough to be asked along for a getaway at Lee's Catskills farm.

Lee spent much of her time upstate writing. She had the final manuscript for one historical novel and was working on her next, for which she had spent time in the British Museum researching, among other things, an immensely powerful woman in Queen Elizabeth I's court. Several years earlier, she and fellow Riverdale teacher Nancy Rosenberg had written *Bellwether*, a comedic story about a prep school. The last full manuscript she finished involved a presidential campaign in the year 2000—a time that, though just eight years in the future, she would not live to see.

Lee Stearns died unexpectedly of a cerebral aneurysm on May 20, 1992.

//////////

Nearly a decade later, Joss would relive the experience of his mother's death—the surreal moments and his seemingly irrational reactions—through one of his fictional female avatars, while writing the *Buffy* episode in which the main character's mother, Joyce, dies.

In the fifth-season episode "The Body," Buffy arrives home one morning to find her mother on the couch, cold and unresponsive. Buffy blindly goes through the motions—calling 911 and then Giles, her surrogate father figure, to come and be with her, watching the paramedics try and fail to revive her mother—until finally she is once again alone with her mother's body.

Over the years, fans have told him that it helped them deal with a death that had happened years earlier. Joss was touched but surprised by how many people reached out to say that they found the episode comforting and cathartic. To him, it was not a story about finding comfort in God or coming to terms with what death means in some grand, preplanned scheme. "At this time a lot of people turn to, as [writer] Tim Minear would call him, the Sky Bully," Joss said. "But since I don't believe in the Sky Bully, and don't really have that to fall back on, I haven't really found any lessons in death other than I wish it wouldn't."

For Joss, the point of "The Body" was to capture the first few hours after someone dies, when there is "no solution, catharsis, or anything else . . . the almost-boredom." At one point, Buffy fixates on something meaningless—the buttons on the house phone—which was something that Joss did when Lee died. It isn't until the moment when Giles arrives and attempts CPR on Joyce that Buffy reacts with an incredible intensity and yells at him to not touch "the body."

"I wanted to be very specific about what it felt like the moment you discover [that] you've lost someone. That moment of dumbfounded shock. That airlessness of losing somebody," Joss said. "Death is a physical thing. . . . Apart from the sense of loss that you inevitably feel, there is the fact of a body. And dealing with that is an experience that really does kind of stop time. . . .

"I had always learned from TV that a death made everybody stronger and better, and learn about themselves. My experience was that an important piece had been taken out of the puzzle, amongst my family or friends, and that that piece would never be replaced and people would never be the same. There is no glorious payoff. There are sometimes revelations, and lessons that are useful. You have to take something out of it, because it's inevitable: none of us [are] getting out of here alive."

//////////

After 20th Century Fox bought the *Buffy* film, the studio offered Joss a development deal. As a part of it, he'd written a script called *Nobody Move*. It was a comedy about a twelve-year-old boy whose girlfriend, the love of his life, and her family are preparing to move away, so he decides to stop them. His schemes, each one bigger than the last, all seem to backfire.

In addition to becoming the Wile E. Coyote in a tween romantic comedy, the boy is coming to terms with having recently lost his mother. Everyone around him, including his father, thinks that he is fine and doesn't pay him much attention. Desperate and alone, he constructs all his over-the-top plans to keep his girlfriend from leaving because of his need to keep anything else from changing.

Joss actually wrote *Nobody Move* before his mother died. At the time, he felt that the boy's actions seemed fake and unrealistic. He didn't know where they were coming from as he wrote them, just that they needed to be done. And then his own mother died, and he did everything the boy did in the script. It wasn't until years later that he put it all together— that he had all the same reactions and had no understanding of why he did them.

It was an intense realization for him, and he referred to this time through a quiet, emotional exchange during an awkward moment between Buffy and her friend's girlfriend, Tara, in "The Body." Tara reveals that her own mother died when she was seventeen and that there were thoughts and reactions that she had that she couldn't understand or begin to explain to anyone else. "Thoughts that made me feel like I was losing it, or like I was some kind of horrible person," she says.

Buffy then asks if Tara's mother's death was sudden. "No, and yes," Tara replies. "It's always sudden."

//////////

Two months after Lee died, *Buffy the Vampire Slayer* opened July 31, 1992. It would go on to achieve decent box office numbers—around $16 million against its budget of about $9 million—but the reviews were less than stellar. It was an additional blow for Joss in an incredibly painful year. He had lost his lifelong role model and feminist icon, and the icon and role model he had created—nurturing the character for years, even drawing a sketch of her at one point—had been twisted into something unrecognizable by the Kuzuis' desire to make a broad comedy. It was a hard and important lesson, and one that he took to heart: in the future, he would need to find a new way to take creative control of his work.

After the *Buffy* premiere, Kai suggested that maybe a few years down the road, Joss would get to tell the story of his Slayer again, the way he wanted to make it. He remembers telling her, "Ha ha ha, you little naive fool. It doesn't work that way. That'll never happen."

//////////

In the aftermath of his mother's death, Joss shifted his focus to spend a lot of time with his father. Both men were out of work at the time; Tom had finished up his run as executive producer on *The Golden Girls* when the series ended in May 1992. So he and his son worked together on some spec scripts and a sitcom pilot. Their pilot was modeled after the show *Siskel & Ebert*, in which two rival Chicago movie reviewers discussed, and often argued about, films that had recently been released. The sitcom version by the Whedons gave that premise an *Odd Couple* spin, with extra mutual loathing. To keep the series current and interesting, the fictional reviewers would comment on real movies during the show, and the scenes in which the characters actually reviewed the films would be shot the day before each episode aired so that they could actually reflect what was coming out the following weekend.

Their pilot wasn't picked up, but working together so closely was quite fun for both father and son. Not only did they have similar sensibilities in their writing, but Joss also learned a lot from Tom. "His very simple advice has always been the best," Joss says. "First one being: if you have a story that matters, you don't need jokes, and if you don't, all the jokes in the world won't save you."

Joss poured additional energy into working on his own new ideas and spec scripts. Agent Chris Harbert had a special technique for pushing his client into action: when another writer sold a project or a script, he'd send Joss the *Variety* article about it, because he knew it would engage his competitive side. "I would go upstairs and start writing. It's that competitive envious thing," Joss said. "I get jealous of anyone who gets to do cool stuff. That's never not the case. It's part of being ambitious."

Joss also got into script doctoring—working on other people's scripts that were already in development to punch up the dialogue or story. In 1993, he picked up his first gig writing "loop lines" for the remake of *The Getaway* starring Alec Baldwin and Kim Basinger. He scripted new dialogue that could be looped in over footage that had already been shot—for instance, when an actor's back was to the camera—to fill in missing connections in the story or just get rid of dead air. "If you look carefully at *The Getaway*," he said, "you'll see that when people's backs are turned, or their heads are slightly out of frame, the whole movie has a certain edge to it." The following year, he would spend a couple of days punching up dialogue for the western *The Quick and the Dead* so that he could meet the director, Sam Raimi, who had written and directed a film very influential to Joss's horror sensibilities: *The Evil Dead*. "That's a movie that goes genuinely insane, on its own terms, without ever violating its terms of reality," Joss said. "The movie itself goes bonkers, and I just think that's a beautiful thing."

/////////

Joss had several meetings with Jorge Saralegui, the junior executive at Fox who had recommended that the studio buy the *Buffy the Vampire Slayer* film. Saralegui had also worked with Joss on *Nobody Move*, and while that script never quite made it through the development process, it had helped to establish a friendship between them. One day over lunch, Saralegui pitched the idea of a "dog movie, a movie with a dog in it," Joss said. "I was writing mostly comedy, and I was being pitched comedies because that's what I had come from. I was pitched so many [examples] like 'It's *Wayne's World* meets *Flubber*.'"

Joss countered with a gag pitch: "*Die Hard* on a bridge." The joke was that in the early 1990s, many scripts were written in the hope of recapturing the blockbuster success of the skyscraper-set action movie *Die Hard* (1988). But Saralegui thought the pitch, and the idea of setting it on the George Washington Bridge in New York City, had real potential that Joss didn't see. However, Saralegui knew that Hollywood would see Joss as the guy who wrote *Buffy the Vampire Slayer* and the kid-centric *Nobody Move* and worked on *Roseanne*, and with that résumé, he'd have little success selling an action movie on a pitch alone. The executive felt that Joss was better off writing a full spec script; once it was complete, Joss could shop it around town, letting the industry see his versatility.

Saralegui became adamant that he go home and write the script. "Don't option it, don't tell anybody about it, go and write it," Joss remembered Saralegui saying. "I guarantee you will never be pitched a dog movie again."

And so Joss did. His screenplay for *Suspension*, as in suspension bridge, followed Harry Monk, an ex-con who has just been released from a New Jersey prison after serving a fifteen-year stint for an armed robbery that included the shooting of a police officer. Harry is desperate to get back to New York, to return to an old haunt, but as he crosses over the Hudson River, he and the rest of the people on the George Washington Bridge are taken hostage.

After leaving his cab and exploring the bridge a bit, Harry connects with Avery, a skeptical female police officer. More officers get pulled into the hostage situation, and they tell her that Harry is not to be trusted. Joss said that due to Harry's crime, "when he hooks up with other policemen, they hate him; they don't trust him and he has to earn their trust." For his first proper action film, Joss explored an idea that echoed back to his classes with Richard Slotkin at Wesleyan: redemption through violence.

There is a *lot* of violence in the script. The mastermind behind the bridge hijack is a psychopath named Chi, who is unstable and unpredictable and, in typical Whedon fashion, quite snarky and funny. The funny, however, does not soften his murderous tendencies. In order to show the police how far he will go, Chi has a young boy shot on live TV. "I wanted a baby for that spot," the character admits, "but having the boy . . . was a nice touch."

With the *Die Hard* comparisons obvious, the *Suspension* script does not do much to change up the action formula that will see Harry and

Avery emerge victorious and alive at the end of the film. Yet Joss did a great job of keeping the suspense at an intense and believable level, and making all of the characters real and relatable—which were skills that he would soon bring to another action film.

In June 1993, *Die Hard* and *48 Hrs.* producer Lawrence Gordon's company Largo Entertainment bought the script for $1 million—a surprising amount for a project with no talent or director attached, from a fairly untested twenty-eight-year-old screenwriter. All of a sudden, Joss was starting to be widely seen not as a comedy guy but as an action writer. *Suspension* was a huge deal that put him on the map.

Joss hoped that the filmmakers would keep him on the project, but as often happens with less experienced scribes, he was replaced by another writer. The preproduction costs kept building, and in the end, *Suspension* was never made. "It's one of those scripts that you eventually put so much money into it that it wasn't worth continuing, which happens a lot," Saralegui says.

//////////

The following year, Joss sold his next script to Sony for $1.5 million. In *Afterlife*, an intense science fiction tale, scientist Daniel Hoffstettor is in the last stages of succumbing to a fatal disease and trying to make the most of his final days with his wife, Laura. After he dies, he awakes with newfound health in a brand-new body. It has all been engineered by a government agency called Tank that "resurrects" dying men whom the agency feels have more to contribute to society, transplanting their brains into young, healthy bodies. Tank wants him to continue his research, but Daniel is desperate to reconnect with his wife. He escapes from the agency's facility to find Laura, and while he's on the run, he quickly finds out that his new body may be healthy, but it comes with some issues of its own. It previously belonged to a notorious and very recognizable serial killer, and the killer's personality slowly emerges to take control.

Like *Suspension*, *Afterlife* was never made, but it, too, showed some of the hallmarks of Joss's successful projects to come. First, while the story contained fantastical elements, Joss grounded them all in reality by focusing on the very human interactions that draw the audience to connect with the characters. Second, the script embodied Joss's deep distaste for large entities that impose their desires on the free will of individuals.

This theme would return several times in his television series, with the Watchers Council, which oversees and attempts to dictate the actions of the Slayer in *Buffy*; the Alliance, the oppressive interplanetary government in *Firefly*; and the sketchy and morally ambiguous Rossum Corporation in *Dollhouse*. It would also become a factor in Joss's personal life, in the form of the Writers Guild of America (WGA), which he would go up against in two separate battles.

////////////

By 1993, Jorge Saralegui had been promoted to vice president of production at 20th Century Fox and was producing his first movie, the Keanu Reeves / Dennis Hopper actioner *Speed*. The film is about Jack Traven (Reeves), a SWAT officer who is pulled into a plot by a deranged bomber (Hopper) in which a Los Angeles city bus has been rigged to blow up if its speed falls below fifty miles per hour. Jack must work with Annie (Sandra Bullock), a passenger who takes the wheel when the driver is injured, to navigate the L.A. traffic, help track down the bomber, and figure out how to get all of the passengers off the bus before it explodes.

The film was set to shoot with director Jan de Bont, who had been the cinematographer on *Die Hard* and *Lethal Weapon 3*. Right before they were about to start production, Fox decided that the dialogue needed to be polished and that Graham Yost, the original writer (who also had been primarily a television screenwriter), wasn't right for the job. They felt that it was time to bring in a heavyweight.

The studio hired Paul Attanasio, who had written the soon-to-be-Oscar-nominated *Quiz Show* and the Michael Douglas / Demi Moore vehicle *Disclosure*. Two weeks later he turned in a draft, but instead of polishing the dialogue, he had drastically changed the script. Attanasio's script was sent to Peter Chernin, the new chairman of Fox Entertainment Group, who was very passionate about the project. Chernin called Saralegui on a Saturday morning and asked what he had done to the script.

"I knew it sucked," Saralegui says. "I don't know why [Attanasio] did what he did, but he did what he did." Chernin subtly told him that he was on the verge of losing control of the project and to look for help. Saralegui brought in big-name producer Walter F. Parkes (*WarGames*, *Awakenings*), who read *Speed* and liked it, and mentioned some writers that he thought would be good to work on the dialogue. Saralegui, remembering how much he'd enjoyed the stylized dialogue in the *Buffy the Vampire Slayer* screenplay, suggested Joss.

Parkes had never read Joss's work before, but he was on board once Saralegui sent him some scripts. "He loved Joss's writing," Saralegui says. The two quickly met with and hired Joss, who came onto the film a week before they started shooting in September 1993. Joss didn't get to see his vision of "*Die Hard* on a bridge" come to fruition, but he did get to play with "*Die Hard* on a bus."

One of the first things that Joss did was to revise the character of one of the bus passengers. Stephens (Alan Ruck) was originally an obnoxious lawyer. He was always set to die, but because he'd been such an unlikeable character, there was no reason for the audience to feel bad for him. "I turned him into a likeable, sort of doofy tourist guy and [they said] 'Well, now we can't kill him,'" Joss recalled. "My opinion was 'Well, now you should, because now people will actually care when he dies.'"

Joss also pared down parts of the script that he felt were artificial. Reeves's Officer Jack Traven was initially a hotshot maverick. But Reeves had shadowed law enforcement agents to develop his character, and he was taken by how polite they were, how they often courteously addressed people as "sir" and "ma'am." He also respectfully asked for changes to particular dialogue and actions that he felt were incongruous with his character. Joss was inspired by the care the actor had put into the character, and he rewrote Traven to be less of a hothead and instead just a cop who thought more laterally than the rest of his squad. "What if he's just the polite guy trying not to get anybody killed?"

"It's all about finding the emotional reality of the characters and getting them from A to B in a realistic fashion," Joss says. "You're connecting the dots. 'OK, he goes from a bus to a train to a plane. Why? What does that mean? What's that gonna do?' It can be great fun. Very stressful when you find the flaws, and you go, 'Ooh!' Make the flaws where the meat is."

//////////

Speed was released on June 10, 1994, and grossed $14.5 million in its first weekend, ultimately bringing in $121.3 million in North America and over $283 million worldwide—an impressive follow-up to *Buffy*'s $16 million. It was also a critical hit; Roger Ebert wrote, "Films like *Speed* belong to the genre I call Bruised Forearm Movies, because you're always grabbing the arm of the person sitting next to you. Done wrong, they seem like tired replays of old chase clichés . . . done as well as *Speed*, they generate a kind of manic exhilaration."

Sandra Bullock, who was still early in her career, stood out in what could have been an especially clichéd role, that of Jack's potential love interest. The *Washington Post* offered Bullock's Annie the sort of praise that would soon become common for Joss's female characters: "If it weren't for the smart-funny twist she gives to her lines—they're the best in the film—the air on that bus would have been stifling. . . . She emerges as a slightly softer version of the Linda Hamilton-Sigourney Weaver heroines: capable, independent, but still irresistibly vulnerable."

///////////

The writing credits for *Speed* were a matter of great contention, with Joss demanding recognition for his contribution and the film's original writer, Graham Yost, insisting that he should receive sole screenplay credit. The dispute ended up in arbitration before the Writers Guild. Under WGA rules, a writer must have contributed to the plot of the story, not just its dialogue, to receive official credit, so the guild ultimately sided with Yost and Joss went uncredited. (His writing credit is listed, however, on a rare early version of the *Speed* poster—a copy of which Joss owns.)

"The arbitration was a great sticking point with me," Joss said. "I've always just disagreed with the WGA's policy that says you can write every line of dialogue for a movie—and they literally say this—and not deserve credit on it. Because I think that makes no sense of any kind." He realized that "writers get very protective of themselves. They're worried that some producer will want to add a line so he can put his name on it. But what they can do is throw writers at it forever without putting their names on it because of this rule. So I actually don't think it works for writers. It certainly didn't work for me."

Saralegui also disagreed with the ruling, even if he understood the WGA guidelines. Joss "deserved credit" because he was responsible for a lot of the feel of the movie, he says, and "the characters felt different after he wrote them," even though these newly fleshed-out characters were still the same ones that Yost had created. "It's really Graham Yost's story idea, but it's also his characters and his plot," he adds. "So, it's a tough one."

It was not until a decade later that Yost admitted in an interview that Joss "wrote 98.9 percent of the dialogue." Yost added, "We were very much in sync, it's just that I didn't write the dialogue as well as he did. That was a hard part of the whole 'Speed' thing. It's my name up there, but I didn't write the whole thing. But I fought hard to get that credit, so I'll live with it."

Even later, Yost expressed how impressed he was with Joss's writing, and said that he would always be grateful to him. "When I read his draft, I went, 'Oh, thank god. Oh, he gets it.' He's a very funny writer, a very smart writer. So I was very, very lucky." He also credited Joss with Hopper's signature taunting line: "Pop quiz, hotshot."

As for Joss, he said that "Graham Yost has always been very polite to me and very sweet but he did say to me, 'You would have done the same thing.' And all I could say to him at the time was, 'Well, I guess we don't know if that's true.'"

Even without official credit, the *Speed* script got Joss's work noticed in the industry. Between it and *Buffy the Vampire Slayer*, he now had two solid projects that showcased his dialogue prowess on screen.

6

TO INFINITY AND BEYOND: *TOY STORY* AND *ALIEN: RESURRECTION*

At first glance, the theatrical version of *Buffy the Vampire Slayer* had nothing in common with the 1995 computer-animated classic *Toy Story*: quippy blonde teenager does battle with evil vampires versus a tale about toys learning how to get along. And yet it was *Buffy* that brought Joss to the attention of Pixar Animation Studios when it was time for the company to rewrite the script for its first film.

In 1993, work was well under way at Pixar on *Toy Story*, a long-form version of its 1988 Oscar-winning animated short *Tin Toy*. John Lasseter, who had been an animator at the Walt Disney Company, led the project. During his time at Disney, Lasseter had become increasingly interested in the possibilities of full-length film composed entirely of computer-generated imagery (CGI), which made him an anomaly in an era when hand-drawn animation was still the norm. After he unwittingly stepped on the toes of some of his direct supervisors with a plan to produce a CGI version of Thomas Disch's 1980 novel *The Brave Little Toaster*, Lasseter was fired. He went on to become a founding member of Pixar Studios, which Apple cofounder Steve Jobs acquired in 1986.

Toy Story was the then-small animation studio's first big project, and it was in dire straits. Disney had agreed to back the film, and on November 19, 1993, it screened a rough draft of the picture, essentially just a filmed version of the storyboards combined with dialogue and music. Disney's verdict: the movie was unwatchable. The story had lost the heart that *Tin Toy* had; the leads, Woody the cowboy and Buzz Lightyear the astronaut, were sarcastic and unlikeable—not exactly ideal heroes for a children's movie.

Ironically, it was Disney chairman Jeffrey Katzenberg who had insisted that *Toy Story* should not be a children's movie at all. In the documentary *The Pixar Story*, Disney's Tom Schumacher explained that Katzenberg "would always . . . be pushing for what he called 'edge' . . . snappy, adult, the edge of inappropriate, and not to feel too young." He worried that the title would repel older kids and adults from the film, and under his guidance, Woody, whom countless children would later come to love and admire, was written as a bitter toy who berated and insulted all the other toys and was bound and determined to destroy Buzz.

Despite Katzenberg's prior instructions, Disney insisted that Pixar stop production and take three months to rethink and rewrite the film. It was the latest reversal in a tug of war between the organizations over the project—including a battle with Lasseter, who was insistent that the film not be a musical, unlike other Disney films of the era such as *The Little Mermaid*, *Beauty and the Beast*, and *Aladdin*.

The Disney regime pointed to one problem in particular: no one on Pixar's creative team was a writer. The group was filled with producers and animators, who were confident that they had good story instincts and could storyboard the film very well. But none of their previous shorts had had any dialogue, and usually a feature-length film needed characters that actually spoke. They agreed that the project needed a professional screenwriter.

So Lasseter's team began reading scripts, in search of someone who could save *Toy Story*. Several writers took a shot at it, but they weren't generating the top-notch material that the project needed. Unfortunately, a creative team that was new to screenwriting also lacked the skills to recognize the lack of experience of the writers that came through. Disney didn't want to leave the project in the hands of unproven scribes, so the company brought in an established writing partnership, Joel Cohen and former *National Lampoon* contributor Alec Sokolow. Cohen and Sokolow worked through seven drafts of the script with Pixar's story team before departing the project.

That's when the story team came across Joss's original *Buffy the Vampire Slayer* script. They loved it—they loved his irreverent style, and that the script was both dark and comedic. "It was fascinating to read the script that we loved, that had us cracking up and put wonderful images in our head," says Pixar's Andrew Stanton. "All the things that you would attribute to Joss now were fresh to us."

As luck would have it, Joss was already in the Disney stable at the time. He had wanted to work on musicals, and what better place to do so, he thought, than the studio whose recent animated blockbusters were inspiring a resurgence of the form? He was working on a new animated film that was supposed to be a musical version of the classic Jules Verne science fiction novel *Journey to the Center of the Earth* and would eventually become *Atlantis: The Lost Empire*. He'd also been deeply invested in a project that he called "Marco Polo Meets My Fair Lady." Through Disney's songwriter program, Joss had not only written the script but also penned the lyrics for three songs set to music by composer Robert Lindsey-Nassif. The studio, however, wanted to pull him off the project to work on a floundering CGI film that would have no singing whatsoever.

//////////

Yet there was a big reason why Joss wasn't entirely available to tackle *Toy Story*. When Disney came calling in late 1993, Joss and Kai were in the middle of an eight-week cross-country road trip. The journey was a bit of a test for their future. They had been together for a couple of years, but with all of the work Joss had been getting as a script doctor, Kai wasn't sure if he'd have enough time in his career to keep pursuing the relationship with the same intensity. She hoped the trek would prove whether they had the compatibility and commitment to make it long-term.

"I often say to people, 'Plan a wedding, take a road trip,'" she explains. "Then you really find out about a person." So they set out on a drive around the country, during which time Joss promised that he would not work, that he would just live in the moment with Kai. After the first five days with bad directions and bad food, there was little that Joss and Kai could hide from each other. Luckily, they were having a blast. "We loved driving across country and just laughing and talking and reading," she says. "We get along really well; we're very compatible." But about two weeks into their trip, Joss got the call about the *Toy Story* rewrite—and Disney wanted him right away.

Put off by the initial script, Kai begged him not do it, but Joss explained that the situation was every rewriter's dream. It was "a perfect structure with a ghastly script. If you have a pretty good script, but there's just something you can't put your finger on and figure out structurally, that's a nightmare," he says. "When you read something where the structure was John Lasseter's story concept, which was rock solid, and you could just go in there and do a strong rewrite, that's good."

Conflicted, Joss called his Wesleyan professor and mentor Jeanine Basinger for advice. He wanted to take the job, but he wanted to spend the time with Kai as he had promised. "Everything can be negotiated except Kai," Jeanine replied. "Negotiate the other end. Tell them you know exactly how to fix it and you'd love to do it—the problem is, they have to wait four weeks."

Joss did exactly that, which was a telling moment for Basinger. "I knew for sure Kai was the one," she says.

The rest of the trip went as swimmingly as the first two weeks. The only bad part of the whole experience was a single incident that Joss never lets Kai forget about. It speaks volumes about her tendency to jump into things impulsively and his hatred of spoilers. In a small South Dakota store, they found a big bag of old Nancy Drew books. They took turns reading the tales of the girl detective to each other in the car as they drove. "One day, we were reading this Nancy Drew, and [when] we got to where we were going, we took a nap. I couldn't help it, and I finished the book," she says sheepishly.

"I don't think Joss has ever been madder at me than when I finished that Nancy Drew. He felt so betrayed that I would go on and finish the book. I was apologetic the whole time: 'I'm so sorry. I don't know what happened. I just lost control. I had to know what was going to happen.'

"Joss responded, 'It's Nancy Drew. You know what's going to happen. It'll work out OK.'"

///////////

When they returned home, Joss left for Oakland to work with Pixar. The project was so much more creatively involved than the script doctoring that Joss had been doing. It was a complete rewrite of the film, one he would have to undertake with a whole group of collaborators. His first step into that world made him nervous: when he was introduced to the team, they were told that Pixar had to shut down production on the film due to the major story issues. "Many of you are going to be laid off, and

Joss is here to fix the script," he remembered someone announcing. "And then I was just like, 'Why are you pointing at me? What's going on? This is horrible!'"

Yet unlike the tense, awkward group dynamics he'd experienced on the writing staffs of *Roseanne* and *Parenthood*, he discovered that the *Toy Story* team members were eager to jump back into the story and strip it down to the essentials. They threw out all of the extraneous ideas to dedicate their focus on the very simple thing that makes Disney so popular: a story that connects with its audience. Lasseter told them not to concern themselves with fancy applications of CGI animation. At the time, not many people had seen computer animation—certainly not at the level that Pixar is now famous for—so it was easy to wow people with early animated tests of Woody and Buzz and footage of green army men walking. But Lasseter insisted that Joss and the team needed to concentrate on *Toy Story*'s narrative instead.

That guidance helped the writers shake off the issues they were having with the script. Or, as Joss explained, they realized, "Oh! We already know how to do this. We've just got a slightly new medium to do it in."

Despite his strong desire to write songs for Disney, Joss agreed with Lasseter's choice to refrain from making *Toy Story* a musical. "It would have been a really bad musical, because it's a buddy movie," Joss explained. "It's about people who won't admit what they want, much less sing about it." A staple of Disney's musicals is the "I want" song, in which the main character plainly expresses how he or she wishes life could change. But "Woody can't do an 'I want' number," Joss said. "He's cynical and selfish, he doesn't know himself. Buddy movies are about sublimating, punching an arm, 'I hate you.' It's not about open emotion." (Members of the Pixar team were surprised that someone who had written such dark, macabre, funny stuff as *Buffy the Vampire Slayer* knew so much about musicals and was proud of it. "He would wear his musical interests big on his sleeve, when most people would hide that fact," Stanton remembers.)

Joss worked closely with Pixar's team as everyone got their heads around the idea of *Toy Story* as a buddy picture. Buzz Lightyear had always been conceived as a Dudley Do-Right: dim-witted but cheerful and self-aware. Joss helped them reenvision the character as an action figure who isn't aware that he's a toy, and who therefore takes his job as an Intergalactic Space Ranger quite seriously. It was a huge epiphany that turned the whole movie around and created the chemistry in *Toy Story*.

Once they had a good grasp on the film's characters, the group built the story back up. Joss loved being in the room with all the animators and getting to try anything. "They were so sweet and so much fun," he says. "Watching them draw caricatures of each other, getting Sharpie headaches and having to leave the room, and come back and draw in pencil. Just throwing ideas back and forth, and really feeling, you know, having your voice heard. My voice has been heard in very few of the rewrites I've done, and this was a different animal. This was really something that I felt like I got to help shape totally."

The feelings of respect and excitement were mutual. "We're all animators, so it's kind of a prerequisite that we know our comic books, we know our toys, we know our movies," Stanton says. "Our references were his references, so he felt like one of us." As storyboard artists and as gag men, the Pixar animators were used to sitting in a room together, spitballing ideas, and pinning drawings on the wall—which turned out to be quite similar to what Joss was used to in a television writers' room. "I think Joss was a little envious that we could draw our ideas so fast; that tends to be the case with a lot of screenwriters when we work with them," Stanton adds. "But we were so jealous that he would come up with these incredible one-liners. The thing that I connect to him so strongly is that I got to see, firsthand, the germ of the idea be created in a group." Sometimes those germs led them down the wrong path for the story. "It's not like he came in and solved it for us," he clarifies. "We made our own mistakes, and we made our own solutions as a group."

Joss would take all the ideas from the Pixar team and go into his office, crank up the music he needed to be inspired, and write. When he emerged, he delivered pages that evoked exactly what they had been trying to describe in the room as a group—but so much stronger, more economical, and so much more concise. "It was this huge epiphany, because [Joss's writing] was beyond just the dialogue—his descriptions and the economy of his scriptwriting forced the exact images he wanted in your head," Stanton explains. "It was this huge lightbulb for me that scriptwriting is not writing novels—it's cinematic dictation. It's having the art of being able to describe what the final image will be on the screen cinematically so well that anybody that reads this script page can't help but see the same image. That was what a great scriptwriter did." Stanton's résumé now includes cowriting credits on Pixar's later hits *Monsters, Inc., Finding Nemo,* and

WALL-E—and he's quick to point to Joss as an influence, having soaked up how Joss worked and wrote during their time together on *Toy Story*.

Eventually, the story took shape. *Toy Story* is the tale of a little boy's toys and their adventures when he isn't around. The group is led by Woody the cowboy (Tom Hanks), a generally stand-up and cheerful fella who enjoys his status as Andy's favorite toy. Things change when Andy's birthday party brings a new player into the mix: Buzz Lightyear (Tim Allen), the astronaut action figure who doesn't realize he's not a real astronaut. When the Space Ranger usurps Woody's position as Andy's favorite toy, Woody decides to get rid of Buzz. His plans go awry, however, when they both get lost. Adding to the drama is the family's impending move. Can the duo work together to get back home before they're left behind—or, worse, before they fall into the hands of Sid Phillips, the evil neighbor hell-bent on toy destruction?

Joss tried to inject some girl power into the testosterone-heavy storyline by suggesting that it be Barbie who comes in and saves Woody and Buzz from Sid. "She's [*Terminator 2*'s] Sarah Connor in a pink convertible, all business and very cool," Joss said. But he wasn't able to get his way; Mattel execs wouldn't allow *Toy Story* to develop an actual action-hero identity for Barbie. In addition, the Pixar team itself preferred to keep the focus on Woody. "We decided we could either be PC and fair about this or bring true toy moments," Stanton explained. Joss had better luck adding a Whedonesque character to the mix with Rex, a boisterous green plastic tyrannosaur who is often taken over by fits of anxiety and the worry that he isn't scary enough.

In addition, Joss "wrote a lot of great lines that stayed in the movie," Stanton remembers. "His best one was under the truck, where Buzz says to Woody, 'You are a sad, strange, little man. You have my pity. Farewell.'"

////////////

In April 1994, about four months after Joss joined the *Toy Story* team, Disney finally greenlit the film to go back into production. Joss had become a hot property and was being pursued for other projects, so he decided to part ways with the *Toy Story* team.

Though Joss left, the rewrites continued; Pixar's staff members are known to never stop refining the script even when a film is well into production. But Joss's influence lingered. He had reset the bar, and the rest of the creative team rose to the occasion. "Joss helped set the tone of sincerity and the reverence that I'd like to think is an amalgamation of him and us—as what everybody in the world knows as Pixar," Stanton says.

The Pixar team didn't see Joss again until a test screening when the film was nearly finished. He seemed a little shocked at how much it had changed. A couple weeks after the movie came out and he had finally seen it two or three more times, he sent a letter to the team. "'I didn't get it at first, but now I GET it'—and I remembered he capitalized *GET*," Stanton says with a laugh. "It just took a while for him to adjust from where he had left the film to what it became."

Toy Story opened just before Thanksgiving, on November 22, 1995. Despite Jeffrey Katzenberg's earlier concerns, fans from every age bracket embraced *Toy Story*. Critics admired the fact that such a warm and engaging tale could be told in CGI, through what the *New York Times* called its "utterly brilliant anthropomorphism" and "exultant wit." *Entertainment Weekly*'s Owen Gleiberman wrote, "I can hardly imagine having more fun at the movies than I did at *Toy Story*," and Kevin McManus of the *Washington Post* said, "For once, reality lives up to hype. With *Toy Story*, gigantic superlatives become appropriate, even necessary. . . . In fact, to find a movie worthy of comparison you have to reach all the way back to 1939, when the world went gaga over Oz."

The film had earned more than $39 million by the end of its first weekend, on its way to becoming the top-grossing film of the year in North America and one of the most successful animated films ever released to that point (behind only 1992's *Aladdin* and 1994's *The Lion King*). *Toy Story* would go on to gross almost $362 million worldwide.

//////////

After the film was finished, Lasseter called Joss to let him know that there was an issue with the story credits on the film. Arbitration with the original *Toy Story* screenwriters was still being worked out, and several animators had taken a pass through the script at one point or another as well. Some had even completely rewritten it, attempting to avoid carrying over the bad ideas they felt were in the previous versions. Eventually, a lot of names ended up on the cover page of the final version of *Toy Story*—many of them writers whose work didn't appear in the final movie. Nonetheless, Lasseter wanted Joss's permission to give story credit to all of the animators who worked on the movie.

More than a year after the WGA arbitration issue with *Speed*, Joss was now in Graham Yost's position. He told Lasseter it was fine to add the writers in. "[It is] gratifying to me because it means I finally have an answer to [Yost's question]. Which is, 'No, I wouldn't,'" Joss said.

Joss's work on *Toy Story* landed him an Academy Award nomination for Best Original Screenplay. The Oscar was later awarded to Christopher McQuarrie's neo-noir mystery *The Usual Suspects*. *Toy Story*, however, is still an Academy Award–winning film; John Lasseter was given a special achievement award (the first for any animated film) for "the development and inspired application of techniques that have made possible the first feature-length computer-animated film."

/////////

Joss's next project wasn't exactly another Oscar winner. In 1994, he was approached to do script rewrites at the end of production for *Waterworld*, starring Kevin Costner and produced by Lawrence Gordon. The film had already been plagued with production setbacks, and costs were running as high as $175 million—a record at the time.

"When they said, 'Do you want to come down to Hawaii next week?' *Mad Max* in the water? Include me in! I was so excited," Joss says. "Then I read the script, and it's a hundred and twenty pages and the last forty pages all take place on land or a ship. 'This guy has gills, man! What were you guys thinking?'"

An assignment that was supposed to last one week quickly expanded to nearly two months. "I was there for seven weeks," he recalled, "and I accomplished nothing." The scenes he wrote weren't filmed, and Costner had his own ideas of how the story should go; when he wasn't giving notes to Joss, he was scripting scenes that the writing staff wasn't allowed to touch. Joss described the experience as feeling like he was incredibly well paid to take dictation.

According to Joss, his favorite thing that he wrote was the first time the Mariner (Costner) sneaks onto a big tanker to confront the bad guys. He promptly freaks out. The female character accompanying him asks what's wrong. The Mariner, a man whose whole life has been on the sea, replies, "I can't see the water."

"Of course it got thrown out," Joss says. "In those situations, what's really happening is they are asking you to make the climax cheaper. They don't actually want you to fix the movie, even if you can."

//////////

When he wasn't off in another city working on other people's scripts, Joss focused his attention on Kai. He would curate movie montages for her: "He puts together these unbelievable bits of movies, little bits, little scenes of movies. And they're spectacular. He'll put clips together and he'll say, 'Shut your eyes,' because I always shut my eyes until they're actually on. I'll be waiting around for a while with my eyes shut, having a drink, and he'll be fumbling about to get the next piece," she laughs.

It started as a way to amuse her, and then grew into both a lovely way to spend the night together and a helpful tool when Joss is working on a character in a script. "Something usually ties them together. But sometimes it's just certain things he wants to watch. He's a film buff— you can't watch five thousand movies every day and have a job and have a life." If he was working on a villain, he'd make a montage of villains from his favorite movies. For a movie montage of examples of genuine romantic love, he would include scenes from *Magnolia* (1999) between John C. Reilly and Melora Walters, the handprint scene in *Twenty Four Seven* (1997), and "absolutely the part in *The Remains of the Day* (1993) where Anthony Hopkins won't let Emma Thompson look at his book. That's just heartbreaking," Joss explains. "Because he just can't do it, he just can't do it and she gives him every opening. The whole scene revolves around the secret of what's he reading, what's he reading, and it's a romance and he's so embarrassed. I'm gonna start to cry. I'm fine. I'll be just fine, just leave me alone."

"Every once in a while, he'll do montages for other people," Kai says, "but it really works better just him and me. He knows I'm not going to judge, he isn't going to have to impress me, really. So he can be freer doing it."

Kai often refers to herself as being spoiled by Joss, explaining that not only does he do most of the cooking, but he also buys all of her clothes, because she hates to shop. One particular purchase led to a very impulsive decision.

They were at her apartment, where she was trying on a red velvet dress he had just bought her. "I put it on, and he just looked at me and said, 'Marry me,'" Kai laughs. "I said, 'Shut up.' He said, 'No, I mean it.'"

The proposal was not planned. In fact, when he started to feel that Kai was "the one" for him, Joss was terrified. Not to mention that this impromptu proposition completely upset his emotional schedule. "I wasn't supposed to meet my wife when I was twenty-seven. That's a bit young. I had all sorts of adventures I was going to have first," he explains. "I'm not sure what those adventures were; I'm sure they involved cockroach racing. This from a man who had stopped dating entirely for a year before I met her."

Kai was equally surprised, as neither one had really thought they'd get married—ever. It was an accidental, out-of-the-blue proposal, quite like their accidental, out-of-the-blue meeting four years earlier. But they'd already checked off "road trip" on Kai's ways of truly getting to know someone, so "plan a wedding" was just a bonus. That day, they went looking for a house, and they found the home that they'd live in for the next fourteen years. It would also be the place where they'd marry, on June 24, 1995.

//////////

That same year, Fox exec Jorge Saralegui was planning to resurrect a film franchise that was very close to Joss's heart. Over the course of more than a decade and three films, the *Alien* series had turned Sigourney Weaver into a science fiction legend as Lt. Ellen Ripley, arguably one of the greatest female protagonists of all time. Ripley wasn't the damsel in distress, defined by her relationship with the men around her (in fact, the part had originally been written so it could be played by either a woman or a man). Ripley led the charge, and fought the battles, and came out victorious.

The series began in 1979 with Ridley Scott's *Alien*, which had terrified Joss so much as a teenager and which he still considered his favorite horror film. In the movie, Lt. Ripley is a member of the crew of a spaceship returning to Earth from a mission when it receives a distress call from a distant planet. They descend to the planet and inadvertently bring back an alien parasite, which quickly grows into a horrifying creature that proceeds to terrorize the crew.

For the 1986 sequel, aptly titled *Aliens*, writing and directing duties passed to James Cameron, fresh off his breakout hit *The Terminator*. *Aliens* picks up fifty-seven years after the first film, as Ripley awakes from suspended animation to learn that a human colony has been established on the planet where her crew picked up the alien. When contact with the colony is lost, Ripley and a team of marines embark on an attack-and-recovery mission. They discover that the colonists have been slaughtered by similar alien creatures, but Ripley finds a sole survivor: a little girl named Newt. Taking the girl under her wing, Ripley assumes a beautiful dual role as a nurturing maternal figure and a fiercely protective warrior. *Aliens* took in more than $85 million in North America and $131 million worldwide, and Weaver was nominated for an Academy Award, only the second time a woman received a nomination for a role in a horror film (after Ellen Burstyn in 1973's *The Exorcist*).

The saga continued with 1992's *Alien 3*, directed by David Fincher, but critics and fans—including Joss—felt that it was a misstep in the evolution of the series. The sequel's path to the big screen was troubled from the beginning; screenplays from two different writers were tossed out before David Twohy was brought on and delivered a story that featured Ripley only briefly, focusing instead on Corporal Hicks, her love interest from *Aliens*. (Weaver was unhappy with the studio's changes to *Aliens* and would only agree to a cameo appearance in the sequel.) But when Fox president Joe Roth read Twohy's screenplay, he objected to the new direction. "Sigourney Weaver is the centerpiece of the series," he insisted, and her character was "really the only female warrior we have in our movie mythology."

Four more versions, including one set on a "wooden planet" inhabited by monks, were nixed before the twenty-eight-year-old Fincher, a music video director, was hired to helm what would be his first feature film. Ultimately, Weaver agreed to return, but she wanted the movie to be Ripley's swan song. First, however, it would kill off her supporting characters from the previous film. As the story begins, an escape pod containing Ripley, Newt, Hicks, and the android Bishop crash-lands on a prison planet. She's believed to be the only survivor—until another alien infiltrates the prison. At the very end of the film, Ripley jumps into an immense furnace to sacrifice herself and kill the alien queen that was about to burst out of her body.

The audience's displeasure with *Alien 3* was reflected in the box office; the film grossed little more than $53 million in North America and $159.7 million worldwide—less then *Aliens*' take when adjusted for inflation. Several of the cast and crew from the franchise would express their open frustration and disappointment; Cameron said that killing several of the previous film's most essential characters was "a slap in the face" to both him and the fans of *Aliens*. As for Joss, he complained that that "the fans were robbed. . . . They actually had a scene where people we didn't know were being killed by the alien."

All of this left Jorge Saralegui wondering if the audience would buy an *Alien* movie without its leading lady. But Weaver had wanted Ripley killed off and had very little interest in returning to the franchise, so Saralegui decided to bring back Newt, the little girl Ripley saved, instead. Although Newt died at the beginning of *Alien 3*, Saralegui's idea was that she would be cloned because of the survival skills she demonstrated in *Aliens*, and would be used by Ripley's former employer to track down the alien for their own research. The cloned Newt, in effect, would become a Buffy-like character—a young girl imbued with special skills and strengths to take out a particular enemy.

After receiving the go-ahead from the studio to develop a treatment, Saralegui reached out to Joss, because the *Buffy* movie script demonstrated his ability to bring just such a character to life. Joss was incredibly excited and agreed to take on the project. This was the chance of a lifetime—an opportunity to right the path of a favorite franchise that had gone astray.

//////////

After reading their thirty-page film treatment, studio executives told Joss and Saralegui that they found the reboot idea exciting, but they were worried about the success of an *Alien* film without Ripley. At first, Joss rebelled against the idea of scrapping their Newt concept to revive Ripley. But he was also a longtime fan of the *Alien* series, and this was his chance to be involved, so he eventually went back to the drawing board. With only the parameters of "Scary like *Alien*. Exciting like *Aliens*. Add in Ripley" to guide him, Joss found it much more difficult than his first go-round.

Joss's script for *Alien: Resurrection* takes place two hundred years after *Alien 3*. Scientists aboard a military spaceship have used a genetic sample from the prison planet to create a clone of Ellen Ripley, in the hopes of harvesting the alien queen that was growing inside of her and breeding more aliens for study. Later, a ragtag crew of mercenaries arrives to deliver human bodies, which the scientists plan to use for the alien incubation. Call, an android with the group, recognizes Ripley and tries to kill her, suspecting the truth about the clone's purpose. Unfortunately, the queen has already been extracted and the breeding process is underway. When the captive aliens escape and kill most of the military personnel, the ship's emergency systems kick in, sending the vessel back to Earth. Ripley and the mercenaries struggle to find a way to destroy the ship before the aliens reach Earth.

Joss knew if he was going to bring such a beloved iconic character back to life and have the audience accept it, he needed the resurrection to feel real, not just like a sci-fi metaphor. Joss had to create "a total identification" between the audience and the Ripley clone; he needed to acknowledge the difficulty viewers would have in accepting the character's rebirth by making it hard for the character herself to accept. "It's very important to me that it's a very torturous, grotesque process so that people will viscerally feel what it's like to be horribly reborn in a lab," Joss said. "Is she human? Has she changed? . . . She was pregnant with an alien. . . . Is there a little something wrong there?"

Joss was worried that Weaver would want to see a more likeable Ripley than the one he envisioned. To great relief on both sides, Weaver told Joss she loved his original script and how he made the concept of cloning very personal. She liked how Ripley, sharing both human and alien DNA, faces new questions about where her loyalties lie. She told him to push her character further and asked, "What if I'm even stranger? What if I have more Alien and less human in me?"

"She created an extraordinary character," Joss said.

Foreshadowing a theme that would later be explored in both *Buffy* and *Angel*, Ripley's rebirth comes with a big cost. She has to confront the question of *why* she's back, and what that means for the rest of her life. Through Ripley's struggle to accept her rebirth, Joss asked the question of what it meant to have an identity. Ripley identifies with both her former human self and the alien that incubated in her body—which she had in some sense given birth to.

Ripley's quest to find an answer to "What am I?" led to Joss's creation of Call, a robot filled with self-loathing. "When Call, who was played by Winona Ryder, who is very beautiful, says, 'Look at me. I'm disgusting,' it hit something that I'd never found before," Joss said. "I was talking about something that was very personal, that a lot of people go through—*and* I was doing it with a robot and a clone, so I was in heaven!" Saralegui, too, thought that one of the story's greatest strengths was that the two most human characters are the two females who are not human. "An android and a clone who's got alien DNA inside her. They are by far the most human and humanistic characters in that movie," he says. "Ripley is brutal, but she's still human. She still has a heart and still does the right thing." These same connections, at once personal and universally human, would soon inform the rebirth of Joss's own iconic hero.

Developing Ripley's resurrection story was a turning point in Joss's storytelling. He's said that as a child he enjoyed spinning yarns, but with *Alien: Resurrection* he began writing as an "adult." His new driving force would be to give his audience that "total identification" with his characters, to have their every action be so honest and real that the viewer would always feel that they were on the journey with them.

///////////

Unlike on the *Buffy* movie, Joss wasn't involved with much of the actual production of *Alien: Resurrection*. Filming took place from October 1996 through February 1997 on the 20th Century Fox lot in Los Angeles. While it was nearby, Joss was deeply involved with a new project, also produced by Fox. In addition, he didn't feel that he had connected with the movie's director, Jean-Pierre Jeunet, the French filmmaker who had previously helmed the black comedy *Delicatessen* and the fantasy drama *The City of Lost Children*. Nor did he agree with Jeunet's casting and directing choices. Despite his concerns, however, he was completely unprepared for what awaited him when he saw the director's cut at the studio screening.

Joss started to cry, heartbroken that Jeunet's vision for *Alien: Resurrection* did not match his own. "Then I put on a brave face because Fox is my home . . . but I can say with impunity that I was shattered by how crappy it was."

The story hadn't changed much from Joss's script. But Joss felt that Jeunet's direction "highlighted" all the problems with his script while "squashing" the strongest elements, like the final battle with the alien. The previous three films had ended with huge, dramatic battles between Ripley and an alien, but this time around, the expense of the alien and other special effects ballooned the budget, costs had to be cut, and Joss had to script several endings. "The first one was in the forest with the fly-ing threshing machine. The second one was in a futuristic junkyard," Joss said. "The third one was in a maternity ward. And the fourth one was in the desert." Each one was cheaper to film than the last, but each one further blunted the emotional impact he wanted the ending to have. The finished film wraps up with a *fifth* ending, in which the alien is sucked out through a small hole in the spaceship's window as it enters Earth's atmosphere. A similar scene appeared in Joss's first draft as an earlier con-frontation between the alien and a soldier, but it seemed anticlimactic as the final scene of Ripley's battle with the creature.

More than the ending, Joss's disappointment came from the fact that what was on the screen was so far from the vision he'd had in his head. "It was mostly a matter of doing everything *wrong*. They said the lines . . . *mostly* . . . but they said them all wrong. And they cast it wrong. And they designed it wrong. And they scored it wrong. They did everything wrong that they could possibly do," Joss explained. "There's actually a fascinat-ing lesson in filmmaking, because everything that they did reflects back to the script or looks like something from the script, and people assume that, if I hated it, then they'd changed the script . . . but it wasn't so much that they'd changed the script; it's that they just executed it in such a ghastly fashion as to render it almost unwatchable."

One visual element that he took great issue with was the art direc-tion of the alien itself. Starting with H. R. Giger's surrealist, nightmar-ish design in the first film, aliens had been truly terrifying creatures, often black or bronze with a skeletal, biomechanical appearance. They had blade-tipped tails that would slash anyone to pieces and highly acidic blood that corroded anything on contact. *Alien: Resurrection*'s alien has been modified with Ripley's DNA, and so some evolutionary change is to be expected. But "I don't remember writing, 'A withered, granny-lookin' Pumpkinhead-kinda-thing makes out with Ripley,'" Joss said. "Pretty sure that stage direction never existed in any of my drafts."

///////////

After the screening, Joss called up Saralegui, prefacing his comments with "Listen, I don't want to be a jerk, but . . ." before launching into his problems with the film. Saralegui understood, but he didn't fully agree. The exec would admit that the cool and funny details that were a trademark of Jeunet's films felt like forced quirkiness in the *Alien* universe. But they didn't bother him as much as they did Joss, possibly because he'd been worried about the film since he started seeing the dailies footage during shooting. "I think the biggest problem with that movie is something that we—literally every single person involved in that movie—didn't foresee," Saralegui says. "You've seen *Alien* too many times already. And by that, I'm saying in your life. You've seen *Alien*, *Aliens*, and *Alien 3*. And now here they are again.

"I had that sick realization one day watching dailies when we were seeing [the alien] for the first time—one of those classic shots where the alien grins and all that drool spills out of its mouth, which you've seen in every movie. I see it for the first time in this one, and I go, 'Oh, cool,'" he remembers. "And then I'm thinking, 'You didn't think that was cool when you first saw it. It scared the shit out of you.'" Whether it was franchise fatigue, tonal issues, or the disappointment of a scaled-back final battle, *Alien: Resurrection* did not resonate with fans as they'd hoped. Yet, while not the most critically lauded of the *Alien* franchise, *Resurrection* pulled in just over $161 million worldwide after its release in November 1997.

For Joss, the experience was the *Buffy* movie all over again. Again, he felt as if a director with a drastically different vision had undone the film he set out to make. "It was the final crappy humiliation of my crappy film career," he said. But if he'd given up on filmmaking, it's only because he'd found another medium in which he could finally enjoy the creative control he'd always craved.

BUFFY: RESURRECTION

In the mid-1990s, few could have predicted that the next teen series phenomenon would come wrapped up in the title *Buffy the Vampire Slayer*. The adolescent fare of the time tended to be more limited in scope, more rigidly compartmentalized. ABC's "TGIF" programming block of family-friendly sitcoms included series such as *Boy Meets World*, which told tales of growing up yet shied away from the more dramatic issues to be found in day-to-day high school life. For drama, the few options for teenagers aired on the fledgling Fox network, where *Beverly Hills, 90210* was still going strong after pretty much launching the teenage soap opera genre in 1990. The series had quickly jettisoned the fish-out-of-water drama of a midwestern brother and sister transplanted to Southern California for more provocative storylines—losing one's virginity, drug abuse, rape, alcoholism, absentee parents, and, of course, the classic love triangles among the young and pretty characters.

Still, there were signs that audiences were ready for series that reflected a grittier, more realistic view of life from a teenage perspective. In 1994, Fox had introduced *Party of Five*, a more sober youth-oriented series than *90210*, which followed a clan of five orphans adjusting to a new life after the sudden deaths of their parents. ABC broke further ground the same year with *My So-Called Life*, which featured newcomer Claire Danes as Angela Chase, a young woman just beginning to maneuver through her relationships with high school friends, her parents, and the cute bad boy. Angela Chase was an icon with whom teens could truly relate—for starters, unlike the characters on *90210*, she was actually played by a teenage actress. And where *90210* took a glamorized look at well-off kids in Beverly Hills, Angela's story focused on the raw emotional trials of trying to figure out who you are at fifteen, and how each decision you make affects your friends and family.

Both series were critically acclaimed yet fell victim to low ratings; only *Party of Five* would make it past the first season. Joss loved them both, calling *Party of Five* "a brilliant show, [which] often made me cry uncontrollably" and saying that "no show on TV has ever come close to capturing as truly the lovely pain of teendom as well as *My So-Called Life*. And yes, I'm including my own."

Mass audiences might still have needed convincing, but by this point there was a passionate niche market of viewers who were waiting, almost aching, to see their own emotions reflected on TV. "I'd been waiting and waiting, too," Joss says. "It was in the zeitgeist. *My So-Called Life* came along and did it perfectly, and *90210* came along and did it dreadfully. I had tried to get the rights to [the movie] *Pump Up the Volume* (1990) and make a series out of it—a soap opera with a DJ as a sort of MC in *Cabaret* motif. Because teenagers needed a soap opera—nobody takes themselves more seriously. I couldn't make it happen. So then *Buffy* came along, and I said, 'Here's the dramatic portion of it, here's the soap opera.'"

Buffy would also respond to another need that was in the air at the time. The mid-1990s saw the rise of women of action on the small screen, in particular FBI Special Agent Dana Scully of Fox's sci-fi series *The X-Files* (1993–2002) and Xena of the syndicated fantasies *Hercules: The Legendary Journeys* (1995–99) and the upcoming *Xena: Warrior Princess* (1995–2001). Both Scully (Gillian Anderson) and Xena (Lucy Lawless) became celebrated role models for women, but both Scully and Xena were adults; television hadn't really provided a teenage heroine in the same vein. In fact, few series of the era featured a young female lead of any kind; there was Angela of *My So-Called Life*, which was quickly canceled, the title character of the NBC sitcom *Blossom*, which signed off the air in May 1995, and not much else.

Joss knew that the television landscape was ripe for a new series that addressed both female empowerment and universal teenage fears. But even though the opportunity had arisen for him to create exactly that, he wasn't quite sure he was ready to go back to television.

//////////

It was Gail Berman of Sandollar Productions who had approached Joss with the idea of developing *Buffy* into a television series. Inspired by the recent film *Clueless*, Amy Heckerling's witty modern retelling of Jane

Austen's *Emma* set in a Beverly Hills high school, with its own unique and immediately quotable vernacular, Berman returned to Joss's blonde, quippy teenager who is far wiser than her initial vapid appearance suggests. She wanted to pitch *Buffy* as a thirty-minute kids' series à la *Mighty Morphin Power Rangers*, to air in syndication, and was working her way through all the associated rights issues. She realized that 20th Century Fox had failed to secure the television rights for the film, so she was free to proceed without their go-ahead, and she obtained the necessary permissions from partial owners of the Buffy character Kaz and Fran Rubel Kuzui. One of the last contractual loose ends she had to tie up was that she had to offer the project to Joss, who had the right of first refusal if *Buffy* was ever redeveloped. Berman reached out to Chris Harbert, knowing that Joss was deeply entrenched in "big movie projects," and explained that he just needed to decline the offer so that the project could move on without him.

It didn't work out like that at all. "A couple of weeks later," Berman remembered, "I got a call from [Harbert] and he said, 'I talked to Joss about it, and the funny thing is, he is interested in it. Why don't you guys get together and see if there's something you find intriguing?'"

Joss was excited by the idea of returning to his beloved character and script, of course. But his previous experiences in television gave him pause. Still, he knew that he would be returning to the medium under far different circumstances than those that affected his tenure on *Roseanne*. He had earned himself some leverage as a highly sought-after script doctor, after all; he could dictate how he would serve on the show. If he came aboard as an executive producer, he would finally get the chance to direct. He would have more control over the creative aspects of the project. Joss realized that this was an opportunity to finally tell the *Buffy* story the way he had always envisioned it: instead of the *Power Rangers*–esque kids' show Berman had originally envisioned, it would be the saga of high school as a horror movie.

Joss signed onto the project, and with such marketable talent aboard, Berman shifted her focus from a syndicated *Buffy* to a network-worthy *Buffy*. She and Joss readied their proposal for the networks' 1995–96 pilot season, the yearly period in which writers and producers pitch roughly five hundred show concepts to network executives, of which seventy or so are bought and go through script development, before a final ten or twenty are given the green light to film a pilot.

Joss needed a pitch with current references that would connect with executives. In an essay he wrote for the *My So-Called Life* DVD release in 2007, he recalled, "When I pitched *Buffy The Vampire Slayer*, I told executives it was a cross between *The X-Files* and . . . and then I always took a moment to judge how smart they were. If they seemed like empty suits, I'd go with *90210*. It was a big hit. But if they seemed like they knew their business, I'd use another example. The example that every writer I know still references. The show that—forget what it did for my writing and my career—I'll love the way you can only love as a youth: with fierce bewilderment and unembarrassed passion."

The first meeting on their dance card was with Fox, where Berman felt *Buffy* could find a home as a solid coming-of-age drama in the family-friendly 8:00 PM eastern spot. To augment his pitch, Joss prepared a short video; like the movie montages he created for Kai, it combined clips from the 1992 film, special effects shots, and "beautiful images" to demonstrate how different *Buffy* would be from the other series on television. Yet despite a strong showing by Joss, Fox executives passed, deeming the concept too close in tone to *Party of Five*. Berman next had Joss pitch the series to NBC, even though she knew it wouldn't fit into the network's schedule, which was populated with series aimed at twenty- and thirty-somethings after their runaway success with *Friends*. The meeting with NBC would be a good way for him to further refine the pitch before they presented it to a new network just launched that year: the WB.

By the time they got to the WB, the pitch had become more open-ended. Joss told the WB executives that at that point, he didn't know what the format of the series should be. Hour? Half hour? More drama? Maybe comedy? Should it have a laugh track? But what he did know was the *Buffy* universe, which he "sketched . . . out in Dickensian detail, explaining what powers the various types of vampires, slayers, and watchers wielded, and why."

The network had been searching for a drama with a teenage girl as the lead—they'd looked into picking up *My So-Called Life* when it was on the bubble at ABC, but it was beyond their budget. In fact, WB exec Susanne Daniels was looking for a female teen superhero series in particular, but she came into the *Buffy* meeting with a "slight bias" against the project: she was not a fan of the film and was wary of spending money to develop a series based on it. However, she was quickly won over by the fact that Joss's pitch "was such a fresh and improved take from the movie" and by "the emotionality that Joss was bringing to Buffy's story and backstory." Joss, she said, was unlike anyone else with whom the network had met, and the "overall vision that Joss pitched was more intriguing than anything I'd seen in the movie, and more compelling than other pitches I'd heard in our search for a strong young female character." On the strength of the pitch, the WB bought a *Buffy* pilot script; 20th Century Fox came on to produce.

//////////

When the WB showed interest in *Buffy* and began talking about what the series could be, Joss came back excitedly to Chris Harbert. "It's amazing that they're really letting me take the reins. They're really listening. They're really interested in the way I want to do it," he told his agent. To which Harbert replied, "Yeah, they have no idea what they're doing."

There was probably some truth to that. At the time, the WB was desperately searching for an identity. Both it and UPN, the other "netlet" that launched in January 1995, were drawing minuscule audiences compared to the major networks. Where UPN had tried to distinguish itself with a programming slate of sci-fi shows led by the latest series in the *Star Trek* franchise, *Voyager*, the WB had developed programming directed at a more urban market with *The Wayans Bros.* and *The Parent 'Hood*, both sitcoms featuring African American casts. But the WB was struggling in the ratings even compared to its fellow upstart.

To change all that, the network's programming executives were willing to buck the conventional wisdom of the TV business—and hiring Joss was a big part of that. The WB was "the great square hole of television," he would later proclaim. It was barely a year old and its programming executives had put their faith, and their money, behind someone who had a great story and knew how to tell it. After his disappointing experiences with the major networks, the chance to do what he wanted at this new netlet was very rare and very exciting.

At the time, most dramatic offerings on American television were medical and police dramas that eschewed season-long narratives for self-contained episodes about the medical emergency or crime of the week. Joss called this "reset television," noting that these shows tended to have fairly minor consequences for the main characters, and any lessons learned were often swept clean in time for the following episode.

Cable channels had begun to develop original programming, but they weren't nearly as acclaimed or as popular as today's offerings by HBO, AMC, FX, and Showtime. Ongoing narrative arcs, with which Joss had been fascinated since his early years of watching British dramas with his mother, on American TV were mostly limited to soap operas—and the soaps tended to focus on relationship melodrama and shocking personal reversals rather than meaningful character development. A teenage vampire slayer from Los Angeles was about to change all of that.

//////////

According to Joss, "TV is a question, movies are an answer." A movie lasts for only a brief period of time and has one goal: to tell a story from beginning to end and then get out. A TV series, on the other hand, needs to fill many hours, many episodes; it needs to make its story last. Thus, while Joss's pilot script for the *Buffy the Vampire Slayer* series picked up narratively where the *Buffy* film had left off, it made a number of changes to sustain the premise indefinitely.

As the story kicks off, a slightly younger Buffy Summers is beginning her sophomore year at Berryman High School as a transfer student from L.A. Buffy's hoping to leave all of the "Chosen One" business behind, but a quiet new start isn't meant to be when there's a suspicious death on Buffy's first day of school. As it turns out, her new Southern California home—which will be named Sunnydale in the series, with Buffy's new school renamed Sunnydale High—is built on a Hellmouth, a portal between Earth and hell. The Hellmouth attracts not just vampires but all kinds of demons and spirits. Basically, if it's supernatural and evil, it sets up shop in town, giving the writers carte blanche when it came to introducing new villains.

In another deviation from the movie, in which Buffy primarily fought vampires alone (as had all Slayers until her time), she quickly connects with two new friends, Willow Rosenberg and Xander Harris, who will become her confidants and evil-slaying cohorts. Willow is a shy girl, unsure and a bit awkward but full of confidence and excitement when it comes to book learning and computer hacking. She has been in love with her best friend, Xander, since kindergarten. Witty, geeky, and uncomfortable in his skin, especially around girls, Xander is basically Joss in high school.

Buffy also meets her new Watcher, Rupert Giles, who will guide Buffy's development as well as serve as a father figure for all three teens. Rounding out the cast of characters is self-involved cheerleader Cordelia Chase, a walking, talking callback to the girl Buffy had been before the Slayer business came along. This odd band of characters—the shy girl, the boy whose strongest weapon is his ready wit, the snarky popular girl, and the repressed Brit, all following the most powerful girl in the world, who desperately wants to be anything but—would become the template for the chosen families so often found in Joss's later works.

The WB was impressed enough by Joss's script to give the go-ahead to film a pilot. As soon as the team got the green light, casting began.

//////////

Joss has said again and again that he created Buffy to be a cultural icon. "Buffy was always intended to be a role model," he insisted in a 1998 video press kit. "It was very important to me that Buffy be the kind of girl that girls could look up to and relate to, and show not only a hero but how difficult it is to be a hero." With such high expectations to fulfill, it took some time for Joss to find the small-screen version of his titular hero. Several teen actresses including Katie Holmes and Selma Blair were considered for the role but didn't work out.

In early 1996, 20th Century Fox approached a young soap opera star to audition for the series. Sarah Michelle Gellar was just seventeen years old but already a veteran of several TV movies and guest appearances, and a Daytime Emmy winner for her role as Kendall Hart on the soap opera *All My Children*. "They said to me, there's this [role] coming up you'd be really right for," Gellar recalls. The pitch went on to highlight Joss's work. "Joss Whedon: He's great. He wrote *Toy Story*—it's going to be nominated for an Oscar."

Although she was intrigued by the idea, they couldn't work out the scheduling before she left for Australia for filming a TV movie and a holiday. "I finally got back and read the script, and I loved it," she says.

Gellar went in to the audition for the role of Cordelia. Casting agents were swayed by her long dark hair and pale skin, convinced that she'd be an excellent fit for the queen bitch of Buffy's high school—a role very similar to her Emmy-winning turn as Kendall Hart. She nailed the audition, and tested for the studio and the network as well. She got a call confirming that the role was hers—and asking if she had any interest in reading for Buffy.

"I thought: Buffy? Well, that's not really me." And her manager cautioned that sometimes an actor could lose the role she initially had by chasing after another one in the same project. But Gellar decided to take a chance and went back to read with Joss and casting director Marcia Shulman.

Before the Buffy audition, Gellar screened the 1992 film as a model for her version of the character, not knowing how much Joss hated that interpretation of his hero. But Joss was impressed when, at the end of the audition, she announced that she was a brown belt in tae kwon do. Still, it wasn't an easy process—she had to audition twice more, watching many other girls try for the role and getting more notes from Joss each time she was brought back. In all, she had to go through five separate meetings and five screen tests. After all that, she was shocked when Joss told her he always knew she was Buffy. "If he knew I was Buffy, why did I have to go through that?" Gellar asks. "I never quite got the straight answer."

Charisma Carpenter, fresh off a starring role on Aaron Spelling's short-lived *Malibu Shores*, had also gone out for Buffy, but her network audition made it clear that she was a perfect fit for Cordelia. She'd been running late and her agent sent her a number of urgent messages during her frantic race through a rainy Los Angeles rush hour. Once she was able to get off the freeway and to a pay phone, Carpenter called her agent, who informed her that everyone running the screen test was ready to leave. "You tell them not to leave, you tell them to order a pizza, you tell them something but tell them to wait," she responded.

For the role of Buffy's Watcher, Giles, Joss was leaning toward casting a foreigner. In his notes, he wrote that the character could be British, Scottish, or West Indian, with a preference toward a "loud, abusive Scot." He also considered casting a Wallace Shawn type, someone who resembled the nebbishy character actor known for *My Dinner with Andre*, *The Princess Bride*, and his role as the Joss-created character Rex the dinosaur in *Toy Story*. "What he is not," Joss wrote, "Is contemporary. What he's not, to belabor the point, is Buffy."

Anthony Stewart Head, an established British actor primarily known in the United States for a quirky series of commercials for coffee, came in to read. "I'd read the scripts in a restaurant a couple nights before, and I'd laughed out loud," Head says, adding that he later told a friend, "I want this gig. This is the first gig that I've read since I've been in the States that knows how to talk like an Englishman, and it's funny, and it's exciting."

He was cautious, but he went into the room and pitched Joss on his idea of Giles falling somewhere between Alan Rickman in *Sense and Sensibility* and Prince Charles. Joss told him to go for it. "I was looking for a guy whose life is only halfway through," the writer recalls, "who's still on a path himself, because I wanted to be in his perspective too." But most of the actors auditioning came in with an "I'm the craggy mentor" approach to the role. "Tony Head came in, and I think every single person in the room had made a note that was just a drawing of a heart."

As far as Joss was concerned, Head had picked up the part, put it in his pocket, and walked away with it. His casting wasn't set in stone, however. First, Head had to get the sign-off from Fox. In order to do that, his agent told him, he should acquaint himself with the *Buffy* movie. Head watched the film and was surprised. "This is completely different from anything that I got from the script," he remembers thinking. "This is a different feel and a different vibe and a different humor." The next day when testing for Fox, he told Joss that he had seen the movie. Joss's face fell and he quickly told Head, "It has nothing to do with that! Forget you saw it!"

As with Giles, Joss felt that Willow was a character defined as distinctively not-Buffy. In a quick character sketch, he explained that she was "shy, clumsy, sensible and sort of plain." But to him they were meant to be best friends—"They're both outsiders, however they might strive not to be. . . . They both have a sense of right." Early on, he knew that Willow would be the "brains of the operation." And so he wanted an actress who felt real, who had her "own sort of shy quirkiness" instead of the "'supermodel in horn-rims' that you usually see on a television show." He fought the network to cast Riff Regan, whose frumpy take on the character fit into his image of a socially awkward nerd uncomfortable in her skin.

The cast was rounded out with newcomer Nicholas Brendon as Xander, the "charming, decent looking romantic" who was "funny and ascerbic . . . totally unsufferable and just useless with girls." The role was first offered to future *Blade*-universe vampire killer and Green Lantern Ryan Reynolds, who passed because he'd just finished high school, where he'd been bullied, and had no interest in living that time of his life all over again.

Added at the last minute was David Boreanaz as a yet-unnamed mysterious stranger. Future Whedon stalwart Nathan Fillion had also auditioned for the man of mystery but didn't get the role. The following year, Fillion would join Reynolds on the new series *Two Guys, a Girl and a Pizza Place.*

With the cast in place, shooting on the pilot could begin. Unfortunately, Joss immediately ran into some obstacles. First, he wouldn't be able to shoot his full pilot script; because the WB had a smaller overall development budget than the larger networks, it usually only commissioned a twenty-minute "pilot presentation" tape instead of a full-length pilot. Second, the network wanted to bring in a more experienced director to oversee the pilot.

Joss was willing to pare down his script, but he balked at the network's other stipulation, because he was looking forward to directing the pilot himself. Not only was this his chance to tell Buffy's story the way he wanted it told, but he would also be able to guide the actors speaking his words to say them the way he wanted them to be said. The ability to direct episodes of the series had been a major factor in Joss's decision to work on the project. *Buffy* was his chance to launch a show, hire himself, and pay himself a good wage. He saw it as an opportunity to finally get the sort of practical, hands-on experience behind the camera that his heavily theoretical studies at Wesleyan hadn't provided. Chris Harbert insisted in a "friendly but pointed" conversation that Joss would direct alone or he would walk away entirely. The WB agreed.

Once on set, however, the eager director was saddled with a crew who didn't want to be there. The assistant director wasn't happy with Joss, and the director of photography didn't like him at all. There was a lot of weird tension on the set. "They had absolutely no time for him," Anthony Stewart Head recalls. "A writer cutting his teeth on his own show? Who cares?" Joss declared his first outing in directing for television a "nightmare, [with] the worst crew imaginable."

Even so, he never doubted the strength of the project. On one of the first days of filming, Head asked Joss if he thought the show would be picked up. He'd been hopeful that his first American series, the Fox sci-fi show *VR.5* (1995), would get a long run, but it failed to pull in a large audience and was canceled after ten episodes. He was surprised and comforted by Joss's reaction. "Definitely," Head recalls Joss saying. "But the suits don't get it. The studio doesn't get it, and the network certainly doesn't get it. But this will be word of mouth. There's going to be a huge fan base that's going to get this, and it's going to be picked up worldwide." Some might call that pompous. But to know Joss is to know that he's just, well, certain. "He's certain of his beliefs. He sticks to them. He doesn't waver," Head explains.

Next, the footage had to be edited together—which at first seemed to go about as well as the shooting had. David Solomon was brought in as editor; though he was primarily a producer at that point, he was approached because he was known to be good with first-time directors. He and Joss met to discuss the editing process, and Joss asked how he handled notes from directors. Solomon replied that he didn't read the notes until after he finished his initial edit, explaining that "it would be like if somebody came to you as a writer and said, 'Don't write anything that has the word *claustrophobic* in it, and try not to describe anything that might end up being red, and don't use anything with jealousy because I don't like that.'"

All Joss heard was, "I don't read the notes." The meeting ended shortly thereafter.

Solomon got a call from the head of production at 20th Century Fox—his declaration that he didn't read notes had transformed into Joss "hating him." He was asked to go back and apologize to Joss, which he eventually did, begrudgingly—once again explaining that he needed to have the freedom to work without a strict list of initial demands. Fortunately, Joss understood the need for personal creativity and saw that this wasn't another situation like the crew on the shoot. Solomon was there to help him, not fight and demean him.

The pilot presentation was cut on the Avid editing system at Solomon's house, with Joss and Gail Berman. Despite the rocky beginning, Joss and his editor developed a creative flow and worked well together. After the final cut was delivered, postproduction moved to an audio house, where Joss and Solomon continued to collaborate on the sound mix for the show. One day, Joss ran out to the parking lot as Solomon was driving off and said, "Hey, if this thing goes to series, I want you to come on it." Solomon agreed, thinking he would never hear from him again.

//////////

Like his student film, the *Buffy* pilot was a twenty-five-minute tape that Joss said he'll never officially release. Unlike *A Night Alone*, however, it would find its way onto eBay's black market of bootlegged VHS tapes by 1999, and ten years later would be easily watchable on YouTube. While Joss's pilot script had to be truncated to fit the abbreviated running time, the wit and compelling storytelling were already evident.

The story begins with a young couple breaking into a high school at night to make out; the girl, nervous and obviously uncomfortable, struggles with the boy's insistence that they go further into the school. It's a dark scene, both visually, as they're cloaked in shadows, and in tone, as there's a distinct predatory subtext. As he repeatedly tries to convince her that they're alone, it's easy to assume that she'll soon be attacked. Upon being reassured that the school is indeed empty, the girl turns back to the boy—*she's* the vampire. She attacks him as the scene fades out. The words *Buffy the Vampire Slayer* appear, superimposed over a bustling high school facade and backed by the punk band Rancid's song "Salvation."

Joss had again flipped the script—it wasn't the girl who needed saving from the lecherous boy. It was the first of many signs that while *Buffy* was a horror series, it would take the genre to a new level that audiences hadn't seen before.

This opening scene will seem familiar to those who have watched the series' actual first episode, "Welcome to the Hellmouth," which would reshoot and expand on many elements of the unaired pilot. Despite the similarities, the pilot doesn't come close to matching the quality level of "Welcome to the Hellmouth." Sarah Michelle Gellar and Nicholas Brendon are clearly the stars—both relatable, believable, and engaging—but Riff Regan doesn't find the right balance between making Willow shy and wanting and keeping her likeable. The sets are less than inspiring, the dialogue snappy and clever but in danger of drowning in slang that would quickly feel dated. Xander leads Buffy around the school courtyard, and in typical teen movie style points out each of the stereotypical student clusters: stoner surfers, theater club, film club—though he does mix it up a bit by pointing out the "dirty girls." (To its credit, the pilot would sidestep the quintessential big expository speech of every cult film when Giles begins to explain the lore of the Slayer and Buffy cuts him off: "Wow, you're going to do the speech and everything.")

The pilot's shortened script also doesn't allow for the strong emotional connection to the characters that is vital in any coming-of-age tale. Buffy's mom, Joyce, doesn't appear, eliminating a conversation that comes early in "Welcome to the Hellmouth" that beautifully illustrates Buffy's underlying need to keep her actions in Sunnydale as typically teenage and Slayer-free as possible so that she and her mother can have a "normal" life. Also missing is David Boreanaz's character—named Angel by the time the series debuted—the enigmatic stranger with cryptic messages for the Slayer. Boreanaz filmed some scenes for the pilot, but they were cut for time and storytelling reasons.

Despite all its shortcomings, the pilot still showed potential that *Buffy* could become a great series. Even with the truncated script, Joss's limited knowledge of directing, and actors still working to fully inhabit their roles, the teen characters felt more relatable and smarter than those in any series on the air at the time. "They all just kind of fit into those parts right away, and it was just going to happen," Solomon says. "Albeit, we never saw [it lasting for] seven years."

//////////

When the WB execs saw the pilot presentation in May 1996, they were underwhelmed. They did not pick up the series for the fall season, opting instead for a show they had initially developed in-house that was championed by WB head Jamie Kellner: *7th Heaven*, a wholesome drama about a preacher and his family. Still, *Buffy* had made an impact at the network.

"I thought that he had captured a distinct and exciting lead character, and not a lot else," Susanne Daniels said. "Sarah Michelle Gellar shined in his pilot presentation as Buffy, and was endearing and fascinating and someone I wanted to go on a ride with, and see what was going to happen with the character and how. And I thought he had established an intriguing world, but I also thought it was messy."

"The pilot was not great," said Garth Ancier, chief programmer for the network at the time. "And we had some better pilots that year. The discussion was, 'Do we make our bet on another show from Stephen Cannell [*21 Jump Street*, *The A-Team*, *The Rockford Files*]? Or do we make our bet on Joss, who we believe in as a writer, even though this pilot will have to be thoroughly trashed?'"

When the network announced its fall schedule later in May, it made no mention of *Buffy the Vampire Slayer*. Gail Berman grew quite persistent, asking Daniels to confirm whether the series would be picked up or whether the network would release it so 20th Century Fox and Sandollar could shop it elsewhere. The WB responded with a list of minor adjustments and one major casting change that they wanted Joss to make, and once all parties were on board, *Buffy* was officially given a twelve-episode run, to premiere in March 1997. Daniels expressed high hopes for the series: "I think *Buffy* will do for The WB what *21 Jump Street* did for Fox. . . . It [attracted] new teenage viewers and got critical acclaim as well."

///////////

Despite David Solomon's recollection, not all of the actors fit into their parts right away. Among the changes between the presentation tape and the series proper was reenvisioning the role of Willow. Per the WB's request, Riff Regan was out—which was perhaps not a surprise to the actress. She told Joss that "part of the reason that she was not right to play Willow is that she's very self confident [and] sexy." Unlike the frumpy character she played in the pilot, Joss said, Regan "came into the room and blew me away. She was so in charge." Had Regan been given the direction to portray Willow in a manner closer to her own personality, it's possible that she would have made it through the series run.

In the end, though, a more established young actress, Alyson Hannigan, was brought on to replace Regan. Hannigan hadn't been able to get an audition during casting for the pilot, as she was very different from the insecure, mousy girl whom Joss had originally envisioned. She got another chance when network executives called for a different take on the character.

Hannigan approached Willow with an optimistic spark. "OK, so she's talking about how guys won't talk to her, but I'm going to put happiness in her," she said. "She's not going to sulk about it. . . . If she's talking about something that's not the greatest love story, she's still happy in the end." And so the dowdy girl in need of rescue was reborn as a cheerful, brilliant computer hacker confident in her academic skills, though still struggling with her crush on her best friend, Xander.

Before long, Willow would join her friend Buffy as a cultural icon and role model. "Willow is a good role model," Hannigan said, pointing to how the character did very well in school, was confident in her talents, and learned to stand up for herself. "Buffy is the girl everybody wants to be, but Willow is more like what they are." In fact, as much as Joss described Xander as a stand-in for himself, there is a compelling argument for Willow being yet another facet of her creator. She's the smart kid who was invisible to the opposite sex, had problems making friends in high school, and thus worked so damn hard to get through the day while feeling alone.

But that's the beauty of *all* the new characters Joss created to populate his *Buffy* retelling, the Slayer support network that would come to be known as the Scooby Gang (a reference to the teenage crime-fighters in the *Scooby-Doo* cartoons). Each one fell into a typical social role while pushing against it, and their varied struggles to find their own path gave audiences, Joss himself, and even the show's actors so many ways to connect with the story. "I'm no more Buffy than I am Cordelia than I am Willow than I am Xander," Sarah Michelle Gellar says. "I'm parts of all of them."

"[Joss is] more of a girl's guy than a guy's guy, and he understands women," Gellar adds. "There's not a lot of male writers that have the respect for women that he does when writing them. This is still a man's world and most of the writers are men, and the characters sometimes feel stiff, one-dimensional. That's where his strength really lies—in creating these female characters because he respects them."

BUFFY PREMIERES

8

When Joss finally got the green light for *Buffy*'s midseason run, it was time to select a staff. He had worked on a couple of TV series earlier in his career, but he had never been a showrunner, a role that would require him to oversee not only the creative direction of the show but also its day-to-day operations. He needed a co-showrunner, someone who could help him get *Buffy* off the ground and guide him through what to do afterward.

Among the contenders for the position was David Greenwalt, an experienced writer/producer who was just coming off *Profit*, a small Fox show that he had cocreated. The series, which was produced by the same Stephen Cannell whom Joss beat out for a slot on the WB programming slate, followed future *Heroes* star Adrian Pasdar as Jim Profit, an utterly amoral main character who worked at a possibly even less ethical multinational corporation. *Profit* took its storylines to very dark places, impressing Joss with its fearlessness, but in 1996, that fearlessness made audiences and Fox network affiliates uncomfortable. It lasted just eight episodes, only the first four of which were aired.

Despite its short run, *Profit* made a big splash within the industry. *Variety* proclaimed that the show had potential cult-hit status and that it "could go down as the creepiest show, with the most anti-heroic protagonist, in the history of television." It garnered a lot of attention for Greenwalt, and a number of scripts came his way, including an opportunity to work with TV legend Steven Bochco, who had created *Hill Street Blues*, *L.A. Law*, and *NYPD Blue*. But the one script that got his attention was the *Buffy the Vampire Slayer* pilot.

"It's got feeling. It's got heart. I have to meet this guy," Greenwalt says, remembering his reaction to the script. "Joss loves to start a story real—you just feel like you're in real life and just when you're about to get bored, he takes your head and slams it onto the concrete and some great thing happens." Greenwalt loved everything about the script—actually, he considered it the best script of the year, bar none. He appreciated that it was understated, and that Joss had made up a whole language for kids to speak. "So I met him, and it was kind of love at first sight." The feeling was mutual, and Greenwalt was offered the job.

According to Joss, his new creative partner was key to his success. "David was more responsible for what *Buffy* was than anybody really understands," he says. "He walked me through everything, acting like a mentor without ever talking down to me, contradicting me. He was my co-showrunner, but he had all the experience.

"I look back on it, and I'm like, 'I can't understand why he wasn't just like, "You idiot!"' I remember very well that we were on a location scout and were talking about building the set for the classroom. David asked, 'Let me ask a stupid question: do we need a translight?' I said, 'Let me top it! What's a translight?'

"I have found many people who've been extraordinary, but at that time when I really had no idea what I was doing, having David there was so important. He was so great that I just figured this was how it would go in life, that you'd just have that guy at your side all the time." However, their relationship already had an expiration date; Greenwalt's contract was to help Whedon see *Buffy* through its initial episode order and then go to *The X-Files* as an executive producer.

//////////

Joss kept his parking-lot promise to David Solomon, bringing him onto the *Buffy* crew as a producer. He also had to assemble a writing staff—which is where he hit his first major snag. Since *Buffy* was a midseason series, it wasn't ready to send out offers to writers until July. By that time, a lot of writers had already been snapped up in May and June by shows with fall start dates. Adding to the uphill climb was the fact that it was a show in an untested niche (teen horror drama) on a little-watched network, with an inexperienced producer leading a young cast. It wasn't really considered a hot career opportunity.

Joss and Greenwalt read spec scripts from practically everybody, whether their experience was in drama or comedy. Given his own background on *Roseanne* and *Parenthood*, Joss didn't want to discriminate. He wound up with a mix of writers from both half-hour and hour-long shows, including the team of Joe Reinkemeyer and Matt Kiene (*Law & Order* and *L.A. Law*) and sitcom writer Dana Reston (*The Nanny*).

Two of Joss's early hires came from the NBC sitcom *Hope & Gloria*, but it may have been a previous credit of theirs that got them in the door. Dean Batali and Rob Des Hotel had written for a Nickelodeon live-action series called *The Adventures of Pete & Pete*, a quirky cult show that chronicled the lives of two brothers named Pete, their friends, and the small town in which they lived. It was a heavily dialogue-driven show that celebrated clever turns of phrase. Due to its wit and intelligence, it appealed to audiences older than the general Nickelodeon grade school demographic—including one Joss Whedon.

"Joss remembered one line we had written in our *Pete & Pete* script," Batali says. "One of the characters says, 'Now begins the age of Pete,' and he thought that was such a great line. I'm convinced that that's why we got the job—because we wrote the line 'Now begins the age of Pete.' Because it's such a Buffyesque line: 'Now begins the age of Buffy.'"

//////////

Once the writing staff was assembled, the writers set about brainstorming story ideas for the first season's episodes. Joss opened up the discussion by saying, "Tell me your favorite horror movie and your most embarrassing moment, and we'll take it from there." Joss's own early ideas for scripts included a sexually aggressive football player who happens to be a werewolf, "controlling parents as Stepford/baby-snatching guys," and a "competitive cute girl as witch." It was David Greenwalt's spin on the last one that made Joss feel that the show was clicking into place, that they were on to something.

Once a writer pitches a story idea that sparks some interest, the staff then "breaks" the story, turning the basic idea into a series of dramatic beats and working out the emotional arcs that underlie the plot. From Joss's witchcraft pitch, the staff broke the story that would become the first-season episode "Witch." In it, Buffy is in desperate need of some normalcy in her life and decides to return to cheerleading. However, things go awry at the team tryouts (as they so often do on a Hellmouth), and Buffy and her friends quickly realize they must stop Amy, a fellow student, from using witchcraft to take competitors out during the audition process.

As they were breaking the story, David Greenwalt pitched the idea that "Amy" is in fact her own mother, a former cheerleading queen who has switched bodies with her daughter in order to relive her former glory years. But Amy's body isn't as adept as her mother's, and in frustration, the mother methodically attacks cheerleader after cheerleader until "Amy" finally moves off the bench and onto the court.

"Oh! This show's gonna be so good!" Joss remembers thinking when Greenwalt made his pitch. "It's the creepiest thing, and it's totally true!"

Greenwalt's contributions in the writers' room helped Joss develop the show's voice. "I like my stuff to have an edge, but I also am desperate for people's affection and kind of a big softie," Joss says. "So is David. Having a voice that was similar to mine but had its own particular spin was invaluable." It was great, he says, to "have that sensibility next to me at all times, the guy who's ready for the most painful twist, the cruelest joke, the most agonizing moment—and then, at times, a redemptive angle. Things could have been very, very different if I hadn't had his whip-smart, completely unflinching, tough, noir kind of sensibility. It took *Buffy* beyond 'Let's talk about our feelings!' and into a real world of both creepiness and idiotic humor. Because David's not afraid to go for the cheap jokes any more than I am."

But what clicked with Joss most of all was that Greenwalt was able to balance his edginess with an old-school approach to narrative. It was Greenwalt, Joss says, who was "constantly pulling us back to 'But do we care about Buffy? But is Buffy in trouble?'"

"We learned early on when we started writing that we've got to have the metaphor," Greenwalt explains. After all, a storyline that's just about a cool monster every week would quickly get old and predictable. "You've got to have the Buffy of it—what does it *mean*?"

For Joss, too, the answer to "What's the Buffy of it?" was of utmost importance to the development of each episode. "He knows what he wants when he sees it, and he's willing to take the time to *wait* to see it," says future *Buffy* writer Jane Espenson. "He has high standards and is sometimes impatient. He puts story first—or maybe I should say *meaning*—he puts meaning first." Rather than taking the procedural approach and focusing on the plot ("What's going to happen in this episode?"), Joss tackled the story through his characters. How would they interact? What's the conflict between them? *Then* he'd tackle the plot points.

He'd do that by breaking stories from the inside out. Instead of looking at a story from where it would start or end, he would come up with an idea and explore what would be really compelling about it when "blank" happens. For example, in the fifth episode of the series, "Never Kill a Boy on the First Date," Buffy is at a funeral home with her date when a vampire appears and corners the guy. "The question then becomes 'How do we build to that? How do you get to that moment?'" explains Batali. "*How*, and then you start filling it out, so it's inside-out story breaking." Howard Gordon, a second-season hire who'd go on to produce *24* and *Homeland*, among other series, agrees. "Joss reverse engineered [stories] from the ending. He was not somebody who was overly enamored with the beginning of a story, which most writers are."

The *Buffy* stories that made it out of the writers' room all had their roots in that central allegory of the series: high school as a horror movie. As Joss explained to his writers, high school was the most horrifying place he'd ever been. The familiar tropes of the horror genre became a prism through which they could explore familiar adolescent anxieties such as peer pressure and popularity.

Greenwalt remembers being especially impressed with the patience Joss displayed at the next point in the development process. After a story has been broken and the beats of the story sketched out, the credited writer for the episode "goes to the board" in the writers' room and writes out the beats. From there, the writer maps out the actual scenes with locations on index cards, creates an outline, and finally begins to write the actual script. Every show and writer breaks a story a little differently, but in general, "going to the board" is where the story is finalized. "When we'd break stories," Greenwalt says, "I'd watch him wait, and wait, and wait to go to the board—writers want to go to the board too soon. Then, finally, he'd get up and write a couple of things on the board, and they'd just be perfect and be right."

However, Joss had several story ideas that the *Buffy* writers were never able to break. In one, he wanted the Scoobies to find a box in the school that they wouldn't know how to open. "We spent four or five hours one night on it," Batali says. "We could never figure it out. There was another story about the idea of a race of demons that are aliens. Joss really liked the idea that demons were actually aliens, that they were from outer space."

On several occasions, Joss would showcase surprising artistic skills to help his writers visualize certain elements of a story. While working on "Killed by Death," he left the writers' room to draw Der Kindestod, the demon who sucked the life out of children who were feverishly ill. Another time, after they'd spent the morning working on a story, Joss returned after lunch with a clay model of the story's monster that he'd sculpted. In both cases, he delivered the demon with the same pronouncement: "Well, here's what it should look like."

//////////

When it came time to shoot the episodes, however, Joss was at first far less in control. "The first year, it was like we were all on Ecstasy. Everybody loved each other, everybody hated each other, and nobody wanted to go home. Because I was literally there all night—I'd sleep on the couch," he said. "I think we were all so young and so fresh and so crazed when we started, that I let a lot of tension on the set. In trying to be everybody's friend, and so excited to be doing this work, and sort of assuming we'd all get along, I let a lot of non-constructive emotion take open sway on the set, when I should have just put the hammer down and said, 'You know what? We're here to do the work. Everybody, just get it done.'"

Still, when Jeanine Basinger visited Joss on set, she was excited to see how much he was taking charge. He ran around to check up on every element of shooting, taking close care to even review the wardrobe choices. She was also quite touched to see how much the staff had picked up his manner of speaking, which would later come to be known as "Slayer slang."

Later, at lunch, Joss asked if Basinger thought the series would be successful. He followed that up by saying that he was glad he finally got to do what he wanted, and even if *Buffy* only lasted two episodes, he'd be happy. Together, they decided to be hopeful but to stay realistic.

//////////

Joss's long hours and all-nighters also proved frustrating for Kai, who'd grown accustomed to her husband's domestic contributions. "I did not cook at all when we first met," she says. "He's an amazing cook, an awesome, natural cook—doesn't use recipes or anything. His mom was a great cook, so he kind of learned at the foot of her. I'm so jealous because he just doesn't think about it. He just kind of knows how to do it. He even makes roast beef and Yorkshire pudding for Christmas."

Their first Thanksgiving together had been a brand-new experience for Kai. She was used to the stressful days of her family gatherings and had seen the holiday as one filled with unavoidable drama. Joss's emotional connection to the day was far, far cheerier, filled with memories of Shakespeare readings led by his mother. He told Kai that he'd take care of everything and spent the day cooking, singing along to show tunes. "Everything's casual. It's the most wonderful holiday and it's all because of him," she explains. "Thanksgiving is his favorite holiday, because it's about family, but it's about the family that you choose—he's always kept Thanksgiving for friends." (Sometimes those friends were quite random; one year, Joss told Kai that she couldn't invite any more random people, but that night she came home and asked if a guy from Russia that she'd met at karaoke counted as a random person, as she'd already invited him over. "It was a really nice guy, and he had nowhere to go.")

But his responsibilities to his new show meant Joss could no longer spend much time in the kitchen. "I felt it was false advertising when I found out that he was going to stop cooking for me when he started to work for *Buffy*," Kai laughs. "I thought that that's what I signed up for."

///////////

The entire first season was written and filmed before *Buffy* premiered on the WB on Monday, March 10, 1997. By then, Joss had fought and won several battles in the journey to bring the series to air—not the least of which was the title. To broaden the show's appeal, the network wanted to call it *Slayer*; Joss insisted on the full *Buffy the Vampire Slayer*. As he explained, each word was crucial to understanding the show: "One of them is funny, one is scary, one of them is action."

The first two episodes, "Welcome to the Hellmouth" and "The Harvest," were packaged together to serve as the series premiere. Originally, Joss had wanted to preface the story with a dream sequence that bridged the gap between the *Buffy* movie and Buffy's first day in Sunnydale. It would also serve as a primer for anyone who'd skipped the film, recapping Slayer lore, the Watcher/Slayer relationship, and the death of Buffy's first Watcher. But the sequence was scrapped due to budgetary constraints.

Instead, the WB's marketing team created a ninety-second trailer combining scenes from series with generic gothic imagery and explaining how, throughout history, a young woman would arrive in a town plagued by mysterious deaths. "For each generation, there is only one slayer," it announced to viewers. "You are about to meet the Slayer." It was not quite the informative prologue Joss had in mind, but despite the cheesiness of the stock gothic footage, it effectively informed the audience that this was no ordinary teen drama—this was a high school series in which the stakes really were life and death.

That fact was reinforced by the on-screen disclaimer that preceded the premiere:

> The following two-hour world premiere is rated TV-PG and contains action scenes which may be too intense for younger viewers.

The warning may seem strange in retrospect, in an era full of *Vampire Diaries* and *Supernatural* occurrences (let alone bed-hopping *Mad Men* and meth-dealing schoolteachers *Breaking Bad* on basic cable). Yet *Buffy* was just the second hour-long drama on the WB, and it was premiering in the 8:00 PM eastern time slot usually occupied by the family-friendly *7th Heaven*. (The following week it would settle in at 9:00 PM.) A similar disclaimer would appear at the beginning of subsequent *Buffy* episodes, but the practice would retire with the series, not carrying over to any of the WB's other science fiction, fantasy, or horror series.

Each *Buffy* episode would end far less ominously, with a crudely drawn white cutout of a monster jetting across the screen in front of the words "Mutant Enemy." It was the "production slate" for Joss's production company, which he had named after a line from the rock band Yes's song "And You and I." (Mutant Enemy was also the name of the typewriter he had in college.) All television series have such slates, which air during the closing credits, indicating such key entities as the executive producer and the distribution company (in *Buffy*'s case, 20th Century Fox). Joss got word shortly before he needed to deliver the slate and quickly both drew and voiced the monster, which grumbled, "Grr. Argh." The Mutant Enemy cutout and his trademark yelp would become almost as synonymous with Joss as his teenage hero.

The premiere episode introduced the season's recurring central villain, or "Big Bad": the Master, a centuries-old vampire who wants to open the portal to hell beneath Sunnydale. But many subsequent first-season episodes were more stand-alone than part of an intricate ongoing narrative, each hitting on a key trial that teenagers experience. "The Pack" explores the pressure to be cool, as Xander falls in with a group of bullies after being possessed by a hyena spirit. In "I Robot, You Jane," Willow is so excited to have an online boyfriend, unaware that he's an ancient demon who has been unleashed on the Internet.

Buffy often took on the difficulties in maneuvering around new emotions and relationships. In the first episode of the series, Buffy encourages Willow to approach a boy, with the advice to "seize the moment, because tomorrow you might be dead"—advice that is pretty much an underlying theme throughout the show. But even though the characters are constantly reminded of their own mortality, they are often swept up in the seemingly mundane, especially when it comes to matters of the heart: Willow has her big unrequited crush on Xander, Xander is infatuated with Buffy, and Buffy falls for the enigmatic Angel, only to discover that their love is star-crossed as well: Angel is a vampire, reformed after a gypsy curse restored his human soul, allowing him to feel remorse for his murderous past.

"You know, we had our television tropes," Joss admits. "In what world is Sarah Michelle Gellar not very popular in high school? I want to know about that magical land! But I think we did genuinely evoke something of an outsider sort of feeling: 'No matter who they are, no matter how popular they are, no matter how pretty they are, no matter what they are. They have that feeling of, you know, I'm on the outs. I'm barely scrambling. I'm trying to figure this out. I'm alone here.'"

(In fact, Gellar did have a difficult time in school. Like Joss, her mother was a teacher and she attended a private prep school with classmates far wealthier than she was, and she felt misunderstood by the classmates who ostracized and harassed her for being "famous." She, like Buffy, had to balance important personal commitments with her schoolwork, only it was auditions and acting gigs instead of slaying and saving the world.)

//////////

Monday nights on the WB began with the wholesomeness of *7th Heaven*, followed by the demon-filled adventures of *Buffy the Vampire Slayer*. It seemed like the network was sponsoring weekly excursions into heaven and hell. And perhaps it was odd that Joss, the professed atheist, had kept the standard Christian imagery of crosses and holy water in the new vampire universe he had created.

"He's atheist, but never seemed to be anti-faith," Dean Batali, himself a Christian, says. Batali was intrigued that, as an atheist, Joss had created a world in which the vampires are afraid of Christian icons and artifacts. In the premiere, Angel gives Buffy a simple silver cross in a jewelry box with the admonition "Don't turn your back on this." Later that season, in "Never Kill a Boy on the First Date," penned by Batali and Des Hotel, Giles holds a cross up to a newly risen vampire. The vampire recoils and asks, "Why does He hurt me?"

"We didn't write that. Joss wrote it," Batali explains. But further exploration of religious themes, particularly Christian ones, was nixed. Early on, Batali pitched a story in which Buffy teamed up with the religious kids at school to fight a demon, because he felt they all would be on the same side. He and Joss had never debated religion and had no desire to do so, but Joss let him know that he didn't want the show to deal with it.

Even without the religious implications, the series was never lacking in allegorical weight. It was the show's careful development of each story's metaphor, the "Buffy of it" that Joss and Greenwalt insisted upon, that helped the show gain a foothold with its earliest viewers. That lesson was powerfully demonstrated with the airing of "Out of Mind, Out of Sight," the eleventh episode of the season. This was the episode in which a girl named Marcie is so widely ignored by her classmates and feels so insignificant in the world that she literally becomes invisible. (The premise, with its roots in Joss's own high school experiences, had been part of his original pitch for the show.) Once Marcie realizes and embraces her invisibility, she indulges her darker side and lashes out against her perceived enemies, including Cordelia. After the episode aired in May 1997, the producers received a letter from an agoraphobic lawyer in her forties. "I'll never forget: she said, 'Last night's show gave me the courage to walk out the door of my house,'" Greenwalt recalls. "I realized we've got lightning in a bottle here."

In the season finale, "Prophecy Girl," Buffy learns of a prophecy that says she is fated to die at the hands of the Master. Nonetheless, she ventures into his lair to confront him. The episode, written and directed by Joss, echoes the original movie in interesting ways. Buffy goes to battle in a prom dress and a leather jacket, just as she'd done in the film; the

Master, like Lothos, hypnotizes her. But in this case, the vampiric trance makes her so vulnerable that the Master feeds on her blood, then drops her into a shallow pool of water to drown. The Master escapes, but Angel has led Xander to his lair, and the latter revives Buffy via CPR—reminding the audience that this Buffy is even stronger because of her friends. When Buffy meets the Master again, he is incredulous that she defied the prophecy: "You were destined to die! It was written."

"What can I say?" she says before killing him. "I flunked the written."

Joss has said that *Buffy* is about showing what it's like to come to terms with power, and he ended the season—and possibly the series, if it never made it past the first season—with the message that despite the demands of others' expectations, despite how easy it is to believe that we're at the mercy of forces beyond our control, we all control our own destiny by the choices we make. By all conventional wisdom, Buffy's story should have ended with a failed motion picture, but now, with the help of his creative team, Joss had breathed the life back into her.

9

THE BRONZE

Buffy the Vampire Slayer didn't immediately become a household name. In the United States, although the ratings were certainly high enough for the WB to be happy, they were never so impressive that they challenged the show's time-slot rivals on the major networks. Joss's new series garnered a lot of praise from reviewers for the emotional and metaphorical depth of its writing—somewhat surprisingly, given that critics initially had been split on *The X-Files* and mostly looked down on more campy sci-fi/fantasy shows such as *Xena* and *Star Trek: Voyager*—but it struggled to find mainstream success.

In fact, *Buffy* owed a debt to those earlier series, for showing a netlet searching for its identity that it could find success with a show that garnered so-so ratings but inspired fervent fan devotion. "We were not a wealthy or respected show for a while," David Solomon explains. "We were kind of like *The Vampire Diaries* [was in 2011]—a show that feels like it deserves the buzz whether it's getting it or not. They kind of just create their own." *Buffy* got a lot of notice really fast, not from mass audiences but from a small, passionate group of hardcore fans—exactly what the WB needed to get the attention of advertisers. "They hit a show that they thought had a perfect demographic, a perfect, good-looking cast, the perfect 'not like any other show' [aspect], something completely unique," Solomon says. It seemed to hit all the buttons all at once, especially with teenage viewers. The ratings in the highly coveted eighteen-to-forty-nine-year-old demographic kept rising, which meant the WB could charge more for commercial time.

Buffy became a flagship show for the network. Not only did it renew the series for a second season with an order of twenty-two episodes (ten more than in season one), but it also began to refocus the rest of its programming in order to court even more of the teen market. Over the next year, it would roll out such teen-focused series as *Dawson's Creek* (from another film writer newly transitioning to series television: Kevin Williamson, the screenwriter of 1996's hit slasher flick *Scream*), *Felicity* (from future sci-fi mogul J. J. Abrams), and *Charmed*.

Joss liked being on the teen network, and the fact that the WB's new series seemed to be on a similar track as his own. But the network's branding efforts meant that *Buffy* tended to be pigeonholed as a show strictly for a younger demographic. Many fans in their forties and fifties have come up to Tony Head over the years and said that they were hugely embarrassed to admit that they loved *Buffy*, because the show was not aimed at them. Head refutes that thought: "Part of Joss's genius is that he encapsulates such a wide demographic—that's the whole point about his writing. It was a disservice to him to try and polarize that and make it only to a young audience, to [the WB's] detriment."

David Greenwalt agrees. "People who never watched *Buffy* or never understood it [would say] 'Oh, *Buffy*, was that a kids' show?' They didn't get it. The way Joss can guide a character through their paces—you won't see it anywhere else. The way he wrings them out and gives them humanity, you want to cry with them and you want to laugh. You root for them—it's like an old-fashioned movie experience watching his characters on screen."

//////////

The show's burgeoning online community was something that Joss could point to as evidence that *Buffy* wasn't merely a faddish teen phenomenon. At the end of each episode, the WB would advertise the show's official website, www.buffyslayer.com (the URL would later change to www.buffy.com). The site had information about the series and characters, and included an "interactive" section with a chat room and two separate message boards where people could come to discuss episodes. One of those message boards was the Bronze, named for the Sunnydale nightclub where the show's characters hung out. It would eventually become one of the largest single-show-oriented forums on the web.

Today, many television producers and writers have their own Twitter and Facebook accounts where they both post their thoughts and communicate with fans. But in 1997, the main pop culture outlets were magazines such as *Entertainment Weekly*, and fans would need to wait each week to see if there would be news about their favorite shows. Instead of spoilers leaking out as scripts were filmed, the most information that fans could get were episode descriptions in the latest issue of *TV Guide*. None of those options were enough to forge a real connection between viewers and the people creating their favorite shows.

The Bronze did just that—but first it created a bond among the community of "Bronzers" who frequented the site. In 1997, the majority of Americans still didn't have a home computer, much less a permanent Internet connection, so many of the Bronzers either were fairly early adopters or worked at desk jobs with little supervision. Considering the qualifications—had a computer and access to the Internet, watched a high school show about vampires and demons on a small netlet (that wasn't available in many areas of the country), and actually were willing to talk to strangers online—the board posters were a fairly small segment of the television-viewing public.

Bronzers discussed *Buffy* episodes in great detail and took care to find out about the show's writers and their specialties. "These are really, really smart people. I always say that Joss's fans are going to be running the country at some point. They are," Kai says proudly. "They're organized. They're smart." They're not just talking about how cute an actor is, she says. "These are people who are really paying attention to what all of Joss's people are writing. It's a completely different universe than what people think it is."

Chris Buchanan, who would later be president of Mutant Enemy, agrees. "So many of the people that I met over the years at conferences were super literate, super well educated and thoughtful. As much as the mainstream media would say that 'it's a bunch of nerds in their mom's basement who don't have a social life,' I said, 'Actually, it's some really amazing people. One of the early people in fandom worked at the Jet Propulsion Laboratory in Pasadena.'" There were also people who *did* live in their parent's basement, but this was never seen as a bad thing by their fellow posters. People were judged solely by how they expressed themselves and participated in the community.

The Bronze was a "linear message board," where everyone posted to a single, chronological series of posts rather than an organized collection of topics. In the same conversation stream, a poster might discuss the most recent episode, the significance of a demon killed two weeks back, or the stress that she was having at work. "It's a place where, in order to really fit in and survive, you *must* be a good written communicator," said Mary Beth Nielsen, a frequent poster. "I think part of that stems from the fact that Joss himself is so witty and the show is so well-written." It became such a highly developed community that almost a decade after it was shut down, several academic papers and sociological studies would be written about it, as well as a 2007 feature-length documentary, *IRL (In Real Life)*.

Once *Buffy*'s production team became aware of the board, they often read the commentary there to see how people were reacting to each episode. Joss followed the conversation regularly. "I remember him frequently talking about the board," Dean Batali says. "He took what they said to account. He didn't let them make the decisions, but I don't think it's fair to say that they didn't have any influence." Joss's fascination with the Bronze made sense to Batali. "All of life is high school, isn't it? You want to be popular; you want to know people are talking about you and liking what you do." And it was the kind of popularity, self-selecting but devoted, for which Joss was especially eager; "I'd rather make a show a hundred people need to see than a show that a thousand people want to see," he once said.

The actors, too, were amazed by the passionate online fan base that the show was developing. While waiting on official word on the show's second-season pickup, Tony Head had called Alyson Hannigan to check in. She quickly asked him if he had a computer; he did, but he rarely used it. "Well, you have to go on and look up your character name, because there are shrines to you," she told him. "We've all got shrines!" Head asked her to clarify, not fully understanding what she was saying. "There are people who post and talk about you," Hannigan explained. "Go check it out!"

"And so I did," Head says. "I was absolutely blown away. I had never encountered anything like it. Now it's probably two a penny, but at the time it was huge. Never, ever, ever encountered anything like it."

On the Bronze, reading turned into posting and soon Joss, a few of his actors, composer Christophe Beck, makeup supervisor Todd McIntosh, and stunt coordinator Jeff Pruitt were contributing to the conversation. Not surprisingly, the writers, too, checked in regularly to see what the fans were saying. Marti Noxon, who would join the series in its second season, was one of the first writers to post on the board. (She, like many on the board, chose a pseudonym: "Scout.") For the writers, it felt like a gift to watch their fans discuss the show with one another—even when their reactions and responses were negative. "Some Bronzers hated everything every week. We knew them by name; we would go 'Oh here he comes, he's going to take thing apart,'" she recalls. "It was really in the early days of this feedback loop, and with the Bronze it was like being in the audience finally and seeing them appreciate that we'd been working hard, so it always felt great."

Joss often jumped into the conversation with personal reflections and insider information on episodes:

> Am interested in showing dreams of past slayers—bottom line, the past is expensive to produce on TV. . . . The past is more expensive cuz clothes, cars, landscapes all change—everything has to be bought or made. I never taught Nickie to dance like that. Xander is based on me but I am a swell dancer (actually, I never danced in high school.) (ever.) (I'm not bitter.) (This series has nothing to do with my bitterness.) (It's not about revenge.) (The names of the girls who would not dance with me are as follows: #1, Wen—) We interrupt this bitterness to answer the folowing question: Yes there will be more dreams. They're fun to shoot.

And when Joss posted, the Bronze would come to a cross between a total standstill and frenzied chaos. "It was always such a BIG DEAL when he was posting," Melanie Morris, another poster, says. "It sometimes brought out the worst in people—those trying to vie for his attention and to get him to respond to their posts and questions."

To the Bronzers, Joss and other *Buffy* insiders elevated the board's importance. These fans weren't just talking to a bunch of strangers about a Vampire Slayer; they had an actual connection to the show. "It was special that [Joss] took the time to post. It made us more loyal fans," says early Bronzer Amanda Salomon. "You could argue there were Machiavellian overtones to their coming there. They get us to spread the word about their show. Still, we got private words from him that the other people watching didn't get to hear."

In the fall of 1997, two posters had the idea to throw a party so that Bronzers could take their conversations offline and actually meet in person. This event was the first Posting Board Party (PBP). It was held at the Planet Hollywood in Santa Monica—a quick ride on the freeway from Los Angeles if any official *Buffy* folk wanted to come by, although expectations were very low on the part of the organizers that anyone from the show would actually show up. On Valentine's Day 1998, the restaurant was filled with roughly one hundred Bronzers and their friends when Joss and cast members Alyson Hannigan, Nicholas Brendon, Seth Green, Tony Head, and David Boreanaz arrived. They were also joined by several *Buffy* writers; stunt coordinator Jeff Pruitt and his wife, Sophia Crawford, who was Sarah Michelle Gellar's stunt double; and the makeup artist responsible for so many vampire faces, Todd McIntosh. For the Bronzers in attendance, it was a little mind-blowing that so many people from a show they loved would come out to a small fan gathering.

The inaugural PBP was first and foremost a party for the Bronzers—people who talked to each other every day but saw each other rarely if at all. The fact that actors, writers, and crew showed up was just a bonus. Unlike at a convention, where people line up in order to get an autograph or take a photo with an actor, at a PBP, people would mingle, dance, and occasionally run into David Boreanaz or Nick Brendon and chat, possibly snap a picture, and go.

After that first successful event, the PBP would be held every Presidents' Day weekend through 2003, and continue to get bigger and bigger each year. Bronzers would travel in from all over the world, creating their own Bronze of sorts in the official hotel.

"It was always lovely to meet fans," writer Marti Noxon says, "because you get into this vacuum where you're [working episode to episode] and you kind of are dimly aware that it's actually being watched. You sometimes forget that that thing you've been editing for days actually has some emotional impact, because it becomes routine to you." Often the interactions between the fans and the crew and the cast went beyond mere appreciation. Noxon remembers being told "really touching, emotional stories about how *Buffy* is helping certain people at stages in their life feel good and feel more hopeful."

To Joss, the connection was perhaps even more valuable. "I don't think people realize, even the Bronzers, how wonderful it was for Joss to have that community," Kai says. "Joss is not a guy who's going to walk around and make friends at the market. He's isolated, and he had a community. That was a community for him too. It was really nice for him to have that feedback and to have that comfort of the Bronze."

THE *BUFFY* WAY

Joss had found a true creative partner in David Greenwalt, a guide to the ins and outs of television production who showed him the respect that he had craved on his earlier projects. Greenwalt, in turn, was inspired and excited by Joss's ideas, how he crafted stories that connected with fans on such a deep, personal level, something he knew from experience wasn't often found on television. So it was a bittersweet moment when *Buffy* was picked up for a second season—because Greenwalt had left the series for *The X-Files*.

Four years into its run on Fox, *The X-Files* had grown beyond the typical constraints of sci-fi television to become a critical and popular hit. Mainstream critics now held it up as great, "classic" television, praising the writing of series creator Chris Carter and the standout performances of its stars: David Duchovny as an FBI agent obsessed with aliens and conspiracy theories, and Gillian Anderson as his partner, a skeptic medical doctor. *The X-Files* was the cult genre show that mass audiences actually knew about; while *Buffy* was drawing an average of 3.7 million viewers each week, *The X-Files* topped 19 million. In short, *The X-Files* was everything that Buffy aspired to be.

However, it was not a fit for Greenwalt, and he left almost as soon as he arrived. "It is a show that I liked and admired but didn't really quite realize until I got there that I couldn't write *The X-Files* to save my life," he recalls. "It was about its fourth year—it was a really good time on the show, and I don't get this show, you know? *The X-Files* was so cerebral and too . . . too mysterious for me, in a way. I get *Buffy*. I get something with emotion and heart and a search, so the deal completely slipped and I came back to *Buffy* right away."

Greenwalt wasn't the only one who wanted to be in business with Joss for the long term. In August 1997, *Variety* announced that 20th

Century Fox had signed a four-year overall deal with Joss. An overall deal is a development contract under which a studio secures a producer's services not just for a particular series but for whatever projects he or she pursues, usually in exchange for a lot of money. Joss's was worth $16 million. He was given $1 million to fund his production company, Mutant Enemy, and he would executive produce its TV projects and write, direct, and produce any Mutant Enemy films. Not only would he get to develop and write his own films, but Joss had finally won the right to direct them.

//////////

Going into the second season of *Buffy*, Joss had a lot more confidence in his ability to run a series. He'd had the experience of putting together his first writing staff, and he had a good sense of what sort of writers would be a good fit: people with "distinctive voices who can blend into the orchestra" of the show, who could write *Buffy* the way he wrote it, with a distinct patois and pop culture sensibility, and who were just good people. For Joss, the best writers were the best people, and "the person behind the words is ultimately how the show is shaped."

Joss had to create the second-season writing staff almost from scratch, as Dean Batali and Rob Des Hotel were the only first-season writers who remained on staff. Fortunately, Greenwalt's return also netted *X-Files* writer and executive producer Howard Gordon, who would join the staff briefly before leaving to create his own sci-fi series for Fox, *Strange World*. In addition, Joss set his sights on a newbie writer who was just breaking into television—and who had the audacity to turn him down.

"I got offered a job on another network show that already had its order," Marti Noxon says. Joss called her and asked if it was true, that she was turning down *Buffy*. When she explained that she preferred *Buffy* tonally but needed the financial security of the other gig, Joss told her that if she wanted to be a better writer, she should wait for their offer. "He said, 'Come on, that show sucks,' and we talked for a while. He was so winning and so sure of himself, by the end of the conversation I had totally changed my mind." Noxon called her agent when they hung up and turned down the other series. She started on *Buffy* soon after.

The remaining scripts were assigned to freelancers, bringing *Parenthood*'s Ty King and the sitcom writing team of David Fury and Elin Hampton into the fold.

On the set, Joss realized that he would have to take stronger control, to avoid the distracting behind-the-scenes drama of the first season. He realized that by trying to be everyone's friend, he had failed to create a position of authority for himself. He also needed to regain a balance of work and personal time—fewer all-nighters away from Kai. He considered a comment Jeanine Basinger had made about film directors, that "a director doesn't have to create anything, but he is responsible for everything," and reinterpreted it as a mission statement for his role as an executive producer on TV. "I don't have to write a line of the script . . . I don't sew the damn costumes, I don't say the words—but I'm responsible for everything in every frame of every show. That's my job, whether or not I'm directing the episode," he said. "So that's why you have to have that complete faith, that kind of blind faith in a leader who has the ability to lead. . . . I just also think leadership is something that is earned. I respected those above me, and demand the same from those below me. I don't think there's anything wrong with that."

To Joss, part of the reason he needed to assert control was to oversee the fantasy elements of the series. "The thing about fantasy is it creates its own seemingly arbitrary rules: 'And then her face turns into the moon.' 'I love it!' 'And then her sister has long fingernails.' 'That's idiotic! That could never happen!' There's always a reason for it. There's a genuine instinct," he explains. "When we did the Halloween episode in season two, I remember actually shouting, 'No, the dwarves are demons! The midgets are vampires!' I was so mad because people were not listening to me and they had done it wrong—because if you turn into a demon, you might change shape. If you turned into a vampire, you wouldn't."

Joss remembers how he yelled, "Take him away, it doesn't work!" then realized, "Wow, I actually just shouted that with genuine anger in my heart. My job is so awesome."

//////////

The second season brought on-screen changes as well. The series' focus shifted from largely stand-alone stories to a narrative more entwined in mythology. Buffy had slain the Master in the first season finale, and much younger, more impetuous adversaries arrived in the form of aggressive punk-rock vampire Spike (James Marsters) and his somewhat psychotic, somewhat psychic girlfriend, Drusilla (Juliet Landau). Spike and

Dru are overjoyed to discover that their old friend Angelus has taken up residence in Sunnydale, but horrified when they learn that their murderous, manipulative ally, once dubbed the Scourge of Europe, has been cursed with a soul and become the do-gooder Angel. On a lighter note, Seth Green joined the cast as the laconic and dry Oz, a werewolf who is terribly smitten with Willow.

Buffy began to hit a creative stride that drew more praise for the series and, more important for the network, more viewers. In January 1998, the WB moved the show to Tuesdays at 8:00 PM eastern time to help launch the new series *Dawson's Creek* at 9:00. That week, it aired a two-part story, with "Surprise" on Monday and "Innocence" on Tuesday. With those two episodes, the "high school as a horror movie" concept opened up to show that the scariest monsters in our lives are often the people we love.

In "Surprise," the gang plans a surprise seventeenth birthday party for Buffy, which gets diverted when they get word that Spike and Drusilla are gathering the pieces to reanimate the Judge, a nearly undefeatable demon with the power to rid the Earth of the "plague of humanity." The Judge awakens, Buffy and Angel narrowly escape him, and they make their way to his apartment, where they make love for the first time. At the end of the episode, after Buffy has fallen asleep, Angel rushes to the street and crumples in pain.

On Tuesday night, "Innocence" opens with Angel recovering—then killing a streetwalker who has come over to check on him. The gypsy curse that gave him back his soul, and thus his humanity, was broken when he experienced a moment of true happiness with Buffy. He has reverted to the evil Angelus, who revels in taunting Buffy when she finds him again in his apartment:

> ANGELUS: You got a lot to learn about men, kiddo. Although I guess you proved that last night.
> BUFFY: What are you saying?
> ANGELUS: Let's not make an issue out of it, OK? In fact, let's not talk about it at all. It happened.
> BUFFY: I don't understand. Was it me? Was I not good?
> ANGELUS: You were great. Really. I thought you were a pro.

Later in the library with the Scooby Gang, Buffy realizes that it was their lovemaking that broke the curse and is devastated that she brought about Angelus's return. (He will go on to become the Big Bad of the season.) But a Slayer cannot take time off for heartbreak, and she again saves the world, this time by blowing up the Judge with a rocket launcher. When she returns home, her mother is waiting with a birthday cupcake. Joyce, who knows nothing of slaying and vampires, asks Buffy what she did for her birthday. Buffy responds, "I got older." Urged to make a wish, Buffy just watches the candle flame burn.

In the DVD commentary for the episode, Joss showered praise on Sarah Michelle Gellar and David Boreanaz for their work. He declared that the exchange in Angel's apartment was "possibly the best" scene they had done, and that Gellar broke his heart in her crying scenes. He has often cited "Innocence" as among his favorite episodes, and said it was "harder edged" and "uglier" than the stories that had come before.

The episode is certainly a major turning point in the series, in which Joss's storytelling reaches new levels of rawness and honesty about a very common experience for many girls—a guy turning on them after they have sex. Even Buffy, the fairly unbreakable girl, is shattered by the experience. In prior episodes, she had disappointments related to other people's expectations—trying to be a "good girl" for her mother, trying not to get kicked out of school—but in this moment, when she gives everything to Angel and he takes it, then cruelly scorns her, it is all about *her*. It isn't about slaying getting in the way or teachers being unreasonable; it is about giving the guy she loves the most intimate part of her and then being rejected. It is the universal truth of that first heartbreak, which makes one wearier and forces one to see the world as a crueler place, that every viewer could relate to. That and the fact that they must get up and make it through the battle of another day, with or without a rocket launcher.

"You have to make sure the stakes are something more than life and death," Joss explains. After all, the series had shown Sunnydale teens dying at the hands of demons for more than a season, and defined its heroine by her ability to fight monsters rather than get killed by them. With "Innocence," he found a way to evoke real fear. "You have to make sure that the stakes have to do with an experience that will break this person, will twist this person," he says. "Luckily, with Sarah we could go there. Breaking her heart was going to be way, way more terrifying than piercing it."

//////////

So often, you'll hear someone who's worked on a TV show describe the experience as "making a little movie every week." Joss, who had come out of film school and didn't have that much experience with hour-long television, really did think he was doing just that. "Not only were we making a movie, we were making a completely different movie every week. It was really fun," he explains. Like at Pixar years earlier, he felt a certain kind of freedom due to his naïveté about what the "proper" way to do things was. "This one's a French farce! This one's a Greek tragedy! This one's just dumb! But we tried. Not knowing those rules and just reaching for something else, something more textural and ambitious, it was actually a help."

Joss found that his time as a script doctor, even with its frustrations, was one of the better training grounds for being a television showrunner. Like dealing with film scripts that had already gone through several rewrites before they came to him, Joss was now working with an ongoing story that had the elements in place and couldn't be changed. It forced him to think quickly and succinctly.

But unlike a script doctor, he had final say over what ended up on screen. "When something was good, we filmed it and it remained good," he says. "That was probably the attraction for the writers as well, knowing if they got it right, I would never rewrite them, because I do not wish to create more work for myself. I don't have to be the guy who did the thing; I'm perfectly happy to be the guy who runs the show with someone else to do the thing. As long as the thing gets done."

Joss did insist, however, on a very top-down writing process. While other series may be more collaborative, even allowing a lot of story influence from the actors, *Buffy*'s central ideas, themes, and structure tended to come from Joss himself. And no story on *Buffy* would ever be broken without Joss's input. Over the course of 144 episodes, that's a lot of stories.

"Joss's shows are really the products of Joss's brain," explains Jane Espenson, who joined *Buffy* as an executive story editor during the third season and would rise through the ranks until she became a co-executive producer in the final season. As a result, his writers' rooms tend to be productive when he's in them, and sometimes a little bit idle when he's not.

There had been changes to the way the *Buffy* writers' room was run between the show's first and second seasons. In the first, it was more of a group experience, with all of the writers including Joss and Greenwalt working together to pitch and break stories. Beginning in the second season, Joss's writers still worked together in the room but would go to Joss to present the story once it had been broken.

"There was almost never a day in which the staff would pitch him a story and he would just take what we'd done," Espenson says. "We'd help, but it tended to be his—mostly, I think, because he was just that good. He wasn't failing to see what we'd accomplished; it was just that he really could come up with something better."

Occasionally, when they had a particularly tough story to break, the whole writing staff would toil away in the writers' room for weeks to get the story on the board. Then Joss would come in and throw it all away, and they'd start over. Or they would end up just waiting until he came in, because they didn't feel like they could make any progress until then.

"Once, I'd worked a long time on coming up with this story that I wanted to pitch," remembers later Whedonverse writer Shawn Ryan, who would spend a season with Joss before creating the highly acclaimed dark cop drama *The Shield* for FX. "I took, like, five, ten minutes to pitch it, and he just looked at me and said, 'You know, that's a real good story, but it's all just moves.' That was his way of saying that it may have some good plot moves, but it didn't engage him emotionally with the characters. And so I really needed to learn to change my thinking. Ultimately, I brought that to *The Shield* and my other shows—to find out what the emotional arc of the episode would be before figuring out the plot."

"Behind all of the intelligence and a great sense of story was always a great sense of the end," Howard Gordon adds. "What was this adding up to? I think that is something that not a lot of writers look at. I mean, you almost have this novelistic approach to these characters, and having just been inside for this brief time and having watched the series recently with my fourteen-year-old daughter, who was too young at the time to watch it, I got to reappreciate just how intricate, how smart, and how special the show is."

If even Joss found a story hard to break, it was because he hadn't yet settled on some important aspect—usually the reason to tell the story or the way in which it was going to emotionally touch Buffy. "He would pace around the room, sometimes climbing on furniture, or lifting furniture, or leading hilarious discussions about everything except the story, while his subconscious sorted stuff out," Espenson recalls. "The telltale sign that a story was going to take a while to break was the degree of distraction and off-topic-ness that Joss would display."

But Espenson adds that there was an upside to such tough break sessions: "We would often just talk in the room, which made us a close group who really liked and understood each other." Noxon agrees, recalling that the writers' room was filled with "delightful, funny people who know way too much about useless topics. So it was sometimes hard to stay on track, because it was so much fun to just talk about what we had seen or what we loved, or sing musicals, which happened too often."

David Fury, who went from freelancer to staff writer in season three and would later become another co-executive producer on the series, described the writers' room during his tenure as a civilized environment. Instead of a conference room in which everyone sat around a long table, as was the case with most of the sitcom writers' rooms in which Fury had worked previously, Joss had a room adjoining his office that was decked out as a kind of den. "Sofas, easy chairs, etc., on which we could also be relaxed and casual, allowing our ideas to come out of banter between us," Fury explains. "Joss would often sit in a rocking chair with a cup of tea and, no matter how pressing the deadline was for the next script, he'd more often than not exhibit calm yet entertaining leadership."

The writers' room usually had toys, which Joss loved to fiddle with. "We had lots of toys in the *Buffy* room—action figures and little things from inside those Kinder Egg chocolates," Espenson says. (Years later, in the *Dollhouse* writers' room, "there were little magnetized ball bearings that could be used to build shapes.") She adds, "The main thing about a Joss room is that it takes on the shape of his personality—you laugh a lot in a Whedon room."

Greenwalt, for his part, has a word of advice for future writers who find themselves in a Whedon writers' room: "If he lies down on a table in the middle of a production meeting, it's always funny if you lie down and spoon him from behind."

//////////

Joss ran an informal school of sorts in his writers' room; he had the writers read *Regeneration Through Violence*, Richard Slotkin's intense academic tome that had inspired him at Wesleyan. For a much lighter balance to Slotkin's discussions about how no great change can come without apocalyptic, violent feeling, Joss also assigned them Scott McCloud's *Understanding Comics*, an illustrated guide to how comic books work. McCloud broke down the storytelling devices of comic books, to which Joss would refer the writers when discussing directorial choices. Since most writers were focused on telling the emotional story, *Understanding Comics* helped them consider the visual elements of how each scene is framed.

Joss would discuss comic book storylines with his writers as well, because he felt that they were great examples of how to locate the real emotion in a story and then find a way to dramatize it that wasn't always so literal. Like finding "the Buffy" of an episode pitch, superhero stories had to be emotionally grounded to create a sense of authenticity within the fantastical comic book world.

Echoing his childhood hours spent watching films with his mother and his college nights watching films in a basement, Joss also brought movies to the writers' room for viewing and discussion. He and his writers examined the language in Alexander Mackendrick's 1957 film *Sweet Smell of Success* and Martha Coolidge's 1985 comedy *Real Genius*. The first is a film noir about a prominent gossip columnist who enlists an unscrupulous press agent to break up his sister's relationship with a jazz musician; the second is a satire about a teenage prodigy and a brilliant but outlandish college student who team up to develop a high-energy laser. There couldn't be two more different movies. "But he wanted us to look at things about language," Noxon says. "In *Sweet Smell of Success*, the way they speak to each other is brilliant, and *Real Genius* has great language, great ways of talking. We got schooled. We had to do our homework, and he would come back after the weekend and say 'I saw this' or 'I read this.' That surely helped me understand where he was coming from."

"I think that is the great privilege of working with Joss—that he makes you better than you are," Gordon says. "It is one of those things where you have somebody running a show and it doesn't always work this way. I hope I share with Joss the ability to recognize a voice who can sing in the key [of the series] and then bring out the best in that person. Emphasize their strength and help them to be as good as they can be and also protect them from their limitations. Joss does that really well and very gracefully."

The schooling also included some playful hazing, putting Joss back into a high school mode—but this time with people he liked and felt comfortable around. And this time he was at the top of the social pyramid. When Noxon turned in her first script, for the episode "Bad Eggs," she went home to sweat and shake from all the nervousness. She had a phone message from Joss and David Greenwalt that said, "Marti, we've read your script and we have some bad news. There's just no easy way to say this." Her heart dropped and panic set in as they continued: "Oh, we're just kidding, they were great—welcome to the family."

Another time, Joss popped his head into her office and Noxon asked if there was something he wanted her to be thinking about. In all seriousness, Joss said "Leprechauns" and then walked away. It didn't sound like the best idea to her, but Noxon dived into some deep leprechaun research, including watching the Warwick Davis / Jennifer Aniston horror movie *Leprechaun*. She presented all her research and Joss just stared at her for a while before telling her, "Yeah, that was such a joke."

Noxon says, "I have never lived the leprechauns down. I still think about that when I'm talking to a new PA or someone who just wants to get their foot in the business. You say something completely facetious and they're like, 'On it, I will go bomb that guy's house.' So that was me—I was just, you know, you say *jump*, I say *leprechauns*."

Jane Espenson was another target of Joss's teaching and his teasing, as a writer whose previous work had been largely comedic. Joss often approaches writers in the way he assesses actors: "I go for the comic ones. If you can write comedy, you can write 'the other thing.'" But that didn't mean that all comedy writers could jump into the waters of *Buffy* and have no issues. Espenson's second script was season three's "Gingerbread." She was terrified of the story they'd broken, because it had dead children in it. "I had just come off of five sitcom jobs in a row and had been trained to avoid topics, like dead kids, that were certain to kill any comedy," she says. *Buffy* was a funny show and she had no idea how to maintain that humor within such an uncomfortable topic. "Instead of leaning into it, I leaned away, trying to compensate with more jokes," she explains. "Joss hated it and still teases me about all my 'dead kid' quips. I learned that there are other ways to be entertaining than to be funny about *everything*. It was still a long time before I became comfortable writing a script without humor, but I took the first steps toward losing the crutchiness of it at *Buffy* because of Joss."

The schooling wasn't limited just to the staff writers. Diego Gutierrez, Joss's assistant from 1998 to 2001, was considering his future and discussed with Noxon the possibility of going back to school. Joss, who had been setting up a shot on a ladder nearby, stopped what he was doing and looked at him as if he'd just said the stupidest thing ever. "That's dumb," Joss said. "This is your grad school right here—this is what's happening right here."

From that moment, Gutierrez shifted his focus to take advantage of the opportunities he had at *Buffy*—the biggest of which was his access to Joss. In addition to his general assistant responsibilities, he shadowed Joss to see how he worked and learn how to break stories. "Joss was definitely a very specific mentorship, because he was so specific the way he did things—he would break the story and then lock himself up for however many hours in his office and he would just come out with a script."

///////////

As someone who wants things done in a very specific way, Joss is predictably idiosyncratic when it comes to the physical act of writing. Pilot Razor Point is the only pen he's written with for the last twenty years, and notepads are very, very important. "Muji made a wonderful notebook that I'm just in love with—they were thick and just the right size. And they stopped making them because they *hate* me." It's all about writeability, Joss explains; the wrong notepad can kill an entire writing session. They've got to open easily, stay open, and be smaller than eight by ten but bigger than five by seven. "Too small and you just can't compose a scene on it. Too big and it's too intimidating and too hard to carry around. The big, thick, bound, precious ones? They never work out," he says.

The perfect notebook must be simple; it can't ever have anything written on it except lines. And it can definitely not have any cute little drawings in the corner. "I make those cute little drawings," Joss says. "If I doodle anything on the page, I'm not getting anything written that day. I already know that page is useless. Faces, shapes, anything—that means it's over." Joss doesn't toss any notebooks out. He has practically filled an entire filing cabinet with notebooks that he tried writing in—some that he's filled, some that he wrote three pages in then gave up.

Another warning sign of an unsuccessful writing session: talking to himself. "If I'm writing by pacing, and I start talking out loud, not like dialogue but like to myself—'Come on, let's get out of here, let's concentrate'—it's over. It's not gonna happen."

Yes, the pacing. If you ask anyone about Joss's writing habits, they all say the same thing: he's always pacing. Joss likes to have an open space that allows him to pace in a circle. Greenwalt says that he's always drinking tea and always pacing. "By the time he sits down to write, he's already thought of every single possible idea and he's picked the best one. He's like a chess master who can think so many steps ahead." Diego Gutierrez describes another writing habit: "He basically taps his thumb with the rest of the tips of his fingers like as if you were about to snap without really snapping. He would just be constantly doing that as he was walking."

"*Oh my God*, he would do this thing we called the crab walk," Noxon laughs. "He would be all hunched over from stress, and he would be like making these little claws with his hands. Sometimes he would like disappear for a day or two—he was in a dark pit of despair and was always like, 'This sucks, it's going to be terrible, you know, I've really done it this time, you know . . .'"

Because no matter how well Joss knew he wrote, he would fall into a "K-hole of self-doubt when he was working on a script," Noxon explains. "It was routine. It was surprising, because he always turned in an amazing script that didn't need any rewriting. He did all the editing and all the fixing himself, so you would get these perfect first drafts. But he would agonize and he would have to go off campus and take a walk or go to lunch and try to jog it loose and then suddenly kind of the dam would burst and he would be OK."

Without knowing what turmoil was going on in his head, observers could be intimidated to see Joss sit down and churn out a script and be done with it in one pass. Because he waited until he had the whole story in his head before he put pen to paper, he rarely rewrote himself. "He hates to rewrite," Greenwalt says. "I've never met a writer that hates to rewrite more than Joss. He will break a story, which is the hardest part, obviously, and then he'll pace for a week. He won't write a word. He'll just pace. He's always pacing." The technique seemed to work for Joss. "You shoot his first drafts. I've never seen anybody else who can do that."

While his work seldom needed to be rewritten, he often rewrote other writers' scripts. "You could always tell when a script would come back after it had been to Joss," Tony Head says. "It was like somebody had sprinkled fairy dust over it. Sometimes it was sparing, but my God, he knew. He always knew it. Just . . . the jokes were sharper. The moments were heightened. He has great, great writing sensibilities. Bless him, but Joss always got that British reserve, that just Englishness—we are a ridiculous race!"

Joss's fellow writers would struggle mightily to rise to his level. "I would get up at five in the morning to try to keep up with this guy and use a thesaurus on every line of dialogue," Greenwalt says. "I really wanted my stuff to be as good as his stuff, you know, or as close as it could be. He'd put checks in the script when he liked a line, and that was always a big, fun deal, to have a check in a script."

Dean Batali also wrote with Joss's reactions in mind. He knew Joss liked a smart twist of phrase, and the young writer crafted his dialogue carefully. "Can we make him smile with our writing?" he asks. "Can we twist the phrases in a way that makes him smile?"

Even *Buffy*'s fans developed an extraordinary admiration for Joss's writing talents. Espenson has mentioned how *Buffy* fans, more than any other fans she's encountered, indulge in the "cult of the writer." Many writers from the show continue to be showered with affection from fans due to their work on *Buffy*, which doesn't tend to happen with scribes from other series. "The Dear Leader of that cult is Joss," she said. "He's the one who determined what a *Buffy* episode was, and in fact, shaped every single story."

Since the end of *Buffy*'s run, Espenson herself has not only served as a writer and producer for *Battlestar Galactica, Torchwood: Miracle Day, Gilmore Girls,* and *Once upon a Time,* but also cocreated the web series *Husbands,* which featured a special guest star in its second season: Joss Whedon. "He sent us all out into our subsequent jobs asking, 'What's this story *really* about? Why are we telling this story? What is the emotional impact of this story on the main character? How is our hero taking a heroic action?' So in that way, certainly, the Buffy Way has spread."

11

FRONT-PAGE NEWS

In its first two seasons, *Buffy* and its cast had enjoyed a certain amount of freedom because the show flew under the mainstream radar on the WB. But by 1999, the network had established hits with its youth-oriented series *Buffy*, *Dawson's Creek*, *Felicity*, and *Charmed*, and was adding soon-to-be teen favorites *Roswell* and *Popular* (an early effort from *Glee* cocreator Ryan Murphy). The WB started producing image campaigns featuring the young casts of these shows in beautiful, highly stylized promos, and magazine editors soon learned that putting them in their photo shoots would quickly translate into high newsstand sales from fans who had graduated from *Tiger Beat* and *Bop* but still had disposable income to burn.

Feature films wooed the WB actors as well. Joss watched the momentum of the teen entertainment machine begin to affect his cast as a pair of 1999 movies not only starred two of Sunnydale's favorite girls but reinterpreted them as sex symbols. *Cruel Intentions*, a retelling of *Les Liaisons Dangereuses* set in a New York private school, showcased Sarah Michelle Gellar as the manipulative Kathryn Merteuil, who sexes, schemes, and manipulates everyone for her own amusement. The scene in which she instructs the very sheltered and inexperienced Cecile Caldwell (Selma Blair) in the fine art of kissing became a pop culture phenomenon, and would go on to win the 2000 MTV Movie Award for Best Kiss.

Alyson Hannigan had a very different role as the nerdy music student Michelle in *American Pie*, whose "This one time, in band camp" catchphrase throughout the film explodes into infamy with the final punch line about where exactly she had put her flute while on her summer excursion. The shock of seeing sweet Willow—who just a couple years earlier had explained that when she was with a boy she liked, "it's hard for me to say anything cool or witty or at all. I can usually make a few vowel sounds, and then I have to go away"—declare that she knew how to get herself off and instruct the main character how to sex her up properly made for another big pop culture splash.

With the success of *Cruel Intentions* and *American Pie*, Joss saw that his cast's focus was shifting from being excited to be on a critically acclaimed series to anticipating the new projects that awaited them in the future. He was happy for their success but was determined to make sure that his set was still as orderly and his series still as strong as they could be.

Jane Espenson noted the relationship he had with his cast in their third season. Long gone was the flexibility of the early days. "My first impression wasn't that Joss was particularly close with his actors, but that Joss was particularly strict with them, in terms of having to say every syllable as written," she said.

"There was a lot of tension," Joss admitted. "Who that bleeds into are the crew, people who come in before—I was the only person coming in before the crew, and staying after the crew, and I get paid better." Still, he said, "my cast always came to play, always came knowing their stuff, doing the work, doing the best. Whatever bad energy they had before the cameras rolled, they didn't put it on the screen." Eventually, "this stuff kind of calmed down, we went seven years, we all kind of grew up."

///////////

Production adjusted more smoothly to another behind-the-scenes change in season three. In the fall of 1998, Joss was looking for a new casting director, and Marcia Shulman, who did the original *Buffy* casting, introduced him to Amy Britt and Anya Colloff. The young casting directors were more familiar with the show's actors than with the show itself, and they were grateful when Joss took a chance by hiring them, starting a relationship that would take them through four of Joss's series and two of his feature films.

Early on, however, Britt and Colloff discovered that even with the series' track record of cult success across multiple seasons, some performers were still reluctant to audition for roles. Britt recalls, "You just had to encourage actors, or more accurately the gatekeepers who were their agents and managers, to see beyond the title of *Buffy* and get to the heart of the written word and mythology that was Joss's universe."

They also found that Joss was just as particular about casting as he was about every other aspect of production. "Joss is decisive," Britt says. "It's a beautiful thing. It also helps balance out the times when he tells me we're just not finding the right person and must continue looking. Joss has a great eye for talent and knows the right thing when he sees it. As casting directors, it's our job to keep looking until the producer or writer or director is happy. And those people almost always have a wicked sense of humor—must be smart and funny."

//////////

Just after the third season premiered, Sandy Grushow, president of 20th Century Fox Television, had a meeting with Jamie Kellner, the head of the WB. Grushow wanted to discuss the future of *Buffy* at the network past its current contract, which took it through the 2000–01 season. Both men had been champions of the series; the matter here was purely financial. Costs had risen greatly from the first season, but it was all due to *Buffy*'s success: the studio had given Sarah Michelle Gellar and the cast big raises and paid to upgrade the film quality from 16 mm to 35 mm at Joss's request. By the third season, the WB was paying $1.1 million per episode to license the series, while Fox was spending $450,000 to $800,000 more than that to produce it. While those were considerable deficits for Fox to absorb, they were in line with overruns that Fox assumed on other series; they would make their money back once the shows were sold into syndicated reruns. Syndication, however, traditionally came once a series hit one hundred episodes, and with *Buffy*'s short first season of twelve episodes, it would run $85 million into debt before the studio could recoup the money in the show's fifth season.

Grushow offered the WB a deal that would extend the hit series for at least two more seasons in exchange for more money per episode from the network. Kellner quickly said no, explaining that the network's greatest interest was profitability, and an early contract renegotiation that would put them more in debt was not the way to go. Since they were still two years out from the end of the current contract, it didn't seem like an urgent issue. Certainly not as urgent as the new projects Joss had in the Mutant Enemy pipeline.

//////////

On June 5, 1998, *Variety* had announced that Joss was diving back into another facet of the Whedon family business with an animated musical based on *Dracula*. Mutant Enemy was also developing several film scripts, including *Grampire*, a family comedy about "two kids who suspect their grandfather is a creature of the night," and *Alienated*, a comedy about someone who is kidnapped by aliens only to turn the tables on his captors. Ultimately, none of those projects would come to pass, nor would *Cheap Shots*, a TV ensemble comedy that would have reunited Joss with his *Parenthood* boss Ty King. The series would have been set at a B movie horror production company; while still entrenched in genre storytelling, it could have been great fun if it farmed Joss's early teen years for tales of low-budget storytelling.

Another TV project had a more promising future. As *Buffy* had developed a broader audience through its first two seasons, Joss started to think about how to expand the Buffyverse. The WB was interested in making a spin-off series, and making Angel the central character made the most sense. David Boreanaz had developed into a star on *Buffy*, and there was only so much more that the writers could wring out of the emotionally fraught Buffy/Angel relationship.

Joss and David Greenwalt had thrown ideas back and forth about an Angel-centric show. Nothing felt right until they began to explore the concept of alcoholism, and the fact that many recovering alcoholics go through the process of atoning for the mistakes that they have made. Angel's story could be about seeking redemption for his past as an evil vampire, about atoning for the person he'd become but shouldn't have. "Because," Joss said, "none of us turn out exactly what we want to be." Once they hit on that idea, Joss knew they had a show, and he started making phone calls about making an *Angel* spin-off a reality.

David Greenwalt was tasked with moving to the new series and getting it off the ground, just as he had done with *Buffy*. The challenge of developing the new show was to appeal to *Buffy* fans while creating a unique identity for the series and a new set of compelling metaphors to explore. *Buffy* was, for all its demons and apocalypses, the quintessential coming-of-age tale. It could explore the typical rites of passage of the young, everything from first kiss to first love to first sex, to first time getting drunk at a party. Angel, on the other hand, had been around for over two hundred years and was essentially an eternal twenty-eight-year-old. For many, their twenties are a time to make mistakes and learn who they want to be and what they want to do with their lives. There aren't the same rites of passage aside from muddling through to thirty and "growing up."

An episode of *Buffy*'s third season previewed the issues of atonement and self-definition that the *Angel* spin-off would address—while also serving as a rare foray into the overtly Christian themes Joss had previously expressed a desire to avoid. "Amends" is a Christmas story in which Angel is confronted with the spirits of those he killed during his many years as a sadistic demon. At the end of the episode, tormented with guilt, he attempts to commit suicide by facing the sunlight at dawn—but he's saved when a sudden snowfall blankets Southern California on Christmas morning. "It's hard to ignore the idea of a 'Christmas miracle' here," Joss said of the scene. "The fact is, the Christian mythos has a powerful fascination to me, and it bleeds into my storytelling. Redemption, hope, purpose, Santa, these all are important to me, whether I believe in an afterlife or some universal structure or not. I certainly don't mind a strictly Christian interpretation being placed on this episode by those who believe that—I just hope it's not limited to that."

///////////

As *Buffy* continued with its third season, it brought Buffy and her friends to the end of their high school careers and confronted them with two new villains: Richard Wilkins III (Harry Groener), the cheerful, polite, and malevolent mayor of Sunnydale, and the rogue Vampire Slayer Faith (Eliza Dushku). As the season neared its conclusion, however, it was met with unexpected controversy.

In the eighteenth episode, Jane Espenson's "Earshot," Buffy develops telepathic powers after a fight with a demon and discovers that she can hear what everyone is thinking. As it starts to slowly drive her insane, she hears one person's thoughts ring out in the school cafeteria: "This time tomorrow, I'll kill you all." She and the Scoobies quickly go to work to find out who is planning the massacre. While the perpetrator turns out to be a lunch lady who poisoned the school lunches, there is a side story in which Buffy finds fellow student Jonathan (Danny Strong)—a perpetually picked-on character, usually relied on for comic relief—in the school clock tower assembling a rifle. Initially, Buffy believes him to be the potential killer, until he explains that he only planned to kill *himself,* and she helps to dissuade him by sharing her frustrations with her own life.

This tale was not out of place for *Buffy*. Once again, Joss had taken his feelings of being an outsider when he was younger and made them into a story that viewers could identify with, even those who may not have felt quite so alienated. That moment when one realizes that all people, even the popular insiders, have their problems is a big moment of maturation. When Buffy confronts Jonathan, she explains that the reason his classmates do not notice his pain is because they are already consumed with their own problems. "It looks quiet down there. It's not," she tells him. "It's deafening."

Unfortunately, the message of the episode was overshadowed by real-life tragedy. A week before "Earshot" was to air, on April 20, 1999, two students at Columbine High School in Littleton, Colorado, went on a shooting rampage. They killed twelve students and one teacher and injured twenty-one other students. Before they could be captured, the pair committed suicide, leaving behind the deadliest attack on an American high school in history.

Immediately the media focused on lax gun laws and violent media marketed to teens as possible contributors to the massacre. Much of the backlash focused on shock rocker Marilyn Manson and shoot-'em-up video games, but *Buffy* was called out for being an inappropriately violent show in a high school setting. And the WB was particularly leery of airing an episode with direct parallels to the shooting in its immediate aftermath.

Sarah Michelle Gellar pushed for "Earshot" to air as planned. She felt it was a great episode and would help those affected by the Columbine tragedy. But the network decided to pull the episode and play a repeat in its place.

Joss took to the Bronze posting board to discuss his feelings about the move:

> On the inevitable subject, as far as pre-empting the ep, I agreed with the decision and when you see it you'll agree, I think, that it was just badly timed. But it WILL air. I'm proud of it. It comments on that type of sitch, and obviously we come down AGAINST massacring people, but ANY comment after so desperate a tragedy would be offensively trite. Needless to type, this BLAME THE MEDIA thing makes me crazy. . . . It's just a way of avoiding the

subject—and of making sense of something too ugly to deal with by latching onto a scapegoat. Sigh. (But it is Marilyn Manson's fault.)

The episode would ultimately air as Joss promised—months later, right before the fourth season began. In the meantime, however, the WB made another scheduling decision about which Joss was far less understanding.

On May 25, mere hours before the second episode of the two-part *Buffy* season finale was set to air, the WB again pulled the new episode and replaced it with a rerun. "Graduation Day, Part 2" was to end with an epic battle at Buffy's high school graduation, in which she and all her classmates battle Mayor Wilkins, who has been transformed into a sixty-foot-tall demon serpent. Apparently the WB was afraid that this premise might inspire another Columbine-style attack. Brad Turell, the WB's senior VP of publicity, told *Entertainment Weekly* that "if anything [violent] had happened at any graduation anywhere, every news organization would've run *Buffy* clips." Going even further to show that he didn't seem to understand the show or the *Buffy* demographic, he later added, "At least we won't be up against the final episode of *Home Improvement*."

Fans were furious. As *Entertainment Weekly* reported, they created protest websites and sent petitions to the WB. The campaign Stand Up for Buffy raised more than $3,000 and ran ads in a Hollywood trade magazine. According to *EW*, "Even Elvis Costello riffed, at a June 2 concert in L.A., about God searching in vain for 'the lost Buffy.' (He then sarcastically praised The WB for keeping teens safe from unholy demons.)"

Unlike "Earshot," "Graduation Day, Part 2" had been pulled too late to affect its broadcast in Canada, so Canadian fans were able to view the episode on schedule—and record it. They then shared their recordings with the rest of fandom, not an easy thing to do in an era before YouTube. The Bronze, as an international hub of *Buffy* fans, suddenly became a makeshift video exchange, where viewers who hadn't seen the episode could connect with Canadian fans with multiple VCRs and a plethora of VHS tapes.

Also unlike with "Earshot," Joss wholeheartedly disagreed with the WB's decision and wasn't going to take their decision quietly. In an interview with *USA Today*, he told fans, "OK, I'm having a Grateful Dead moment here, but I'm saying, 'Bootleg the puppy.'" With Joss offering his blessing in a large, mainstream media outlet, what had been a quiet sharing of tapes across the border and beyond took on a life of its own.

The Bronze set up an underground railroad of sorts to get the tapes dispersed as quickly as possible. Impatient fans with money and no connections turned to eBay, while those with more technical savvy could find the episode posted online in RealVideo format, which required the video to be broken into several smaller segments that took hours to download. By mid-June, at least one leaked copy of "Earshot" was also making the rounds, disseminated via many of the same sources. (Joss would later post on the Bronze that his rallying cry got him into "hot water" with the WB.)

By the time "Graduation Day, Part 2" finally aired in the United States on July 13, 1999, even the most marginally Internet-savvy fans had already seen it. They knew that Buffy had led the students in a successful attack on the mayor in his demon-serpent form and headed off the apocalypse. They knew that although Willow had lost her virginity to Oz in the first part of the finale, she didn't have to face the usual tropes of death or heartbreak afterward. And they watched Angel and Buffy's mature but agonizing breakup, and Angel leaving Sunnydale, bound for his own series.

The WB was quite familiar with fan protests by this point. Fans of the series *Roswell* had sent them packages of Tabasco sauce, a favorite of the lead characters, to try to convince the network of its large base of support. But the fan network built up to bootleg and distribute "Graduation Day, Part 2" was more than a movement to show support for a series. It took people who had previously only had an online relationship and gave them an offline connection, as they gave their names, addresses, and trust to strangers who simply shared one thing: a love for *Buffy the Vampire Slayer*. It transformed fans from quiet consumers into active participants in a series' success. One fan wrote on the online newsgroup alt.tv.buffy -v-slayer, "We are the people. We have the Internet. We have the power. Any questions?" And it illustrated that Joss's fans were eager to support *him*, not just the work he had created.

But Joss's experiences with both "Earshot" and "Graduation Day, Part 2" were a reminder that even though he'd achieved creative control over the stories he wanted to tell, he was still beholden to the whims of network television. Anyone who works in Hollywood knows that he or she must deal with its quirks and shortcomings—the half-truths, the indiscriminate decisions seemingly based on whim and questionable facts. But Joss was in his third year at the WB and in the process of developing a second series for them, so he felt respected and assured at the network. Nevertheless, he was always mindful of how fleeting and frustrating that relationship could be.

Joss had decided long ago that financial security was an important goal, and he wasn't going to get blinded by his multimillion-dollar deals and blow a lot of money on toys. "Joss had an old black Toyota Supra convertible," Nicholas Brendon, who played Xander, recalls. "I think he had it when he was writing for *Roseanne*." His new show had become a hit, but Joss "was still driving this little black Supra around. Meanwhile, the cast is all driving around Land Cruisers, BMWs, and here comes Joss, the creator of this empire, in his little Supra. He was really very, very modest."

The financial modesty also served another purpose: to keep him from having to take a job just to be able to pay the bills. He wanted to always be in the rare position to walk away from a project that he didn't believe in. He believed in *Buffy*, but as his recent experiences had illustrated, he still didn't have full control. That would require complete autonomy over all aspects of production and distribution, which was something he hadn't achieved—yet.

GROWING UP: *ANGEL*

Angel made it through losing the love of his life, a near-apocalypse, and the WB hysterics and landed in a place filled with more drama than all three wrapped together: Los Angeles.

Joss and David Greenwalt had decided to set the series in L.A., a few hours down the road from Sunnydale. As with *Buffy* a few years earlier, Joss introduced the network to the new setting not in a full pilot episode but with a short presentation tape. This time, however there was no full story to be told—the six-minute pitch tape is narrated, often directly to the camera, by Angel as he explains his past through clips from *Buffy*. A handful of new scenes show off the new setting, introduce Doyle (Glenn Quinn), a half-demon who will receive regular visions of damsels and dudes in distress for Angel to rescue, and hint at the series' eventual Big Bad: the evil law firm of Wolfram & Hart, which both defends and employs unscrupulous and often otherworldly clients—many of which will be sent to kill Angel over the course of the series.

Another familiar face makes an appearance in the pilot: Buffy's tart-tongued high school rival, Cordelia Chase. The producers had made the choice early on to bring Cordelia into this new corner of the Buffyverse. "When Joss [brought up the idea] to spin off *Angel*, the first thing I said was that we've got to bring Charisma Carpenter," Greenwalt says. "We've got to have that comic relief."

The visual pitch convinced the WB to order an initial thirteen episodes of the series in June 1998. However, at this point Angel had yet to appear in the third season of *Buffy*, which would lay the groundwork for the new show. Once the spin-off deal was confirmed, David Boreanaz's representation called and wanted more money for his role on *Buffy*. "David was a great guy, and one of my favorite guys, but this didn't have anything to do with him," Greenwalt explains. "It had to do with his representation. They wanted a huge amount of money for him that would have been impossible for us to meet, because we were still little shows. We didn't have *The X-Files*' budget, certainly." People gathered in Joss's office, worried that Boreanaz would not be available and the show would not happen.

"Joss sat very quietly and he said, 'I want you to call the agent. I want you to tell them we're going to add a new character to *Buffy* called "Bob Fanooti, Demon Hunter" and we're going to spin him off into his own series,'" Greenwalt recalls. "There's a Michael Corleone side to Joss, which is, if you want to play rough with him, don't fucking cross him and do something immoral or bad to him, because he's a very smart guy who thinks things through—he responds rather than reacting." It took just one phone call for Boreanaz's representation to come around.

//////////

Over three seasons on *Buffy*, Joss and Greenwalt had built a strong team of writers who understood the voice and the tone of the show. *Angel* was planned as a darker series with more adult themes, but the tone would be very much the same, so it made sense to hit the ground running by enlisting *Buffy* writers to script episodes of the new series. They did hire a few dedicated *Angel* scribes—the most notable of whom, like Marti Noxon, needed to be convinced to apply.

Tim Minear was already an experienced staff writer, a veteran of the *The X-Files* and ABC's romantic comedy take on Superman, *Lois & Clark*. About a year earlier, he had met with Joss on *Buffy* and pitched some ideas. If a spec script is a writer's audition to get in the door, the meeting with a producer is his or her one chance to shine. While Joss was "blown away" by Minear's talent, his demeanor during the pitch convinced him that Tim Minear was the angriest man he'd ever met. Joss felt that he couldn't spend a significant amount of time in a room with someone so full of rage. On *Angel*, however, Joss had given David Greenwalt his blessing to run the writers' room as he saw fit, and Greenwalt wanted Minear.

However, Minear was not terribly keen to do *Angel*. "I frankly didn't think it was that good," he says. "I didn't think it even remotely compared to *Buffy*—it felt like a pale knockoff to me." He also hadn't enjoyed his recent staff experiences. "I was coming off *The X-Files*, where they didn't let me do anything," Minear remembers. "Interestingly enough, the show that I never dreamed I would actually get a job on, the only show I watched, had hired me"—but his year on that show "was miserable. I was never on the inside with that group, no matter how hard I tried. I was coming from *Lois & Clark*, where they couldn't give me enough to do, to the show of my dreams where they wouldn't allow me to do anything. I just got so frustrated that I actually quit. The inertia at *The X-Files* was too stressful. So I quit at the end of the year with nowhere to go, but I felt great about it."

After that, Minear had turned down an opportunity to create a syndicated show for Tim Burton based on the *Oz* books. Greenwalt pursued him for the *Angel* writing staff, but Minear turned down several of his offers until former *Buffy* producer Howard Gordon, who was returning to the Mutant Enemy fold himself after the cancellation of his Fox series *Strange World*, urged Minear to join him in the *Angel* writers' room. Gordon was a fan of Minear, having previously hired him to write for *Strange World*. The series didn't last long, but he learned Minear's voice, and knew it could sing in the key of Whedon.

"Marti Noxon, Jane Espenson, and David Fury really sang in that key and I never felt like I quite sang in that key," Gordon explains. "That tone was very tricky, so singular and so specific to Joss—the irony and the ability to turn on a dime between emotion, comedy, and scary is really a hard degree of difficulty. You see it when people try to imitate it—it is just so counterfeit. I think all of those writers that have flourished were very funny. There was a kind of intelligence, too. A cleverness and also a love of language. I don't think you could write *Buffy* and not love language—and maybe that goes to anybody who is a writer, but even more so with people on *Buffy*."

Gordon told Minear, "'Trust me. I don't sing in this key but you do, and I guarantee you are going to thrive in this and this is going to be where you cut your teeth and learn.' I knew that it was going to be a great match. It was like knowing two people who fall in love, and even though you like the girl yourself, you knew you could never get her. I knew Tim would be great, and it happened just as I imagined it would."

Minear signed on to Joss's new show, but it was hardly love at first sight. *Angel* might have been designed to be a more mature show than *Buffy*, but sometimes it seemed as if the writers were still in Sunnydale High. The Mutant Enemy building had two floors, with the *Angel* offices downstairs and the *Buffy* team upstairs. "There were the freshmen,"

Minear remembers, referring to the the *Angel* staff, most of whom were mid- or lower-level writers, "and then you had the upperclassmen—the *Buffy* writers who had been with Mutant Enemy for a couple years or more. Everybody had been 'attending classes' there for years before we got there. We're the new class coming in, and David [Greenwalt] felt way more comfortable with the old class. So while we were his writing staff for *Angel*, for the first several episodes of the show, they had *Buffy* writers writing those scripts."

While it was understandable—the *Buffy* writers were familiar with these characters, and Joss and Greenwalt were familiar with the writers—the *Angel* writers were a little disconcerted. They felt that while they were breaking and rebreaking stories for what seemed like interminable weeks, the staff of another show was doing the real work. "Jane Espenson wrote an episode, Doug Petrie wrote an episode, David Fury wrote an episode, and Greenwalt wrote an episode," Minear says. "All these other writers were writing the episodes and we're sort of not getting our turn at bat, and that's making us feel like the redheaded stepchildren."

Adding to that stress, Joss seemed to spend more time on the *Buffy* floor. "As gregarious, entertaining, and as brilliantly as he can hold a room full of people's attention, he's also oddly shy," Minear says. "He didn't really know us, and there was a whole bunch of people there that he knew, that were sort of like his extended family, which were the *Buffy* people, so I think it took a while for him to warm up to us." At first, in fact, "Joss didn't like me," Minear recalls. "I didn't like Joss. He wouldn't talk to me, he wouldn't look at me."

//////////

Angel's premiere episode, "City Of," opens with a voiceover that both immediately acknowledges the series' connection to *Buffy* and informs viewers that they are now in a new world:

> Los Angeles. You see it at night and it shines. A beacon. People are drawn to it. People and other things. They come for all sorts of reasons. My reason? No surprise there. It started with a girl.

Then Angel comes into view, sitting at a bar, nursing a drink, and drunkenly attempting to make conversation with another patron. Soon it becomes obvious that the inebriated monologue was just for show as

Angel follows a couple to a nearby alley and protects a blonde girl—but not *that* blonde girl—from a vampire attack. When she tries to thank him, he sees the blood on her forehead and growls at her to leave, then returns to his apartment, alone.

"We wanted a much darker show and for it to be different in tone from *Buffy*. . . . [It] is set in Los Angeles because there are a lot of demons in L.A., and a wealth of stories to be told," Joss said. "We also wanted to take the show a little older and have the characters deal with demons in a much different way."

However, the initial cut of the premiere went so far into the dark that a portion of it never saw the light of day. "One time, Angel arrives too late to save a girl who's been attacked by a vampire," Greenwalt describes. "She's dead, and he starts licking the blood off her. We scared the bejesus out of the WB." The moment was removed from the final cut. The script for the second episode was even darker in tone: "Corrupt" was to introduce Detective Kate Lockley (Elisabeth Röhm), a police officer who has gone undercover as a prostitute and become hooked on crack cocaine. The WB shut down show production for a few weeks, and the episode was completely rewritten. "They were right, because we hadn't earned that level of darkness in the show," Greenwalt says.

The writers pulled back from simply being "dark" and struggled to refocus the series. The basic premise remained the same: throughout the third season of *Buffy*, Angel was looking to atone for his murderous past, and he finds a calling in Los Angeles to help the helpless. "Buffy is always the underdog trying to save the world," Joss said, "but Angel is looking for redemption." Unfortunately, that premise was expressed through largely episodic storylines in which Angel either chased after the subject of one of Doyle's visions or took on a paying client as a supernatural private eye. Joss joked that it felt like "Touched by an Equalizer"—a mix of *Touched by an Angel*, a wholesome drama about angels who are tasked with a "case" to bring a specific person a message from God, and *The Equalizer*, a 1980s drama about a retired intelligence officer who provides service as a protector and an investigator, free of charge, to people in trouble. Joss found these types of stories more difficult to write than *Buffy*'s episodic "monster-of-the-week" tales, so he moved the series away from the weekly case format and "turned it into another ensemble soap opera drama with monsters in it."

///////////

One way the producers shook up the series' initial status quo was when they decided that the major character Doyle, played by Glenn Quinn, would be killed off in the ninth episode, "Hero." Joss had always wanted to kill off a main character early in a series, the way he'd introduced Xander and Willow's friend Jesse in the first episode of *Buffy* only to turn him into a vampire and stake him in the second. But here he had another motive: Quinn had a substance abuse problem, which was starting to disrupt production. The producers spoke with him about it, informing him that if he didn't get it under control, he would be fired. Quinn was "terrific but troubled, and we had to let him go," Greenwalt says. "It was a really sad turn of events." They hoped that the firing would force the actor to find help for his addiction, but sadly, he would die from an accidental heroin overdose in December 2002.

Quinn's final episode also became a turning point in the writers' room. Joss was in the room a lot more, breaking stories with the *Angel* staff, but people still weren't getting along. There was a "weird uncomfortableness," Minear says. "It's a little intimidating—he can be intimidating, because you want to impress him but you only have a certain amount of time to do it in because he's not there all day. Even though they had been using this other staff, even though they weren't letting us do that much work at that point, we get to episode six and suddenly we're behind."

There was no script for episode nine, no story up on the board. Tim Minear and Howard Gordon were assigned the episode, and they went into Joss's office to break the story in the most rudimentary way. They ended up with a general outline of what happens in each act and how Doyle will sacrifice his life at the end, and were given the weekend to write the script. Like they had done on *Strange World*, the two split up the story and went their separate ways to write. While they checked in to be sure that all the character names were the same, they really didn't have much time to properly integrate the two halves before they turned in the script. They knew that some of it would not quite line up, but it had all the right scenes in the right order with the right elements. In just over a weekend, they had delivered a script that was ready to go into preproduction.

"We turned this in on Monday," Minear remembers. "Neither one of us has slept for like forty hours, we're plainly fried, but we've done it. We've accomplished this thing. We're big heroes, we think." David Greenwalt called Minear in and gave his frank assessment of the script:

half was pretty good and he wanted to wipe his ass with the other half. Minear responded, "Well, when you wipe your ass with it, be sure to keep the brads in," and went back to his office to pack up his things.

For Minear, *Angel* had started to feel like *The X-Files* all over again; he couldn't write anything and he couldn't really talk directly to Joss, just like he hadn't been able to talk directly to Chris Carter. Adding insult to injury, as they left to write the script, Minear had learned that the following Tuesday, October 5, 1999, Joss was having a big party at his home for the premieres of *Buffy* and *Angel*. However, none of the *Angel* writers had been invited. Again, he felt like they were being treated like an afterthought. "There was sort of a high school atmosphere," Minear says. "There were cliques, the popular kids, and then the ones who weren't. It was just like, 'We're not eating lunch with you.'"

Minear then told Greenwalt that he was going to have a free parking space in the back. "I quit," he said. "I'm not doing this for another year. I just had an experience like this, I'm not doing it again." When Greenwalt asked Minear to talk, he decided that he had nothing to lose and completely went off about everything that had been bothering him. "I don't like Joss, he won't look at me, he won't talk to me, and there's just going to be some big premiere at his house tomorrow night and none of us are invited," Minear said. Greenwalt was shocked and asked how he found out about the party. Minear said that it didn't matter who told him, that Joss should have known it would get out.

Greenwalt tried to explain that Joss was very shy, and that the party was in his home and he didn't really know the *Angel* writers. Minear reminded him that this lack of a relationship wasn't the writers' fault. "We've been here for months! Look, I understand that this man has created a brilliant television show about high school because he felt like he wasn't popular in high school," Minear said. "Now this office is like a high school and he is popular, but let me just explain something to you: I didn't like high school either and I have no desire to repeat it."

Minear went home, but he didn't quit. After catching up on sleep, he came back in to work on the edit of an earlier episode he had written, "Sense and Sensitivity." In the episode, Kate Lockley's precinct is forced to go through sensitivity training, set up by Angel's nemeses at Wolfram & Hart. The officers are put under a spell that compels them to be uncontrollably empathetic and unable to stop sharing their feelings. As this new touchy-feely, emotionally wrung-out police force ignores their duties and tries to connect with their prisoners, criminals run rampant. This thrills the mobster who put it all in motion in order to assassinate Kate.

Before the drama of breaking "Hero," the staff had watched the cut of that episode together. Joss declared it unairable. "Great," Minear says. "The first episode that has my name on it, Joss Whedon feels like it's the first episode in the history of Mutant Enemy that is so bad that America must never see it."

Minear had asked to sit in with the editor and work on a new cut of the episode. At the time, it was rare for writers to regularly go into the editing room. They did a tremendous recut, and everyone felt that the results were actually pretty good. Minear himself felt that it never got great, but it definitely got better. Later Greenwalt would tell him that Joss said that he had done a great job and saved the episode.

Over the next weekend, however, Minear started to replay all the things he had said to Greenwalt and thought that when he repeated them to Joss, it would solidify Joss's theory that Minear was the angriest guy he'd ever met. And most likely, he'd be fired on Monday. Monday came, and lo and behold, Minear still had a job.

Instead, Greenwalt invited him to lunch on the set at Paramount and asked him about his time on *The X-Files*, and how Minear had quit that series. "That's a really big show, a lot of money and prestige. It's a top-ten show, it gets nominated for Emmys. But you said no," said Greenwalt, who had also walked away from a turn on *The X-Files* to return to *Buffy* season two.

"Because I wasn't happy," Minear replied. "The two things that don't matter to me, David? Prestige and money." At that moment, Greenwalt knew that none of the things that people are so afraid of losing really meant enough to Minear to be miserable—quite like Joss. And in the same way that Greenwalt had chosen to come back to work with Joss, Minear decided to stay.

///////////

After Glenn Quinn was written off the series, Doyle's plot-motivating visions were transferred to Cordelia, but Joss and Greenwalt still wanted to add another character to replace him. One idea was to bring in Alexis Denisof as Wesley Wyndam-Pryce, a straitlaced, jittery Watcher who had been introduced in *Buffy*'s third season. "I don't even think it was my idea," Joss says. "One of the writers said, 'What if Wesley came?' and I was like, 'Done! Solid. Sold. Beautiful.'" Joss had been impressed by his work on *Buffy*; he says that Denisof's awkward kissing scene with Charisma Carpenter in the season three finale "may be one of my favorite scenes I've ever filmed. We just thought, 'He'll bring lightness, he has gravitas.' And as is always the case in these shows, my goofiest character becomes my strongest."

Joss met Denisof for breakfast and told him how things were going on *Angel*, how they'd like to make Wesley a part of it. The character, after being fired by the Watchers Council, becomes a self-described "rogue demon hunter" and finds his way to Los Angeles. Denisof was very excited. "I had already fallen in love with the character, and I had certainly fallen in love with Joss, so it was a great marriage, as far as I was concerned," he says. "I didn't know the journey that was ahead. I knew we'd have a trajectory for the character, but I had no idea the range that we would discover with that character over the five seasons."

This was just the beginning of Joss reaching across series to bring the people he loved working with together again. He had been building his own family of friends for years, and going forward, he would often staff his projects big and small from that ever-expanding community. One recent addition to Joss's on-screen family actually had his first experience with the Whedonverse years earlier, when he guest-starred in the first-season *Angel* episode "Somnambulist." Jeremy Renner was one of over fifty actors who came in to read for the part of Penn, a vampire whom Angel sired in 1786 and must confront when he comes to L.A. on a killing spree. It was extremely unusual for that many actors to read for a guest role, says casting director Amy Britt. "We just couldn't figure it out, as finding a worthy toe-to-toe adversary for Angel is tough. When Jeremy Renner came in we knew we'd finally found the guy. Even though Renner is smaller than Boreanaz physically, he has formidable in spades. About a decade later the rest of the industry figured that out as well."

The notion of chosen family became an important part of the *Angel* story, too, just as it had with *Buffy*. In the season-one finale, "To Shanshu in L.A.," Cordelia is cursed with horrible, incessant visions that drive her so mad that she has to be tethered to a hospital bed. When Angel finds her, he pushes past the doctor asking if he is family with a fierce and insistent "*Yes*."

Later that same episode, another established character makes a shocking return. "I ran into David Boreanaz on the Paramount lot, where I was working at the time. He grabbed me in a big hug and said, 'Benz, we're bringing you back,'" laughs Julie Benz. Her character, Darla, the vampire who sired Angel, had appeared in the very first scene of *Buffy* and was killed off several episodes later. "I got a phone call asking if I could come in and do a couple of flashback episodes." She had been working on *Roswell*, and being on two separate WB shows became an issue for the network. "Both shows catered to the same audience, so they ended up kicking me off of *Roswell* to put me on *Angel*." She had also done a pilot for Tom Fontana (*Homicide: Life on the Street, Oz*) that year, so they didn't know her future availability when they sent her the script for the season finale. "They didn't tell me what was happening, so I was halfway through the script and Darla hadn't shown up yet, and I called my manager: 'I think they sent me the wrong script.' I got to the last page and it was like 'Oh my god.'"

Darla is resurrected, in Wolfram & Hart's latest attempt to get to Angel and take him down. Joss had kept it very hush-hush, as they didn't know if Benz would be available to stay on. "If you're available, we're going to do a great arc with you," Benz remembers being told. "If you're not available, we'll kill you in the first episode [of season two]." She, and Darla, would make it through the next two season premieres.

The first season finale also introduced an important new element in the mythology of a series that was quickly developing its own identity separate from *Buffy*. A new prophecy is revealed that a vampire with a soul will play an important role in the apocalypse and then be rewarded by becoming human once more. That prize for redemption grounded Angel's journey and the series, allowing the writers to push the limits of their storytelling in a way that hadn't worked for them in their first few episodes. "*Angel* got very dark, but when it got dark, it was usually in a horror movie way, or even in an emotionally complicated way," Tim Minear explains. "The first script couldn't do it well, because we couldn't do it realistically."

Angel's Nielsen ratings seemed to confirm that the series was on the right track. Its first season averaged more than 3.2 million viewers per episode—the same numbers that *Buffy* was garnering. There was no question that Joss had again delivered the WB a solid hit. It seemed a safe bet that the network would long be Joss's home.

//////////

Over the first season, the relationship between Minear and Joss had developed from an adversarial one based on mistrust to a surprising kinship of like minds. While Minear had already produced about fifty hours of television when he started on *Angel* (somewhat unusual for someone who had only recently started working in network TV), Joss gave him the gift of a new world of expression. "When he talked about a story that we were breaking and putting up on a board being just a bunch of plot moves, as opposed to being *about* something, getting to the heart of what's the Angel of it, what's the Buffy of it, what's the emotional center of this story, what we're trying to say about this character—that process gave me language to articulate what it was I had already been doing," Minear explains. "Once I knew what to call things, I got better at it. That's one thing he gave me."

Joss also bestowed on Minear his favorite title: the first person at Mutant Enemy to break stories without him. Minear found a way to synthesize what he thought Joss wanted and would corner him with his pitch. He knew that he'd have as much time as it took to pass Joss in the hallway to bounce an idea off him, and he would get him to either say "yea" or "nay" to it. If he got a "yea," Minear would then go into the writers' room and break the story, put it on the board, bring Joss in, and walk him through it as Joss made one or two adjustments.

"We ended up getting this rhythm together where we could go out to dinner or we could just be in the room and just start riffing," Minear says. "We went to dinner once and broke like two or three episodes in the course of one dinner. That was pretty great."

(Shawn Ryan, who worked on *Angel* the following season, recalls that sometimes Joss would decide that problem-solving was better done with food. "I had always had the belief that you're in the writers' room and you're a prisoner there until you come up with what works," Ryan explains. "Joss likes to contemplate big story problems at nice restaurants. There were a lot of times that we'd be discussing [a plot turn] and he'd say, 'Well, why don't we go to this restaurant to figure it out?' The next morning, I'd come in and David [Greenwalt] would say, 'Oh yeah, by dessert we kind of figured out what we're gonna do.'")

Minear also reached out to Joss when he needed help, especially when it came to the Buffyverse canon. When writing season one's "Sanctuary," in which Buffy comes to Los Angeles seeking revenge against rogue Slayer Faith, Minear was suddenly blocked when it came to writing the Buffy moments. He asked Joss to write them instead. Joss did so, and when Minear submitted the script, he included the byline "Written by Tim Minear and Joss Whedon." Buffy was not really in that many scenes, so Minear had written at least 70 percent of the script, but he thought Joss's Buffy scenes were important enough that they merited a coauthor credit. When Joss saw the script, he told him that he didn't have to do that. Minear said, "Look, I've been lucky enough up to this point in my career where pretty much everything that's gone on screen with my name on it, I've actually written."

That was something that was not all that common, which Joss knew from his time on *Roseanne*. "I definitely want to get credit for my work," he told Minear, "but I also don't want to get credit for work that's not mine. I am in the unusual position where I can make that stand. You're the first person that's ever insisted that my name go on something."

Minear retorted, "Let's be honest. Mostly I just wanted a 'co-' screen credit with Joss Whedon and I wanted my name to go first." It was a ballsy move that Joss found hilarious.

"At the beginning of season one, I think Joss Whedon is a dick. But at the end of season one, he's my bestest girlfriend," Minear says. "I want to sit around with him and braid his hair and make cheese balls. By the end of season one, I'd completely proven myself to him, and he had likewise proven himself to me. Part of it is that he respects my talent. It goes without saying that I respect his, but not only does he love talent, he loves for you to succeed, because it makes his life easier."

Two years later, Tim Minear would be offered an overall deal at 20th Century Fox, for which he gives Joss a lot of credit. Minear says that the president of the studio called Joss and asked if Minear was the one he really wanted. Joss said, "Absolutely, you should make a deal with him." When it was announced in the press, Joss was quoted in *Variety*: he called Minear a "genius writer" and said that "if there was no Tim Minear, there would be no 'Angel.' . . . He's the unsung and unbelievably necessary hero of the show."

Minear was shocked. "That's the thing. It's not hyperbole—it's effusive. And I realize that here's a guy that has earned his reputation for his talent and his excellence, but also he's a guy who is really quick to give credit to the people that work with him," he says. "There are a lot of guys in Joss's position who are not quick to do that. He's very generous with making sure that people get recognition for the things that they do. So I know now that this is exactly where I want to be."

13

A NEW CHALLENGE: SILENCE

In the fall of 1999, as Angel moved off to Los Angeles and his own show, the remaining members of *Buffy*'s Scooby Gang faced a new challenge of their own: freshman year of college. Their creator, too, found that it was time for something new; Joss decided that he needed to challenge himself more as a director. Gone was the ambitious rule-breaker who wanted to explore a new movie genre every week. Instead, he felt he had started to fall into the typical television patterns of "just get his coverage, just get her coverage," and move on.

Joss resolved to write a *Buffy* episode that would require him to up his directorial game. His script for "Hush" would forgo the snappy and innovative dialogue for which he and the show had always been heralded. Instead, it would convey the story almost solely through visual information, which Joss would then have to bring to the screen as the director. He knew that it was a risk—could a Slayer-slang-free episode hold his viewers' attention?

"Hush" frames the altogether unfamiliar lack of speech within the comforting contours of a *Buffy* monster-of-the-week episode. A group of ghoulish fellows named the Gentlemen come to town and steal everyone's voices, which leaves their victims unable to call for help when the ghouls cut out their hearts. Joss devoted much attention to their presentation. He conceived them as fairy tale monsters, heralded by a sing-song rhyme of warning ("Can't even shout, can't even cry / The Gentlemen are coming by . . ."). Physically, they were modeled after classic pop culture villains with disturbingly sharp edges and pointed features such as Nosferatu and Pinhead from *Hellraiser*. The Gentlemen were dressed in proper Victorian fashions, their metallic teeth set into permanent grins. They were cast with actors who were also professional mimes; their training gave each movement, from floating down the street to wielding a scalpel, a deliberate and almost delicate grace.

Joss wanted the Gentlemen to "remind people of what scared them when they were children." They may have been influenced by a specific childhood memory that frightened him. When asked about the first piece of popular media that had made an impression on him, Joss mentioned *Help, Help, the Globolinks!*, a horror opera by Gian Carlo Menotti that he saw when he was five. The Globolinks are dangerous alien creatures that disable a school bus and attack the riders but are scared off by the sound of the bus horn, and later by music played by the children. "The Globolinks came, and the only thing that would keep them away was music. A young girl had a violin and she would play the violin at them and they would go away," Joss said. "It just terrified me. But, at the same time, I adored it." In "Hush," Buffy plays a role similar to Emily, the lone girl with a violin who drives off the Globolinks. The Slayer is the one girl who has the power to fight the Gentlemen and recover their box of stolen voices, and once her own voice is restored, she uses it to defeat them. Joss and composer Christophe Beck also looked to the past to inspire the episode's score, playing tribute to the live musical accompaniment that old silent films employed to carry the viewers through the story.

Amid the glorious music and "genuinely disturbing imagery," as one critic would term it, Joss used the episode to cast a spotlight on the limitations of speech. Before the Gentlemen cast their spell, the characters' conversations mostly consist of attempts to avoid speaking the truth. Buffy and her new love interest Riley (Marc Blucas) struggle to flirt while keeping their mutual secret identities as demon hunters from each other; Xander's girlfriend Anya is frustrated that he won't express what she means to him; and budding magic-user Willow is fed up with the fact that the college's Wicca group is all talk and no action. But once they lose their voices, the characters find themselves expressing how they feel physically, with a sense of urgency and almost desperation. For Joss, this was one of the scariest things he could write: to strip away a form of communication we often misuse and take for granted and explore how easy it is to slip into isolation without it.

"Hush" was highly praised when it aired on December 14, 1999. Critic David Bianculli described it as "a true tour de force, and another inventive triumph for this vastly underrated series," and Robert Bianco from *USA Today* wrote that "in a medium in which producers tend to grow bored with their own creations, either trashing them or taking them in increasingly bizarre directions, Whedon continues to find new ways to make his fabulously entertaining series richer and more compelling. With or without words, he's a TV treasure." The episode has since often been referred to as one of the best *Buffy* episodes of all time—as well as one of the scariest episodes in TV history. As Jane Espenson put it, "'Hush' . . . redefined what an episode of television could do."

What isn't obvious from the shivery recollection by fans, critics, and colleagues is just how very funny the episode is. Each character has a particularly amusing reaction to the realization that they have lost their voices (Willow, for instance, initially thinks that she's gone deaf), and the scene in which Giles presents his research on the Gentlemen to the gang results in some hilarious misunderstandings (Buffy suggests staking their enemies, miming the action near her lap, which her friends mistake for a masturbatory gesture). Even without Joss's trademark Buffy-speak, his witty voice comes through loudly.

"Hush," with just seventeen minutes of dialogue in the entire forty-four-minute episode, earned *Buffy* its only Emmy Award nomination for Outstanding Writing for a Drama Series. (*Buffy* earned several nominations in the makeup, hairstyling, and musical direction categories, and "Hush" was also nominated for Outstanding Cinematography for a Single Camera Series.) Joss lost to Aaron Sorkin for an episode of his political drama *The West Wing*.

//////////

"Hush" also represented a milestone in the ongoing narrative of *Buffy*, as it depicts the beginning of a relationship between Willow and one of her fellow Wicca group members, Tara (Amber Benson). Until this point, Willow had only been involved in heterosexual pairings, harboring a longtime crush on Xander, and pursuing a relationship with Oz until his struggles with his werewolf nature forced him to leave town. The early intimations of Willow and Tara's same-sex attraction are largely subtextual—in "Hush," they simply join hands to cast a spell, then exchange significant looks. But their relationship status is solidified for both the audience and the characters themselves nine episodes later in "New Moon Rising," when Oz returns and Willow realizes that she has moved on with her life and given Tara her heart.

Between the airings of "Hush" and "New Moon Rising," the Bronze had seen sporadic surges of angry posts in opposition to the Willow/Tara relationship. Most were from outsiders; since the Bronze was an official fan board frequented by the show's own staff, conservative church groups told members to go there to register their disapproval. But even within the fan community, some parents announced that they would no longer let their kids watch *Buffy* if Willow "turned gay." The uproar reached a crescendo when "New Moon Rising" aired on May 2, 2000, and sympathetic members of the community decided they needed to counter the protests by sending the *Buffy* crew a tangible sign of their support.

Bronze poster "Kristen" suggested that they should send Joss Whedon, Alyson Hannigan, and Amber Benson a toaster—a reference to the famous "coming out" episode of the sitcom *Ellen*. Many other fans loved the idea. They raised enough to purchase a big, expensive toaster from Williams-Sonoma, which Kristen had engraved with an exchange between Willow and Tara that closed out "New Moon Rising": "You have to be with the one you l-love." "I am," May 02, 2000, When Subtext Became Text. It was hand-delivered to Mutant Enemy, and later the fans "heard from other people [that] from then on the toaster was kept behind his [Joss's] desk, right where everyone could see it," said Bronzer Paula Carlson.

The next day, Joss posted an original song about his esteemed award to the Bronze:

LESBIAN TOASTER
LOVE YOU THE MOST
ALTERNATIVE LIFEstyle CHOICE TOASTER
HOT GIRL-ON-GIRL TOAST
(DRUM SOLO)
LESBIAN TOASTER AH-WHOOOOO!
(TRIANGLE SOLO)
TOAST FOR YOU AND FOR ME. . . .

Got an Emmy nom, all very well but my beautiful engraved (ENGRAVED, for the love of God) toaster is far far cooler. . . . So thanks, and thanks, and thanks. Bread shall be warm. . . .

Kristen—"like" is not the word. ("pudendous" is not the word either, but it's a damn fun one.) NO ONE i know has an engraved toaster. Plus, coolness aside, the fact that you cared that much about what we've been doing with Willow and Tara . . . sniff sniff, something in my eye . . . Can't wait also to show JANE, who wrote for Ellen back when. Thank you.

//////////

In *Buffy*'s past few seasons, as its ratings grew and home Internet access exploded, more and more people had started posting on the Bronze. Word spread about the board's big annual get-together, attended by the cast and crew, so the Posting Board Party grew in attendees each year. It quickly lost the intimate feel of the first party. "Somewhere along the line," says "Missi," a Bronzer, "the PBP stopped being about the people and started being about the cast and who was going to be there and what was going to go on. People got really angry about that."

By 2000, the PBP had become a charity event with corporate sponsorship. The event raised money for Make-a-Wish, a noble venture, but it meant that tickets were far more expensive, out of the price range of many Bronzers. And as the organizers established partnerships with Fox, the WB, and other official corporate entities, the party moved away from its initial identity as a gathering by and for the fans themselves.

Theoretically, the event was still supposed to offer Bronzers unfettered access to any *Buffy* insiders who chose to attend. The PBP was supposed to be a safe space where all attendees—Bronzers and show VIPs alike—were shown the same respect. But the venue now set aside a separate area for the VIPs to escape the crowds. And crowds there were, especially around the actors. At the 2000 PBP, new cast member Marc Blucas was surrounded in a huge semicircle about fifteen people deep throughout most of the night, making maneuvering through the venue impossible at times. People were knocked over by the swarming fans, and many attendees were embarrassed by the way Blucas was groped.

Disillusionment with the event grew. Bronzers complained that it had become a celebrity circus where "you could see the stars of the show, usually from a distance . . . hiding in the VIP lounge drinking free alcohol," said poster "Leather Jacket." It was starting to take on the overwhelming, impersonal feel of a current-day San Diego Comic-Con.

//////////

The message board itself retained its free-flowing character, the sense that it was a space where people could talk about personal matters as easily as they did the series. But that quality was tested when a member of Joss's crew took to the Bronze to discuss his series' behind-the-scenes tensions and politics.

Right before the season-four finale aired, stunt coordinator and second unit director Jeff Pruitt was fired. It came as a great surprise to the fans, as his work had been highly respected in the industry, and he had greatly elevated *Buffy*'s fight choreography upon joining the series in season two. He and his wife, Sarah Michelle Gellar's stunt double Sophia Crawford, had established themselves as an incredibly integral part of the show.

On May 17, 2000, Pruitt decided to air his issues with his dismissal, the show, and Joss on the Bronze. That night, the board was heavily trafficked by VIPs, with posts from Joss, Amber Benson, and writer David Fury. Pruitt answered a few questions from the fans, and in response to being asked if he'd return for the fifth season, he posted a link to a story he wrote called "The Parable of the Knight." It was a thinly veiled allegory of his experiences on the show—so thinly veiled that it was more like a windowpane. Pruitt alleged that he'd been pushed out due to infighting among the cast and crew, likening himself to a long-suffering Knight who, along with his Handmaiden wife, served a young King (Joss), who turned on them once the Princess (Gellar) and her evil cohorts (the show's crew) began to conspire against him.

As a long-standing member of the Bronze community, Pruitt found that many posters were sympathetic about his firing—until they started reading his tale. The board had often been a place to connect with the show's creators in a truly unique way, but this mudslinging among the staff had never happened before. The situation only got worse when Joss and David Fury both returned to the board to refute Pruitt's accusations—and get in some jabs themselves:

Joss says:

. . . I read the Parable of the Knight. Felt I ought to comment on the situation. Yes, Jeff is leaving. It's sad. Jeff was a huge asset to Buffy—he took it to a new level of action and grace with Sophia, and his style will always be a part of the show. But this isn't a fairy tale. Or a thinly veiled "parable." It's a hard, gruelingly hard job, ten

months a year, thirteen hours a day, with fifty or more people strain-
ing, working, getting in each other's face, stepping on each other's
toes, driving each other crazy. It happens. And the only thing that
keeps it together is the effort people make to work together. Doesn't
always happen. There are conflicts, raging egos—and even occasional backstabbing, I'm sorry to say. There are very few "plots," and
as far as I can tell, no jousting of any kind. People just wear on each
other and eventually sometimes you have to make a change. No
one's to blame—or everyone is. But either people get into a groove
of working as part of the whole or they don't. And seeing yourself as
a noble knight being plotted against by evil courtiers really doesn't
help. Remember that.

Fury says:
Hey, Joss—Does this mean I should call off my legions who at this
moment are preparing to storm your castle and overthrow your
kingdom? Damn. There goes my weekend.

Joss says:
Fury, do not storm my castle, for I have read that I am a weak King,
and I would probably get a nervous tummy.

The Bronze was not immune to squabbles. But now the posters were
being dragged into a fight they wanted no part of. Pruitt felt betrayed and
chose to take his feelings to the fans, but instead of garnering support, he
alienated Bronzers, who felt like they now had to watch their divorcing
parents have a nasty fight in their bedroom.

Kathy Hein, a Bronzer, remembered, "Joss came on and he and Jeff
were arguing with each other on the Bronze, and we had the creator of
the show and the second unit director arguing with each other like *children* on a *public Internet forum* in front of fans." As the Bronzers would
police bickering among themselves, they eventually insisted that Joss,
Fury, and Pruitt take their arguments elsewhere.

///////////

Over the next few months, Pruitt gave more candid interviews, and most
of his ire was aimed at Gellar for her actions on set, her attitude toward
fans, and, in particular, her insistence in interviews that she did her own

stunts. Joss told her about Pruitt's parable, but she refused to read it, already feeling weary from all the online criticism she saw daily. "There's no other word except *crushing*," Gellar said of her reaction. "It's one thing to hear people you don't know saying lies about you on the Internet, but when it comes from a disgruntled former employee. . . . It really, really, really hurt."

Unsurprisingly, Pruitt's actions destroyed the relationship he had with Joss. He found out that over the previous year, venting e-mails he had written to friends had been shared with Joss. "He was very upset at my revealing personal things about him in them," Pruitt said. "I thought I was talking 'privately' just as he did when he'd vent to his friends about our private world."

Pruitt's choices hadn't endeared him to the fans, but no one came out of the situation cleanly. There was residual anger at both Pruitt and Joss for staging their battle in what was supposed to be a welcoming community for fans. The incident knocked Joss off his pedestal just a little—but in some small way it also made him a true Bronzer: someone who was smart and witty but could be petulant and pissy at times. Kai said that Joss had looked to the Bronze for a sense of comfort and community himself, and perhaps he found that he could let his guard down and say what he was thinking—for better or worse.

14

SHAKESPEARE FANBOY

As *Buffy*'s fifth and *Angel*'s second season went into production, the writers and cast found new ways to stretch their wings. The previous year, Tim Minear had asked Joss if he could direct an episode—something only two other Mutant Enemy writers, David Greenwalt and Joss himself, had done up to that point. Joss had created the *Buffy* series in part so he could gain experience as a director when no one else would give him the chance, and now he was in a position to offer that same opportunity to his staff. He knew that the best way to learn how to direct is just to do it, and that with learning comes a lot of moments of getting it wrong. Joss told Minear that he would let him direct an episode of *Angel* under one condition: if he failed, and he might, Minear couldn't quit the show. "You can't get upset and you can't quit, because I need you as a writer and producer on this show," he said.

Minear's first directorial effort would be the seventh episode of season two, which he also wrote. "Darla" would explore the history of Angel's vampiric creator, from her own siring by the Master in 1600s Virginia through China's Boxer Rebellion at the turn of the twentieth century. Until her resurrection in *Angel*'s season-one finale, Darla was primarily known as Angel's lover and guide through his years as a murderous demon, but earlier episodes of season two would reveal that she was brought back to life as a human. In his episode, Minear wanted to explore who Darla was before she was vamped and how that was reflected in the vampire she became, and compare how she deals with her restored humanity to Angel's actions after his own human soul was returned.

Minear pitched his idea for the episode without knowing that over on *Buffy*, the writers had already broken the story that would air the same night—about another vampire, James Marsters's Spike. The character had lost the ability to feed on humans the previous season thanks to government experiments, and season five would find him struggling with unwanted romantic feelings for his enemy Buffy. Like "Darla," *Buffy*'s "Fool for Love" would compare Spike's current situation to his century-long history of vampiric mayhem. Joss liked Minear's idea, too, but was hesitant to do both stories, since they covered similar ground. Minear insisted that they not shy away from the similarities; they should develop both episodes in parallel, not as a single crossover tale but rather as companion pieces that tell the story from two points of view.

"What we decided to do was completely separate stories, although there would be natural instances in which [the vampires] would cross paths," Minear said. "There are a few scenes in both that are not in each episode, and there is actually one point in history where they all came together. In the Spike episode, it has a particular meaning for Spike, but in the *Angel* episode we discover that there were pieces in *Buffy* that make it mean something else." Minear's ambitious ideas led to two of the most highly regarded episodes of their respective seasons, and the success of his directorial debut opened the door for other writer/producers, including Marti Noxon and David Fury, to direct future episodes.

//////////

To portray Spike's complicated history in "Fool for Love," James Marsters needed to take the character to a lot of different places in a short time frame; he went from a punk on the subway one day to a poetry-writing dandy the next. While shooting, Marsters mentioned that it was like being back in repertory theater. This comment excited Joss, who hadn't acted much since his days on the Winchester stage. He said, "You know what we should do? Let's have Shakespeare readings!"

Joss, of course, had studied the Bard in depth while at Winchester, and he had fond memories of his mother's Shakespeare readings. When the BBC produced Shakespeare's entire canon of plays in the late 1970s and early 1980s, it had also made a lasting impression on him. "It's hilarious, how little money they had," Joss said. "But at the same time I still think some really good stuff went on there." To Joss, successful productions didn't necessarily require a lot of bells and whistles. "I think Shakespeare works when it's emotionally true," he said. "It can be done on a bare stage . . . [or] it can work completely gussied up, as long as everything is working towards emotional truth."

What's more, circumstances had left him with time on his hands and nothing to do: Kai, a master's student at the Southern California Institute of Architecture, was studying in Japan, so Joss was lonely on Sundays. Thus, in the fall of 2000, Joss invited many of the cast and writers of his shows to join him at his home for a reading. There was a great buzz right off the bat, particularly after Joss assuaged some initial nervousness. If people balked because they felt that they couldn't read Shakespeare, Joss told them, "No one cares. Just come and have fun. We'll have a few drinks and get some food in."

Those drinks were quite indispensable at first, as everyone was rather nervous, particularly those who were not actors. Once alcohol was introduced, things seemed to loosen up. Everyone eventually got pretty drunk, and that emboldened Joss to sit down at the piano. He told Tony Head that he could play some chords if Head would sing along. Head's vocal skills were not a surprise, as he had a background in musical theater (at one time playing Dr. Frank-N-Furter in a stage production of *The Rocky Horror Show*) and had sung in several Buffy episodes during season four. James Marsters, who had been in several bands and performed his own original music, and Amber Benson joined in first—leading to Joss's realization that much of his cast could sing. It was a discovery that would jump-start Joss's long-simmering plans for a very special episode of *Buffy*.

In the meantime, the readings at Joss's home continued. About two or three plays in, Joss, Head, and Marsters were discussing Shakespeare in depth and made a pact to read their respective favorites. "James had always had a real thing about playing Macbeth, and I had recently done a couple of scenes from *Richard III* in acting class," Head says. "I had been given the brief of 'make him sexy,' and I loved it—it was a really interesting way of looking at him." As for Joss, he had always wanted to perform the lead in *Hamlet*, the play he had worked hardest on and studied most deeply at Winchester.

"I waited, waited" to play the role, Joss confesses. And then their readings finally gave him the chance. "That was my dream and that was *doooope,*" he says. "I learned so much about it just from that experience." How was his performance? Head said that Joss's Hamlet was one of the best he's ever heard. "He found nuances in it that I've never heard before. I mean, he's too old for it, but he had a hang of the lines that just made it really personal and really, really powerful," he explains. "It's not an easy part; it's one of those parts that even when it's somebody who's really good, it just misses either at the beginning or at the end." But Joss's take "was uniformly brilliant."

When Kai returned home from Japan, Joss told her what he'd been up to while she was gone. He was very defensive about it, perhaps worried that she would make fun of him, and he told her that he wasn't going to stop. She wouldn't have made him stop, but she was surprised; she knew it was not something she and Joss would have decided to do jointly, since she was very shy. "When you're in a couple, you adjust yourself a bit for what is comfortable for the other person," she explains. "You don't go out [together] and do something that the other person really isn't going to like. [Sometimes] it does take being separated in order to try something that you've always kind of wanted to do and you didn't even know it."

Kai wanted to support Joss in his new endeavor, but she did not want to read herself. A rule of the Shakespeare readings was that everyone in attendance had to perform, whether by reading or holding a spear. Kai was one of the few who were allowed to attend without performing. She would, however, agree to take part in one reading in which she got to pick the play: she suggested that they do "a happy one," *The Merry Wives of Windsor*. She read alongside Alyson Hannigan, who was also not comfortable performing Shakespeare, and Nicholas Brendon's then-wife, actress Tressa DiFiglia.

///////////

Joss's readings were designed to be fun get-togethers, but Joss was very particular about how he cast each one. He had his standard players, such as *Angel*'s Alexis Denisof ("He knows I love it, so I'll always say yes"), but it wouldn't be the same group every time. According to Denisof, Joss would cast his next play by considering who was available and deciding who might be especially suited to a particular role—or especially amusing in it. "It's not always the part that you would be good at that you get given, which is part of the fun of it," Denisof says. "There's no holds barred; nobody's there to give a Royal Shakespeare Company performance."

When Joss reached out to Julie Benz, she was initially concerned about her role on *Angel*. "He called me at home and I thought I was in trouble—anytime a producer calls me at home, I'm in trouble. He said,

'I'm having people over on Sunday and we're reading Shakespeare,'" she recalls. He explained the idea of the readings, and she was immediately on board. "He had me read Lady Macbeth, which I thought was fitting, playing Darla. I was a New York theater-trained actress, so I've been exposed to it, but a lot of the other actors there hadn't been, and he included the writing staff too, and this was just how he socialized with everybody. It just revealed so much about who he is."

"If you're working with him and you express any interest or he knows that you've done Shakespeare or have a desire to, then he would [invite you]," says Amy Acker, who joined the *Angel* cast as Fred in the second season. "The first time, I didn't realize there was as much drinking involved. My wine glass kept getting filled up, and by the end of it, I'm not sure I was reading [too clearly]."

"We had amazing, amazing readings," Joss says. "I learned as much [from them] about acting and theater and Shakespeare as I had studied in school." Head agrees: "Suddenly you saw a whole different side of people." In fact, Kai was disturbed by the side of Joss she saw in his turn as the *Othello* villain Iago. She found herself creeped out a bit and couldn't even look at him for a little while after. "I told him 'I can't talk to you right now,'" she recalls. "I needed a little time off, because he just so became that person."

Denisof had a distinctly different turn in *The Merchant of Venice*. "I was 'nonspecific duke with a long speech,' and that was kind of it for the whole play," he says. "A very high-pitched, strong lisp seemed to be the order of the day for that, which was probably shocking for any Shakespeare academics. But it got some laughs, which is what the readings are really about."

"It's just the fun of hearing these amazing stories," Denisof says, "and having some surprises of some people playing certain parts and an over-riding enjoyment of how amazing Shakespeare is. If you're a Shakespeare geek like I am, then it's always pleasurable to hear Shakespeare read aloud. It's what it's designed for."

//////////

Even as years passed and Joss moved on to new projects or saw old ones end, the readings continued, becoming a well-known and much-loved tradition. When Joss was working on something new, he would get a feel for which members of his cast and crew were into Shakespeare, so he'd have new people to add to his unofficial repertory, alongside those he knew had enjoyed his readings in the past.

Many repertory members have shared the story of a particular performance of *Much Ado About Nothing*, which also happens to be Joss's favorite. Shakespeare's popular comedy is about two couples on very different journeys to a romantic happy ending. The first pair fall in love quickly and then are torn apart by nasty rumors, and the second bicker constantly and swear never to fall in love. In this performance, Amy Acker and Alexis Denisof played the latter couple, Beatrice and Benedick. Kai recalled that the settings included a tea party on the back lawn with quilts and finger sandwiches.

Singer and Whedon friend Angie Hart played the role of the musician Balthasar. When another character called out to Balthasar to sing them a song, Hart's then-husband, Jesse Tobias, pulled out his guitar, Joss took up a lute, and Joss's brother Sam pulled out a mandolin, and they began to sing "Hey Nonny Nonny." Aside from the four of them, no one else knew what was coming—Joss had written music to the songs in the play. He had taught it to his small band about a half hour earlier. Neil Patrick Harris, who was brought along by his *How I Met Your Mother* costar Alyson Hannigan, was taken by the entire experience. "It made me want to eat a giant turkey leg until I'm sick and watch people joust," he says. "It was an amazing Santa Monica bohemian afternoon"—which he admits makes them all sound "like we were much more hippies than we all were."

Harris would do four plays at the Whedon home, and each time he'd do his best to come prepared. "I didn't study Shakespeare, and so I just didn't want to look like an asshole who didn't know what I was talking about," he explains. "So for whatever part he would give me, I'd go out and read it Cliff Notes style as quickly as I could and sort of get the gist of it, and then show up and do it."

Jane Espenson was particularly excited to act with Harris. "It's crazy! I loved it but it was also terrifying. I'm not very good, but I jump in with enthusiasm and I'm very useful, because I used to have a set of clamp-on Eeyore ears from Disneyland that were very necessary for any production of *A Midsummer Night's Dream*," she says. "I've been to three different readings of that play at Joss's house—I read big long scenes opposite Tony

Head once! I am no actress and this is well beyond my comfort zone. But it was also one of my most cherished accomplishments."

The readings were always a lot of fun, and as they went on, ideas were bounced around about capturing them somehow. Joss started using a still camera to take shots of the performers, as a record if nothing else. "It was that that got him thinking maybe there's a way to capture the fun and feel of one of these readings in some kind of medium that other people could enjoy," Denisof says.

////////////

The Shakespeare readings had become such a part of their lives that when Kai, having earned her master's in architecture, was rebuilding the new home they bought in 2004, she thought about the spaces and how they could be used for different readings. They could read in the courtyard and then go up on the balcony. There was also a space in the backyard with a big drop of a slope that went down into the hills of a golf course and protected parkland. (Joss describes it as Vietnam in the morning and Tuscany at night.) She decided to surprise Joss with a little stone amphitheater.

"I just pictured it in my head that Joss could have that and how much he would love it," she says. "I was the happiest person in the world when he had a Shakespeare reading out there. I was taking pictures. I was serving people. I was too distracted, loving watching them all read Shakespeare down here."

Choosing one's family—going beyond blood, beyond marriage to create a support system—is not only a strong theme in Joss's writing and his professional life, it is a centerpiece of his personal life as well. He has fun bringing all different kinds of people together to create something. "He loves it so much," Kai says. "Probably the happiest I've ever seen him is during a Shakespeare reading."

15

BUFFY GOES BACK TO HIGH SCHOOL

When the fifth season of *Buffy* premiered on September 26, 2000, it marked a huge shift in focus for the series. At the end of the first episode, viewers are introduced to Dawn, Buffy's previously unmentioned little sister. Much of the season to come will focus on the Slayer's relationship with her younger sibling; though easily irritated by her immaturity, Buffy will put protecting Dawn above everything and everyone else in her life.

Joss created Dawn as a way to "have a really important, intense emotional relationship for Buffy that is not a boyfriend." He also modeled Buffy and Dawn's interactions on Kai's early relationship with her own younger sister, Dawnmarie. Kai's mother and stepfather brought the baby home on Kai's birthday, an event that everyone had forgotten about. "She was all cranky about it," Joss said. Then "they put Dawn in her arms. . . . She said she just felt like, 'I have to take care of this.' " Initially, Buffy's Dawn was written to be much younger than her sister, but she was aged up once fourteen-year-old Michelle Trachtenberg was cast.

Joss did establish an in-story reason why Buffy suddenly had a teenage sister. Subsequent episodes reveal that Dawn is actually a mystical object called "the Key," which its guardians placed in human form and sent to Buffy to protect. Buffy learns that these guardians also altered her memories and those of her friends and family, causing all of them to believe that Dawn had been there all along. It was a development Joss had been planning for a while, dropping the occasional cryptic hint as far back as the season three finale.

But many viewers were still resistant to the sudden appearance of a whiny interloper. To them, Dawn was an example of "Cousin Oliver

Syndrome." Named for the annoying eight-year-old added to the cast of *The Brady Bunch* in its final season, a "Cousin Oliver" is a young character shoehorned into a series to add a youthful energy the existing cast members are growing too old to provide. Even though Dawn had a more meaningful purpose within the *Buffy* narrative, the sudden focus on her teenage angst was grating to fans used to a more nuanced portrayal of adolescent life. Whether Joss's idea was a miscalculation or the writers simply didn't know quite how to write for the new character, Dawn ended up on a number of "hated characters" lists, including *Entertainment Weekly*'s "Most Annoying TV Characters Ever" and *TV Guide*'s "Most Loathed TV Characters."

Another member of Buffy's family evoked an intense reaction of a different sort. It was in the sixteenth episode of the fifth season that Joss killed off Buffy's mother, Joyce, mirroring the death of his own mother nearly a decade earlier. To Sarah Michelle Gellar, herself the daughter of a single mother, portraying Buffy's grief "was probably the most awful experience of my life—and I mean that in the best way. . . . It was gut-wrenching for me, and though it cut to the heart of the character and the show, I never want to do it again." Millions on the other side of the screen were also devastated—though the fact that many viewers also drew comfort from "The Body" was one of the many gifts the series has given its fans that Joss could not have predicted.

After his first Emmy nomination for writing "Hush" the season before, Joss hoped that "The Body" might again be honored by the Television Academy. He had two chances, having both written and directed the episode, but this time he was snubbed altogether, as *The West Wing*, *The Sopranos*, and *ER* swept the nominations in both categories. "It's my own fault for getting my hopes up," said Joss. "Every now and then, I'll go, 'Damn.' But if I wanted Emmy nominations, all my characters would be doctors."

//////////

Dawn was not Joss's only attempt to return *Buffy* to its teen-centric roots. While the Scooby Gang had moved on to college and other postadolescent pursuits, Joss had formulated a plan to take them back to high school and, this time, make their adventures a bit more colorful and a lot more animated. With two series on the air already, Joss sought out talent beyond the Mutant Enemy family to make *Buffy: The Animated Series* a reality.

Buffy was well into its fifth season when writer Jeph Loeb got a call out of the blue to have a meeting with Joss. Loeb had spent many years working on different Marvel comic book series: *Avengers*, *X-Force*, *Captain America*, and *Iron Man*. He didn't know what Joss could want to meet with him about, but he was excited by the request, as he was already a fan of *Buffy* and of Joss, who he felt was doing astonishing work in the challenging field of genre television. "*Buffy* had cut a swath into this world with humor, pathos, and a voice that was singular," Loeb says. "Which are critical elements in being successful in network television."

Loeb showed up for the meeting, and while waiting for Joss to show up, he noted all the comic books in Joss's office—a lot of comic books. He figured that was why Joss wanted to see him—that this was a guy who liked comic books and wanted to talk to someone who wrote them. When Joss arrived, instead of explaining why Loeb was there, he sat down and began to strum his guitar. They talked about comics for a bit, until finally Joss got to the point: he was thinking about doing an animated *Buffy* series and was curious what Loeb thought about it.

"I'm not sure if he's asking because he wants me to do something on it or he just wants my opinion," Loeb says. "But immediately I can see the exciting opportunity of what this could be. And then he asks what I think is a trick question: 'What would the series be about?'"

Loeb hedged until he finally said, "Buffy the Vampire Slayer?" There was a visible look of relief on Joss's face. Encouraged, Loeb pitched that the series could take place during Buffy's first year at Sunnydale High. That would allow Joss to return to the series' early metaphors about the demons of growing up that the live-action show had outgrown. "I guess those were the right answers," Loeb says. "Joss lit up and started talking about the show as if it had already aired. He had ideas for stories and explained them like he had watched them. It was . . . enchanting."

What Loeb didn't know at the time was that other people had already come in to pitch for the series, and their answers to Joss's questions had been less encouraging. "One wanted to star Giles as the headmaster of a wizard's school in England with a boy with glasses who wanted to fulfill his destiny as a warlock. For a show called *Buffy: The Animated Series*"? Loeb was dumbfounded. "*Potter* much?"

Before Loeb left that first meeting, Joss had offered him a job. Development on *Buffy: The Animated Series* began soon after, with Joss and Loeb as executive producers. Most of the cast signed on to voice their characters, with the notable exception of Sarah Michelle Gellar, who opted out and was replaced by voice-over actress Giselle Loren. Several of the show's writers took on script duties: Joss and Loeb wrote the pilot, while Jane Espenson and Doug Petrie also wrote episodes. A new writer, Steve DeKnight, was hired for the animated series on the strength of a *Buffy* spec script that he had written in which Xander gets Slayer powers, and in doing so demonstrates why men can't handle such strength. Joss felt it was the best spec script he'd ever read. It was "funny, clever, had twists and that's all well and good and very important," he said, but "the most important thing is that he found the underlying emotion. To me, there's no other reason to be writing. He found what it felt like for Buffy [to be the Slayer], what it felt like for Xander—he found extraordinary character insights."

Buffy: The Animated Series was written with the same basic tone—the same humor, action, and excitement—as the live-action series, but with the drama and sexual content toned way down to appeal to kids. It returned to the familiar relationships of *Buffy* season one: Willow pining after best friend Xander, who pines after Buffy, who pines after the mysterious Angel. "Unlike the series, it's not about change," Joss said. "It's a chance to tell all of the high-school stories that we couldn't tell because they were only in high school for two and a half years."

While the content would be familiar, Joss wanted to break new ground with the show's visual style. The challenge was to give the series a look that hadn't been done before in an animated action-adventure show, while still capturing that Whedonesque humor and mood. "That's a tall order for a Saturday-morning cartoon, but that was Joss," Loeb says. "If he was going to get into this business, it was going to be something that changed the game the way *Buffy* had changed network TV and *Batman Beyond* had changed animated shows."

Batman Beyond was a series that aired from 1999 to 2001 on the WB. The acclaimed cartoon was conceived as a kid-friendly, futuristic version of Batman, but it was considerably darker than most other children's programs at the time: in 2039, Bruce Wayne is an elderly and bitter recluse who reluctantly agrees to allow a newly orphaned teenager to take over the Batman persona under his tutelage. To Joss and Loeb, the series was less of an inspiration for *Buffy: The Animated Series* than a bar for them to reach for and surpass. They brought in Eric Radomski, who had been very responsible for the look and feel of *Batman Beyond*'s moody, noirish predecessor *Batman: The Animated Series*, to run production. Radomski, an Emmy Award–winning producer, was working at Film Roman, an American animation studio that produced content for such shows as *The Simpsons* and MTV's *Beavis and Butt-Head*. He, in turn, enlisted Eric Wight, who had worked on *Batman Beyond*, to join the *Buffy* animation team.

Tonally, Eric Wight explains, his new series and his previous one "were very similar. We had to strike a very difficult balance of being a little bit dark but not too edgy. On *Batman Beyond*, we were taking an established mythology and evolving it into a completely unique direction. With *Buffy*, we were trying to honor the original series as closely as possible."

With scripts in hand, the team set about creating character sketches and storyboarding. "One of my favorite stories Jeph told me was how they had the art hanging up at the offices and on one occasion he looked over and saw Michelle Trachtenberg staring at her character design, unknowingly standing in the exact pose I had drawn her in," Wight says. "He knew I had a strong attention to detail, but that blew him away." Wight hoped to bring aboard many friends from his *Batman Beyond* days. He also had preliminary conversations with Mike Mignola, the creator of *Hellboy*, about creating some monster designs. "Both Joss and I are tremendous fans of his work, and he was a huge influence on the style," Wight says.

Joss and the writers were also excited about the stories they could tell without the limitations of live-action budgets; in animation, a dragon crashing into a library costs the same as people sitting in a room talking. One episode involved Buffy having to deal with a demonic driver's ed instructor; another was about Buffy getting shrunk down to a super-tiny size. "It's a very silly show," Joss said. "We refer to it as *Simpsons Beyond*."

But to Jeph Loeb, "the scripts were like fine pastries in a sea of cafeterias. It was the Murderers' Row of writers—the *Buffy* and *Angel* staff writers at the height of their game writing for Saturday-morning cartoons. They all wanted to work on this!"

//////////

For all the enthusiasm, the development of *Buffy: The Animated Series* did not proceed smoothly. The plan was for 20th Century Fox to produce the series, to air in its Fox Kids block on affiliates across the country. But in July 2001, Fox Family Worldwide, which oversaw Fox Kids, was sold to Disney. Joss and Mutant Enemy didn't feel that anything would change—at first. But then they finally got a call: Disney wasn't interesting in proceeding with the series.

"We were met with a lot of—I don't want to say resistance, because it was just more of no response," explains Chris Buchanan, whom Joss hired to run the business end of his production company in early 2002. "[Disney] just didn't really respond to us." The irony, of course, is that years later Disney would very much be in the Joss Whedon business, when they bought Marvel Comics and produced *The Avengers*.

It was an enormous blow to the team. They'd worked hard and were ready to ship the first episodes overseas. The animation test had come back promising. "It was like getting ready for a birthday party and then the cake never arrived," Jeph Loeb says. "Only worse."

They hoped they could find another home for the series. But "because of the sale, there were larger issues between Disney and Fox," Buchanan says, which made it difficult to obtain permission to shop the show around. "We finally got over the hump on it and made a little presentation, which is different from a pilot because it's just much shorter. It was really cool—and it was a great style of animation that Joss was really into, and it started that round of conversations with different distribution partners like Cartoon Network. We talked to pretty much everybody."

The challenge was that in the time between when work on the show began and when the team sorted out the issues with the Fox Family changeover to Disney, the animation market had changed dramatically. Joss had modeled *Buffy: The Animated Series* after shows such as *Batman Beyond*, which featured high-quality animation and demanded a fairly pricey per-episode cost. By the time *Buffy* was back in negotiations, most animated fare on TV was much less ambitious, demanding perhaps only half the budget of something like *Batman Beyond*.

"Essentially what that means is instead of having fifteen days of production in Asia and Korea on your show, you were down to ten days," Buchanan says. "It was just not the same creative model, and the offers that we had coming in didn't really make sense. It just ultimately kind of died the death where we didn't have enough demand on the distribution side to get enough money to execute it the way that Joss and Jeph wanted to creatively. It was just really unfortunate, because the scripts were great, and I thought it was a fantastic way to kind of bring a new generation of *Buffy* fans into the fold."

In addition, the networks they approached in 2002 had trouble imagining how they would schedule such a series; *Buffy: The Animated Series* was deemed "too adult" to be placed in a more traditional children's animated block of television, yet it didn't have broad enough appeal to be worthy of a prime-time airing. Today the media landscape has shifted further, and there are far more adult animated series airing in prime time. It raises the question: could an animated *Buffy* series be a viable property once again?

"I've always said—sometimes to Joss's teasing dismay—that the best Buffy stories had to do with resurrection," Jeph Loeb laughs. "So why not bring this back again? Joss has never been more popular and Buffy is firmly implanted as a TV icon. Who knows, we might even get Sarah [Michelle Gellar] now."

///////////

As the saga of *Buffy: The Animated Series* was making its way toward its premature conclusion, back in the live-action world, its parent series was headed toward an unexpected end point of its own. In 2001, the show found itself caught in a battle between two things far more fierce than anything to come out of a Hellmouth: a television network and a production studio.

Buffy was nearing the end of its contracted run at the WB. If the network wanted to continue running the series past season five, it would have to agree on new terms with 20th Century Fox. It wouldn't be easy; during their earlier negotiations, the studio had already offered up veiled threats to take the show elsewhere if the WB didn't agree to its demands for higher licensing fees. When asked if he would consider moving *Buffy* to the studio's own network, Fox's Sandy Grushow had hedged his comments—"The first time we move a show like that is the day our business is in serious jeopardy"—but added that if the WB's Jamie Kellner "attempts to lowball and refuses to step up to fair market value," such a scenario would certainly be possible. "Fair market value is fair market value."

These comments had not engendered goodwill between the two men. Kellner had long been concerned about the WB's financial stability and was frustrated that Grushow was muddying the waters of public opinion at a time when *Buffy* still had two seasons left on its contract. He felt that Fox had a potential franchise on its hands and could capitalize on syndication deals, spin-offs, and merchandising instead of pushing for more money from his network. In fact, the WB had already bought the spin-off *Angel* and solidified a two-hour block of Joss-produced television each Tuesday night. In Kellner's opinion, the studio should have been grateful for all of the attention and promotion lavished on *Buffy*, instead of expecting more money.

Through *Buffy*'s third and fourth seasons, the financial disagreements had quieted, but in spring 2001, with the network's contract nearing its end, the parties readied themselves for battle once again. And this time, Joss himself would be drawn into the fray.

16

ONCE MORE, WITH FEELING

The first shot in the battle over Joss's flagship series came from the WB's Jamie Kellner at the Television Critics Association press junket in January 2001. He told reporters that if his network went along with 20th Century Fox's plans to raise *Buffy*'s licensing fee from roughly $1 million to $2 million per episode, it would actually lose money by airing the show. Kellner suggested that the WB's final response would be to say, "We will take all the revenue we can generate with 'Buffy' and we'll give it to you in a giant wheelbarrow. . . . And if that's not enough, then take it to somebody else, and you've demonstrated that you're not the kind of partner we should be doing business with."

Sandy Grushow, now the Fox Television Entertainment Group chairman, snapped back in his own executive Q&A session at the TCAs, "They don't have wheelbarrows at the WB, they have Mercedes."

While the two men aired their grievances in the press, Joss tried to stay out of it as much as he could. He liked being on the WB, the small network that had taken a chance on him and his stories. His girl hero was not too keen to make a move, either, and she chose to go public with her feelings. "The WB has been so supportive, such a great network over the past four years," Sarah Michelle Gellar told E! Online. "It feels like home. I don't want the show to move, because I feel that we belong on the WB. It's where our fans are." She added, "I will stay on *Buffy* if, and only if, *Buffy* stays on the WB. And you know what? Print that. My bosses are going to kill me, but print that. I want them to know. . . . If *Buffy* leaves the WB, I'm out."

The renewal drama was spreading, but with no clear sense of when a decision had to be made, Joss focused on the more urgent task of guiding two series with complex narrative arcs toward satisfying season finales.

By March, however, Joss could no longer leave the fight to other people. On March 23, 2001, Kellner landed a devastating blow in an interview with *Entertainment Weekly*. "Nobody wanted the show," he argued. "It didn't perform [at first] but we stuck with it. . . . It's not our No. 1 show. . . . It's not a show like *ER* that stands above the pack." He also claimed that *Buffy*'s audiences were getting too old to warrant a heftier price tag. "Our audience is a younger audience," he said. "Maybe what we should be doing is to not stay with the same show for many years, and refresh our lineup."

Joss responded in the same article, countering Kellner's slams about *Buffy*'s aging demographics by pointing out that he had been told that the show's median age was "26 to 29 years old in year 2 of the show," so it shouldn't be a bargaining point in year five. He also pointed out that *Buffy* might not have been the network's highest-rated show (that was the wholesome *7th Heaven*), but it "put the WB on the map critically" and remained their second-highest-rated series. The WB, he argued, should "step up and acknowledge that financially."

In light of Kellner's disrespectful and dismissive comments, Joss no longer felt such a strong pull to stay at the WB. He explained his views on leaving: "Other networks reach more people, but other networks also have more hit shows they need to promote. We could be exposed to a new audience, but we could also be buried. But if we decide to move, I'm fine with it."

Many assumed that 20th Century Fox would move the series to the Fox network. That move, however, would create an even bigger drama in the television industry. While television series had jumped networks in the past, those moves were precipitated by the original network's choice to cancel a fading series, not the studio's desire to make more money from a successful show. Fox didn't want to endanger its ongoing relationships with ABC, NBC, and CBS by suggesting that it might pull other hit series from those networks to air on its own.

Instead, Fox offered *Buffy* to the big three networks. But while the series was a hit by WB standards, its average audience of 4.4 million viewers per episode in the 2000–01 season was not comparable to the ratings of their hits, which regularly netted around 18 million viewers. A better fit was the other small netlet, UPN. At the time, UPN aired four nights of original programming a week, and its biggest hits were the male-skewing wrestling series *WWF Smackdown!* and *Star Trek: Voyager*.

Even though *Buffy* brought in fewer viewers than either, it had a strong core female audience that the UPN wanted to court. The netlet immediately became the front-runner to be the new home of the Slayer, even as Fox executives made it clear that they would give the WB the chance to match any UPN offer to acquire the series.

According to then–WB programming chief Susanne Daniels, the WB's staffers couldn't believe that Kellner would let *Buffy* go, and the more panicked their pleading became, the more obstinately resolute Kellner was that the WB would not pay a higher cost per episode. "The studio did everything it could to keep the show at the WB," a Fox source told E! Online. "But the more Jamie opens his mouth, the more he says things like 'this is a niche show,' 'maybe we should replenish our schedule every year.' We started to realize our vision for the show was not the same as [the WB's]."

//////////

As Joss was directing "The Gift," *Buffy*'s one hundredth episode and fifth season finale, he still hadn't received final word as to whether it would also be the show's final episode on the WB. The network sent yet another mixed message by requesting that Joss and crew take part in a publicity stunt; they'd bring press on set to celebrate the hundredth episode with cake and a photo shoot. "The whole thing made me so angry, I had to stop shooting," Joss said. "I was like, 'Shut it down! I just can't be here right now!'"

The WB's final offer was roughly $1.8 million per episode, and on April 20, Sandy Grushow called Jamie Kellner to offer him the chance to counter UPN's offer of $2.33 million and a two-year contract. UPN's deal also included a commitment to pick up *Angel*, should the WB cancel it after the last year on its contract expired. Kellner declined, even passing on Grushow's offer to knock the fee down to $2.25 million per episode. *Buffy* and Joss had been evicted.

With three episodes left to air, the supportive network that Gellar had revered quickly changed its attitude. By May 2, *Buffy* stock photos had been pulled from the WB's official website, in a move that a spokesperson explained was to protect their "contractual right to exclusively promote the show." Also pulled was an advertisement in the *Hollywood Reporter* to congratulate the series on its hundredth episode. (UPN quickly jumped into the vacancy with its own congratulatory ad.) While it was well within its rights to no longer support the series, the WB behaved like a teenage girl burning all photos of an ex-boyfriend after a breakup.

On May 22, 2001, the WB aired "The Gift," in which Buffy sacrifices her own life to save her sister and stave off another apocalypse. (The last shot of the season is her tombstone, which reads, SHE SAVED THE WORLD A LOT.) This ending lent the last WB episode a disturbing sense of finality; the Bronze posting board exploded with discussions of *Buffy*'s death and speculation about the new season at UPN. Joss took to the board to assure fans that Buffy's death would have taken place whether the series jumped networks or not, and that the writers had planned out much of the next season well in advance of the season finale. He insisted, as he had many times before, that the viewers should trust the tale:

> The STORY is in charge, the story that keeps on speaking to me, that says there is much more to tell about all these characters. An ensemble this brilliant could easily carry the show even without the Slayer—but the fact is, even though she reached some beauty closure, Buffy's story isn't over. When it is, I'll know. And we'll stop. Till then, have faith.

Soon thereafter, when the WB shut down www.buffy.com, the Bronze, too, ceased to exist. UPN set up a new official site with its own message board, but its more complicated layout, with organized topics instead of one chronological stream of posts, didn't appeal to most Bronzers. They moved to a new, privately run board at BronzeBeta.com that replicated the linear structure of the board they had lost. The fate of the community was finally in the hands of the users themselves, but the replacement site never quite gelled. Whether it was the loss of the connection to the official *Buffy* site or just the inevitable erosion of interest after being so deeply involved in a community for so long, fewer and fewer fans showed up to participate in the discussion. The most devoted Bronzers would remain, and Joss and the writers would still post from time to time, but their intimate connection to a vibrant fan community was fading.

"The community, [their debates about events in the show] and everybody being pretty darn smart about their comments was wonderful for him. It was his salvation at the same time, and it came at a time that he needed it," Kai says. "Because he wasn't getting it from the executives.

People didn't know what he was doing—luckily, they just let him do *Buffy* before they understood that they didn't want him to do it anymore."

//////////

Over at UPN, the executives were quick to lavish gifts on their prized new addition. They gave Joss a nineteenth-century edition of the collected works of Shakespeare, Gellar got a new Gucci jacket, and the supporting cast received Cartier watches. After all the insults hurled at *Buffy* by Jamie Kellner, the recipients greatly appreciated the acknowledgment that the series and they themselves were important to the network. Those not in the title role were especially grateful; a cast member told *Entertainment Weekly* that it didn't seem as if the WB "realized there was anyone else on the show but Sarah and David [Boreanaz]."

While Buffy's death was a surprise to fans, Joss had let UPN in on the plans to resurrect his hero. "They were actually really excited," he said, "because rebirth is kind of the theme they're going for; they want to re-create the image of their network. It's very fitting Buffy would be coming back from the dead."

Joss's idea was to bring back Buffy as a different person than the one who gave her life for her little sister in the fifth season finale. In the sixth season premiere, an increasingly powerful Willow succeeds in casting a spell to raise the Slayer from the dead—but it turns out that in doing so, she has dragged Buffy out of heaven. Buffy's time in the afterlife finally brought her peace, and now she is faced with paying bills, raising her sister, and keeping Sunnydale safe from demons. She chooses to keep the fact that she was in heaven from her friends in consideration of how much they did to get her back, but the isolation and desperation push her into a deep depression and a series of terrible mistakes.

"The college years can be supremely self-destructive, particularly for women who have a dark side—that's when a lot of bad choices can get made," Marti Noxon says. "Speaking from my own experience, bad things will happen if you go to the dark place, and so I was definitely pushing that kind of stuff." Noxon had been a writer/producer on the show since the second season, and in the sixth she was elevated to showrunner, overseeing issues such as "reading new writers, making wardrobe calls, and all the day-in, day-out of the production" that Joss or David Greenwalt had handled in earlier seasons. Greenwalt was now occupied with *Angel* season three, and Joss had taken a small hiatus to work on two projects: a new space western series that he was developing for Fox—and a very, very special *Buffy* episode.

//////////

Joss had always wanted to write a musical episode of *Buffy*. He and Tony Head had discussed the idea for years, ever since they were shooting the pilot presentation back in 1996. As they were waiting for the lighting to be set up for the initial meeting between Giles and Buffy, Head and Joss were chatting, and the discussion turned to the fact that they both loved musicals. "Sarah Michelle piped up and said, 'I like musicals too!'" Head remembers, which led them to muse that if the series ever got picked up, it would be fun down the line to do their own musical.

It was perhaps a natural inclination for Joss, a man whose life had been scored by Broadway soundtracks. After all, both his father and grandfather had written musicals at Harvard and staged original musical theater in New York, and he himself had written three songs for a musical film that never came to pass. "He's a huge musical theater aficionado. He seems to know every musical ever written," writer Dean Batali says. "I think, deep in his heart, he'd rather win a Tony [Award] than anything else."

Although Joss had never been known as a musical lyricist, many of his colleagues recognized, consciously or subconsciously, the musical quality of his writing. Howard Gordon pushed Tim Minear to take a job on *Angel* because he knew that, like Marti Noxon, Jane Espenson, and David Fury, Minear could "sing in the key" of Joss. Fox's Jorge Saralegui compares Joss to a composer in the way that he can balance darkness with humor. "That's really almost kind of like music, it's a rhythm thing in your head," he says. "Most writers don't have that. They're more like a songwriter that knows how to put together a song: verse, verse, chorus, bridge, whatever. But they don't hear everything in that way where one thing balances the other—counterpoint, in effect. I think you either hear it or you don't. Joss is excellent at it."

So the skillset was always there. But Joss faced a huge obstacle: practicality. He was always so involved as the show's creator and showrunner that he couldn't take more than two weeks off in a row. That was not enough time for him to write an entire score. Joss also felt that in the established universe of the series, he'd have a hard time justifying a musical's heightened reality—that is, why everybody suddenly starts bursting into song. If there wasn't a justification for it in the story, Joss felt, it would look like they just ran out of ideas and reached for a gimmick. Consequently, every season Head would ask if they were doing a musical that year, but Joss always replied, "No, it doesn't feel right."

That didn't keep him from bringing his love of musicals, particularly Stephen Sondheim, to the set. When Danny Strong was playing Jonathan in "Earshot," he remembers, "I was doing this jump backwards that was a bit too choreographed looking. Joss came over to me and said 'Can you make the jump a little less . . .' and I jumped in and said, '*West Side Story*?' He totally freaked out and said, 'That's exactly what I was going to say!' Then we realized that we had both played Baby John in *West Side Story* and bonded over our mutual love of Sondheim."

Finally, during the impromptu sing-along at one of their early Shakespeare readings, Joss had been inspired by his cast's singing abilities. He decided that it was time to challenge himself again. With the show moving to UPN, it was the perfect time to remind people why *Buffy* was such a pop culture touchstone—and what better way to do that than to write a musical completely from scratch?

Joss had finally found a compelling reason why his characters would break out into song. In "Once More, with Feeling," Sunnydale is plagued by a demon with the power to compel people to express hidden truths musically. Though it's far from the most extraordinary thing to occur in Sunnydale, Joss made a point to have his characters remark on the strangeness of their choreographed musical outbursts, in a nod to any viewers who might not be particularly fond of musicals and might resist the notion that the characters will suddenly start singing about their feelings. Joss also took care to tie this mystical development into the ongoing emotional arc of the characters. As in "Hush," there has been a great lack of honest communication within the Scooby Gang, and everyone has been keeping secrets—the biggest one being Buffy's revelation that her friends ripped her out of heaven. The demon revels in the chaos and misery that's caused when those secrets are finally revealed. "Say you're happy now," he taunts them in song. "Once more, with feeling."

Joss crafted the episode's songs over the course of six months, with much of his work taking shape during a month-long vacation at Joss and Kai's vacation home in Cape Cod. Joss had taken pains to figure out all of his actors' musical ranges before he and Kai left; he had the foyer set up as a recording studio and used all of the other resources at his disposal. "I was basically his slave," Kai laughs. "I had nothing creatively to do with it except that he bossed me around because I was the only person who would sing, the only girl, because we were on vacation. He'd come downstairs and say, 'OK, I need you to do this part,' and I'd respond, 'OK, but can I finish the dishes?' He's like, 'No.'"

At one point, they had dinner plans with Kai's sister. "We were going to go out, and we couldn't go until I got this thing right. And I couldn't get it right. I went out to the carriage house," Kai recounts. "Because I was kind of shy too. I never sang in school. I'd just sing in the shower. But he needed me, and so it was kind of wonderful to have someone so specifically need you and push you to be better than you ever thought you could be. It was hard, but we had a blast. It was the only thing that we ever really did where he was like the boss of me, and I loved it. I loved it. I was so happy to help him, but I felt . . . I felt really proud of the work that he did."

Once the songs were locked, they created a demo of the two of them singing all the parts. "We listened to that over and over and over. It was so funny—we were obsessed with it. He always says it's the original soundtrack." Joss had created songs in a variety of different musical styles. For instance, Buffy's first number, "Going Through the Motions," was heavily influenced by "Part of Your World," *The Little Mermaid*'s version of the traditional Disney "I want" number, which Joss had rejected as too straightforwardly emotional to include in his earlier project *Toy Story*. In this episode, however, it seemed perfectly appropriate to start things off with a celebration of the "I want" trope—Buffy fights demons as she sings about the secrets that she's been keeping: "I can't even see / If this is really me / And I just want to be / *Alive*."

Joss sent the finished songs out to the cast. Tony Head received a CD in the mail, labeled simply ONCE MORE, WITH FEELING. "I started to listen and went, 'Oh my God, it's the musical!' And [my partner] Sarah said, 'This is really quite good!' and I said, 'It is!'" Head excitedly remembers. "It was like, 'Bloody hell, this is viable!'"

Not everyone was as positive. On set, James Marsters found a tape waiting for him instead of the new script that he was expecting. "It's obvious now that they were good songs but the thing was Joss and his wife Kai, they don't sing very well. And they don't play piano very well. The songs sounded really cheesy and horrible. Absolutely horrible," he said. "I remember coming out of my trailer, blinking in the sunshine and seeing the other cast members coming out of theirs with the same looks on their faces because they had been listening to their cassettes. Everyone was completely confused. There was this period of about four days where everyone realized this was the new episode and we were expected to perform these songs in front of the camera and freaking out."

Several of the cast members were so terrified that they tried to get out of the episode. It was a huge artistic risk, and they feared that if it failed, it would ruin their careers. But Joss was firm that the musical was going to happen and they all were going to be in it—they were under contract. "At that point the cast knuckled down and really started to make it work. We stopped complaining and really just married to the material," Marsters said. "As an artist you want to leap off the cliff and once you leap you better start flapping because there are only two possibilities, you are going to fly or you are going to splat."

The latter outcome may have seemed more likely to some of Marsters's castmates, who unlike him hadn't done much singing before. Several of them, including Alyson Hannigan, would have greatly reduced singing roles, but as the star, Sarah Michelle Gellar had no choice but to be front and center. At first she wanted a voice double to handle her part, but she changed her mind once she realized how important the songs were to her character's arc. "I basically started to cry and said, 'You mean someone else is going to do my big emotional turning point for the season?'" she recalled.

To get up to speed, Gellar and the rest of the cast trained with voice coaches for three months; Gellar herself had two vocal trainers. "It took something like 19 hours of singing and 17 hours of dancing in between shooting four other episodes," she said. "I hated every moment of it." Ultimately, however, she deemed the effort "an incredible experience": "I'm glad I did it. And I never want to do it again."

On the other hand, Head, a veteran of several musicals, would have happily worked on the episode for several more months. "I was rather sad in the recording process," he recalls. "Knocked mine out relatively quickly then hung around like the saddest ligger while other people came around to do theirs, because I loved being in the studio: 'Any help? Can I help?' 'No thanks, Anthony! That's enough! You can go!' 'Well, I haven't got anywhere to go, particularly!'"

//////////

During shooting on "Once More, with Feeling," Joss found himself exasperated by something related to neither music nor dancing. A scene called for Dawn to pour her books out of her bag, and the props department showed up with a Louis Vuitton purse. Joss was appalled at their choice of accessory for the teen.

Tim Minear explains, "He has exquisite taste, and by that I mean everything from culinary taste to art to music." And yet, "Joss is a fourteen-year-old girl who wears his heart in his purple clear Hello Kitty backpack. I think he'd be the first to admit it."

Joss wants to clear up a popular misconception about his backpack: "It wasn't Hello Kitty"—though it was purple. He had it for years, and every time it would fall apart again, he'd bring it to the wardrobe department to sew back together. Which is why the bag was in good shape to step in and play Dawn's own in the episode.

//////////

Worries about the musical started to abate when Joss gave the cast a first look at the footage. He wheeled a television onto the set to show them his first cut of Xander's number. "At that point we were overjoyed because it was brilliant," Marsters said. "We went from the depths of despair to the heights of self-pride in eight days."

But one question remained: how the audience would respond to it. It was certainly a risk—producing an episode full of all-original songs by someone who'd never written a musical before, married to a storyline that represented a crucial turning point in the ongoing narrative of the season. If it worked, Joss would be praised for his creativity and skill in brand-new fields. If it didn't, it would be a high-profile failure that gave credence to the WB's decision to cancel the series.

Fortunately, the episode was well-received by audiences and critics, with reviews noting that the characters stayed true to themselves even within the musical format. Joss's careful work to justify the musical conceit had paid off. To Marti Noxon, this was not an unprecedented feat but merely the latest manifestation of the basic principles Joss and his writers relied upon to craft every episode. "Being able to navigate the swing from real to hyperreal, without showing the wires and the pulleys," she says, "it's being able to keep a groundedness in this hyperreal world so people feel like, 'God I'm watching something that's really that feels emotionally very real to me.' To me that was always the song we were singing: 'Monster, monster, monster, joke, joke, joke, now we're going for the jugular.' While you're distracted we're going to build something that's actually going to make you feel something."

The musical wasn't without its critics, though. At *Salon*, Stephanie Zacharek wrote that "the songs were only half-memorable at best, and the singing ability of the show's regular cast ranged only from the fairly good to the not so great." And the point on which the episode's entire plot hinges—the revelation that Xander deliberately summoned the musical demon to ensure that he and his fiancée, Anya, would have a "happy ending"—was criticized as out of character for a guy who learned in previous episodes that messing with magic leads to bad things like a mob chasing him down and Buffy turning into a rat.

These few weak points couldn't solely be blamed when the episode failed to garner Joss a second Emmy nomination for Outstanding Writing for a Drama Series. In yet another snub by the Television Academy, the nomination ballots sent out to Emmy voters mistakenly omitted it from consideration in the writing category, and the academy had to send out follow-up postcards reminding voters of its eligibility. The episode did receive a nomination for Outstanding Music Direction, though it failed to win. It was also nominated for a Best Dramatic Presentation Hugo Award and a Best Script Nebula Award, both given for excellence in science fiction and fantasy writing.

///////////

Despite the high of Joss's special episode, many fans found other aspects of *Buffy*'s sixth season to be problematic—particularly the bleak turn taken in several beloved characters' storylines. "Once More, with Feeling" ends with a typical musical moment: Buffy and her onetime mortal enemy Spike sharing a passionate kiss as the music swells. But it's a moment that sends Buffy on a progressive downward spiral. In earlier episodes of the season, Spike served as her confidant of sorts, the only one in whom she could confide that she'd been pulled out of heaven. After their kiss, he becomes a cruel tempter instead, pushing her into acts of debauchery and seeking to widen the growing gulf between her and her friends. Yet Buffy is drawn to him, their connection soon manifesting in over-the-top sex scenes that are quite graphic for a network television series. In one episode, the two have emotionless sex next to the Dumpster outside the fast-food restaurant where Buffy works.

Many viewers recoiled at these developments, feeling that the writers were making dramatic alterations in the characters without first providing a strong, believable foundation for those changes. They felt similarly about the character of Willow, who over the course of the sixth season becomes increasingly reliant on dark magic. While some were receptive to the idea that Willow might want to escape her shy, awkward past by embracing the power that dark magic gave her, they disagreed with the writers' choice to frame her obsession instead as a physical addiction to magic, as if she were a drug addict jonesing for a fix.

Fans knew that Joss was spending much of his time developing his new Fox series, so they laid much of the blame for the failings of the season at the feet of Marti Noxon. "There are websites devoted to how I ruined *Buffy* in season six," she says. She had been a strong advocate of darker storylines—including the Spike/Buffy relationship—and she had become more involved in the production aspects of the series that Joss no longer had time for. But the season, she says, followed the creative direction Joss laid out. "The reports of his demise in season six were greatly exaggerated."

In fact, not only did she never take over full creative control of the series, she says, "to be honest, I didn't really want it. It belongs to him, and I'm the last person who wants to, like, ruin it. I wasn't waiting in the wings for my opportunity. I was like, 'Thank God Joss is in control.' I was scared to death."

The complaints about the season, however, were not without merit. Even Sarah Michelle Gellar had concerns about the well-being of her alter ego. She was not known to try to control the story direction for her character, so when she did have an opinion it mattered more. Gellar told Noxon that she felt that Buffy was losing her "hero-ness" and losing her way. "It wasn't who Buffy was, or why people loved her. You don't want to see that dark heroine; you don't want to see her punishing herself," Gellar told *Entertainment Weekly*. "It didn't feel like the character that I loved."

Gellar singled out the episode "Dead Things" as her least favorite of the series. On a rare night off from all her responsibilities, Buffy joins her friends at the Bronze. She makes her way up to the balcony for a quiet moment alone and is soon joined by Spike, who physically takes her from behind and forces her to watch her friends down below as they have sex.

"I really thought that was out of character. And I didn't like what it stood for," she said. "Joss always explained that season as being about your 20s, where you're not a kid anymore, but you don't know what you want to do [with your life]. He always said that I didn't understand . . . because I've always known what I wanted to do, and I didn't have that confusion, [that] dark, depressive period. But I think the heart of the show lies in the humor of the drama. I felt like Buffy's spirit was missing [in the sixth season]."

Joss's comment seems dismissive of Gellar, someone who had lived and breathed the television Buffy for almost as long as he had. It is certainly true that Gellar never had to kill her boyfriend, blow up her high school, or return to a miserable life on Earth after being pulled from heaven, but she brought Buffy through all those emotional journeys believably. Once again, it feels as if the writers were so determined to tell a story about a young woman's descent into extreme depression and self-abuse that they didn't fully consider the world or the characters they were telling it in.

In fact, all of "Dead Things" seems like a huge disconnect from the positive and empowering emotional core for which *Buffy* is known. Its storylines seem to smash away at the morals of the series minute by minute: The Trio, the three nerdy college students who serve as the season's previously comic Big Bads, develop a "cerebral dampener" that removes its target's free will. They then go out to pick up women to turn into sex slaves. Buffy beats Spike to a bloody pulp while railing at him for being evil and soulless. And finally Warren, the leader of the Trio, kills his ex-girlfriend when the "dampener" effects begin to fade and she became aware that they're attempting to rape her. The Trio get away with the murder, although their attempt to pin it on Buffy fails.

As the season proceeded in this grim fashion, online fandom responded with overwhelming disapproval. "That's where having feedback from the fans can be really useful—when you start to see a kind of consensus that stays consistent through episodes," Noxon says. "Certainly there are times when you just have to say, 'We know you don't like this, but we've got a plan, don't worry.' There are often episodes where you're like, 'This is the medicine. You're not going to like it, but it's good for you.'" But there was enough of a critical groundswell from fans who loved the show and had supported it for six years that, combined with

Gellar's concerns, convinced Joss that they needed to course-correct a bit. "A little less descending," Noxon says. "A little more ascending."

//////////

Before it began ascending, however, the show would hit rock bottom in many ways, with "Seeing Red," the nineteenth episode out of twenty-two. In an infamous scene set in Buffy's bathroom, Buffy returns from a rough night of patrolling and is looking to relax with a long soak. Spike shows up uninvited, and in a wildly misguided attempt to convince her that she does in fact love him, he overpowers Buffy and attempts to rape her. Though wounded, she fights him off, ending their battle by kicking him through a wall. He is immediately horrified and apologetic, but Buffy insists that the only reason he halted his attack was because she had the physical strength to stop him.

It is a painful scene to watch—and it was a painful scene to portray. James Marsters has called it the worst day of his professional career, one of the hardest things he ever had to do and something he will never do again. "The truth is the writers on *Buffy* were being incredibly brave," Marsters said. "Joss was asking each of them to come up with their most painful day, their most humiliating day, the day that they made the biggest fools of themselves or the day they hurt someone else the most, and then put a patina of fangs and blood over that. Basically that's why I think the series is so delightful, because of the bravery of the writers on that score." But even though he understood why the writers did it, "I still think it was a mistake."

Several writers have insisted that the attack was crucial to Spike's emotional arc. "Spike's a villain," Noxon says. "At his core he is bad, let's not forget." Jane Espenson saw the attempted rape as the impetus for Spike to look at himself and truly see the demon inside, and then make a choice of what to do—which is to search for a way to restore his own soul and become a man worthy of Buffy.

To be sure, Spike's arc needed a vivid climax to push him onto such a dramatic new path. But it's questionable that it needed to be the attempted rape of the series' main character. Joss and his writers, ordinarily so devoted to the "Buffy of it," seemed to have subordinated her role in these events to the needs of a supporting character's storyline. And in doing so, they reframed the Buffy/Spike relationship, changing the hero of their story from a willing if conflicted participant in their sexual exploration into a mere victim. It comes off as a cheap and narratively inept way to start the next chapter in Spike's life.

In seven seasons, "Seeing Red" is one of *Buffy*'s most controversial episodes, if not the most controversial. It also angered viewers because at the very end, Trio leader Warren shoots and kills Willow's girlfriend, Tara. Fans were devastated and furious that Joss had allowed such a groundbreaking, beloved example of a happy lesbian couple on television to come to such a brutal end—after they sent him a toaster to thank him for it! Angry viewers claimed that *Buffy* had fallen into the "dead lesbian cliché," by which TV series often introduced lesbian characters just so they could be killed off. As with the attempted rape, the writers insisted that Tara's death was necessary to the larger story—she needed to die so that Willow would be motivated by grief to return to dark magic and go on a murderous rampage, setting her up as an antagonist for Buffy in the final episodes of the season.

Yet Tara's death—and the deaths of Joyce Summers, Doyle, and quite a few other ill-fated characters over the course of Joss's writing career—are not merely narrative necessities. They all speak to Joss's need to ground his tales in truth and human experience. Prior to *Buffy*, television series, especially sci-fi series, often put their characters in danger but rarely exposed them to true peril that might lead to death. *The X-Files* regularly set up Mulder and Scully to be attacked by assorted monsters and creatures, and they always made it through to the following week. Viewers had become conditioned to this; they would watch each episode through the veil of "she's a main character, she won't die"—their emotional attachment still strong but their fear muted.

But in real life, everyone dies eventually, and many will die suddenly, leaving loved ones behind to deal with an intense devastation in a very personal way. Joss knows what it's like to be forced to deal with such a loss, with no possible explanation that can make sense of the pain or ease it in any way. He lost his mother to a brain aneurism, and several years later a Riverdale friend, the writer Joe Wood, went missing on Mount Rainier and was never found. Joss designs each death in the Whedonverse to make viewers feel the despair and ache of loss—because he spent so much time creating an emotional connection that brought them joy and love in the first place. When Joss kills a character, it hurts because it is designed to hurt.

Still, fans took Tara's death particularly hard—in part, perhaps, because of a trick Joss played on viewers at the beginning of her last episode. He added Amber Benson, who had played Tara on a recurring basis for the past three seasons, to the opening credits, a position usually reserved for full-time cast members. "I realized, just the other day, that I have this terrible reputation for killing people not just because I killed Tara, but because I was such a dick about it," Joss laughed. "[Adding her to the credits] was just *mean*. Tara may be dead, but she haunts me still, because now all anybody ever talks about is the fact I kill characters off, and I think, 'I do other things as well!' "

//////////

Another episode from late in season six felt like a return to form for the series—and it came from outside the current writers' room. Diego Gutierrez had left his job as Joss's assistant at the end of the previous season to pursue his own writing career, but years earlier, he'd pitched the idea for "Normal Again." He'd been fascinated by the idea of psychosis and mental breakdowns, which led him to imagine how Buffy would look to someone unaware of the hidden world of magic and demons. "If you heard her talking [about her life] at a restaurant, you'd think she's totally nuts," he says.

He conceived of a story in which Buffy is attacked by a demon whose venom puts her into an extreme hallucinogenic state. She then floats between two worlds: one in which she's a Vampire Slayer in Sunnydale; the other in which she's a patient in a mental hospital, where she has been in a schizophrenic catatonic state for six years. Both of Buffy's parents attend to her at the hospital, hoping that she'll break free from her deranged beliefs that the world is filled with demons and she is a Vampire Slayer.

Joss liked the pitch, but for a long time, nothing came of it. He told Gutierrez later that he'd been trying to find a plausible way to do the story. When Gutierrez's assistantship was nearing its end, he was working on a packet of spec scripts in hope of landing a staff writing job, and one of the scripts was a spec version of his asylum idea. He was excited when Joss agreed to read the script and give him notes. However, he did not expect Joss to say that he wanted to buy the script and bring him back the following season to work on the episode.

A year later, Gutierrez took a short break from his new job writing for *Dawson's Creek* to return and work on the script with Joss. He suggested that they scrap his original, ambiguous ending, which instead of showing Buffy in Sunnydale, fully recovered from the demon's venom, closes on a shot of her in the mental hospital. Joss surprised him when he said, "Let's end it in the asylum . . . let's fuck with them."

"Joss never undermined the intelligence and the respect between the fans and the show," Gutierrez says. "He was always making sure that even if he wasn't giving you what you wanted, you were always getting something that was cool and interesting."

In the end, Buffy chooses to leave her parents and a chance at happiness behind to live in a nightmarish world filled with demons and daily battles. The final scene, in which she has returned to her catatonic state in the hospital and the doctor declares her "gone," is indeed jarring. The viewers are left to wonder which of the two worlds is real for Buffy, and thus *Buffy*.

"Normal Again" would have been a brilliant ending to an uneven and uneasy season. It could have set up questions about sanity and reality that echoed throughout the following year. Instead, the brain-twisting events were confined to a stand-alone episode, like Joss's despised "reset television," in which storylines never really progress and characters never learn any lessons.

//////////

The actual conclusion to season six returns to the key Whedonverse notion of chosen family, asserting that it's this community who will support us even when we falter, love us when we don't feel like we deserve it, and stand by us in our worst moments. In Willow's worst moment, she tries to kill those responsible for Tara's death and then attempts to destroy the world in order to bring an end to her agony. And it is Xander, the one without great strength or magic, who comes to her, letting her lash out at him physically and verbally, and repeats over and over that he loves her no matter what she has done. His love lessens her fury and she breaks down in his arms.

But to many fans, this heart-tugging redemption story was too little, too late. At this point in the story, Willow and Xander hardly talked to each other. They were not the best of friends they had been in the series' first few seasons. And yes, people change and grow, and relationships transform after high school. But for two people who still spent a significant amount of time together, they barely seemed to register what was going on in each other's lives. (A few episodes earlier, in "Hell's Bells," Xander and Anya call off their wedding; Xander mourns the breakup alone in a motel, while Willow, Buffy, and Dawn discuss the couple elsewhere.) So it's difficult to accept that this Willow, who had been so devastated from the loss of Tara that she wanted to take out the entire world, could be talked down by someone who *was* her best friend and confidant, many years earlier.

Still, there is undeniable poignancy in watching these two friends, who have known each other for a lifetime and whom the audience had known for six years, reconnect so purely and transcendently. After a season in which so many characters lost their way in convoluted and clumsy storylines, it gave fans hope that the next season would be a return to form, and a restoration of the characters and relationships that mattered. In that way, season six had finally started to ascend.

17

WE AIM TO MISBEHAVE: FIREFLY

Joss created *Buffy the Vampire Slayer* to introduce a character he had always wanted to see in a horror movie but never had. For his next television series, he turned his attention toward something he found lacking in televised science fiction: "a gritty realism that wasn't an 'Alien' ripoff." In *Firefly*, he combined his love of outer space sci-fi with his affection for a much more rough-and-tumble genre—westerns, "particularly the '70s westerns, the immigrant stories, the ones about 'this is all we have out here, so we might be dead soon.' "

He first conceived of the series when he wasn't supposed to be thinking about television at all, during a nonworking trip to London with Kai. Joss had brought along Michael Shaara's Pulitzer Prize–winning historical novel *The Killer Angels*, which told the story of the soldiers in the 1863 Battle of Gettysburg in the American Civil War. What drew him in was how Shaara recounted the minutiae of the soldiers' lives; it made him think about how everyday people got by in an age when their needs weren't prepackaged and instantly available.

Under his deal with 20th Century Fox, Joss needed to deliver them a new series. He suddenly knew that this was the idea that he wanted to explore. "I wanted to play with that classic notion of the frontier," Joss said. "Not the people who made history, but the people history stepped on—the people for whom every act is the creation of civilization." And he wanted to do it on a spaceship.

That concept, he hoped, would elevate *Firefly* above the average sci-fi series. Though he'd clocked countless hours watching movies set in faraway worlds, most TV examples of the genre failed to engage him.

Even his love of British television didn't extend to science fiction. "Never watched any British sci-fi," Joss says. "People were always talking to me about *[Blake's] 7*, *Red Dwarf*, even *Doctor Who*, and I just never watched them. I watched one episode of *Doctor Who* and I was like, 'Did they film that in my basement?' because it looked cheesy." His series aimed to be anything but.

Firefly would be set in a distant future in which the Earth has been "used up" and can no longer support the whole of the human race. Humanity survives by homesteading terraformed outposts in a new planetary system, simply called "the 'verse" by its inhabitants. Joss would introduce us to not just one but a series of worlds recovering from a civil war between an antiseptic, Orwellian government called the Alliance and a band of outgunned rebels called the Browncoats.

Joss characterized his story as an exploration of "how politics affect people personally. And the *personal* politics are the only politics that really interest me. I'm not going to make this big, didactic polemic—I'm just going to say, 'When there are shifts in a planet, those tiny little guys are the ones who are affected. So let's hang out with them—not the Federation heads or the Jedi Council.'"

True to that mission statement, *Firefly*'s heroes are the nine crew members and passengers aboard a ramshackle "Firefly-class" spaceship called *Serenity*. The crew barely scrape by on odd smuggling jobs and the rent they charge their regular passengers, who all have reasons to retreat to deep space to escape the authorities of the Alliance. Joss had originally conceived of a smaller ensemble, but he increased the character count after being inspired by another western, John Ford's 1939 movie *Stagecoach*, which likewise follows nine characters—a driver, a marshal, and seven strangers—as they cross the open and fairly unsettled frontier between Arizona Territory and New Mexico Territory.

In fact, literature professor Fred Erisman later identified quite blatant parallels between Ford's film and Joss's new tale: "Buck, the serio-comic driver, becomes Wash, the pilot," an unabashed geek who plays with dinosaur action figures set up on *Serenity*'s console during his downtime. "Drunken Doc Boone becomes the up-tight surgeon Simon Tam," who is in hiding from the Alliance along with his sister, River, after he rescues her from a government lab that was engaging in horrific human experimentation. "'Reverend' Peacock is replaced by an actual cleric, the enigmatic Shepherd Book," a preacher with a mysterious dark past. And "in an especially telling reversal, the prostitute Dallas becomes Inara Serra," an elite sex worker known as a Companion "whose presence aboard the ship gives it 'a certain respectability.'"

Rounding out the ensemble are *Serenity*'s captain, Malcolm "Mal" Reynolds, a former sergeant who fought on the losing side of the civil war; and pilot Wash's wife, Zoe, who fought alongside Mal and remains his loyal second in command. When the ship breaks down or needs repair, Kaylee serves as its able, salt-of-the-earth country mechanic. And Jayne is a hired mercenary with questionable loyalties. Finally, Professor Richard Slotkin's influence on Joss can once again be seen as he transformed the looming threat of the Apaches into the Reavers, the brutal savages who live on the outskirts of civilized space.

Although *Firefly*'s dystopian sci-fi elements might seem a drastic departure from *Buffy*'s world of fantasy horror and privileged teenage angst, its central theme is quite familiar: A group of seemingly disparate individuals, each just trying to get by in a universe that really isn't smart enough to appreciate his or her exceptional talents and quirks, are tossed together by extraordinary circumstances. Occasionally, and sometimes by accident, they manage to save the world(s).

Firefly's cast of characters is filled with the archetypes that pop up in much of Joss's work: the loner with a distinct sense of justice, although his sense of right and wrong may not mesh with society's; the stalwart and dependable comrade, who may question the hero but will always have his back; the stuffy, book-learned one who finds that real life often does not adhere to the facts he was taught; the one with faith, who has left an organized group but still works to apply its tenets for the benefit of those around him; the mercenary who's always up for a fight; the confident one who is often just trying to get through the day in the most pleasant way possible; the well-trained one whose strength is not fully understood until she is pushed; and, of course, the young woman coming to terms with her new power and the responsibility that it entails.

In the case of *Firefly*, that last archetype is filled by Simon's sister, River, a onetime child prodigy whose mind has been damaged by the experiments to which the government subjected her, but who in her rare lucid moments over the course of the series will shock the crew with her fighting prowess and psychic predictions of doom. It would be the most familiar element of an unfamiliar concept, akin to Joss's numerous movie ideas that all tended to revolve around adolescent female superheroes.

Joss designed *Firefly* to be different, "about Joe Schmo, everyday life," he said. "And then of course I introduce River, the young female superhero. Let's face it, I'm just addicted."

But he was glad that, for once, his female superhero would be merely one character among many. "It was nice to have a show that was about different perspectives and to really get to explore all of them. I was excited that I was going to have a happily married couple that was not boring. Because that's just so rare in fiction and it's such an important thing in life. And yet apart from [the] Thin Man [film] series, I think it's never really been adequately represented. And I had a preacher on board, to explore the concept of faith, people who don't have it and people who do."

That exploration of faith would become an important aspect of the series, embodied in the relationship between the pious Shepherd Book and the lapsed believer Mal Reynolds. Captain Reynolds "is a man who has learned that when he believed in something it destroyed him," Joss said. "So what he believes in is the next job, the next paycheck and keeping his crew safe." The series pushes past the idea that a belief in God is necessary for a moral life, and questions the definition of morality that others want to impose. Mal, to Joss, is a "guy who looks into the void and sees nothing but the void—and says there is no moral structure, there is no help, no one's coming, no one gets it, I have to do it."

Mal is also a character his atheist creator strongly identified with. "Of course the captain was the me figure," Joss joked, "because he's very tall and handsome, but cranky and also slim." But in actuality, *all* of the characters, all the archetypes they embodied, are facets of Joss himself. And perhaps that's why he would fall in love the hardest with *Firefly*—because he poured every bit of himself into these characters, and developed relationships between them that mirrored the relationships and friendships in his own life.

He was even willing to walk away from the show rather than alter one of those relationships, the marriage between Zoe and Wash. "Wash is an absolute contrast to Zoe, yet a perfect mate for her," he explained. "Rather than playing out every little romance in its infancy the way shows usually do, I thought it would be nice to show a happily married couple, who would have their fights and their troubles, but would stay married." But when Fox executives were deciding whether to pick up the series, they saw a stable marriage as dramatically limiting, and they pushed him to break up the couple. "The last thing that Fox said was,

'We will pick up the show, but they can't be married.' And I said, 'Then don't pick up the show, because in my show, these people are married. And it's important to the show.' "

//////////

Gail Berman, the former Sandollar Productions executive who brought Joss the idea of a *Buffy* television series back in the mid-1990s, had joined the Fox network in 2000 as its president of entertainment. In December 2001, she greenlit *Firefly* with an order for thirteen episodes. A month later, Mutant Enemy was given $10 million to develop and shoot the pilot. But before he could go behind the camera, Joss had to find the right cast.

Every ship needs a captain, and *Serenity* was no different. Nathan Fillion was coming off a recently canceled ABC sitcom, *Two Guys, a Girl and a Pizza Place*, and had been offered a "talent holding deal" by 20th Century Fox; the studio wanted to keep him on retainer so that they could find a new role for him on one of their upcoming shows. He was brought in to meet with Joss about the Mal Reynolds role.

After failing to get past the first cut for the part of Angel on *Buffy* in 1996, Fillion had run into some of the actors who were cast in the series at parties, and they would talk about the adventures that they were having and the stories the show was telling. He was intrigued, and tried to catch the occasional *Buffy* episode. But he never met Joss until casting director Amy Britt brought him in for *Firefly*.

"I walked into an office," Fillion recalls. "Amy was there, and she said, 'Hi. OK, I'm just gonna let you guys sit down and chat.' There was this little guy in the corner, in a purple sweater with a rip in it. With scraggly hair and a scraggly beard and I thought, 'Nice guy, but when's Joss Whedon gonna get here?' "

He realized quickly that this scraggly little guy *was* Joss Whedon, and they chatted for about forty-five minutes about work, about other shows, and about *Firefly*. Joss told Fillion that he'd love for him to come in and audition for the part of his captain. "This'll be great," Fillion remembers Joss saying. "I think you'd do well with this part."

The audition process wasn't as smooth. He was asked in to read over and over. The fifth time he went in, he told them that he didn't quite understand what was going on. The casting people told him that he seemed to be reading it the same way each time. "Which I am," Fillion told them. "Is there something you'd like to see differently?"

"These poor people are thinking, maybe I'm an idiot, I can't take direction. I can only do the one thing; I'm a one-note guy. But here we go." With a little input, he changed up his approach, showing them that he could take direction and give them different reads. "We did it differently and we had a great time," he says. "There was a bit of a breakdown in communication there, but I was tense. I'll tell you that, I was tense."

After that, Joss had Fillion wait in an office. To his relief, he was told that he had the part. He was shown costume designs and sketches of his ship. It was thrilling. He was a fan of westerns and of sci-fi—and this was both. "When I get a project, I don't look at it and say, 'Boy, the impact this is gonna have!'" Fillion explains. "I have no idea. When I look at a project, I look at a character that I'm playing, I look at the story that we're telling, and I think, 'Am I going to have any fun? Can I bring something to this? Am I right for this? Does it excite me?' And *Firefly* was exciting."

At the time, Joss didn't even have a finished pilot script; *Firefly* was only a treatment of roughly eighteen pages, a play-by-play outline of the events the script would cover. Fillion had a lot of questions, and he sat down with Joss to discuss them. He was so impressed at how completely Joss had imagined the entire *Firefly* universe, down to the minutiae. "He would describe something in the universe, and then describe how they were going to depict it. He would describe lighting; he would describe music." Joss had everything planned for the way that they were going to shoot the special effects shots. He even explained how one group of guys would wear hats and another wouldn't.

Joss was equally articulate about the big ideas, explaining to Fillion the idea of a "found experience": how the characters were out in space because they were each searching for something in life they couldn't find. "I've had a lot of meetings with a lot of show creators. And I have a lot of questions for them," Fillion says. "No one has been so complete in their vision as Joss Whedon. And that much about Joss has never changed since the first day I met him. He's always complete in his vision."

Gina Torres, who was cast in the role of first officer Zoe, was grateful to receive more open-ended direction from Joss. The two main things that she took away from their conversations was that Zoe is "career military" and that she loves her husband, Wash, who would be played by

Alan Tudyk. "After that, it was up to me to add the flesh and bone and heart," she said. "It was lovely to be trusted to do that."

Adam Baldwin won the role of the mercenary Jayne. He later found out that Joss had seen some of his earlier work and already felt that he was a strong fit for the part. The direction that he was given was that Jayne was not the sharpest tool in the shed but that he was always self-centered and self-directed. "You wouldn't want to cross him and you couldn't trust him as far as you could throw him," Baldwin explains, "but he was the guy you want on your team."

Jewel Staite had just arrived in L.A. after sending in a taped audition for mechanic Kaylee. Before heading to a screen test at Fox Studios, she had to audition in front of Joss at the Mutant Enemy offices. "I was petrified," she says. "*Buffy* was about to celebrate its millionth episode or something, so there were all these congratulations posters up in the office, and I was just kind of in awe that I was even there at all.

"Joss came out of the audition room to greet me with this big, warm smile on his face, and right away I was put at ease. I felt like he was in my corner from the get-go, and later at my screen test, every time I got overwhelmed with nerves, I'd just find his face in the crowd of Fox executives, and he was always smiling that warm smile at me. I kind of wish he could be there for every screen test I have to do."

Former *Doogie Howser, M.D.* star Neil Patrick Harris was in contention for the role of surgeon Simon Tam, but the role ultimately went to actor Sean Maher. Before being cast, Maher had very little interest in the series, as he'd never cared much for *Buffy* and wasn't particularly a sci-fi fan. He agreed to go in to talk about the project simply because he wanted to meet with Joss. Since the pilot script still wasn't written, all he was given were "sides," discrete scenes used for audition purposes. But they were enough to change Maher's mind about the show. "This whole moment in the pilot where Simon explains to the crew the backstory about his sister River. I was so immediately intrigued, the first thing I said to him was, 'Please tell me about this show,' " he said. "So I got to hear about the world of *Firefly* from Joss' mouth. . . . I almost fell off my chair."

Summer Glau joined the cast as River, and Ron Glass was hired as Shepherd Book. In the role of the Companion Inara, Joss initially cast Rebecca Gayheart, who left the project after production began in March 2002. Morena Baccarin came in to audition as her replacement. After her initial read-throughs, casting director Britt decided to stop and call in

Joss, who was on set at the time. Baccarin thought that was a good sign, and she felt even better when Joss arrived, super casual in his cargo pants. She ran through her lines and Joss told her that she did great.

"He immediately started joking around with me, asking, 'Can you do it in a Polish accent?'" Baccarin remembers. "And I was like 'Sure!' So we just had this rapport and started joking around together, and I thought 'Wow, this would be so much fun! To get to work with somebody like that.'" When she tested for the studio and network the next morning, Joss was in the room. As with Jewel Staite, "he was smiling at me and, like, giving me the thumbs-up and just being really sweet and very supportive, which was really nice.

"I left the room after my audition, and they have to confer and talk about you, and sometimes they ask you to go back in and do the scene again a little differently. When they asked me to come back inside, Joss came out to get me and I went inside and I thought, 'OK, I'm going to have to prove myself again, have to do this again,' and he just said, 'Congratulations, you have the job.' It was incredible! The day after that I was on set shooting, so it was like three or four days between auditioning and being on set."

Nathan Fillion fondly remembers *his* first day on set. He was in his trailer when he was called to the stage. "I put on my coat and walked into the studio. The big cargo bay door was open, and I walked up into the cargo bay up this ramp. Someone [called out] 'Captain on deck!' And everybody turned and stopped and did like a little mock salute. A couple of people applauded. And I thought, 'Oh my God. I just got on a spaceship.' The moment was not lost on me. Every kid wants it."

That spaceship, *Serenity*, is in many ways the tenth character in the *Firefly* ensemble. Its vast, winding sets, filled with rusted metal and signs of duct-tape-and-a-prayer repairs, give the series a lived-in feel. Its CGI-generated exterior, on the other hand, would evoke the *Millennium Falcon*, its glowing engine like a beating heart, pulsing with just enough juice to allow our heroes to escape the clutches of evil in the nick of time.

//////////

Like many actors in their first Whedon roles, the cast of *Firefly* needed to adjust to Joss's signature rapid-fire, snarky dialogue, peppered with invented slang. Adam Baldwin admits, "I had trouble in the early going with the whole 'Nothing into nothing carry the nothing' [line in the pilot], the rhythm of the language in a couple of the scenes, before it really clicked in. I would go to Joss and say, 'What's the rhythm of this?' Joss is a very good actor, so it was very easy for him to give me a line reading.

"I found that was effective," he adds. "I worked for Stanley Kubrick— Stanley was not as good a communicator with actors as Joss is. Stanley would just have you do it again and yell at you that you were lame and bad and need to be a better actor, whereas Joss would say, 'Well, try this' or 'Try that,' and he would care. Being a good actor, he was able to give all of us guidance toward his vision of how the scene would play. And that was a huge, huge benefit."

Beyond the trademark Whedon-speak, the *Firefly* actors had to contend with a new linguistic complication. In the Firefly universe, the English language is peppered with Chinese—in particular, long and inventive bouts of swearing, created by Joss. The idea was inspired by Kai's experience of living and teaching English in China, combined with Joss's own interest in the country and culture. "It does make perfect sense," Joss said. "China is going to be the greatest world power on the planet within this decade." But he soon discovered a surprising limitation of the complex, tonal language: "You can say something that's paragraphs long in like two syllables, so I kept having to write longer and longer curses, just so people could hear the Chinese."

His actors may sometimes have found it frustrating to memorize and repeat long curses in an unfamiliar tongue, but they were otherwise deeply grateful for Joss's creative leadership. "When Joss directs, he has a way of saying no that you don't care that your idea was rejected," Nathan Fillion says. " 'I have an idea. What if I do it like this, and I jump around and I take my time, and do a little—,' and he says, 'Oh, that's a great idea. Or . . .' His idea is so much better, realistic, and clever. And then, I go, 'Oh my God, that's brilliant, yes! Yes, of course that's how I should do it.' Then it goes on screen and people give me the credit: 'Oh, when you did this thing, it was so great, and it was real, it was so cool and clever.'

"Yeah, that was me, all right, up there doing that thing that Joss told me to do."

//////////

As *Firefly* proceeded from pilot to series, Joss knew that he was going to be spread thin overseeing three shows simultaneously. *Buffy* was in the middle of its sixth season, *Angel* its third. Joss had enlisted Marti Noxon to run the day-to-day operations of the former, and David Greenwalt was still doing the same with the latter. But he needed someone to fill that role on *Firefly*—someone with whom he could develop the show and to whom he could entrust it when he wasn't able to be on set or in the writers' room. "If you don't have a second-in-command who can control the set when you walk away," he remembered being told, "you never will."

His strongest inclination was to draft *Angel*'s Tim Minear, who had distinguished himself by becoming the first writer to break stories without him. But he had promised Greenwalt that he would never pilfer him from *Angel*. He searched for a *Firefly* showrunner outside of Mutant Enemy, to no avail; he felt that he "could not find anybody even remotely of the caliber of Tim." Determined to keep his promise, he kept looking, until someone convinced him that if he didn't move Minear to *Firefly*, Joss would have no time or energy for *Buffy* or *Angel*.

Minear had already read the *Firefly* pilot script, and Joss had told him about some of the stories he wanted to do over the course of the series. He was very excited about the show. When Joss showed him an early cut of the pilot, Minear gave him notes in the editing room—he loved the episode but kept himself from becoming emotionally invested in it, because he was working on *Angel*.

Finally, Joss showed up on the *Angel* set at Paramount, where Minear was directing the episodes "A New World" and "Benediction" back to back. He sat down with Tim and said, "I want to give you a spaceship." As a longtime *Star Trek* fan—who had filmed and starred in his own *Trek* films in high school and screened them at comic cons—Minear was thrilled. "Oh, for God's sake, that's the whole reason I'm doing this!" he said.

The offer led to some turmoil at *Angel*. David Greenwalt "did not take it lightly, nor should he have," Joss said. Greenwalt chose to leave *Angel* at the end of season three; he had a chance to develop a new show outside of the Buffyverse as the showrunner for the new ABC series *Miracles*. That wasn't the only upheaval in the Whedonverse; Marti Noxon left *Buffy* to have a baby and would be gone through most of the seventh season.

Joss suddenly had three shows and had lost two showrunners. But he knew that this kind of pressure could actually be a good thing for him—it had helped him refocus his life for the better before. In the early years of *Buffy*, he'd pull all-nighters all the time, because they were always behind. "When *Angel* came around, I was so tapped out," he explains, "because every second I wasn't working on *Buffy*, I would turn around and there would be work to do on *Angel*. I was much healthier, because I just was so worn out that I couldn't wear myself out." He got eight glorious hours of sleep every night, because his brain was so full.

In the same way, he says, "when three shows came on, I was very fierce and ridiculously focused." *Buffy*'s upcoming seventh season was likely to be its last, so "I can let it slide," Joss reasoned. "It's the first year of *Firefly*, there's nowhere to slide from"—and there was a risk that it wouldn't succeed—"so I've got to bust it out." He decided that "*Angel*'s where everyone's going to expect me to drop the ball, so I have to make that super awesome. You get into a mode where you can just keep going, and just, you know, clicking over and clicking over. It was taxing, but in a way, it was almost simple."

Joss did realize, however, that he could no longer oversee the day-to-day dealings of his production company. It was at this point that he reached out to his friend Chris Buchanan, who had quite the varied résumé as, among other things, a film producer, literary agent, and senior VP of production (one of his projects was 2001's *Ocean's Eleven*). On March 31, 2002, he announced Buchanan as the new president of Mutant Enemy.

Buchanan saw himself as the person to guide Joss's creative ideas into concrete projects. "He's done his thing," Buchanan told *Variety*. "Somebody was needed to pick up the ball and run with it, figure out how we make things happen, how do we move it to the next stage." He hinted that in the future, Mutant Enemy might not limit itself to only Joss-penned TV and features. "Joss has surrounded himself with people who are very creative," Buchanan said. "He'd like to be the platform on which they build their own empires. It all goes back to world domination."

Two weeks later, Joss reemphasized his commitment to *Firefly* and its Mutant Enemy siblings. The longtime comic book geek dropped out of talks with New Line Cinema to direct their upcoming film *Iron Man*.

////////////

Joss's new approach to all things Mutant Enemy had another impetus behind it: Kai was pregnant with their first child, due in December 2002.

She had waited through five years of him pulling long hours in order to get his shows in production, and now, with a baby on the way, she was determined that he be a part of the new world they were creating together.

"OK, you did your time," Joss remembers her declaring. "We said you were going to do your time and then we were going to start a family. So we're starting! You have to be in it!"

//////////

In the meantime, Joss attended to the birth of his new series, a process replete with its own pressures and anxieties. His star Nathan Fillion, however, never lost his initial giddiness, even with all the pressure of being the lead on a one-hour television program. Fillion had been part of a sitcom ensemble, but this was something that he'd never done before. He tried not to think about the responsibilities it entailed. "I didn't feel a daily pressure of, 'Hey, you're carrying the show,'" he says, "because it was very much an ensemble piece. And when you're on a television set and you see the kind of work that goes on, the lead actor is not doing the majority of the work.

"Certainly your face is up there, but the majority of the work has been done before you even get to work. There's a lot of hard work going on in a television program, and the majority has been done long before I ever step foot on a set. The writing, the organizing, building a set, the decoration, the costumes, casting; it's a lot of work. What I do is icing on the cake." But if anyone around him tried to remind him that the success of the series was riding on him, "I'd start to feel it. Start to look around and think, 'I can't blow this. I can't blow it. Don't blow this.' That was my mantra."

Joss most likely didn't want Fillion to take on all the pressure for the series' success. But perhaps the prospect of starting his own family with Kai, coupled with knowledge of how intricately involved he was in the intense episodic schedule, led him to initially keep his latest on-screen family at a greater distance than usual. In fact, he warned the cast early on that there was a reason why he named the show *Firefly*, after the spaceship, and not after any central character. Adam Baldwin recalls Joss declaring, "Because I've had experience with that before and I don't want that. You're all expendable. If I choose, you can go at any time."

18

CURSE YOUR SUDDEN BUT INEVITABLE CANCELLATION

On paper, the fall of 2002 was to be a banner television season for Joss Whedon. With *Buffy* on UPN, *Angel* on the WB, and *Firefly* starting up on Fox, he would have three series on as many networks. And his success wasn't limited to TV. On Tuesday, September 24, the same day as *Buffy*'s seventh season premiere, Joss Whedon released a CD.

The *Once More, with Feeling* soundtrack album, from the independent music label Rounder Records, included all fourteen original songs from the *Buffy* musical. Although Joss had closely overseen every creative element of the musical, he left the marketing in the hands of new Mutant Enemy head Chris Buchanan. "My marching orders [from Joss] when I got to the company, literally the first day, were 'I want to be able to go to Tower Records and have the original cast recording CD there,'" Buchanan says. When he started to ask about the musical rights, Joss reiterated that he was just concerned with Tower Records stocking the CD. The rest was up to Buchanan. "That was great; I think that made for a good partnership, because that's what I took care of.

"Think about it—that's from somebody who's an incredible micromanager on the creative side. On the business side, he wasn't at all, because he didn't care about that. That gives me a tremendous amount of flexibility in accomplishing the goal, and it was a really hard process to do it, but I remember being able to say, 'Hey, dude. Go to Tower Records. Your CD is on the shelf and it's really good.'" *Once More, with Feeling* would sell 150,000 copies in the United States by December 2004—an impressive number for a soundtrack from a "cult" show. In the United Kingdom, *Buffy* merchandise had already been selling particularly well, as DVD and VHS box sets were the only (legal) way for British fans to watch the series without dealing with the erratic scheduling and censorship of local broadcasters, but even so, everyone was surprised at how well the album sold internationally, especially in the United Kingdom and Germany.

"Once More, with Feeling" would go on to another life off the small screen. Taking a cue from *The Rocky Horror Picture Show*, fans began staging public screenings of the musical, where they could dress up like their favorite characters, sing along to the musical numbers, and shout out sardonic commentary. By 2007, it would become such an event that Marti Noxon and Joss attended a sing-along at the Los Angeles Film Festival. However, in October of that year, after 20th Century Fox received a bill from the Screen Actors Guild for unpaid residuals from the screenings, the studio pulled the licensing, putting an end to the events. Joss called the move "hugely depressing" and promised to do anything in his power to convince the studio to reconsider. "Of course," he added, "the words 'my power' might confuse my gentle readers into believing I have any."

//////////

In lamenting his powerlessness, Joss was perhaps recalling an earlier conflict with Fox's broadcast arm, which led to the swift unraveling of one of his three TV projects for 2002. Joss's struggles to keep *Firefly* flying are legendary among Whedon fans, and they all came down to one central problem: the Fox network didn't get the series that it was expecting—a pithy *Buffy*-esque action series set in space—and didn't know what to do with the series it actually got.

The first warning signs came in May, when the network was putting together its 2002–03 schedule for its "upfront" presentation, the annual meeting at which a network previews its fall schedule for advertisers. Fox was about to lose two of its flagship series, *Ally McBeal* and *The X-Files*, and it had two sci-fi shows on tap to fill the void left by the latter. A few days before the upfront, there was talk that the other series, the James Cameron–produced *Dark Angel*, would be renewed for a third season and placed on the fall schedule, while newcomer *Firefly* would be held until 2003 as a midseason replacement. But by the time of the Fox upfront on May 16, Joss's series had been added to the fall roster and *Dark Angel* had been canceled.

With the good news came some more bad news. Gail Berman had scheduled *Firefly* in what is often referred to as the "Friday-night death slot." Series often have a hard time attracting an audience in a Friday time slot, most likely because that's when the coveted demographic of viewers ages eighteen to thirty-four are going out to start their weekend. Ominously, it's the very slot into which *Dark Angel* was moved prior to its cancellation.

What's more, before it could even premiere, *Firefly* needed a new first episode. Berman did not like what Joss had delivered in his two-hour pilot, "Serenity." Fox executives outlined a list of reasons why they felt that it didn't work, including that it was too dark and not filled with enough action to keep a younger audience engaged. Their complaints frustrated Joss, who had made the show he wanted to make—a story about people living on the edge and the small moments that make their lives meaningful. For him, the most important scene in the whole pilot was the one in which Kaylee is alone eating a fresh strawberry, a rare treat for those always on the move in a spaceship. "That's what we do in our homes—we're creating our lives, our ethics," Joss said. "Whether or not we have a template or someone gives us money, everything we create, we do ourselves." *Firefly*, he added, "is about these quiet moments in between the gun battles."

Still, Joss did reshoots to address every one of the network's doubts as best he could. To grab young viewers with action, he shot an opening war scene. To make sure the main character didn't come across as too grim, he put in scenes in which Mal displayed a sense of humor. Fox remained unsatisfied. The network asked him to produce another episode with which to introduce the series—one that was less "*Stagecoach* in space" and more like an action-oriented futuristic spin on Sam Peckinpah's violent 1969 western *The Wild Bunch*.

Joss and Tim Minear had two days to write a new premiere script. It needed to do all the heavy lifting of introducing the characters and setting up their situation that had already been done in the pilot, while also presenting a new, more action-packed story. They scrambled and produced "The Train Job"—which, compared to the original pilot, does provide a smoother welcome for those coming to the series through their love for *Buffy* and *Angel*. The episode immediately sets up Mal's tendency to walk willingly into a fight when he could avoid it, Zoe's unwavering support for her captain even when she knows he's being stupid, and the fact that our heroes will take as many hits as they dish out. By the end, it's clear that while this crew of smugglers is not happy getting by with very little, its members will risk crossing a sociopath and losing out on a bounty in order to return needed medicine to those stuck in a situation far worse than their own.

The concessions the writers made in their "Train Job" script were early examples of the constant tug-of-war about the "darkness" of the show. Joss didn't want everyone drawing their guns in every episode, and he certainly didn't want Mal to be killing people indiscriminately. But he got notes that Mal needed to kill more people. "This is something that was problematic," Joss says. "[Fox's] insistence that it be less dark made it, on some level, more offensive. I wanted Mal to have to make really horrible decisions that were tough and that he would have to live with." Fox instead said that they would like for Mal to shoot a guy and make a joke. So at the end of "The Train Job," Joss had the captain kick a guy into the ship's engine. As Joss puts it, "It's hilarious! I just compromised my morality. Woo-hoo!"

He adds, "They tried to strangle it when it was in the womb. You forget, [creating a television show] is like childbirth. 'Sure, I'll squeeze another one of those things out! It doesn't hurt, right?' Well, of course, it does. None of them have been easy."

In truth, *Firefly* was much darker in Joss's imagination than it would end up being on screen. One of his first pitches, which he gave to Minear as he wooed him away from *Angel* to be *Firefly*'s executive producer, would never see the light of day. Joss explained that as a Companion, Inara has a special syringe. She injects herself before meeting a client, so that if she is raped, the rapist will die a horrible death. In this story, Inara is kidnapped by the savage Reavers. When Mal finally reaches the Reavers' ship to save her, he finds them all dead. At the end of the episode, after she's been horribly brutalized, Mal gets down on his knee and takes Inara's hand, treating her with the respect of an esteemed lady (which he was usually reluctant to give her) as he takes her home to *Serenity*.

"It was very dark," Minear remembered. "[Joss] said, 'These are the kind of stories we're going to tell.' " But as they had learned with *Angel*, they couldn't start the series out with such grim and gritty tales without earning it.

//////////

Firefly's troubles didn't end when the series finally made it to air. Episodes almost immediately began to be preempted by Fox's coverage of the Major League Baseball playoffs. Then Fox started airing the episodes out of order, disrupting the character and story arcs that Joss and Minear had carefully planned out. But one of the biggest ways Fox mishandled the series was how it chose to market the show.

Instead of advertising *Firefly* as a space western or a gritty sci-fi show, the promotional campaign suggested that it was a wacky genre comedy—"the most twisted new show on television." Several promos strung together jokes about a "flighty pilot" (Wash), a "space cowboy" (Mal), a "cosmic hooker" (Inara), and a "girl in a box" (River, referencing a plot point from the pilot episode the network refused to air), tied together with the tagline "Out there? Oh, it's out there!" Another reduced the show's complex premise to a tired cliché about a "band of renegades" for whom "the only thing that mattered was profit until they discovered something worth fighting for." Much like the directors whom Joss had resented for mishandling his feature film scripts, Fox marketing was twisting Joss's vision to fit their own, promoting *Firefly* as the Kuzuis' campy version of *Buffy the Vampire Slayer* if it were inhabited by the poorly realized mercenaries from Jean-Pierre Jeunet's *Alien: Resurrection*.

"We knew we were in real trouble before the show debuted," Chris Buchanan says. Fox sent them a promo reel of the spots they'd cut for the show, and the first opened with Smashmouth's hit song "Walkin' on the Sun." They first thought that the promo was for *Fastlane*, Fox's highly stylized police action drama. "Then all of a sudden it was like '*Firefly*, the cosmic hooker and a whacked out space cowboy.'" Buchanan recalls, horrified. "My mouth just dropped open. When the marketing guy called back to ask what they thought, I said, 'Well, it's really great, but that's not what our show is.' I don't remember exactly what he said to me, but it was along the lines of 'Our job is just to get people to watch it, and then they'll figure out what it is, and they'll stay.'" Buchanan replied, "So you're selling them this goofy comedy thing, and then they're gonna get *Firefly*."

Sure, there's funny in *Firefly*, but it's not a wacky space comedy. (Just as *Buffy* wasn't a wacky horror comedy either; in its attempt to appeal to *Buffy* viewers, Fox had misunderstood that show as well.) While Joss's fans were excited and ready to turn out for the premiere, the promos were so off base that anyone else who might have been interested in what the show actually had to offer was turned off, while those who liked the show that Fox was promoting would be greatly disappointed by the real thing.

//////////

At times, Joss's new show seemed to be considered the bastard stepchild even within Mutant Enemy. While his other two productions were successful, long-running series, *Firefly* was the little show that couldn't. And yet "we got the best people from those other two shows," Nathan Fillion recalls—something the people on those shows didn't always appreciate. "They're looking at us going, 'What's happening? What's *Firefly* got that we don't got? You're taking our best guy? C'mon!'"

As the other Mutant Enemy casts may have suspected, *Firefly* had quickly found a special place in Joss's heart. He was passionate about the universe he'd created and—even though he'd impressed upon the actors that they were all replaceable—about the cast he'd assembled. "I never worked with an ensemble that meshed like that," he recalled. He'd never felt so sure right from the pilot how a show was going to work. "It was Camelot. It was the best experience of my career."

His actors were just as enamored with the experience. "I've always pulled at least one friend out of everything I've done. With *Firefly*, I think I pulled about thirty-five friends out of that thing," Fillion says. "Not just cast, but writers and producers and crew. People I still call and people I still chat with. People I still hang out with," Fillion says. "Joss did this great job of saying, 'You're going to be great at interpreting these words and you're going to be great to have around.' I made so many good friends. That was ten years ago and I'm still close to these people. I still love these people."

The feelings of cast and crew are perfectly embodied in the episode "Out of Gas," which aired on Fox on October 25, 2002. It was a "bottle episode," filmed entirely on existing sets to spare the show the time and expense of location shoots. The plot is simple: *Serenity* has stalled in space and is running out of oxygen thanks to a broken part, compelling the crew to abandon ship. As the captain, Mal stays behind to meet another group of smugglers, purchase a new part, and make the repair. Wash sets a red recall button on the ship's helm, instructing Mal to press it when it is safe for the crew to return. Unfortunately, Mal gets shot and almost bleeds out before he can hit the button. His crewmates return anyway, coming back home to their captain.

Joss's mother, Lee Jeffries, receives her diploma from Radcliffe in 1957.
Courtesy of the Schlesinger Library, Radcliffe Institute, Harvard University.

Joss with his family. Back row, from left to right: brother Matthew, stepmother Pam, brother Sam, father Tom. Front row, from left to right: cousins Deke and Tucker, Joss, brother Jed.
Courtesy of Jed Whedon and Maurissa Tancharoen Whedon.

Photos from H. Bramston's boarding house at Winchester College. In both the 1981 photo (left) and the 1982 photo (right), Joss is at the center of the front standing row. *Courtesy of Winchester College.*

Eclectic

With the Eclectic Society at Wesleyan in 1985. Joss is seated at center, on the couch arms. *Courtesy of Wesleyan University Library, Special Collections & Archives.*

Sarah Michelle Gellar as Buffy the Vampire Slayer, the heroine who made Joss's artistic dreams come true. *Photofest, © WB.*

Joss and the cast of *Buffy* at the 1999 Posting Board Party. Above left, from left to right: David Boreanaz, Seth Green, Anthony Stewart Head, Eliza Dushku, Joss. *Courtesy of Brad Zweerink.*

Angel's one hundredth episode celebration, December 4, 2003. From left to right: Charisma Carpenter, James Marsters, Amy Acker, Alexis Denisof, Joss, David Boreanaz, Andy Hallett, J. August Richards. *Justin Lubin/WB/Photofest, © WB.*

Joss with some of the cast and crew of *Firefly* on the show's tenth anniversary, at San Diego Comic-Con 2012. Above, from left to right: Alan Tudyk, Tim Minear, Sean Maher, Summer Glau, Joss, Nathan Fillion, Adam Baldwin, writer Jose Molina. *Chuck Cook Photography.* Right: Nathan Fillion and Morena Baccarin with Joss on the set of *Serenity* in 2005. *Universal Studios/The Kobal Collection.*

Joss presents his Wesleyan professor Jeanine Basinger with
an honorary degree from the AFI in 2006. *AFI Conservatory*
Commencement photograph courtesy of American Film Institute © 2006.

Joss with *Dollhouse* cast members Eliza Dushku, Fran Kranz,
Dichen Lachman, and Miracle Laurie at PaleyFest 2009.
James Riley/GeekShot Photography.

Mutant Enemy Day
at the WGA strike,
December 2007.
Ivana Olson.

Joss with some of the folks who helped make *Dr. Horrible's Sing-Along Blog*
at PaleyFest 2009. From left to right: Joss, Nathan Fillion, Felicia Day, Zack
Whedon, Jed Whedon, Maurissa Tancharoen. *James Riley/GeekShot Photography.*

The official introduction of the *Avengers* cast at San Diego Comic-Con 2010. From left to right: Chris Evans, Samuel L. Jackson, Jeremy Renner, Mark Ruffalo, Joss, Kevin Feige. *James Riley/ GeekShot Photography.*

Joss talks to Scarlett Johansson on the set of *The Avengers*. *Marvel Enterprises/ The Kobal Collection.*

At a Can't Stop the Serenity screening in June 2011. From left to right: Felicia Day, Tim Minear, Jane Espenson, actress Heather Fagan, Kai Cole, Joss, *Firefly* guest star Michael Fairman, Nathan Fillion, and Jessica Neuwirth and Amanda Sullivan of Equality Now. *James Riley/GeekShot Photography.*

Kai in the Whedons' garden amphitheater. *Los Angeles Times Staff. Copyright © 2013 Los Angeles Times. Reprinted with permission.*

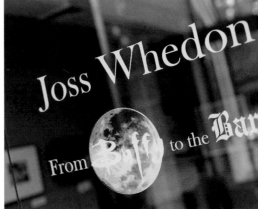

Left, the writers behind *Agents of S.H.I.E.L.D.* Joss, in back; in front, from left to right: Jeph Loeb, Maurissa Tancharoen, Jed Whedon, Jeff Bell. *Courtesy of Jed Whedon and Maurissa Tancharoen Whedon.*

Above, the 2013 exhibit at Wesleyan University in honor of Joss Whedon. *Courtesy of Olivia Drake / Wesleyan University.*

Written by Tim Minear, "Out of Gas" is *Firefly*'s origin tale, with flashbacks that explain how each person came to be part of the *Serenity* crew. The last image of the episode is the moment when Mal sees *Serenity* for the first time. That moment is shot with all the love-struck anticipation of "seeing this beautiful woman across a crowded room," Minear said. "That was Joss and us saying, 'We fell in love with this thing too.' There was already a sense that it was slipping away from us at that point. And the sense of that is in that episode."

///////////

In November 2002, Fox buoyed hope for the series by ordering two more scripts into production. Four days later, the network preempted the show yet again, this time for an Adam Sandler movie. It was clear that the series was in a precarious position. Its creators reached out to their online fans for help.

If you watch just about any show on television today, you'll see an ad with a Twitter hashtag encouraging fans to discuss the episode they just watched online. It's strange to think that just a decade ago, Mutant Enemy's Chris Buchanan had to struggle with Fox's marketing department to shore up *Firefly*'s online presence. "I went to Fox very early on in the process and said, 'What's going on with the Internet? We need to get the site up—it's got to be multimedia, and we need a lot of video.'" Fox felt that he was jumping too far ahead too quickly, considering the series hadn't even premiered yet, but Buchanan pushed back, asking why they would wait.

"*USA Today* did an article about Internet and television, like how influential the Internet was for TV," he remembers. "I was quoted saying something like, 'I actually think that the Internet communities are going to be able to make or break a show.' They kind of hung me out there like the optimist of 'This Internet thing's gonna work.' Fox, to their credit, said, 'OK, if you want to. Yeah, great, knock yourself out. Go and get this thing rolling.' They let us put a lot of video and stuff up before the show aired, which was not done at the time."

The official message board was poorly designed and wasn't terribly user-friendly, but it quickly became a central location for people to express their love for the series, pore over the episodes, and discuss the characters. Another common topic: the ratings. In recent years, television viewers had become savvier, checking the Nielsen ratings after each airing to see how their favorite shows were faring. For *Firefly*, it wasn't looking good.

Another place to follow all things *Firefly* was the new fan site Whedonesque.com, a sort of clearinghouse where people could share news and updates about anything Joss Whedon–related. Caroline van Oosten de Boer and Milo Vermeulen had launched the site in June, and it quickly became a source of breaking Joss news, CNN style. The simple text site linked to articles and videos about Joss's projects new and old, as well as projects from other Whedonverse writers, actors, and crew. Once someone was in a Mutant Enemy project, he or she was brought into the fold and soon learned that acceptance came with a passionate and supportive fan base. "Without Whedonesque, Joss wouldn't even know what was going on in his own life," Kai says. "He goes there to find out what's going on with his friends. Whedonesque is like his Day-Timer [appointment book]." For *Firefly* fans, Whedonesque was the place to read everything from cast interviews to ratings breakdowns to the latest on the fan movement to "save" the show.

By November, several cast members were posting messages directly to fans on the official *Firefly* site, while Kai reached out to the webmaster at another fan site, JossWhedon.net, asking for help in getting the word out about the show. Soon after, a fan-led campaign called "Firefly: Immediate Assistance" mobilized, and an army of fans calling themselves Browncoats after the show's rebel resistance organized to plead for *Firefly*'s continuation. They sent postcards to news outlets asking journalists to cover *Firefly* in their columns, raised funds for the placement of a full-page ad in *Variety*, and organized viewing parties throughout the United States. Mutant Enemy kept in touch with the fan organizers and even provided the hosts of viewing parties with publicity photos and a copy of Nathan Fillion's recipe for seven-layer bean dip.

On December 9, the *Variety* ad ran, featuring the headline You Keep Flying, We'll Keep Watching. Joss posted his thanks on the fan site Buffistas.org:

> I'm only posty for a moment to say . . . (starts to cry . . .) I promised myself I wouldn't cry . . . That Variety ad . . . I have the coolest fans ever. So classy, so passionate (the ad AND the fans), I must be doing something right. Or paying Tim to do something right.

Unfortunately, despite the passion of the series' creators and fans, the campaign hadn't convinced many other viewers to tune in to Fox on Friday night. By mid-December 2002, *Firefly* was averaging 4.7 million viewers per episode—more than even the highest-rated episodes of *Buffy* and *Angel* but a dud by Fox standards at the time; the series was expected to pull in almost triple that amount. With three of its fourteen episodes still unaired and two of them still in production, *Firefly* was canceled.

//////////

The official news of the cancellation came on Thursday, December 12, 2002, while they were filming the episode "The Message." In it, a former soldier (Jonathan Woodward) who served with Mal and Zoe in the war with the Alliance has his corpse sent to them with the request that they bring him home. The taped message that he includes with his body recalls an oft-quoted mantra of their unit but breaks off early: "When you can't run anymore, you crawl, and when you can't do that . . ." Mal and Zoe silently acknowledge the missing ending to the line and, always loyal to their men, decide to honor his request.

"We were on the bridge shooting," Tim Minear says, "and Joss showed up on the set and he pulled me aside and he's like, 'They just canceled the show.'" Joss then asked if he should announce it while everyone was gathered or wait until shooting was done. Minear said to tell them immediately and they'd all wrap for the day.

"I've never seen him so mad," Adam Baldwin recalls. "He looked at me and said, 'I don't have good news. They pulled the plug and this is the last episode. And I wanted you all to know immediately.'" After Joss informed his cast and crew, nobody felt like working, so they all went to Fillion's house to get drunk and drown their broken hearts.

"It was right before we were going to break for hiatus and go home to our families for the holidays," Jewel Staite recalls. "We all had a good feeling that we were the underdog that year, but it always felt like our impending cancellation was just looming over our heads, and I think we were all waiting for some sort of shoe to drop. It was still devastating, though. Kind of like when you jump off a diving board, and instead of going headfirst in the pool, you twist your body the wrong way and hit the water with your belly instead. It felt like that."

But they still had to finish production on the remaining episodes. The next day everybody was hung over, and the first thing they had to shoot was a scene in which Mal, Zoe, and Inara sit around the dining room table laughing hysterically as Mal tells funny war stories about their comrade. "We've just been canceled and they have to pretend like they're having a laugh," Minear remembers. Ultimately, Joss and his cast and crew decided that joking around was exactly what the situation called for. They were going to have the best time they possibly could have, and then it would be over. "We would screw things up, you know—like, not get something right—and the joke was always 'What are they gonna do, cancel us?'" says Morena Baccarin.

Baccarin also recalls how during the later days of filming, Joss helped her reach a deeper emotional truth and find an emotional release. In "Heart of Gold," Inara tells Mal that she will be leaving *Serenity*. "I understood how that scene was really sad, and I did it a few different ways. Joss said, 'That's really, really good and we have those takes, but now try one where you have to put on your best face and you have to pretend that you don't give a shit that you're leaving, because if you show him that you care, he's going to convince you to stay.' That brought a whole other layer to that scene—it made me sadder, it made me have to fight harder against showing that, which in turn made me cry," she says. "You know, it was like the oldest trick in the book, you know—don't cry, and you cry. But it was such a great piece of advice."

On the last day of shooting, the cast and crew had to finish scenes for both "The Message" and "Heart of Gold." When filming an episode of a TV series, on the last day of a guest star's shoot, the assistant director will announce that it's "a wrap" for the guest star. Everyone will clap, and the guest star will thank everyone and go home. Ordinarily, the regular cast members don't get such a send-off, since they'll be back the next week. But on this day, there was nothing to come back to. So every time an actor shot his or her last scene, the assistant director declared, "That's a *Firefly* wrap" for him or her. The rest of the cast and crew applauded, the actor gave a sad speech, and then it was onto the next scene. But no one left when they were done. They all waited for the others to be finished, because, like on *Serenity*, the cast and crew of *Firefly* had become a family.

At the end of the day, Tim Minear headed home, emotionally exhausted. "It's Friday. The show is finished. They are now tearing down the spaceship," he recollects. "I get home, turn on the TV, and what's on TV? The pilot. They're finally airing 'Serenity.'"

//////////

The spaceship was being torn down, but bonds of its crew were stronger than ever. Many cast members talked about the fact that not only was Mal the captain of *Serenity*, but Nathan Fillion was also like the captain of the cast. They called out his wonderful disposition and how well he worked with everyone, and said that they looked to him as a leader behind the scenes as much as on camera.

"God bless them for that," Fillion demurs. "I don't know how much responsibility I can take for that; I don't know how much credit I can take for that. I was grateful to be there—not only to have a job, I had to tell the story I was telling. I was thankful for each and every one of them. I was surrounded by talented, wonderful people. What could you be except happy?

"They've said these things about me being a leader. I say, they carried me. I didn't have to do the work to be a captain, because when I walked around, they treated me like the captain. I was on a spaceship, dressed like a space cowboy walking around. Everybody had their own attitude toward me and authority itself. I didn't have to do any work. I just had to listen, I just had to watch them. I just had to be there. It's funny how our perspectives are different. I didn't feel like the leader. That's actually another thing that my adventures with Joss Whedon have taught me: pick the right coattails to ride. There are some amazing, incredibly talented people who are kind and generous. Grab 'em! Grab 'em."

The *Firefly* cancellation hit Joss hard. "I promised these [actors] that if this was good it would go," he later said. He kept telling the cast that it wasn't over, that he would take the show somewhere else. "I went crazy; I would not accept cancellation," he said. He had a production deal with Fox and got together with Minear, agent Chris Harbert, and his lawyer in hopes of finding a way to continue the story. "Joss was so dedicated to the show," Adam Baldwin recalls, "and so heartbroken, as we all were, that when it went down he was going to try to keep some of the sets, and put them up in a warehouse and keep filming on his own. That just wasn't in the cards. But he kept fighting." The cast was sad that Joss seemed to be in so much denial. "I love him," Baccarin says, "but I was like, 'This show is gone. Nobody wants it. It's dead.'"

As his series ended, another story in Joss's life was just starting. Five days after Fox announced that the show had been canceled and two days before it finally aired the pilot, Kai gave birth to their son, Arden, on December 18, 2002.

Though it was a new beginning for Joss, it was perhaps not quite an ending for *Firefly*. After the series was canceled, actor Alan Tudyk took an item from the set: the recall button from the episode "Out of Gas." In the spirit of the crew and their love for their captain, he sent it to Joss, with the instruction to hit the button when his miracle finally arrived.

END OF (*BUFFY'S*) DAYS

In a November 2002 interview, Joss described the differences among the sets of his three shows: "Every set has its own sort of tenor. The thing about *Firefly* is . . . that this whole cast . . . they're extremely kind and professional, and they get along, and they help each other, and they work hard. I'm not saying my other casts don't work hard. And some of them get along, and it's great. But there's a star, and then there's the ensemble. And there's tensions on the set. . . . It's not one big happy family. It seldom is on a television set. [In *Firefly*,] I've got nine people, all of whom are great in a scene . . . all of them doing their best to help each other out. It's early on still. But they really feel like an ensemble [more] than any bunch I've worked with." Today, Joss's comments—which even with his vague attempt at being diplomatic imply significant tensions on the sets of *Buffy* and *Angel*—would have spread like wildfire through social media and become gossip fodder among fans and industry insiders alike. But at the time, they were barely noticed. Perhaps that's why the talk of canceling *Buffy* came as a shock to many.

The series was in the middle of its seventh season, the end of which would mark the expiration of both UPN's and Sarah Michelle Gellar's contractual obligation to the series. While *Buffy*'s ratings were down to roughly 3.8 million viewers per episode from the 4.6 million of the previous year, UPN execs were still very interested in renewing the series, because it still did well in the key demographic of eighteen-to-thirty-four-year-olds. However, it seemed unlikely that the story would continue without its lead, and Gellar appeared ready to move on. Joss and UPN discussed several options, including continuing with Gellar in a recurring role and spinning off an entirely new series without her.

In February 2003, Gellar narrowed their options when she told Joss that she would not be returning to her defining role. It was a decision many months in the making, starting with a conversation she'd had with Joss at the beginning of the season. "We both kind of felt that this was the end, that we should make that decision and say it publicly. And then . . . we didn't. We didn't even talk about it for a while," she said. Perhaps Joss didn't want to talk about it because he was consumed with the pressure of overseeing three television series each week and he chose to delay the inevitable. But he could put it off no longer.

On February 25, 2003, *Variety* announced that Gellar would not return for an eighth season. Three days later, *Entertainment Weekly* published an interview in which she explained why she thought it was the right time to bow out of her defining role. After the darkness of season six and the criticism that followed it, Gellar said, she and Joss felt that the series was back on its game in season seven. "A lot of people were ready to tear us down [in season six. So when] we started to have such a strong year this year, I thought, 'This is how I want to go out—on top, at our best,'" she said. "It feels right, and you have to listen to that. The show, as we know it, is over."

The public impression that *Buffy*'s end was a mutually supported decision, however, started to fray a month before the finale was set to air, when Gellar's husband, Freddie Prinze Jr., told the press that the reason she walked away was because she hadn't been thanked enough for her contributions. "A lot of people owe Sarah a lot for doing that show and she doesn't always get the credit she deserves," he griped. "She's a very strong woman, because she deals with a lot of nonsense, and instead of that nonsense, she should be thanked—and she's not. . . . If that environment would have remained the way it [was] six years ago, she would go back, because she's loyal. But things change, and people's egos get in the way sometimes. They make poor decisions."

Joss later blew off Prinze's comments, saying that he had never seen Prinze on set, so he didn't know what he could be referring to. He did acknowledge a little more publicly this time that there were tensions on the set: "Not everybody was best of friends, and in fact we did not link arms and sing 'La Marseilles.' But we made the show as well as we could for seven years, and you know, everybody made it together."

Tensions weren't helped when Alyson Hannigan claimed that she'd learned of the cancellation from Sarah's interview. This exasperated Joss, who later said, "There was a whole thing about it being in *Entertainment Weekly* and the crew wasn't informed and everybody was unhappy, and I was just like, 'There was somebody who didn't know?' Some of the actors were upset and I said, 'You guys I've talked to specifically about this.' The crew I actually went and apologized to. I said, 'I don't know how this isn't already public knowledge and I apologize if you guys felt the carpet pulled out from under you.' But I kicked the actors off set before I did it because they knew."

///////////

It was the end of an era, and while it was difficult for fans to hear, it shouldn't have come as a huge surprise. From its first episode, season seven seemed to be taking the series full circle. The show with the initial driving premise of "high school is hell" brings Buffy back to a rebuilt Sunnydale High as a counselor. While prior seasons drove the characters apart, this one focuses on reunification and redemption: after trying to end the world, Willow returns from an enforced sabbatical with Giles in England, anxious to reunite with her friends and keep her powers under control, while a newly ensouled Spike holes up in the school's basement, tormented by guilt for all his evil and murderous actions.

The Big Bad of the season is the First Evil, originally introduced as Angel's tormentor in the third-season Christmas episode, "Amends." The First is a living embodiment of evil, incorporeal but omnipresent, which has existed since the dawn of time and plans to be the only thing standing after the world ends. It usually takes the appearance of dead people, allowing the series to revisit departed friends and foes such as Joyce, Warren, and Mayor Wilkins, but it also takes the form of Buffy herself. It has realized that Buffy's death and resurrection caused a glitch in the Slayer line, allowing it to find all of the Potentials, the girls all over the world who have a chance of being called as the next Slayer when the previous one dies. It sends its agents—eventually including a misogynistic preacher named Caleb (*Firefly*'s Nathan Fillion)—to kill each Potential.

The role of Caleb required Fillion to shift gears from swashbuckling hero to sinister serial killer, a change that pushed him out of his comfort zone. Previously, the actor had often lost out on villainous roles because people felt that he came across as "too nice." And perhaps there was some truth to that; Fillion credits Joss with finally teaching him the proper tenets of villainy. "Villains don't think they're evil. Villains don't believe they're the bad guy. Villains believe in what they're doing. Villains think they're righteous, and that's what makes them dangerous," Fillion explains. "There's a trap in wringing your hands together and going '*Mwahaha*'—that's not villainy. The villainy to be afraid of is the villainy you don't see coming. He's sweet, he's pleasant and polite. He sneaks up on you. And you don't know he's a villain until he's got a knife buried in you. Now that's a villain."

The stage was set for a definitive showdown, but exactly how would Joss bring a satisfying end to the series and character that had changed his life? Killing Buffy wouldn't work—he'd already done that a couple times. He realized that he could convey a new message through the Potential Slayers, girls who had yet to go through Buffy's journey of receiving power and then learning how to deal with it. Throughout the final season, the Scooby Gang tracks down the Potentials and gives them shelter in the Summers home. As the First's plan to wipe out the entire Slayer line comes to light, Buffy is joined by her fellow Vampire Slayer Faith, and together they train the girls in preparation for an epic final battle.

In readying her troops for the showdown, Buffy gives several speeches about how she's in charge because she knows better than all of them what's right and what needs to be done. They all need to fall in line, she says, and she'd sacrifice each one of them if she had to. ("Honestly, gentle viewers," another character remarks in one episode, "these motivating speeches of hers tend to get a little long.") One wonders how much Buffy's speechifying reflects Joss's own feelings about the conflicts behind the scenes of the series and his view of his role in the Mutant Enemy world. Joss later told the *New York Times* that "Buffy also became a little bit closed off from the other characters, in the same way that a star is kind of separated from an ensemble, so we dealt with the idea of the isolation of the Slayer, of the person who has to lead." This characterization is quite different from the Buffy of the first four seasons—the Slayer who was stronger because of her friends and the support system she had built together with them.

But the season finale, "Chosen," written and directed by Joss, returns the series to a more inclusive notion of empowerment. As a battle with the First Evil's minions rages in the newly opened Hellmouth, Willow performs a spell that grants *all* the Potentials the full powers of the Slayer, defying the "one Slayer in every generation" rule set forth millennia ago by the progenitors of the Watchers Council. As Buffy puts it:

> Here's the part where you make a choice. What if you could have that power, now? In every generation, one Slayer is born, because a bunch of men who died thousands of years ago made up that rule. They were powerful men. This woman [Willow] is more powerful than all of them combined. So I say we change the rule. I say my power should be *our* power. . . . From now on, every girl in the world who might be a Slayer will be a Slayer. Every girl who could have the power will have the power. Can stand up, will stand up. Slayers, every one of us. Make your choice. Are you ready to be strong?

It is definitely one of Buffy's better speeches, and the subsequent montage is a monumental one: girls around the world overcome with a new strength and sense of power. These girls will go on their own hero's journey, like Buffy herself.

The loveliest moment in the episode comes just before the final battle, as Buffy, Giles, Willow, and Xander stand in the halls of Sunnydale High School making small talk, with the unspoken understanding that none of them are certain to make it through alive. It mirrors the final scene in the two-hour series premiere, in which Buffy and her high school friends walk off, ignoring Giles's warnings of upcoming danger, leaving Giles to say in exasperation, "The Earth is doomed." Here Buffy, Xander, and Willow again ignore Giles as they head down the hallway and off to their separate battle stations. Giles, watching them go, confirms that "the Earth is definitely doomed."

//////////

Once "Chosen" aired on May 20, 2003, *Buffy* was finished. Possible spin-offs were discussed, including one starring Eliza Dushku as Faith, who would become a traveling do-gooder in the mold of *Kung Fu* or *The A-Team.* "It would have been Faith, probably on a motorcycle," Tim Minear explained, "crossing the Earth, trying to find her place in the world. I'm sure it would get an arc at some point, but the idea of her rooted somewhere seemed wrong to me." Dushku passed on the pitch, eager to move on from her character and onto a new Fox sci-fi series, *Tru Calling.* Another idea, a spin-off set in a Slayer school for the former

Potentials who were imbued with Slayer power in the *Buffy* finale, also failed to come to fruition.

For now, it was time for *Buffy* and its characters to rest—as it was for Joss. When asked what he would have done if he'd had one more year with the cast, he answered, "Honestly, if I had a strong answer for that question there probably would be another season. I think it's time they all went their separate ways. And so my answer is, I can't possibly think of anything, I'm simply too tired. That's the end, thanks very much."

Yet some time after Buffy aired its final episode, Joss was having lunch with Tim Minear and the subject turned to *Buffy*'s final two seasons on UPN. "I realized that there was a scene I had never written that I wished I had thought of at the time, which was simply Buffy expressing gratitude about power," Joss explains. "It was such a burden for her, and we were always turning the screws, and I realized that to complete the statement of the show, it would have been better to have a moment where she just said, 'It's awesome that I have this. It matters.'"

//////////

With the end of *Buffy* and *Firefly*'s cancellation, *Angel* was suddenly the last man standing in Joss's TV regiment. When the WB announced that the series would return for a fifth season, it turned out that Joss would be doing it with one fewer woman. Charisma Carpenter, who had played Cordelia Chase since *Buffy*'s first day, had become pregnant during season four, and her character was placed in a coma at the end of the season so that she could take time off to have her baby. Viewers expected that Cordy would wake up and return to the show when the new season began, but Joss confirmed to *TV Guide* that Carpenter had been removed from the cast list.

"We had taken that story . . . about as far as it could go," he said. "Some choices are ultimately kind of controversial about who stays and who goes and who we focus on. But obviously, we had to have her out of a bunch of episodes toward the end of the year because she was having a baby . . . so what we had [leading] up to it wasn't a dynamic I wanted to play out that much. . . . When you have an increasingly large ensemble week-by-week, and you come in in your [fifth] year kind of having to revamp the show and trim the budget and also think creatively, 'How am

I going to service all of these people?,' sometimes the people who have been around the longest, you've done the most with them."

Carpenter was shocked and hurt by the turn of events. In 2009, she elaborated on how she felt things had transpired: "My relationship with Joss became strained. We all go through our stuff. . . . I was going through my stuff and then I became pregnant, and I guess in his mind [Joss] had a different way of seeing the season go in the fourth season. . . . I think Joss was, honestly, mad at me—and I say that in a loving way. It's a very complicated dynamic working for somebody for so many years. As you've been on a show for eight years, you've got to live your life, and sometimes living your life gets in the way of what the creator's vision is for the future, and that becomes conflict," she said. "I found out in a really horrible way. . . . I never got a phone call from anybody. I actually got a phone call from somebody in the press."

Carpenter had also been unhappy with the way her final season had gone. David Greenwalt was the one responsible for bringing Cordelia onto the spin-off in the first place and had been protective of the character, so when he left at the end of season three, she no longer had a champion on the writing staff. Perhaps as a result, season four had seen her character make some very questionable decisions. As her pregnancy progressed, they locked Cordelia up in a love nest with Angel and Darla's teenage son, Connor (Vincent Kartheiser), who was born in season three but aged rapidly after being kidnapped and taken to a demon dimension. Season three had teased a romance between Cordelia and Angel, so the idea that she would then romance his son was more than a little creepy.

As for Kartheiser, the future *Mad Men* star later admitted that he wasn't a fan of Joss's work and felt miscast in the role of Angel's son. He did not like the direction the writers took with Connor, either. "The character lost its thrill about four episodes in. . . . I felt like I was doing the same scene over and over and over. Every week I'd show up and have a scene with Cordelia, then Angel would show up and I'd have some sort of conflict with him. There'd be a couple of fight scenes where I'd fight with them even though I didn't want to and then I would sulk and leave. That to me was every episode," he said. "Ultimately, they wrote him into a corner. . . . I think the majority of the fans really hated Connor and really hated me and getting me off the show was the highest priority. And I don't blame them."

If *Buffy*'s sixth season was the one in which fans felt the show most lost its way, many viewers felt the same way about the end of *Angel*'s fourth season. Angel's demon-fighting comrade Gunn (J. August Richards) makes the comment that he "spent most of this year trapped in what I can only describe as a turgid supernatural soap opera"—which is an apt description of the season. Cordelia is saddled with a number of soap opera tropes, from amnesia to the aforementioned love triangle to an unexplained pregnancy, to a sudden personality change that turns her evil. Several other characters are stuck in another love triangle, while Angel temporarily reverts to the evil Angelus, a version far less cunning and charismatic than his earlier *Buffy* incarnation. By the time Joss brought on *Firefly*'s Gina Torres as Jasmine, a goddess birthed by Cordelia who brings inner peace to all who gaze upon her, the season felt wrung out and ready for an end.

Whether it was because two of the people who had been steering the ship—David Greenwalt and Tim Minear—were gone or because Joss had been consumed with launching *Firefly* and ending *Buffy*, the *Angel* storylines seemed to have gone off the rails for a bit. But now Mutant Enemy was down to just one series, and both Joss and Minear returned to give *Angel* a reboot. Minear penned the fourth season finale, "Home," in which the team was offered leadership of the evil law firm of Wolfram & Hart. Season five would ask what would happen if the Big Bad they'd been fighting for the past four years suddenly agreed to do their bidding, and whether working within a corporation with immense resources and reach would be worth making a literal deal with the devil.

AN ASTONISHING RETURN TO HIS ROOTS

The summer after *Buffy* was canceled, Marvel Comics editor in chief Joe Quesada considered reaching out to Joss about writing for the company. It would be his second recruitment attempt; he'd first approached Joss nearly two years earlier, when he decided that one of his first projects as editor in chief should be to reinvent the X-Men universe.

The X-Men are a group of mutants with special powers in a world where "normal humans" fear and mistrust them. This conflict is often compared to the struggles of real-life minority groups in America, such as African Americans and the LGBT community. The property was created by writer Stan Lee and artist Jack Kirby in 1963, and Quesada thought it was very much in need of an update. So in late 2001, he decided to get in touch with Joss, whom he had never met but who was working with his friend Jeph Loeb on the *Buffy* animated series. Quesada cold-called Joss and basically said, "Hey, Mr. Whedon, you don't know of me, but I was wondering, how would you like to write an [X-Men] book?"

There was a pause, and Quesada felt that his pitch was not going well. Perhaps it gave Joss flashbacks to a previous entanglement with the property, when he served as a script doctor for Bryan Singer's 2000 *X-Men* film. He'd been asked to punch up the last fight sequence, but he felt that the story had bigger problems than just the ending and did a major overhaul of the script. To his chagrin, only two exchanges from his draft made it in the final film.

Joss finally gave Quesada his response: "Can I take a day or two to think about it?" Quesada was floored that Joss would even take the time to think about it. He told him to take a week.

Joss was surely tempted. This was his chance to produce official stories for the comics publisher that had so consumed him since he was young. But when Joss looked at his schedule—*Buffy* and *Angel* on the air and *Firefly* in the pipeline—he was forced to gracefully decline. Well-known writer Grant Morrison picked up the X-Men run instead, but Quesada realized that his instinct to draft Joss into the Marvel family had been a smart one.

Now, in 2003, Quesada was doing a signing at San Diego Comic-Con, when he learned that Grant Morrison had publicly announced that he was leaving his *New X-Men* series. Morrison hadn't discussed it with him previously, and as Quesada sat there disappointed, trying to put on a good face for the fans lined up to see him, he was consumed with what he would do next. He tried to remember if he had Joss's number, and wondered if Joss would consider writing for the X-Men again. "I wish Joss Whedon were here in San Diego. I'd pull him aside and talk to him," Quesada remembers thinking.

"I swear, I looked up and there in front of me on the line was Joss Whedon with his hand extended, saying, 'Hey, man, how are you doing?'" Quesada recalls. "I didn't see Joss walk up to the table, so I assume he just metamorphosed or transported there—whatever sort of Joss Whedon magic contraption that he has at home, as brilliant as he is." Quesada, shocked, put his arm around Joss and pulled him behind the booth. He explained his predicament and asked if Joss would want to write an X-Men series now. Joss again asked for time to think about it. "Then I went back to the table and started thinking, 'Gee, I wish Angelina Jolie were here at San Diego Con.' I looked up and she wasn't there." Apparently that's a special kind of Joss magic.

//////////

With *Buffy* and *Firefly* off his plate, Joss now had time on his hands. A couple days later, he let Quesada know that he was in. He'd get a new outlet for his storytelling skills, and Marvel would get a writer who might attract new readers to the franchise—whether it was people who were fans of Joss or those simply looking for a fresh voice who hadn't written for Marvel before. The initial plan was for Joss to write for one of two existing X-Men series, *Uncanny X-Men* or Morrison's *New X-Men*, but the more they got into the project, the more they realized how special

Joss's run was going to be. Ultimately, they decided to give him his own series, and so *Astonishing X-Men*, a title that had been used for limited runs in 1995 and 1999, was born again.

"What Joss is popular for and what people admire him for is his ability to take characters and breathe life into them, to make the characters feel like they're people that you and I know, and because of that, we get to care about them so much," says Mike Marts, the regular group editor for the X-Men series when Joss signed on. "Then he brings these characters that we've fallen in love with on these exciting journeys with huge ups and huge downs and twists that we never expect. He did that so well on *Angel* and *Buffy*, and then to apply that to the X-Men—that's great."

Marts was already a huge fan of *Buffy*, *Angel*, and *Firefly*. "I loved his writing. I loved the way that he ran his shows and, without a doubt, he was someone I would have loved to work with," he says. "But being realistic, I always thought it was an impossibility, just knowing that he was a Hollywood guy, that his schedule was extremely demanding and he was always working on new projects. So when it happened, it was really just like a dream come true."

Joss, in turn, was an X-Men fan who had been keeping up with Morrison's run on *New X-Men*. He didn't see a need to make dramatic alterations in the continuing storylines, and most of the characters he wanted to work with were already a part of *New X-Men*. In addition, Marvel asked if he could find the right storyline to bring back Peter Rasputin, a.k.a. Colossus, a Russian mutant with the power to turn himself into steel. The character had died in a 2001 storyline when he sacrificed himself to stop the spread of a deadly plague roaring through the mutant world. Joss also wanted to include Kitty Pryde, a young mutant who can phase through solid matter and often serves as the moral center of the X-Men, but she was starring at the time in a different ongoing series, *X-Treme X-Men*.

Joss has often discussed how much his creation and development of Buffy owed to Kitty. "If there's a bigger influence . . . I don't know what it was," he said. "She was an adolescent girl finding out she has great power and dealing with it." Unsurprisingly, now that he was in the Marvel fold, he had a specific story in mind for the character.

"We started talking not only about how we could revive Colossus, but also about how we could separate Kitty Pryde from *X-Treme X-Men*," Marts says. That series was being penned by renowned writer

Chris Claremont, who had started at Marvel in 1969 and wrote the *Uncanny X-Men* series from 1975 to 1991, the longest run of any writer. He cocreated a number of beloved X-Men characters, including Rogue, Emma Frost, and Gambit. Paul Levitz, who served as president and publisher of DC Comics, said that the complexity of Claremont's stories "played a pivotal role in assembling the audience that enabled American comics to move to more mature and sophisticated storytelling, and the graphic novel."

Joss was a huge fan of Claremont—and the feeling was mutual. Claremont agreed to relinquish the character of Kitty. "It was fun to see these guys admire each other's work and then to see the baton passed with Kitty Pryde," Marts says, "Chris wrapping up the storyline that he had with her in *X-Treme X-Men*, and then Joss moving on to doing something great with her in *Astonishing X-Men*."

John Cassaday, an artist known for his work on *Captain America*, *Hellboy*, and *Uncanny X-Men*, was assigned to *Astonishing X-Men*, and he and Joss developed a wonderful working relationship. Still, Marts was concerned about how clean Joss's scripts would be and how kindly he'd take to editing. When someone has written primarily in other mediums, it can be difficult to learn how to write for comics. But Marts needn't have worried about the man who had been reading comics for over thirty years, who had made all his writers study Scott McCloud's *Understanding Comics*, and who, perhaps most important, hated to rewrite so much that he would wait until he had the story exactly the way he wanted it in his head before putting it to paper.

"When Joss's scripts came in, they were so pristine," Marts says. "I would look for things to try to change, but I couldn't find them. He was so meticulous with his scripts that I don't think we ever had a second draft—unless Joss, somewhere along the way, decided that there was a better way to pull off a certain scene or a certain moment. The scripts came in and they were near perfect."

Nick Lowe, then–assistant editor under Marts, remembers a particularly frantic time when Cassaday was about a day away from finishing an issue and they desperately needed a script. The next day, he got a fax with handwritten pages—Joss's computer had crashed and he didn't have one to use, so he'd written the script out in longhand. "The craziest thing was that while the handwriting wasn't the neatest, it was *really* clean," he says. "So he either did a whole handwritten draft or he just had it all in his head exactly how he wanted. There were only a handful of things scratched out on that whole thing. It was nuts."

/////////

From December 2003 to February 2004, Joe Quesada teasingly denied the "rumors" that Joss was taking over the X-Men series. Then, on February 18, Marvel announced that Joss and Cassaday would launch the new *Astonishing X-Men*, to the great excitement of Whedonverse fans.

Joss's first *Astonishing X-Men* arc, "Gifted," introduced the idea of a "mutant cure." It explored a very simple but very profound premise: "What if somebody had a cure for your being different? Would you take it?" The premiere issue hit the street on May 26, 2004.

Kitty Pryde was a core member of the X-Men team from the first issue, and shortly thereafter it was revealed that Colossus wasn't dead. Joss ensured that the storyline in which the beloved character was resurrected was emotionally driven and character-centric. Each issue still featured a lot of action, but Marts felt that the strength in Joss's run was how he handled the relationships between the characters. Readers immediately felt the love and affection Joss had for them. "More than the plots themselves," says Marts, "when people talk about *Astonishing X-Men* and his run on it, that's mostly what people remember—that it was a time where we fell in love with these characters again and we cared for them. We laughed and cried along with them.

"That's exactly what a publisher and editor is looking for: someone like Joss with a great creative vision to come in and to breathe new life into these characters that we all love and to do unexpected things with them and to take chances with them and to really bring the readers on this journey where hopefully we get some laughs and tears, some anger, some frustration—but in the end, this feeling that, wow, we accomplished this great journey together with these characters and we're so satisfied with the story."

Nick Lowe was impressed by how Joss was able to service preexisting character arcs and hit "fan buttons," while at the same time he injected a lot of new characters and new life into the X-Men's world. "Joss's run was a pitch-perfect mix of old and new that no one before him had accomplished," he says. "He played with the Kitty Pryde / Colossus relationship, messed with the Danger Room, continued the Cyclops / Emma

Frost relationship, but he and John Cassaday also created Breakworld and S.W.O.R.D., which are still big parts of the Marvel U. And Agent Brand, the head of S.W.O.R.D., is still one of my favorite characters in the Marvel U."

IGN.com called Joss's first run the "best X-Men title published in over a decade" and praised his ability to write believable team dynamics while letting each character shine in his or her own unique way. *Astonishing X-Men* won the prestigious Will Eisner Award, the "Oscars for the comics industry," for Best Continuing Series in 2006.

But his tenure was not without its criticism—mostly for its delays. Joss's contract with Marvel was to produce twelve issues in one year. But starting with issue #6, they started coming out every month and a half, pushing the final issues to September 2005 (issue #11 came out two weeks after #12). *Astonishing X-Men* started a new arc in February 2006, which was not as well received as "Gifted." Marts left Marvel for rival DC Comics in August 2008, while Joss and Cassaday continued on the project through issue #24, ending their run on January 23, 2008.

Joss had breezed into his *Astonishing X-Men* run with his own fan base built up over three television series, but with some wondering whether his interest and ability would translate to the pages of a comic book. When he left, he'd proven himself in yet another medium—and paved the way for future forays into the Marvel universe.

NOT FADE AWAY

By late 2003, a year after its cancellation, Joss was still fighting for *Firefly*. Although fan campaigns hadn't succeeded in getting the series renewed, the community sent a stronger message with their wallets, when the *Firefly* DVD set was released on December 3, 2003. Fox hadn't even been sure they were going to bring the series to DVD at all; prior to that point, few series had been released on home video if they hadn't at least lasted a full season. But the studio took a chance on the release, and as the numbers started coming in, it found that the fans were buying the DVDs in droves. They stepped up to support Joss and his *Firefly* team, jumping at the chance to finish the line from "The Message": "When you can't run, you crawl, and when you can't crawl—when you can't do that . . ." "You find someone to carry you." The Browncoats were carrying *Firefly* home.

The strong DVD sales demonstrated that there was a real commercial value to the property—something Mutant Enemy had been saying all along. It gave Joss an opening. He also had another card he could play: the head of Universal Pictures at the time, Mary Parent, wanted to be in business with Joss. "She would come in and offer him work on movies and ask him what he wanted to do," Chris Buchanan says. When she first approached him, Joss would tell her that he had three shows on the air and didn't have time to do anything. "To her credit," Buchanan continues, "when the show got canceled, which was a very dark moment for all of us and the next period of time was not good, Mary came to Joss and [asked what he wanted to do]." Joss told her that he wanted to do a *Firefly* feature film.

Joss also reached out to Barry Mendel, a producer who had worked with M. Night Shyamalan on *The Sixth Sense* and Wes Anderson on *Rushmore* and *The Royal Tenenbaums*. At the time he was producing Steven

Spielberg's *Munich* under a deal with Universal. Mendel let Parent know that he was on board for the *Firefly* movie. She in turn told Joss that if they could keep the budget within a certain range, and if Universal could secure the rights from Fox—which could prove tricky, since Fox would have to agree to let a property that it had spent tens of millions of dollars on go to another studio—then they could do the film.

//////////

As the chances for *Firefly*'s revival were unexpectedly rising, Joss's last remaining TV series met with an equally unanticipated reversal. On February 12, 2004, Joss was hanging out with one of the *Angel* actresses, Amy Acker, when he told her he'd be meeting with WB CEO Jordan Levin for dinner. She was concerned, asking if Levin was planning to cancel the show. Joss allayed her fears—after all, there'd been no long lead-up or public war of words as there was at *Buffy*'s end—and the two joked about it.

Joss called her a little later. "So, [Levin] canceled the show," he told her. "I don't really know what happened."

Things had shifted greatly in the *Angel* universe during its fifth and final season. Angel and his friends agreed to take over the Los Angeles branch of Wolfram & Hart, trading their lives as scrappy underdogs for the corridors of corporate power, their complicated serial entanglements for more episodic adventures. And since *Buffy* had finished its run on UPN, the WB wanted to bring a fan favorite back into the fold: James Marsters's Spike.

There was a bit of upheaval behind the scenes as well. Tim Minear chose not to return for season five, signing on instead as the showrunner of the new Fox series *Wonderfalls*. The day-to-day running of *Angel* fell to Jeffrey Bell, who had been promoted to co-executive producer the previous season after Minear moved to *Firefly*, and David Fury, who had split his time between *Buffy*'s last season and *Angel*'s fourth but now also moved up to co-executive producer on *Angel*. Although the two had more than six combined years writing and producing in the Buffyverse, they found that being on top didn't go as smoothly as they initially hoped.

"Unlike early *Buffy* seasons, or even seasons of *Angel* when there was a consistent hierarchy like with Greenwalt and Minear, we weren't really able to map out the season the way we really wanted to," Fury said. "Jeff

Bell and I pretty much mapped out a season where we could see how it would work and we were planning on doing that, but once Joss came into the mix [and] put his own mark in it, unfortunately, it blew a lot of our stuff out of the water." And "ultimately, a lot of the direction of the series went by Joss' whim—as it should, it's his show."

The writers also had to deal with a decreased budget from the WB—though their limitations forced them to push themselves creatively. One memorable episode was "Why We Fight," which flashed back to Angel's adventures aboard a sinking German U-boat during World War II. And for *Angel*'s one hundredth episode, they decided to do a big story to celebrate the milestone.

Bell and Fury reached out to Charisma Carpenter, asking her to return as Cordelia for the hundredth episode. Though she still harbored resentment over how she'd been let go from the series, she agreed, knowing that the fans, and Cordelia herself, needed closure. Carpenter just had one stipulation: if she came back, she didn't want them to kill off her character. Once she had their assurances that Cordelia would make it through the episode firmly on the mortal coil, she signed her contract. Then they told her that Joss planned to kill Cordy in the episode after all.

"I started bawling: 'I knew you guys would do this to me, why did I agree to do this?' . . . I felt totally betrayed," she recalled. "It's such a big part of my life and it was just so awful to think about her dying. And it was shocking and I was sad and I grieved, and then I'm like, 'I'm not doing this!'"

Fury asked for a chance to explain Joss's idea for the episode: Angel decides to quit his job running the evil law firm, because he feels that he's failed in fighting the powers of darkness from within, that he's just helping the evil get more evil. But before he can officially resign, he learns that Cordelia has miraculously awoken from her coma. After a joyous reunion, she explains that she's been brought back to keep him from going off-track. Battles ensue, as they always do, and Angel makes peace with his new position, knowing that he can succeed, especially with Cordy by his side. But it turns out that her return was one last favor from the higher powers of the universe, and she can't stay. "I'm just on a different road, and this is my off-ramp," she tells him. "We take what we get, champ, and we do our best with it." They share one final kiss, broken off when Angel needs to take a call. It's the hospital, reporting that Cordelia has died without ever waking from the coma. He looks back to find that she's gone.

Carpenter was still heartbroken that the writers had blindsided her with such deliberateness. But she was won over with the poignancy and levity of her exit. "I heard it and I was like, 'Ugh, that's good. Joss is good,'" she said. "That's the story. It sucked that I died but I really felt it was a hell of a way to go."

And it was. The episode, credited to David Fury, reflects the best of Joss's work—poignant and funny, drawing viewers even deeper into their emotional connection with the characters and leaving them with a deep yet glorious heartache. The final scene between Angel and Cordelia is a beautiful, bittersweet moment of closure for Carpenter and Cordelia, and for the fans who felt she was cheated out of a proper ending in the previous season.

//////////

When "You're Welcome" aired on February 4, 2004, the landmark episode was celebrated with much press fanfare. So it was a shock to many when the series was canceled just over a week later. Even *Variety* was confused: "Move on the surface is a head-scratcher: [*Angel*] is the net's second highest-rated hour among viewers 18-34 . . . and fourth among auds 12-34. Its numbers have been solid this year, even against brutal competish on Wednesday night." Ratings for the season averaged 3.97 million viewers, up from 3.65 million the year before, and there was much critical acclaim for the new direction of the series.

According to David Fury, Joss had actually gone to Levin to ask for an early pickup in light of the season's ratings spike and positive critical response. "Joss did not want his writers to lose out on job offers from other shows if ANGEL wasn't coming back. The prior year, some writers turned down offers, and could have ended up jobless if ANGEL was cancelled. . . . He didn't think it was fair to them to wait to know if they had a job for a sixth season."

But why did the WB cancel a show that may have aged but was aging well? Speculation abounded, zeroing in on the fact that the WB was developing a pilot based on the 1966–71 ABC series *Dark Shadows*. This reboot, a dark and stylized soap opera with vampires, werewolves, and a parallel universe, had been bought from John Wells (*ER*, *The West Wing*) and the original series' creator, Dan Curtis. Perhaps the WB wanted to avoid putting two vampire shows on the fall schedule—though it ended up being a pointless consideration, as the *Dark Shadows* pilot was not picked up. And the two dramas the WB *did* order for the 2004–05 season, *Jack & Bobby* and *The Mountain*, barely made it a full season, making *Angel*'s cancellation seem even more ill advised.

However, the WB was also looking to cut its budget and join the other networks in the reality show game. UPN had found success the summer before with Tyra Banks's kitschy and compelling competition series *America's Next Top Model*. The WB's offerings didn't catch on as strongly in the pop culture zeitgeist, but reality series are cheaper to make than genre shows that require special effects and monster makeup.

Levin had learned from predecessor Jamie Kellner's questionable decision to attack the other side when *Buffy* was in renewal negotiations between its fifth and sixth seasons—he was far more respectful as he explained his decision. "This isn't about the WB bailing out on one of its top shows," he said. "The show had a loyal core following, but it didn't have a tremendous amount of new audience upside." He noted that the series didn't do well in reruns, and while he knew that fans would be unhappy, the network was considering its schedule as a whole. "We have a lot of veteran shows that are aging, and we're going to have to make room for new programs."

The night the news came out, Joss took to BronzeBeta.com to share his feelings about the cancellation:

Yes, my heart is breaking.

When Buffy ended, I was tapped out and ready to send it off. When Firefly got the axe, I went into a state of denial so huge it may very well cause a movie. But Angel . . . we really were starting to feel like we were on top, hitting our stride—and then we strode right into the Pit of Snakes 'n' Lava. I'm so into these characters, these actors, the situations we're building . . . you wanna know how I feel? Watch the first act of "The Body." . . .

I've never made mainstream TV very well. I like surprises, and TV isn't about surprises, unless the surprise is who gets voted off of something. I've been lucky to sneak this strange, strange show over the airwaves for as long as I have. I don't FEEL lucky, but I understand that I am.

Thanks all for your support, your community, and your perfectly sane devotion. It's meant a lot. I regret nothing (except the string of grisly murders in the 80's—what was THAT all about?) Remember the words of the poet:

"Two roads diverged in a wood, and I took the road less traveled by and they CANCELLED MY FRIKKIN' SHOW. I totally shoulda took the road that had all those people on it. Damn."

It was a reminder of the special relationship between Mutant Enemy and its online fans that in a few short years would be gone. "I miss those days, to be honest with you," says writer Drew Goddard, who'd started as a fan of the show, joined the *Buffy* staff in season seven, and gone on to write for *Angel* in season five. "It still felt like this sort of weird clubhouse that only the people in the club knew about—and no one else cared about. We all had so much fun. I could post things on the Bronze and not worry about other people quoting those posts in the news. It was just sort of acknowledged, like, 'Oh, no. This is private. This is just for the people that are here.'

"Which doesn't happen anymore," he explains. "I see people posting on Twitter, and now they're quoted in news articles. I miss those places where it felt like it was just for us. I don't think those exist anymore."

//////////

"Smile Time," the first episode to air after *Angel*'s cancellation was announced, prompted a new outpouring of criticism that WB was axing such a clever and innovative series. In this episode, Angel gets turned into a puppet—an idea that arose from Joss's longtime desire to do an evil *Sesame Street* episode. He'd had Muppets and "Muppet people" in his life from the time that his father worked with the Children's Television Workshop, and he had some very intense convictions about them: "I thought Muppets were cool. Now, I'm not talking about the ones that had their own show, I'm talking the *Sesame Street* ones. I was one of the people that felt that Kermit was a sell-out when he started his own show. I was never really into it. Fozzie Bear is just a wannabe Grover," he said. "I always thought there should have been war between the East Coast and West Coast Muppets. . . . They were a serious part of what I remember from my youth. . . . Does my son have a Grover? Yes he does. Because Grover is the finest of all of them."

In "Smile Time," Angel investigates a popular children's TV show after learning that its puppet stars are stealing the life force of their young viewers. While poking around the studio, he inadvertently activates a spell that turns him into a puppet. The episode was written by Joss and Ben Edlund (*The Tick, Firefly, Supernatural*) and directed by Edlund. It is replete with slapstick puppet humor, fight scenes, and catchy songs.

"That was great, entertaining television that, like all good Joss Whedon things, has this great emotional core to it," Fury said. "As silly as it is, it's got this great little story about self-esteem in there." "Smile Time" was later nominated for a 2005 Hugo Award for Best Dramatic Presentation, Short Form.

///////////

Just over a month after learning that *Angel* would be no more, Joss got some of the best news of his life. Universal Pictures had managed to secure the necessary rights to a *Firefly* movie from 20th Century Fox. Fox did retain the rights to the title *Firefly*, however, so on March 3, 2004, the studio announced that it had greenlit *Serenity*, named for Mal's ship in the original series. Joss himself would direct. Considering he had no previous experience directing feature films, Universal demonstrated great faith in Joss by giving him the job of helming a multimillion-dollar action movie. It was a bounty of riches: Joss got to continue telling tales for a universe that he loved dearly, and as a director, he would have an autonomy not offered with his previous feature film scripts.

"I've been in Hollywood a long time, and it's a highly, highly, highly unusual story," Chris Buchanan notes. "The fact that *Serenity* ever got made is amazing."

The riches did not include a generous budget. At the time, many space adventures and fantasy films were budgeted for $100 million or more. Universal had followed that pattern and lost money in 2003 with its live-action version of *The Cat in the Hat*, which had recouped just over $133 million worldwide against its $160 million budget. Its adaptation of *Peter Pan* that same year fared a little better, bringing in over $121 million to cover its $100 million budget, but the studio's 2004 sci-fi flick *The Chronicles of Riddick* would be a big box office disappointment. With such a spotty track record with genre films, Universal found *Serenity* to be an attractive proposition—because Joss was sure that he could finish all of principal photography in less than two months and way under the budget Universal usually gave to such films. With a budget of less than $40 million and a shooting schedule of fifty days, production was set to begin in Los Angeles on June 3, 2004.

Jewel Staite was working on Tim Minear's *Wonderfalls* when she learned of *Firefly*'s return. "I was in the car on my way to the airport to shoot another episode. My phone rang, and it was Joss. He said, 'I just want to tell you that we've been greenlit for our very own movie.' I was totally shocked. I didn't dare hope that it would ever really happen. I think I was just stunned for the entire plane ride to Toronto."

Adam Baldwin had been skeptical that this day would ever come. "There had been rumors and rumblings about it, but until it's official, it's not official," he says. He had picked up a few guest-starring roles since *Firefly* ended, but he was looking for more work; he admits that "2003 was a tough year for me. I didn't land a pilot, and did a couple of small things. I pretty darn near close ran out of money. So when he finally did get the green light, I said 'Joss, I gotta do some things, you know, to get ready for you, but, um . . . I need a job.' And he said, 'Well, funny you should call, because we got a guy on *Angel* that you'd be perfect for. He's kind of like Jayne but smarter and in a nice suit.'"

With that, Baldwin walked into a recurring role in the final episodes of *Angel*: Marcus Hamilton, liaison to the Senior Partners of Wolfram & Hart. "That was a lifesaver. There are a few jobs over the course of a long career in Hollywood that are career lifesavers. Whether they're high profile or not, they put food on the table, they pay the rent, and that was one of them. He really stepped up and helped me out. He's met my family and I've met his and we appreciate what it's like to be fathers," he laughs. "Big responsibilities."

When Morena Baccarin got the call from Joss saying that *Firefly* was back, she couldn't believe it. "It was one of the happiest days of my life," she says. "I just thought . . . wow. We get to come back, all of us. And that was in his contract—that we all had to be back, we all had to do this movie and play again. And this time we knew that it was going to be over, so we savored every second of those three months we were shooting."

//////////

Perhaps inspired by the success of the *Firefly* campaign, *Angel* fans didn't give up on their show so easily. They organized letter-writing campaigns and online petitions, bought advertisements in trade magazines, and even held a "Save *Angel*" blood drive for the Red Cross in the United States and Great Britain. They lobbied other networks to pick up the show, especially UPN—despite the fact that it had canceled *Buffy* the previous year. It was a passionate outpouring, but the WB's decision stayed the same, and no other network came to the rescue.

Star David Boreanaz was relieved by the show's impending end. "I don't wanna sound like I was cheering, but when Joss broke the news, it was almost more like the burden of pressure came off me after five years," he said. "It's a lot of responsibility [carrying a show], and you don't realize how much that is until they say it's done and then you can breathe. . . . Look, it's a f—in' show, and it was a great experience. I think we can be very proud of what we've accomplished. Now, you just move forward." No doubt the passage of time had a much bigger effect on his human self than it did on his immortal vampire character, and he said that he had no interest in returning to the character once the final credits ran. Many fans, however, were a bit stung by how gleeful he seemed about leaving a show they'd loved and supported so much.

Garth Ancier, then-chairman of the WB, laid the blame for the cancellation on 20th Century Fox. "They had pushed for an early decision on whether the show should come back or not," he said. "I think the mistake that was made is that between us and 20th, we didn't wait until May. We just made the decision early based upon their request."

On May 19, 2004, *Angel* aired its final episode, "Not Fade Away." Unlike *Buffy*'s finale, in which Angel made a brief appearance, Buffy does not show up. Sarah Michelle Gellar had declined to guest-star earlier in the season, and while she was open to returning once it was announced to be the final season, she was available only for the final episode. Joss didn't want the finale to focus on a guest star; he wanted to celebrate *Angel*'s own cast and characters. "I want to end the show with the people who've been in the trenches together," he explained.

"The original goal [with *Angel*] was to do a story about redemption as an adult looking back on a bad decision and atoning for that," Joss said.

"But we ended up doing even more than anticipated. It was first designed as a stand-alone mystery show, but the characters were the most interesting. So we explored them in great depth and complexity and it exceeded my expectations."

There was no question what the next step in Angel's redemption story was going to be had the series continued. "We knew [season six] was going to launch into [a] post-apocalyptic show," Fury explained. "It was going to be Angel in *The Road Warrior*, which I thought would be awesome. In the ruined city of LA or out in the desert or something, it was just going to be kind of a really cool, different, show."

The writers had many discussions about the upcoming apocalypse, who would survive it, and which characters could return in season six. But without that next season, the writers had to find a way to bring closure to the series and its characters. The idea of a world-changing apocalypse remained. The final scene revealed Angel and his remaining friends in an alley, preparing to fight an army of demons big enough to overtake L.A. The ambiguity of their last moments gave hope to fans that this would not be the final chapter in Angel's story. "The last thing you will see of Angel is the last thing you should see," Joss said. "'Angel' is about redemption, and redemption is ongoing."

Eighteen months earlier, Joss had had three series on television. Now he had none. But he was about to take his storytelling skills back to the big screen—and this time, he would be in control of how the tale would be told.

GRANT ME THE SERENITY

Crafting *Serenity* was a challenging proposition even for an experienced screenwriter like Joss Whedon. Joss had to keep two audiences in mind as he wrote: *Firefly* fans who already had watched and rewatched the entire fourteen-episode series and moviegoers who had never seen the show. Too much dependence on the established mythology and the new viewers would be lost and alienated; too few connections to the series and the diehard fans who supported *Firefly* and campaigned for a film continuation would feel cheated and bored.

The task was made even more difficult by the fact that *Firefly* had a particularly complex backstory. Joss had to work with ten very different characters who all had a history together; he couldn't use the standard screenwriting technique of introducing the characters to each other as a way of introducing them to the audience. He also found it difficult to put the rather western Mal and the noirish River in the same story and make it work. He discussed his concerns with Jeanine Basinger, who guided him back to two films he had studied at Wesleyan: *The Furies* and *Johnny Guitar*.

Initially, Joss cribbed together a story for the film based on some ideas that he'd had for a second season of *Firefly*. The original draft was a "kitchen sink" version, in which he tried to touch on all of the major plot points from the series. All of the characters are on the ship (save for Inara, who left *Serenity* at the end of the series), and Joss struggled to give them all meaningful storylines. This draft came in at 190 pages, well above the average screenplay length of 90 to 120 pages. Universal was supportive of Joss but was not prepared to bankroll a three-plus-hour movie based on a little-seen television series; the studio asked him to cut the script down to a more manageable length. He trimmed more than sixty pages—removing, in particular, a lot of extensive exposition, often replacing it with simply a line or two, or sometimes just a simple look between characters. These revisions made for more powerful moments and a much cleaner and more concise film.

The final draft of *Serenity* focuses primarily on one particular element of the series' mythology: the story of River Tam, the young prodigy who was subjected to traumatic government experiments before being rescued by her brother, Simon, and brought aboard *Serenity*. Set a few months after the *Firefly* finale, the film pits the crew against the Operative, a shadowy assassin for the Alliance government who is sent to kill River before she can access and share the government secrets buried in her head. Captain Mal Reynolds is faced with the daily question of how far he'll go to protect River and her brother, who are now part of his crew.

Joss was also able to streamline the story by cutting back the involvement of several of the characters. Universal had wanted all nine main actors to sign multi-film contracts, but Alan Tudyk (Wash) and Ron Glass (Book) could not commit to sequels. So Joss needed to find a sensible way to take them out of the story while honoring the relationship that fans had with the characters. Joss moved Book off the ship and gave him a storyline previously assigned to a side character, adding weight to a big moment that motivates Mal to take action against the Operative.

///////////

On June 14, Nathan Fillion took to the official *Firefly* forum to announce that Joss and Kai had taken the cast out to dinner to celebrate the news that the movie was a go. Joss also enlisted Jack Green, who was also the cinematographer on the Clint Eastwood western *Unforgiven*, and editor Lisa Lassek, who had worked on all three of the Whedonverse series.

Joss had very specific intentions when casting the new characters in the 'verse. For the determined Operative, he chose British actor Chiwetel Ejiofor, because "he brings such depth and soulfulness and regret to everything." In the small but essential role of Dr. Mathias, the pompous Alliance researcher working on River's case, he cast comedic actor Michael Hitchcock. Mirroring his approach for *Buffy* writers, Joss picked "comedians, because they have the chops that I will need."

Another essential character, the ship itself, needed to be rebuilt from scratch. "I'll always remember the walk-through of the new *Firefly/*

Serenity set on a gigantic stage at Universal," Adam Baldwin recalls. "Just to see Joss's face and how happy he was that it was reborn, sort of a resurrection—he was just like a kid in a candy store. I was so happy for him. This was his baby and . . . his baby got killed, but he gave it his Midas touch and brought it back. He was so happy again, and he had that little dance in his step, and a smile on his face, this little sheepish grin that he has, like, 'We did it! We did it, guys!' And it's like, 'No, Joss, *you* did it. Thanks for bringing us along.'"

The vibe on set was a combination of the joy of being back together, getting to play in a world that they all knew and loved, and the relief at not having to deal with the threat of cancellation that had hung over their heads when they last shot together. "We didn't have to worry about losing our jobs or not being able to pay our mortgages," Jewel Staite says. "We had this beautiful piece of unfinished business to attend to, and for six glorious months, we got to play it out in just the fashion we wanted to. It was total bliss."

Though the principal actors wore their characters like a second skin, Joss's direction gave them new facets to explore. "There was a scene where I had a very infamous line about using a vibrator ['Goin' on a year now I ain't had nothin' twixt my nethers weren't run on batteries!']," Staite recalls. "Initially I played it in sort of a whisper. Joss asked, 'Why are you whispering? Kaylee isn't inhibited! She'd shout that as loud as she could to get her point across, no matter who was listening!' And I was like, 'Oh yeah. Of course she would.'"

Early in the film, Mal and his crew land on a planet to undertake a heist and end up in an intense chase sequence with a vicious band of Reavers. One of the Reavers harpoons Jayne's leg as he clings to the side of the crew's small hovercraft, and Mal must shoot the rope off the harpoon to set him free. Nathan Fillion gave a lot of thought to how he would play that moment. "I thought I was going to crick my neck and take my time to do a really slow aim," he remembers. "Joss said, 'Or, after this blade comes whipping past your face, it's like, "You almost hit me with that blade," *bam*, he shoots. It's like the angrier Malcolm Reynolds gets, the better he shoots.' And I thought, 'Oh, that's so much better.' I was going for this overly dramatic, ridiculous, stereotypical, unrealistic moment. And his moment was just so much better. And I get the credit! Until just now."

It was in this same scene that Joss loosened the reins on being the supreme overlord of his dialogue. He was busy with all things directing, so with the Reavers roaring up on them, Joss told Fillion to "say something that Mal would say." Fillion then ad-libbed a now-classic Whedonverse line: "Faster, faster, faster would be better!"

As director, Joss had some learning of his own to do. He'd honed his producing skills over eight years and three television series, continuing the informal schooling that he started in the *Buffy* writers' room. "You're basically teaching people how to write your show and how to make your show and how to act it and how to direct it and everything else," he said. Directing a feature film forced him back to square one; he went from seasoned teacher to floundering student.

Fortunately, he found another mentor in Mary Parent. Joss credits the Universal executive, who was also a producer on the film, with teaching him more about making movies than anyone since Jeanine Basinger at Wesleyan. "That was very humbling and very difficult, and sometimes very frustrating, but ultimately the best thing in the world."

ELECTION 2004

On September 17, 2004, Joss announced that *Serenity* had finished shooting. But that didn't mean that he was taking a break. In the fall of 2004, with an intense American presidential election nearing its November crescendo, Joss felt that he needed to get involved.

The incumbent president, Republican George W. Bush, was locked in a close race with his Democratic challenger, Senator John Kerry. Joss believed that Bush's administration had made America less safe, that under his guidance the country was "regarded with more contempt by other countries than it had ever been," and that "nothing in this country [was] going right, and the president [was] acting as if none of that matters." Joss was concerned that so many people seemed apathetic toward the election and saw little difference between the candidates. "If you're for Bush I doubt I can sway you," he said. "But if you're one of those people grumbling about politicians all being the same I'm begging you to look hard at the facts and at the smirking face of the man who is doing more damage to this country than any president in my lifetime. We cannot let apathy decide our fate."

Joss decided to host a fund-raiser for Senator Kerry in conjunction with the website Ain't It Cool News. The popular and highly trafficked site had gained attention for posting insider news and reviews about film and television projects before they were released—much to the irritation and sometimes anger of the production studios. The initial plan was for fans and supporters to participate in a conference call with Joss in exchange for a thirty-five-dollar donation to the Kerry campaign. Joss promised to talk about politics, his series, and anything his fans wanted to discuss.

To get the word out, Joss officially joined the fan site Whedonesque.
com, creating a profile that read:

> A svelte and mysterious Jewel Thief, Joss Whedon has appeared
> as Batman's nemesis in several embarrassing fantasies. He also
> goes by the names "El Hombre," "The Shadow-guy," and "Hoppy
> Hoppy Bunny." He likes long walks on the beach if they're brief
> and nowhere near water. He prefers blondes, brunettes, redheads,
> bald people or people with big hats so you're not even sure. Turn
> offs: insensitive men, people who smoke and then burst suddenly
> and horribly into flame. He is often very dizzy. Location: I'm inside
> your house.

As with his "Bootleg the puppy" battle cry of 1999, the troops were ready
to be rallied. Interest soared, and plans quickly changed. The conference call evolved into a party, attended not only by Joss but by several
Whedonverse cast members as well, with tickets selling for a fifty-dollar
donation to the campaign. Joss would also answer questions on a conference call with forty-two fan parties across the country.

On October 24, Hollywood's Cinespace nightclub hosted High
Stakes 2004. More than two hundred fans attended in person, donating
to the Democratic ticket for the chance to hang out with Joss, Alyson
Hannigan, Alexis Denisof, Nathan Fillion, Nicholas Brendon, Amber
Benson, Danny Strong, Amy Acker, and J. August Richards. On the
conference call, Joss fielded questions about subjects ranging from *Buffy*
storylines to the upcoming *Firefly* movie to Joss's involvement in the third
X-Men film, though he made a concerted effort to bring all of his answers
back around to the impending election:

> Q: You mentioned in [an interview] that the invasion of Iraq caused
> some changes in the story arc of *Buffy*'s season six. What was the
> original storyline, and [how did it change?]

> Joss: The fact is, there wasn't a huge change in the story for *Buffy*,
> but when we were writing the story, we decided that we were going
> to shake up the paradigm of the show by having her fight evil at its
> source, attack evil instead of waiting for it to attack her. And then
> we started hearing a lot of rhetoric from the president that sounded
> very similar. We as a writing staff got very nervous and very upset,
> and we were worried that some of those rhetorics might overlap.

We'd like to remind the president that he is not a high school girl who kills vampires. Ultimately, what happened was when Buffy crossed the line and she became an ineffective leader who endangered the persons around her, they kicked her out of the house. . . .

Q: You said that the *Angel* finale was not a cliffhanger. If the last episode of *Angel* had [the characters] literally hanging from a cliff, would you consider that a cliffhanger? . . .

Joss: If they were all hanging from a cliff, I would probably call it a cliffhanger—unless, of course, I had started the show with all of them hanging from a cliff. The fact of the matter is, the reason I always maintained that the end of *Angel* was not a cliffhanger, even though we don't ultimately know the fates of the people involved, is that the message of that show was very simply, you have to keep fighting.

And once again, there is no more relevant message for what we are here for today than that. You have to keep fighting. One thing about this country, you never get to sit back and just let things happen. When you do that, well, we all see what you get. You have to keep fighting every single day to make things better if you want to call yourself a moral, decent, responsible person. It's extremely hard, and that is the story that I was telling.

It was not lost on Joss that he was now enlisting in a political campaign the same people who had often campaigned on his behalf. The spirit of his fans inspired him, and he felt that his fan base had "always been motivated by altruism and by the desire to make things better and by a willingness to get out there and do what's right." And he and his fans continued to be optimistic: "Sometimes you work on a campaign that cannot win, and ultimately that's the only way to win the ones that can be won, so when you work on campaigns, sometimes they work, sometimes they don't . . . but to our fans, it never seems to matter. This is one campaign that we can, and will, and must win."

/////////

The day after the event, 20th Century Fox Television announced that, at Joss's request, it was suspending his overall deal with the studio. Under the agreement, Joss couldn't work on television projects for any other studio, and if he returned to TV, Fox would get first look at the project. It was the first time since 1997 that he was no longer under contract with the studio. Mutant Enemy closed its office. The production company was not dissolved, however, and although Chris Buchanan left his position as company president, he continued producing and promoting *Serenity*.

Joss's decision to leave television came as a surprise to many, considering he was just a year removed from a five-year run with *Angel* and he had only a year left on his contract. But with no new series ideas, he wanted out of the television game for a while. "I spent a lot of time trying to think what my next series would be," he said. "I couldn't think of anything. When that happens, it generally means something is just not working. I didn't feel like I could come up with anything that the networks would want." With a "bitter taste" left by the burgeoning reality TV market, plus his frustration and devastation over *Firefly*'s cancellation, his choice seemed more like a declaration of freedom than a white flag of defeat.

Ten days later, on November 3, 2004, George W. Bush defeated John Kerry to win a second term in the White House. Joss was disappointed, but his personal campaign against apathy was not dampened. He had reached out to his fans to broaden their activism. In the conference call, he had said that it was time to speak out. "Even if you're worried that someone else is going to be more articulate than you are. Even if you're worried that you may not have all the facts," Joss said. "Nobody has all the facts. . . . This is a time when . . . you can stand up and make yourself heard. And I believe this is the one time when we simply have no choice. We must be heard." It would not be Joss's last stand against a powerful status quo.

///////////

Joss and Kai were now expecting their second child, and Kai was put on bed rest for the last three months of her pregnancy. Normally, she was the one to keep their house in order—an arrangement that had never bothered her before, since Joss was in charge of all the cooking. But now, she was frustrated by her inability to do so, and her new need to put everything in Joss's hands. "Joss didn't really know how to load a dishwasher," she says. "Or really ever notice if things were messy."

Joss has shared a story that makes shockingly clear the degree to which he can be unaware of the immense clutter around him. "My study was filled with crap. . . . I would literally have to walk this byzantine, video-game path through all the junk to get to my desk to write," he said. One weekend while he was away, "Kai and our housekeeper went and cleared out everything completely. I went upstairs, went to my desk and Did. Not. Ever. Notice." But in mid-2004, with a movie in postproduction, a house to clean, and family to tend to, he needed to step up his game.

Joss's disappointment over the election gave way to joy when his daughter, Squire, was born on November 7, 2004. Squire was named for his mother's paternal grandmother's father, Squire Huguely (1843–1922). Joss noted the irony that Lee's great-great-grandfather fought in the Civil War on the side of the South (Huguely was in the Seventh Regiment, Kentucky Cavalry, of the Confederate Army), while his father's great-grandfather, John Whedon Steele, was awarded the Congressional Medal of Honor for "extraordinary heroism" while fighting for the North. (As a major and aide-de-camp, he "gathered up a force of stragglers and others" to defend against a night attack on the wagon and ammunition train of his corps at Spring Hill, Tennessee, in 1864.) "No wonder [my parents] got divorced," Joss muses.

24

I WROTE MY THESIS ON YOU

The same year that hundreds of fans gathered in Los Angeles to support Joss Whedon's political fight, approximately four hundred people assembled in Nashville, Tennessee, for another event that attested to Joss's extraordinary influence beyond the typical bounds of genre entertainment. The event was the first-ever *Slayage* Conference, a gathering of academics discussing *Buffy the Vampire Slayer*.

As a child of a teacher, who delved with equal excitement into comic books and Shakespeare, Joss had made research and academic study an essential part of his first two television series. In *Buffy*'s early seasons, the Scooby Gang's home base was the Sunnydale High School library, where they pored over ancient texts to learn how to defeat the supernatural threat of the week. Unlike a lot of teen shows, the series embraced the idea that old-fashioned book learning was cool. It makes sense, then, that the show's architect would inspire his fans to delve into the symbolism and deeper meaning of his work, and that Joss and the Whedonverse, like his beloved Shakespeare, would be given their own chapter of academic study.

By 2001, there had been enough scholarly interest in *Buffy* to warrant several books of essays on the series. These collections explored the show, its characters, and its underlying themes through the lenses of such academic disciplines as psychology, philosophy, theology, and sociology. One such collection, *Fighting the Forces: What's at Stake in Buffy the Vampire Slayer*, had received so many quality submissions that there was no way that the editors could include all of them. One of the book's editors, David Lavery, suggested to his coeditor, Rhonda V. Wilcox, that with "a not-soon-to-be-exhausted international critical and scholarly interest" in *Buffy*, they follow in the footsteps of *Whoosh! The Journal of the*

International Association of Xenoid Studies, an online journal that had been established for the series *Xena: Warrior Princess*. In January 2001, Lavery and Wilcox published the first edition of *Slayage: The Online Journal of Buffy Studies*. It included five articles written by PhDs and doctoral students, ranging in topics from "Dissing the Age of Moo: Initiatives, Alternatives, and Rationality in Buffy the Vampire Slayer" to "Undead Letters: Searches and Researches in Buffy the Vampire Slayer" to "Teen Witches, Wiccans, and 'Wanna-Blessed-Be's': Pop-Culture Magic in Buffy the Vampire Slayer."

Wilcox, an English professor and the editor of the journal *Studies in Popular Culture*, had been writing about television long before she started to watch *Buffy*. Initially she brushed off the show as cute, funny, and lightweight entertainment and had no plans to explore it any further. But the longer she watched, the more impressed she was with it. She loved the language of the series (a subject covered by another book, Michael Adams's *Slayer Slang: A Buffy the Vampire Slayer Lexicon*), and she saw Joss as a pioneer who recognized the untapped potential of long-term television narratives. "*Twilight Zone* or *Star Trek* had wonderful symbolism, but you didn't have the kind of narrative that Whedon did," Wilcox explains. "He paid attention to the continuity and therefore he was able to grow the characters. That's something that, as a person who did her dissertation on Charles Dickens, I could really enjoy. When Dickens wrote, he wrote serialized novels, and those were kind of looked down on during the time period that he was creating those. I think that Whedon did some of the same kind of work."

//////////

From 1998 to 2012, various publishers would release no fewer than thirty books of essays exploring different facets of each of Joss's TV series. No other series or creator has inspired such an intense and expansive body of academic work—not even *Star Trek*, which has been around since 1966. Why such interest? "There are many audience members who were proud of getting the symbolism and invested themselves in the show more because they could see that it had more than one meaning at once," Wilcox posits. "It was clear that Whedon was counting on having an intelligent audience, which is probably one of the reasons that it worked better on one of the smaller networks, because he never did have that large an audience."

The world of Whedon studies has yet to win over all academics as a worthy endeavor—which probably says little about Joss and more about the general resistance to accepting television studies (and sometimes even film studies) as important. At this point it may be difficult to convince more traditional academics that Joss's work belongs in the literary canon, but broadly popular works are often dismissed as unserious by the intellectual class. "You have to wait for about a hundred years or more for it to be realized," Wilcox argues. "That applied to Dickens, it even applies to Shakespeare, and you would think by now that people would've noticed a pattern, right? Harvard would not allow American literature to be taught in the nineteenth century, because, my goodness, that's beneath us."

But other academics were eager to discuss Joss's work, and they began gathering regularly to do just that. The first academic conference on *Buffy* was held in October 2002 at the University of East Anglia in Norwich, England. "Blood, Text and Fears: Reading Around *Buffy the Vampire Slayer*" was initially planned to last only one day. However, as Lavery and Wilcox found with *Fighting the Forces*, there were so many submissions that they had to extend it to a full weekend.

"That was one of the most wonderful experiences of my life," Wilcox says, "because I'm standing up in front of hundreds of people giving my *Buffy* paper and every single one of them knew exactly what I was talking about." She didn't have to argue about whether studying *Buffy* was a worthwhile pursuit; everyone in attendance was eager to talk *Buffy* well into the night. Two years later, the first *Slayage* Conference was held in Nashville; with its four hundred attendees, it was impressively large for a conference of academics. It would later become the biennial *Slayage* Conference on the Whedonverses.

25

SERENITY LANDS

On April 26, 2005, Universal issued the first trailer for *Serenity*, which was scheduled for release in September of that year. But Joss's fans would not have to wait until the fall to catch the *Firefly* movie they'd long been waiting for; shortly after the trailer's release, Universal announced an unprecedented plan to promote the film. On May 5, the studio would start screening a rough cut of the film for fans in three US cities, in hopes of building an early buzz to interest non–*Firefly* fans. Even though the film wasn't finished, ticket sales were brisk. Over the next two months, screenings were held in thirty-five US cities—often selling out as soon as tickets became available.

Joss knew that the enthusiasm of the Browncoats was an important factor in Universal's decision to greenlight *Serenity*. During the preview screenings, Joss inserted a message before the film: "All the work the fans have done have helped make this movie. It is, in an unprecedented sense, your movie. Which means if it sucks, it's your fault. . . . If this movie matters to you, let somebody know—let everybody know. Make yourselves heard. If you don't like the movie, this is a time for quiet, for months of silent contemplation."

Fan interest was certainly high, but some questioned whether the buzz for such a niche sci-fi film could be sustained for five whole months. And if the movie's core audience had already seen the film at a special screening, how likely were they to return when opening weekend rolled around?

Joss had a different concern: whether the film would make sense to the uninitiated. He'd been so close to the world for so long that he had a difficult time seeing it from the point of view of a complete *Firefly* newbie. Surprisingly, he found a helpful resource in the generally hated process of film test screenings, in which the studio shows a film to general audiences and uses their feedback to suggest adjustments to the filmmakers. In this case, testing highlighted where Joss had overexplained and underexplained important information, and where he actually did need to adjust things to help uninitiated audiences connect with the film. One key takeaway from the testing was that because *Serenity*'s opening scenes focused on the character of River, audiences didn't understand that Mal was the central character. Joss went to the set of cinematographer Jack Green's new movie, *The 40-Year-Old Virgin*, and they shot a new early scene in which River "hands over" the movie to Mal.

//////////

July 2005 was a good time to be a *Firefly* fan. Indie publisher Dark Horse Comics released the first book of a three-issue tie-in comic, *Serenity: Those Left Behind*. The Sci Fi Channel (which was owned by NBC Universal) brought the original *Firefly* episodes back to television, airing them right before its hit series *Battlestar Galactica*. And at San Diego Comic-Con, Joss showed the final cut of *Serenity*, which he had just finalized the day before.

In August, Joss went in front of the camera for the latest entries in *Serenity*'s viral media campaign. The "R. Tam Sessions," a series of five short videos, was a prequel to *Firefly* that shed light on River's life before Simon rescued her. The grainy videos show interviews with River at the Alliance "learning facility" where she studied and was then experimented on, depicting her transformation from the sweet, brilliant girl that Simon remembered growing up with to the mentally unbalanced young woman we meet on the series. Although he's only shot from the back, Joss played the counselor interviewing her.

Joss and the cast also visited several other countries to promote the film. As the film's lead, Nathan Fillion was well aware of how essential he was to the marketing of the film. He was humbled by this new big-screen role. "Until Joss Whedon and *Serenity* came along, I was never considered for a lead," he says. "I had some small parts, some small roles in films, but no one would give me a crack in this town. I would go in to audition for something, they'd say, 'He's very good. We don't know if he can handle a lead.' Unless someone lets me, no one will. I'll never get that chance. I was here for five years before Joss said, 'You are the guy. I'm gonna give you the chance.' Joss Whedon opened a lot of doors for me. He was my champion. He was my mentor. I owe so much to Joss Whedon."

Fillion's appreciation did not color their friendship with too much gravitas. While bouncing from city to city in Europe on the promotional tour, he and Joss came up with superhero alter egos Strong Man and Brain Boy to play with. "He would take pictures of me, standing big, chest out, with my hands on my hips looking into the future," Fillion remembers. "And him, kind of crouched down next to me, pointing at his head like he's thinking really hard. Concentrating. 'Tell you what, Brain Boy. With your brains, and my not-so-brains . . .' He loves to play."

After a screening in Sydney, Australia, the tour took a more serious turn when a fan asked Joss what he had against being a Christian. He replied with what was, up until then, his most detailed and straightforward treatise on his atheism:

> I don't actually have anything against anybody, unless their belief precludes everybody else. I am an atheist and an absurdist and have been for many, many years. I've actually taken a huge amount of flak for that. People who have faith tend to think that people who don't, don't have a belief system and they don't care if they make fun of them. It's actually very difficult: atheists are as a group not really recognized by the American public as people to be taken seriously. This does not mean that I rail against religion; however, the meaning of life and the meaning of what we do with our lives is something that is extremely important to me. . . . I think faith is an extraordinary thing. I'd like to have some, but I don't, and that's just how that works. . . .
>
> There's one other thing I would mention, which is from *Angel*, actually. One of the few times I really got to sort of say exactly what I think about the world was in the second season of *Angel*, episode sixteen ["Epiphany"], when [Angel had] gone all dark, because he does that, and that he was getting better, and he basically decided—he'd been told—"The world is meaningless, nothing matters." And he said, "Well then, this is my statement: nothing matters, so the only thing that matters is what we do." Which is what I believe: I believe the only reality is how we treat each other. The morality comes from the absence of any grander scheme, not from the presence of any grander scheme. . . . So the answer is: "Nothing, unless you've got something against me."

///////////

Back home, *Serenity* had a red-carpet premiere on September 22. Universal invited some of the fans who had done exceptional work to promote the film and gave them the chance to walk the red carpet as special guests. Those fans were probably among the many who purchased tickets for midnight screenings on the night of the film's September 30 release.

The reviews for *Serenity* were generally positive, even from critics that hadn't been deeply entrenched in *Firefly* fandom. With the encouraging critical reception and the roaring fandom support, box office expectations were high—especially for a weekend with little competition. However, the final numbers were disappointing. *Serenity* took in $10.1 million on its first weekend, eventually earning just $25.5 million domestically. The worldwide total was $38.9 million, which barely met the film's $39 million production budget and didn't begin to cover the marketing costs, which were upward of $30 million. Any hope of a big-screen sequel was dashed.

It seemed as though the film, while a storytelling success for Joss, failed to pull in non–*Firefly* fans, just as he'd feared. Universal had granted him creative control, his biggest budget ever, and a strong marketing push, but again he'd created a work that spoke mostly to a devoted niche audience. What would it take for the cult auteur to find mainstream success?

STRONG FEMALE CHARACTERS

As Joss was shepherding his beloved *Firefly* toward its rebirth on the big screen, he fell hard for a new TV drama: *Veronica Mars*. UPN's neo-noir mystery series follows the eponymous teenage sleuth (played by Kristen Bell) who faces the daily pressures of high school life while simultaneously investigating cases for her private investigator father and her fellow students and attempting to solve her best friend's murder. The series, though low-rated (ranking 148th out of the 156 series of the 2004–05 season), was highly acclaimed, landing on a number of "best fall television" lists. Joss had been wrapped up in production for *Serenity*, so he came late to the series, but once he discovered it he was almost immediately consumed by it. By August 2005 he'd watched the whole twenty-two-episode first season in a "crazed Veronica Marsathon," and he took to Whedonesque to declare his love:

> Joss Luvs Veronica. . . .
>
> Best. Show. Ever. Seriously, I've never gotten more wrapped up in a show I wasn't making, and maybe even more than those. Crazy crisp dialogue. Incredibly tight plotting. Big emotion, I mean BIG, and charismatic actors and I was just DYING from the mystery and the relationships and PAIN, this show knows from pain and no, I don't care, laugh all you want, I had to share this. These guys know what they're doing on a level that intimidates me. It's the Harry Potter of shows. There. I said it. . . .
>
> Some of you may already be all up on this, and some may disagree, but I'm urging peeps to check it out, 'cause there is great TV afoot, and who doesn't want that? Thank you for your time.

The news quickly spread to the *Veronica Mars* writers' room, where the staff was working on the show's second season. Series creator Rob Thomas remembers the excitement everyone felt as they gathered around to read Joss's post; it was a benediction of sorts from one cult phenomenon to the next. "We're both sort of writing in the 'Heathers' school of stylized teen dialogue, pretty quippy and bantery," Thomas said. "We both imposed metaphors on a high school setting. He did high school as a horror show, and we're doing high school as a noir piece. In our own ways, we re-imagined high school to fit a distinct style of storytelling."

And like *Buffy*, *Veronica Mars* was a phoenix rising from the ashes of another acclaimed series that had been canceled way too soon. Just as Joss was still reeling from the cancellation of *My So-Called Life* when he developed his iconic show, Thomas felt the need to create his own teen show to ease the pain of the swift cancellation of NBC's *Freaks and Geeks* (1999–2000). "The most beautiful final episode of a show ever," he says. "That one killed me. When [the show] got canceled, I felt like it was the death of a small-story television. I can get a sexy soap opera like *Gossip Girl* on—but to just get a show about normal teens with small stories like *Freaks and Geeks*? It wasn't going to last. And they weren't going to take their chances with another one." The fact that Veronica, like Buffy before her, found a home not on one of the big four networks but on one of the smaller netlets speaks to the truth of Thomas's statement.

Even by the more modest standards of UPN, *Veronica Mars* was hardly a breakout hit, so the Whedon love was much appreciated. Joss continued to bestow praise on the series, writing a review of the season-one DVD set for *Entertainment Weekly*, in which he characterized the show as much more than just a modern update of the treasured Nancy Drew tales that he'd shared with Kai on their cross-country trip:

> Last year, Veronica Mars' best friend was murdered. Some months later, she was drugged at a party and raped in her sleep. Welcome to the funniest and most romantic show on TV. . . . The teen-soap element of the show is just as compelling as the season-long murder mystery. Nobody is who you think they are. Everyone shifts, betrays, reveals—through their surprising humor as well as their flaws. The show is filled with deft, glorious wit. Creator Rob Thomas and his scribblers give *VM* more laughs than many sitcoms, and they never grate against the emotional brutality. . . . What elevates it is that in

a TV-scape creepily obsessed with crime-solving, *VM* actually asks why. It knows we need our dose of solution as a panacea against the uncontrollable chaos of life's real mysteries. And it shows, feelingly, that having the answers is never enough.

Joss also called out Enrico Colantoni's role as Veronica's father, disgraced former sheriff turned private investigator Keith Mars, dubbing him "the world's greatest dad. (Seriously. Greatest. There should be a mug.)" Keith is indeed Veronica's rock throughout the series, and their bond is one of the best father-daughter relationships ever realized on screen. Keith also stands out against the long line of *unsupportive* fathers in Joss's own work; even as his series celebrate the value of chosen family, blood relatives and particularly fathers are more likely to be portrayed as absent or abusive.

Even so, the similarities between *Buffy* and *Veronica Mars* were striking, including witty writing and a smart girl hero. Rob Thomas's show seemed sure to appeal to many fans of the earlier series, if only they would give it a try. By the beginning of its second season, the show had already cast former Whedonverse actors Alyson Hannigan and Charisma Carpenter in recurring roles, but it wasn't until Joss went public with his love that Thomas thought of the ultimate way to reach more of the Whedonverse audience. Through his friend Marti Noxon, Thomas had met Joss a couple of times, and he knew that he had a background in theater. Thomas figured that it wouldn't be totally strange to ask Joss to take on an acting role in the show.

Joss took him up on the offer. In November, he played a car rental agent in the episode "Rat Saw God." Thomas was impressed with his skills in front of the camera. "Trust me, I cast guest star actors all the time who I find myself having to cut around. It's a little nerve-racking to cast a writer in a role and think, 'Oh, we can't have a real scene,'" he says. "It was really remarkable—he was great." Star Kristen Bell agreed: "Joss is such an intelligent guy and he gets the show completely and he was just very funny. It was so cool to have him on set because we're hopefully following in his footsteps, and he really knows how to write for cult fans."

In addition to drawing his fans' attention to *Veronica Mars*, Joss had another lasting effect on Thomas. He took note of how Joss stood out as "a face of a series" at a time when most writers and producers were unknown, and he was inspired by how willing Joss was to engage in conversation with his fans. It's an example he would still be following almost a decade later, when he reached out to the *Veronica Mars* fan base to help resurrect the long-canceled series in another medium.

//////////

Joss had embraced *Veronica Mars* largely as a fan, eager for another writer's creation to find the success he thought it deserved. But 2005 also saw him become more than a fan of another female-centric franchise, one that had inspired him just as he was now inspiring others.

DC Comics' Wonder Woman, like Marvel's Kitty Pryde, was one of the comic book heroines on whom Joss had drawn when he crafted the character of Buffy. The famous Amazon princess from Paradise Island, who was created by William Moulton Marston during World War II, first comes to our world when US pilot Steve Trevor crashes nearby and she rescues him. When she finds out about the Nazis, Wonder Woman leaves Paradise Island with Trevor to help take down Hitler. She brings with her a set of magical golden accessories that give her superhuman strength in man's world: bracelets that deflect bullets, a tiara that she uses as a boomerang, and a golden lariat that forces people to tell the truth. And she flies an invisible plane. Wonder Woman was the first female superhero to score her own comic book, and for a long time she was the only female member of DC's top-tier superhero team, the Justice League.

Of all the superheroes to make the jump from the comic book page to live-action media, Wonder Woman has had the most difficulty. While she has starred in countless cartoons, attempts to create a flesh-and-blood retelling of her story have resulted in only a single television series: the iconic Lynda Carter version that ran in the mid-to-late 1970s. "Wonder Woman was the first great female superhero to emerge from comic books and later inspire millions of fans in her television incarnation, but unlike her counterparts Batman and Superman, this groundbreaking heroine has yet to be reinvented for the feature film arena," producer Joel Silver (*Die Hard, The Matrix*) said in a 2005 press release. Silver was determined to finally bring the character to the big screen.

"It was after I made 'The Matrix' when I saw the response of the first tests and I realized the Trinity character was the highest-tested character," he recalled. "This was before they had done 'Charlie's Angels' or 'Elektra' or any of these movies, and I thought, 'Let's just go out and try to make

Wonder Woman work." The project had gone through several writers from 2001 to 2005, but Silver was never satisfied with any of them. So next he went after the creator of another iconic female superhero. "I just thought [Joss] would be the perfect guy to write it. I love Buffy and he's a great writer," Silver said. "I sat down with him and asked if he'd do it."

Joss was hesitant. Not only was he in postproduction for *Serenity*, but he knew that *Wonder Woman* was a difficult project that had been in development for years. Still, he felt that Silver had a vision for the film, and although the idea was unformed, as with *Toy Story* years before, he thought it was an idea he could work with. "He wrote me a note where he passed, and in the note, he explained what the movie had to be," Silver remembered. "There was no way I was going to let him pass, so I hammered him until he said, 'Yes.'"

///////////

This wouldn't be Joss's first attempt to bring a comic book to the big screen. Though he'd been discouraged when his script doctoring work on *X-Men* was largely rejected, he'd jumped back into the superhero world in 2002, when Chris Harbert told him that Warner Bros. was thinking about doing another Batman movie. Harbert knew that Joss wanted to concentrate on his own original work, so he mentioned it only as a formality. Joss was ready to brush it off until Kai, very much not a comic book fan, said, "Are you kidding? It's Batman!"

Joss thought about it for a while and fell in love with the idea he had for an origin movie to reboot the Batman tale. "In my version, there was actually a new [villain], it wasn't one of the classics," he said. "It was more of a 'Hannibal Lecter' type—he was somebody already in Arkham Asylum that Bruce went and sort of studied with. It was a whole thing—I get very emotional about it, I still love the story." A crucial moment was based on the beat-down he'd suffered on the way to the newsstand at age thirteen: a young Bruce Wayne battles a group of older kids and wins. "It was the key to the whole movie," he said. "Where he goes from being 'I'm just morbidly obsessed with death' to 'I can work the problem; I can actually do something about it.'"

The studio, however, seemed less interested in a small film focused on personal epiphanies than in a summer blockbuster to kick off a new franchise. "I was clearly not on the same wavelength," Joss said. "So I got in my car and headed back to the office and I literally said to myself, 'How many more times do I need to be told that the machine doesn't care. The machine is not aware of what is in your heart as a storyteller.' I got back to the office and they cancelled 'Firefly'. So I was like, 'Oh! So, uh, just once more. OK!' That was not a happy day."

////////////

With two failed superhero experiences behind him, would the third time be the charm? Or would Joss find that defeat comes in threes? His main concern was making Wonder Woman a relatable character. Joss felt that DC superheroes like Wonder Woman and Superman tended to be written as old-fashioned heroes, perfect and bigger than life. "There are great DC books and they write about human things in the [Justice] League, and they get into the big iconic characters, but they don't have the connection that 'I'm a nerd in high school who has the powers of a spider' gives you," Joss says. Marvel superhero stores, by contrast, are "based on 'Oh my God, we're all so fucked up!' " which he felt was more relatable.

"Batman is the only Marvel character in the DC universe," Joss explained. "He's got the greatest rogues gallery ever, he's got Gotham City. The Bat writes himself. With Wonder Woman, you're writing from whole cloth, but trying to make it feel like you didn't." And while other members of the Justice League have enemies that have become part of the pop culture lexicon—Lex Luthor, the Joker, Catwoman, the Rid-dler—none of Wonder Woman's nemeses (Circe, Cheetah, Ares) are well known. "She doesn't have good villains," Joss says. "So you pretty much have to start from scratch there."

One of the things that convinced Joss to finally take on the project was his own unfamiliarity with Wonder Woman's extensive backstory. Except for her origin story, most of the Wonder Woman tales he was familiar with centered not on the individual character but on the Justice League as a whole. He also felt that there had been a lack of development to show how she came to be such a force for good. "I think she sort of sprang out fully formed, much like Athena herself," he said. "In the '40s, when it was first done, she came to the world from Paradise Island and then went about her business, and so that experience, which is really a rite of passage, which is the same as any hero has to go through, has never really been investigated the way I want." In discussing Wonder Woman with Silver, he realized that the woman behind the legend was just as important as the legend herself. She's "fascinating, very uncompromising and in her own way almost vulnerable. She's someone who doesn't belong in this world, and since everyone I know feels that way about themselves, the character clicked for me."

His plan was to write an updated origin story about how Wonder Woman moves from the female-centered society on Paradise Island and into man's world. "She comes from a civilization where she's rather perfect, so she's the opposite to Buffy in many ways," Joss said. "She's going through an adolescent rite of passage because she's new to the world." For him, Wonder Woman's vulnerability is her "outdatedness," and her inability to understand why human beings are "so lame." In his version, he explained, Wonder Woman is very powerful and travels the world— but remains very naive about people. "The fact that she was a goddess was how I eventually found my in to her humanity and vulnerability," Joss said, "because she would look at us and the way we kill each other and the way we let people starve and the way the world is run and she'd just be like, *None of this makes sense to me. I can't cope with it, I can't understand, people are insane.* And ultimately her romance with Steve was about him getting her to see what it's like *not* to be a goddess, what it's like when you are weak, when you do have all these forces controlling you and there's nothing you can do about it. That was the sort of central concept of the thing. Him teaching her humanity and her saying, OK, great, but we can still do better."

While Joss was hammering out the story, actresses were lining up to throw their golden tiara into the ring. *Buffy* vets Charisma Carpenter and Eliza Dushku expressed interest, and A-list names like Angelina Jolie, Beyoncé Knowles, Sandra Bullock, and Megan Fox would be linked to the project at different times. *Firefly*'s Gina Torres called Joss to tell him, "If they will allow for you to have a middle-aged, ethnically ambiguous Wonder Woman—I'm your girl. Most importantly, I'm the only damn Amazon you really know." The question of who would don the bulletproof bracelets was possibly more popular than the question of what the film would be about. Joss and Silver insisted that no one would be considered until the script was finished.

///////////

Wonder Woman and Veronica Mars weren't the only ladies Joss was thinking about. One week before *Serenity* officially opened in the United States, Universal Pictures announced that it had bought a Joss Whedon spec script, *Goners*, which he would also direct. Joss provided *Variety* with a description that was purposely cryptic, unsurprising for the spoiler-wary writer, but it seemed to promise that the film would tread familiar ground: it was, he said, a very dark rite-of-passage tale, a "young woman's journey" that featured a "great deal of horror and some heroics."

Universal's Mary Parent was still determined to be in the Joss Whedon business; as with *Serenity*, she came aboard to produce. The studio had enough faith in Joss's storytelling to lock him into a seven-figure deal for *Goners* without seeing what the *Serenity* box office would bring. But even with a script in hand, Parent and Universal knew that his commitment to *Wonder Woman* came first.

And it took a long time for that script to be finished. Before he turned in his second *Wonder Woman* draft in July 2006, he took a moment to honor another great feminist icon in his life. On May 15, the day after Mother's Day, the women's rights organization Equality Now presented Joss with an award at their "On the Road to Equality: Honoring Men on the Front Lines" event. Equality Now had been founded by Jessica Neuwirth, a former student of Joss's mother's at Riverdale Country School.

Neuwirth had been inspired by the work they did at Riverdale with Amnesty International, in particular when they adopted a prisoner of conscience in East Germany. "When he was released from prison, he wrote back to us, which was an incredible experience for all of us," Neuwirth says. "In addition to the basic research and writing skills, Lee Stearns tried to develop in her students the ability to think critically, to ask questions, and to be active in the world."

Neuwirth went on to graduate from Yale and Harvard Law School, then joined the staff of Amnesty International, where she worked from 1985 to 1990. In 1992, along with two other lawyers, Navanethem Pillay of South Africa and Feryal Gharahi of Iran, Neuwirth founded Equality Now to promote the rights of girls and women around the world. She reached out to Lee soon after and was buoyed by Lee's excitement for the project and her desire to work with it in her Riverdale classes, as she had with Amnesty International.

In May 1992, Neuwirth and Pillay were in London for the first organizing trip of Equality Now. When Neuwirth came home, there was a message on her answering machine from Lee, "full of light and energy" and "keen to hear how the trip had gone." It was followed by a grim-sounding message from another teacher at Riverdale, a close friend of Lee's. "I knew something was wrong, and she told me the tragic news when I called her back," Neuwirth remembers.

The news of Lee's death was devastating, and as she continued her work with Equality Now, she realized how much of it she had done in Lee's honor. Lee's memory, she says, "is with me all of the time. She had a huge influence on me, which carried very much over into Equality Now. I learned human rights from Lee through Amnesty International, but Lee was also a great feminist, which only came to me much later in the course of the creation of Equality Now. I know that Lee would have had so much to contribute to the development of Equality Now, and I have really missed her, though I see so much of her thinking in Joss and his work."

Joss quickly took up his mother's support of the organization. "Joss has been involved with Equality Now for as long as I can remember," Neuwirth says. "He immediately understood what we were trying to do and has always been helpful in many different ways." His vocal support brought tremendous visibility to the organization and its work, and thousands of his fans were motivated to join the group and support it financially.

Firefly fans in particular developed a special relationship with Equality Now. At San Diego Comic-Con 2005, they set up a table where they raised $12,000 for the charity, while producers of *Done the Impossible*, a documentary about *Firefly* and its fans, pledged a portion of their profits to the group. In January 2006, with the approval of Universal, fans began organizing *Serenity* screenings, all the proceeds of which would be donated to Equality Now. The Can't Stop the Serenity screenings spread worldwide, and by 2013 they had raised over $800,000 for charity, with the majority donated directly to Neuwirth's organization.

It isn't just the financial and promotional support that Neuwirth is grateful to Joss for. "Indirectly, his work—such as *Buffy the Vampire Slayer*—has had a massive impact on our work, creating new role models of strong women and girls that have inspired so many young women and men to reach for a new paradigm of equality in everyday life. Joss makes gender equality seem like such a natural thing, something taken for granted, which is of course as it should be, but isn't quite yet."

//////////

At the Road to Equality event, Joss was introduced by Meryl Streep, who also paid tribute to Lee and her influence on him, his work, and Equality Now. In his own speech, Joss chose to address the one question that he'd been asked repeatedly at press junkets for years. He took on the role of reporter to ask himself, "Why do you always write these strong women characters?"

> I think it's because of my mother. She really was an extraordinary, inspirational, tough, cool, sexy, funny woman, and that's the kind of woman I've always surrounded myself with. It's my friends, particularly my wife, who is not only smarter and stronger than I am but occasionally taller too. But only sometimes, taller. And, I think it—it all goes back to my mother.

> *So, why do you write these strong women characters?*
> Because of my father. My father and my stepfather had a lot to do with it, because they prized wit and resolve in the women they were with above all things. And they were among the rare men who understood that recognizing somebody else's power does not diminish your own. When I created Buffy, I wanted to create a female icon, but I also wanted to be very careful to surround her with men who not only had no problem with the idea of a female leader but were, in fact, engaged and even attracted to the idea. That came from my father and stepfather—the men who created this man, who created those men, if you can follow that. . . .

> *So, why do you write these strong women characters?*
> Because equality is not a concept. It's not something we should be striving for. It's a necessity. Equality is like gravity—we need it to stand on this Earth as men and women, and the misogyny that is in every culture is not a true part of the human condition. It is life out of balance and that imbalance is sucking something out of the soul of every man and woman who's confronted with it. We need equality, kinda now.

> *So, why do you write these strong female characters?*
> Because you're still asking me that question.

That speech struck a chord with fans, who would continue to quote it for years—although like most complex arguments, it would usually be reduced to the punchy sound bite of the last exchange. His mention of Lee would sometimes be added to give context, but few would mention his salute to Tom and stepfather Stephen. Yet their influence, too, is clearly evident in Joss's work. Though his series may lack a "world's greatest dad" like Keith Mars, they're filled with male role models who support and admire the strong women in their lives, from Xander and Giles in *Buffy* to Zoe's commanding officer Mal and husband Wash in *Firefly*.

//////////

While on the East Coast for the event, Joss spent a day with Jeanine Basinger in Connecticut. It was a rare opportunity for Joss to step away from his work, given how much of his time it demands and how consumed he becomes with the stories he's writing. The two had a most lovely day, walking around and discussing his script for *Wonder Woman*. Basinger was a huge fan of the character, and knowing that Wonder Woman's next adventure was in the hands of her prized student made her proud. Joss was not as confident, confiding in his mentor that he felt that his story was stupid.

Basinger had wooed him out with the promise of a surprise, and she took him to New Haven for a veterans association event at which she was speaking. The event honored 1940s film star Joan Leslie, who starred with Fred Astaire in *The Sky's the Limit*, a favorite of Joss's. "He's very fond of the songs and dances in it," Basinger says. She introduced Joss to Leslie, saying, "You know, Miss Leslie, this is one of my former students who's now a TV writer. I'd like to introduce you to Joss Whedon." Joss was thrilled. As Leslie responded graciously, the actress's daughter was visibly shocked. She asked to speak to Basinger privately. "Is that the *Buffy the Vampire Slayer* guy?" she said, gasping. "I'm such a huge fan!"

Kai recalls a similar story involving Joss's icon Stephen Sondheim. The couple attended a performance of Sondheim's play *Company* in New York, with plans to meet the playwright afterward. Backstage, Sondheim mentioned to his cast that he was going to have dinner after the show with "Joss Whedon and his wife." Sondheim had no idea that they knew who Joss was; to his surprise, it turned out that several cast members were avid *Buffy* fans. "The people who liked it crashed our dinner and were gushing over Joss," Kai laughs. "Sondheim sitting here and they're like, 'Tell us another story, Joss.'"

A couple of months after his visit with Basinger, Joss turned in his second draft of *Wonder Woman*. Breaking the story had proven unusually difficult; he felt like he was pulling teeth to get the pieces to come together. "Plot-wise, I was like, 'Uh . . . I don't think I've cracked this,'" he recalls. "I went back and did an outline and said, 'I've got it!'"

Unfortunately, while Joss was fairly happy with the draft he turned in, the producers didn't seem to agree. "I wrote a script. I rewrote the story. And by the time I'd written the second script, they asked me . . . not to," Joss said. "They didn't tell me to leave, but they showed me the door and how pretty it was. 'Would I like to touch the knob and maybe make it swing?' I was dealing with them through Joel Silver, who couldn't tell me what they wanted or anything else. I was completely in the dark. So I didn't know what it was that I wasn't giving them."

While waiting on final word from Silver and executives at Warner Bros., he returned to rewrites on *Goners*. He was struggling to get it into the "perfect structure." Universal had asked for script changes, and while he was hoping to just move forward with the project, he felt that he finally had a basic story that he loved and could work out the specifics instead. That was a relief compared to being in limbo for eighteen months with no constructive direction on the *Wonder Woman* project.

With *Wonder Woman*, Joss felt that he never got to tell the story that he wanted to. "I never wrote my definitive version of the *Wonder Woman* script," he said. "I wrote one that had all the characters but the plot was super-lofty just structurally. So there is no sort of definitive *Wonder Woman* script that I would say, 'This is how I would have done it.' Although there are a lot of things in it that I wrote that I adore."

On February 3, 2007, Joss took to Whedonesque to make an official announcement about withdrawing from the *Wonder Woman* film:

Joss will not be fighting for our rights after all.

You (hopefully) heard it here first: I'm no longer slated to make Wonder Woman. What? But how? My chest . . . so tight! Okay, stay calm and I'll explain as best I can. It's pretty complicated, so bear with me. I had a take on the film that, well, nobody liked. Hey, not that complicated.

Let me stress first that everybody at the studio and Silver Pictures were cool and professional. We just saw different movies, and at the price range this kind of movie hangs in, that's never gonna work. . . .

The worst thing that can happen in this scenario is that the studio just keeps hammering out changes and the writer falls into a horrible limbo of development. These guys had the clarity and grace to skip that part. So I'm a free man. . . .

But most importantly, I never have to answer THAT question again!!!! And you don't have to link to every rumor site! Finally and forever: I never had an actress picked out, or even a consistent front-runner. I didn't have time to waste on casting when I was so busy air-balling on the script. (No! Rim! There was rim!) That's the greatest relief of all. I can do interviews again! . . .

ps All right, it was Cobie Smulders. Sorry, Cobes.

"I think that was more of a wink to me," *How I Met Your Mother* star Smulders explains. She'd become friends with Joss through her costar Alyson Hannigan. "I never met with anyone involved in the project. I was never up for it. But because he was a friend of mine, I think he was just playing around. Joss is one of the most loyal—I want to say friend, but also most loyal coworker. If he likes you, and if he thinks you're talented, he will fight for you."

In the end, Joss felt that *Wonder Woman* had been a waste of his time, because he "was so ground down. Second-guessing *everything*, unable to focus," he said. But he later added, "I would go back in a heartbeat if I believed that anybody believed in what I was doing. The lack of enthusiasm was overwhelming."

//////////

Joss was "ground down," but not completely hopeless. He was excited to finally be able to devote all his time to *Goners*. The year and a half he spent on *Wonder Woman* was emotionally exhausting, and for more reasons than just the stress of trying to deliver the perfect story in a vacuum.

"I really kept *Goners* at bay because of *Wonder Woman*. There's also a lot of . . . there's personal stuff that I'm not interested in talking about that was difficult," he said in August 2007. "There's also wonderful stuff that was difficult, which was my children. I had to create a system whereby I could get a full day's work [done] and still be the father that I want to be."

It felt like it would be just a matter of time until *Goners* moved out of development and into production. But the rewrite he turned in to Universal later that year "was not incredibly well-received," he said. So with his major-studio projects failing or stalling and no television series on the horizon, Joss starting thinking about developing "a real production company" that could create and produce smaller projects independently.

"I'm tired of not telling stories," he said. "It's really hard to get on television and birthing any television show is the most painful thing imaginable. Once you have one, you love it so much you forget, so you try to birth another one. Much like the female body. . . . Right now, the thought of trying to get a TV show off the ground is a little daunting. But the thought of making things that are smaller, a little more streamlined and a little more indie, so that I don't have to spend three and a half years telling every story. It doesn't feel like who I am. I feel like there are too many stories to tell."

He added, "That's part of why I've been working in comics so much, because the turnaround is so quick."

A NEW WAY OF STORYTELLING

By 2007, Joss was entering his final year as steward of Marvel Comics' *Astonishing X-Men* series, but his work as a comic book writer was far from over. For his next project, Joss returned to the defining hero of his career, four years after her television swan song. On March 14, Dark Horse Comics released *Buffy the Vampire Slayer Season Eight*.

This was not the first time that Buffy had fought her way through the panels of a comic book. Dark Horse had premiered a monthly *Buffy* comic in 1998, initially without much involvement by Joss or his writers. At the time, it was rare for a television scribe to work on a tie-in comic while the show was still on the air. In fact, Dark Horse had obtained the license through Fox, not Mutant Enemy, and the series' editor, Scott Allie, initially knew little about the program it was based on. As time went on, however, writers from the show such as Doug Petrie and Jane Espenson began to work on the comic, and it started to feel more in line with the show. With the success of these crossovers, bringing series writers into the comics fold became more common in Dark Horse's tie-in properties.

When Joss was developing the spin-off series *Angel*, he approached Dark Horse with the idea of doing another tie-in comic, and this time he wanted to be more involved. Scott Allie met with several Mutant Enemy writers, including Joss and Doug Petrie, to discuss what a comic for the series should be. By this point Allie had a much better understanding of the Buffyverse, so he was able to strike up a good rapport with the shows' creator. Their meeting opened the door to a lot more interaction between Joss and Dark Horse.

Next, Allie and Joss met to discuss doing a comics series centered around the Vampire Slayer Faith. He had a specific story that he wanted to tell—and he wanted to write it himself. He also had a particular artist he wanted to work with. They discussed it off and on for a little while, until Joss decided that he wanted to work on a new idea instead: a futuristic *Buffy* spin-off called *Fray*.

The series follows a Slayer named Melaka Fray who lives in twenty-third-century Manhattan. The city, not unlike the 1970s New York Joss grew up in, is crime-ridden and dangerous, but it has also been taken over by mutant mobsters. Fray is a young thief working for Gunther, a mutant boss who's willing to accept any and every job. Much like the ragtag crew of *Firefly*, Gunther and his crooks do what they need to do to get by in a harsh and unfair world. Fray accepts her lot in life until she, like a certain blonde cheerleader hundreds of years earlier, learns that she comes from a long line of Slayers.

Joss picked artist Karl Moline for the series. They were both very early in their comics careers, and thus there was a lot of back-and-forth discussion as they created a brand-new world with all-new characters. "Karl would give me thumbnails and we would go over them because there were certain things I was looking for specifically," he said. "But I loved what he came up with." The series was first published in 2001 and concluded in August 2003, with Joss's TV writing causing publishing delays. Joss has stated a number of times that he has plans to one day return to the world of Fray—beyond the time-travel story that would see Fray and Buffy cross paths as part of *Buffy the Vampire Slayer Season Eight*.

//////////

By the time they were working together on *Season Eight*, Joss and editor Scott Allie had developed a strong collaborative relationship. By talking over stories with Joss, reviewing his scripts, and going over artwork with him, Allie had gotten great insight into Joss's process and his vision. "His writing chops translate really well to comics," Allie says. "The number-one thing for me that transcends comics and film and TV, the thing that goes across everything he does that I find so compelling, is the way that he tackles genre fiction in a way that's all about character. Genre fiction, particularly in comics, tends to just be a quagmire of plot, and [Joss's work] is funny."

To the editor, Joss's work stood in sharp contrast to many of the superhero stories that made up the bulk of the industry's output. Allie has long said that one of the things wrong with superhero comics is that a lot of writers come up with a story they want to tell that has no real connection to any specific character. For example, they might pitch an idea for a Batman story to the *Batman* editor, and if that person says no, the writer will say that it works just as well as a Green Lantern story and pitch it to the *Green Lantern* editor. "What that tells me is that the story isn't remotely about the character," Allie says. "The story is just the writer saying, 'Well, maybe I can get some money out of the *Batman* guy.' If the story works equally well for Batman as it does for Green Lantern, then it probably doesn't work at all for either one of them."

Joss, on the other hand, brought his intense focus on the "Buffy of it" to this new medium. "Once you focus and make sure those elements are integral to the story," Allie says, "then it's a *Buffy* story and you can't equally [say that] it's an *Angel* story. You can't just take that story and say, 'Oh, well, we've already got something going on *Buffy* this week. Let's just do this on *Angel*.'" Allie also appreciated that Joss's fantastical adventures were always grounded in relatable human concerns. "Not many of us have had the experience where our 'stepfather' actually turns out to be a robot [as in the *Buffy* episode "Ted"], but we can all really relate to what's really at work there. We can really relate to feeling threatened by our stepfather and all our friends not understanding it and our mother seeming like she's under some kind of spell. And that's what happens to Buffy every week, or every month in the comic."

///////////

Buffy the Vampire Slayer Season Eight didn't just carry forward Joss's focus on "the Buffy of it"; it was a direct continuation of the *Buffy* TV show. It picks up a year after Buffy shared her powers with all the Potential Slayers in the television finale and finds her and Xander running the operations of a worldwide network of new Slayers. It would become a five-year, forty-issue series exploring this new status quo. Before *Season Eight*, canceled shows like *The X-Files* and *Star Trek* had continued telling their stories in feature films, but no one had attempted a full seasonal arc in comic book form. The project's success set a new trend in television-to-comics adaptations, as several other series launched comic book sequels, including *Buffy*'s onetime WB neighbor *Charmed*.

As with the unproduced *Buffy* animated series, the comics format enabled the writers to include moments that would have been too costly to produce in live-action television. They set issues in fantastic worlds beyond the earthly domain and brought back numerous guest characters, some thought long-gone. But the enlarged scope of *Season Eight* also presented problems: with Buffy so preoccupied with running an army of Slayers, many of her concerns were problems that the average reader couldn't actually relate to. As the series went on, it lost sight of the deeply personally stories Allie had so admired. "There were definitely things set up from the beginning of *Season Eight* that were very relatable," he says. "But we found ourselves bogged down in some of the plot stuff that takes you away from the small personal stuff that I think really makes *Buffy* so extraordinary.

"There are places where I think, and [Joss] would say the same, we kind of strayed from the true path. At the end we brought it all back, and it was through a great deal of hard work that we did a good job of pulling it together at the end, but when you're trying to figure that out, it's always going to go back to character."

//////////

Also in 2007, Joss again teamed up with Dark Horse to produce an online comic for MySpace.com. *Dark Horse Presents* had initially been a print anthology series, the first comic book that the indie publisher produced. Running from 1986 to 2000, it featured a mix of established and new writers and artists, giving many of them a much wider audience. Dark Horse decided to relaunch the series in the digital world as part of MySpace's comics portal.

Joss's contribution to the new collection, *Sugarshock!*, debuted in July 2007. It's the tale of an "all-girl/robot rock band" that unwittingly gets pulled into an intergalactic battle of the bands. The band is fronted by Dandelion Naizen, the hyperspastic lead singer and guitarist, with an extreme and somewhat inexplicable hatred of Vikings. "She's . . . more like me than anybody I've written," Joss said. "She's insanely bipolar and completely capricious but very dedicated to something or other." Rounding out the band are "Wade, the drummer, who's really sexy, kind of chubby and always takes a groupie home because she's awesome"; L'Lihdra, the "very tall, very ethereal and very beautiful" guitarist who is always clad in men's pinstriped suits; and Phil, the bassist robot.

Fábio Moon drew the world of *Sugarshock!*, and together he and Joss won an Eisner Award for Best Digital Comic of 2008. Joss scored an additional Eisner for Best New Series that year for *Buffy the Vampire Slayer Season Eight*, which he shared with artists Georges Jeanty and Andy Owens and cowriter Brian K. Vaughan.

//////////

Brian K. Vaughan had also created, with artist Adrian Alphona, the comics series *Runaways*, of which Joss was a big fan. The series follows a group of six teenagers who decide to run away together after they discover that their parents are supervillains. Their lives are fraught with both mundane difficulties and ethical challenges as they figure out how to fend for themselves and deal with their own emerging superpowers. The characters inhabit the same universe as Marvel's higher-profile superheroes such as the X-Men and the Avengers, but they see them as a bunch of "old guys" who don't understand what they're going through. A "growing up is hell" story about headstrong and snarky teenagers steeped in Marvel mythology—it's no wonder Joss fell in love.

The series debuted on Marvel Comics' smaller Tsunami imprint in July 2003 and ran for about a year; Joss penned a letter begging Marvel to continue it. (The letter was later published in the series' first hardcover compilation.) The Tsunami imprint was shuttered, but Marvel chose to bring *Runaways* back in 2005, after sales showed what a strong fan base it had. Vaughan and Alphona returned, but a year later they announced that they would be leaving when issue #24 came out in 2007. Vaughan was being wooed to join the ABC series *Lost*, where former *Buffy* and *Angel* scribe Drew Goddard had taken up residence. In light of *Runaways'* popularity, Marvel was desperate to find a new writer who could step in and fill Vaughan's shoes. Nick Lowe, the series editor, thought he knew the perfect person.

At the time, Lowe's boss was Mike Marts, who was also Joss's editor on *Astonishing X-Men*. Knowing that the writer was a *Runaways* fan, Lowe reached out to Marts to see if Joss would be interested in taking over the series from his *Season Eight* cowriter. Marts sent the offer over and Joss thought about it, but he ultimately turned it down. Lowe accepted defeat as gracefully as he could and left for the weekend.

"I came back on Monday to find an e-mail from Joss telling me that he'd changed his mind and would like to do *Runaways* after all," Lowe says. "Apparently the thought was eating away at his brain and he ended up calling Brian K. Vaughan over the weekend. A week later he shot what the story would be over to me and I was over the moon. He nailed it right away and he had me tearing up in an outline. *That bastard!*"

Joss's six-episode arc, "Dead End Kids," brings the Runaways to New York City to meet with a long-running Marvel villain, the crime boss known as the Kingpin. There, the kids come across an artifact that unexpectedly sends them back in time. Trapped in 1907 New York, they fall in with the "Street Arabs," a mishmash crew who also have superpowers, as they search for a way back to the present day. Joss created several memorable characters, including Lillie McGurty, a woman who can dance on air if there's music playing, and Klara Prast, a young girl with the power to control plants, who has been married off to a much older man who is abusing her. Klara joins the Runaways when they return to the twenty-first century and remains with the series as it continues.

Joss's first issue came out in April 2007, and in July, Marvel gave Whedonesque.com readers a look at the full issue in digital form. As with *Astonishing X-Men*, putting Joss on *Runaways* had given Marvel the opportunity to appeal to Whedon fans who weren't necessarily at the comic book store every Tuesday. And setting the tale in a previously unseen past made it more accessible to those who were interested in Joss's work but intimidated by the idea of catching up on a lot of backstory.

Among existing *Runaways* fans, reception to Joss and artist Michael Ryan's run was mostly supportive, especially considering that Joss was the first new writer to step into an acclaimed series that already had a strong authorial voice in Vaughan. While many enjoyed the new world that Joss created, some felt that it was less a proper extension of *Runaways* than a well-told tale by a fan who clearly loved and knew the series but didn't quite capture the characters' original voices.

Nonetheless, Joss's involvement certainly did increase interest in the comic. "The sales were great," Lowe says.

WGA WRITERS' STRIKE

As Joss was enjoying the streamlined production process that allowed him to write and release multiple comic book series over the course of just a few months, he was eager to translate those same quick turnarounds to the world of feature film. In spring 2007, he approached former Mutant Enemy writer Drew Goddard with an idea: he wanted to write a movie with him—in a weekend. The two of them, he proposed, would hole up in a hotel room and not leave until they had knocked out a script. It would be like they were back on *Buffy*, when they often fell behind and had to finish a complete script in just a few days.

At the time, Goddard was working on a feature script for another writer/producer wunderkind: J. J. Abrams. Goddard had freelanced for Abrams's juggernaut *Lost* during its first season in 2004, then joined his spy series *Alias* in 2005 as a writer and coproducer for its final season. He returned to *Lost* for its third and fourth seasons and was now following *that* up with writing duties on Abrams's upcoming horror film *Cloverfield*.

Cloverfield would be Goddard's highest-profile project to date, a movie budgeted at $25 million that would go on to make nearly seven times that upon its release. But he knew well how slowly the film world worked, and he shared Joss's desire for the energy and fun that could come from writing quickly and to a hard deadline. He also missed working with Joss. "I've told passionate Whedon fans, 'Look, I know you guys think you're the biggest Joss fans, but you're not bigger than I am,'" he laughs. "I loved him so much that I actually weaseled a job with him. That's how crazed I was. I actually got into his inner circle."

So they decided to go for it.

First, though, the logistics needed to be worked out. The story had to be something they could realistically write under the strict time parameters—an intricate murder mystery, for instance, was out. But a horror film, they thought, could be written quickly without sacrificing quality. They both loved horror movies, and they both wanted to make one. Horror it was.

//////////

It was the right time for a horror movie, too; at the time, the genre was experiencing a resurgence. As with most returning trends, however, the newest generation of horror auteurs sought to put a new spin on the genre. Thus, the horror movies of the mid-2000s went for scares by placing a strong emphasis on graphic violence, nudity, torture, and mutilation. Critics labeled the subgenre, made popular by such films as *Hostel* (2005), *The Devil's Rejects* (2005), and the *Saw* series, "torture porn." Established horror writers and directors were split on whether torture porn was a legitimate new subgenre or dehumanizing exploitation. Despite the criticism, the movies had many fans, and Lionsgate, the studio behind *Hostel* and the *Saw* films, found them to be very profitable.

Joss himself had recently jumped into the torture porn debate, to criticize the publicity for another Lionsgate film, 2007's *Captivity*. The billboards and posters for the movie featured four images of actress Elisha Cuthbert being tortured, each with a caption: ABDUCTION, CONFINEMENT, TORTURE, and TERMINATION. On March 22, 2007, Joss posted an open letter on the *Huffington Post* in support of a campaign asking the Motion Picture Association of America to withhold the film's rating:

> To the MPAA,
> There's a message I'm supposed to cut and paste but I imagine you've read it. So just let me say that the ad campaign for "Captivity" is not only a literal sign of the collapse of humanity, it's an assault. I've watched plenty of horror—in fact I've made my share. But the advent of torture-porn and the total dehumanizing not just of women (though they always come first) but of all human beings has made horror a largely unpalatable genre. This ad campaign is part of something dangerous and repulsive, and that act of aggression has to be answered.
> As a believer not only in the First Amendment but of the necessity of horror stories, I've always been against acts of censorship. I

distrust anyone who wants to ban something "for the good of the public." But this ad is part of a cycle of violence and misogyny that takes something away from the people who have to see it. It's like being mugged (and I have been). These people flouted the basic rules of human decency.

God knows the culture led them there, but we have to find our way back and we have to make them know that people will not stand for this. And the only language they speak is money. (A devastating piece in the New Yorker—not gonna do it.) So talk money. Remove the rating, and let them see how far over the edge they really are.

Thanks for reading this, if anyone did.

Sincerely, Joss Whedon.

Creator, "Buffy the Vampire Slayer"

He later took to Whedonesque.com to discuss the parallels between the stoning of Du'a Khalil Aswad, an Iraqi Kurd murdered in an "honor" killing, and the trailer for *Captivity*, in which "pretty much all you learn is that Elisha Cuthbert is beautiful, then kidnapped, inventively, repeatedly and horrifically tortured, and that the first thing she screams is 'I'm sorry.'"

He'd also recently revealed that his mysterious spec script *Goners* was a story that had poured out of him in response to the popularity of torture porn films in which "kids we don't care about are mutilated for hours." The script, he said, is "about a girl named Mia . . . who sort of sees in a mystical way the underbelly of the city and of human society, and goes through a kind of extraordinary hell." For Joss, *Goners* was "an antidote to that very kind of film, the horror movie with the expendable human beings in it. Because I don't believe any human beings are." His story, by contrast, "is much more a story about human connection and whether or not it's possible."

But with *Goners* still mired in the rewrite stage, perhaps his new horror project with Goddard would be the one to do right where Joss had seen so much wrong in the industry. Perhaps it would show moviegoers they could still be scared on a more cerebral level—by looking critically at the inescapable horror formula by which a group of kids are faced with a killer and proceed to make the worst, stupidest choice at every turn.

//////////

Of course, before all that could happen, he and Goddard had to write it. Joss had been musing on an idea for a horror film for a couple years, and he already had a clear vision for the third act of a story. (The only other time he'd ever seen a story so clearly before writing it was for his unproduced early sci-fi script *Afterlife*.) He pitched the idea to Goddard, who was quickly on board. They spent several months talking about the story and working up an outline for the script, and then checked themselves into a two-floor hotel room—Goddard was upstairs, Joss downstairs—and swore not to leave until it was done.

They wrote for three days straight. "It was a crazy three days," Goddard says. "Just our laptops, and our appetites. We ate a lot of room service. We definitely tried to treat ourselves, because we were working from 6 AM till 1 AM every day. You need some creature comforts."

The writing flowed smoothly as they divvied up pages and scenes and met up later in the day to mesh them together and figure out the next batch of assignments. They got to argue about who would win in a battle between werewolves and zombies—shades of Joss's "The dwarves are demons! The midgets are vampires!" arguments in his *Buffy* days.

Goddard was stuck on a certain scene in which the characters needed to read from a young girl's diary. He called downstairs to Joss to see if he was interested in taking a crack at her words. "Six minutes later, he ran upstairs with it, this full page [of] a beautifully written horror diary of a prairie girl," he said. "He cranked that diary out faster than I've seen anyone write anything. I couldn't write my own name repeatedly as fast as he wrote that diary." Joss had once again found his calling in giving voice to a young girl.

What emerged from the marathon hotel session was *The Cabin in the Woods*, a comedic horror tale following a group of young people who head to a remote cabin for a quick weekend getaway. One by one, they're each killed off in typical horror movie fashion. In this case, though, it's not just the usual knife-wielding maniac behind the mayhem. The youths have been lured into a secret facility, where unseen technicians manipulate them into succumbing to horror clichés ("We should split up—we can cover more ground that way"), then serve them up as part of a ritual sacrifice.

With the bones of the story formed into a workable skeleton, Joss and Goddard checked out of the hotel knowing that there would be more rewriting to come. But the project they'd wanted to move forward with as quickly as possible soon came to a complete stop—along with the rest of the storytelling in Hollywood.

/////////

When Joss joined *Roseanne* in 1989, he'd missed by a year being caught up in a contentious strike by the Writers Guild of America. The 1988 WGA strike had focused on expanding writers' creative rights in television and, more important, providing them with enhanced residuals when an hour-long program aired in syndication. Networks, studios, and production companies, represented by the Alliance of Motion Picture and Television Producers (AMPTP), wanted to put the writers on a sliding scale for residuals, citing lower ratings for syndicated repeats. The WGA pushed back, angling for a larger percentage when a series' foreign rights were sold. This was a new arena in 1988—no one knew exactly how American series would fare abroad—but writers didn't want to be cut out of valuable royalties if the emerging market started to soar.

The 1988 strike was the longest in the guild's history. Starting March 7 and running through August 7, it revved up just as production on the 1987–88 television season was coming to an end. While it didn't affect that season greatly, it delayed the start of the fall 1988–89 season by about six weeks, at a time when networks were chained to the cycle of show premieres and viewers had little option other than to view episodes live if they wanted to see them. The broadcast networks filled their WGA-writer-less slates with more newsmagazines in the style of CBS's *60 Minutes* and ABC's *20/20*. The lack of scripted series ushered in the beginnings of today's reality programming boom, as NBC upgraded *Unsolved Mysteries* from an occasional special to a weekly series, and Fox premiered its unscripted, voyeuristic *Cops* series. The more immediate result, however, was that ABC, CBS, and NBC saw their prime-time ratings drop 4.6 percent that fall.

After five months, both sides came to an agreement and the WGA won a better percentage on foreign sales, while the AMPTP convinced the writers to accept its sliding residual scale. That was the last Hollywood strike for almost twenty years.

In July 2007, regular negotiations between the WGA and AMPTP had already begun. On the table was the three-year Minimum Basic Agreement (MBA)—the contract that covers writers' "salaries, benefits, pensions, working conditions, residual payments, and creative rights" in television, film, and new media. Advances in digital technology had only recently made it practical for viewers to download or stream TV episodes online, and the practice was still in its infancy. But the networks were already using new media as a way to grow their broadcast audiences, requesting supplemental video content from their series' writers to distribute as online exclusives. And as with foreign rights in the 1988 strike, the WGA knew that online access was an outlet with the potential to become quite profitable as soon as networks and studios developed deals to monetize viewing directly.

In the negotiations, the AMPTP acknowledged that online viewing was increasing, but insisted that it was too early to judge how profitable it would be. As it stood, writers were only paid when a show was streamed, with their compensation being 1.2 percent of the sales revenue. If someone downloaded an episode from iTunes with an exact price point, they received nothing from that sale. For three months, negotiations were at an impasse over the issue.

When the WGA's contracts expired at the end of October 2007, the negotiating committee formally recommended that the writers go on strike. Committee chairman John Bowman told the members that "the Internet has to be one of our most important issues. That's our future." On November 5, picketing WGA members focused on fourteen Los Angeles studios and several locations in New York (including NBC's headquarters, Rockefeller Center), and many SAG members and Teamsters refused to cross the picket lines in solidarity with the striking writers.

//////////

Just days earlier, on November 1, it was announced that Joss would soon be returning to television, with a face quite familiar to Whedon fans. *Dollhouse*, a series about a group of "dolls"—young people who exist as bland, blank slates in a spa-like laboratory until they are "imprinted with personality packages" and sent out on all kinds of morally ambiguous missions—would star former Buffyverse guest star Eliza Dushku as Echo, a doll who begins to see beyond her programming. "We call it a suspense-drama-mythology-comedy-action-horror musical," Joss joked. "The main thrust is the thruline of Echo as a sort of newly born character who goes, 'Wait a minute—I exist. Wow. So who would I be? And how dangerous is it for me to let anybody know that I know that I exist?' Not unlike the Frankenstein myth, it's, 'Who made me, who am I, and why am I?'"

Joss's return to television had come about unexpectedly, thanks to a lunch meeting a few months earlier between him and Dushku. Joss thought it would be just another one of their check-in meetings; they had met to talk about her career path a few times over the years, ever since Joss reached out to her after her run of "crappy horror movies" in the early 2000s. He'd asked to meet for tea and then started in with the mentoring: "I said, 'I love you. I think you have something that no other actor that I've worked with has. What the f**k are you making these movies for? Why are you doing this to me? You're killing me. I just think you're better than this.'" At the time, Dushku had been in a state of self-examination, trying to figure out what she wanted and where she wanted to go in her career. It was soon thereafter that she scored the lead in Fox's *Tru Calling*, and when it ended after two seasons in 2005, she took a role in an off-Broadway play. They would reconnect from time to time, including one night after a performance. The two sat up until 2 AM discussing a new opportunity that she had.

Now, however, as Joss and Dushku met to discuss what her next career steps should be, especially in light of a development deal she had with Fox, he was suddenly struck with an idea for a new show. "It was a mistake!" Joss told *Variety*. "I sat down with her to talk about her options, and acted all sage, saying things backwards like Yoda and laying out what I thought she should do. But in the course of doing it, I accidentally made one up. I told it to her, and she said, 'That's exactly what I want to do.'" Inspired by Dushku's life as an actress, Joss came up with the premise of people who were hired out to be someone else's fantasy. He described the show to her over their four-hour lunch and delivered her an outline two weeks later.

"He had my back," Dushku says. "We pitched it to Fox, and it was a complicated, controversial, and deep project. Through all of the press, criticism, and acclaim, he was my partner." The network gave them a seven-episode order without even seeing a pilot.

But Joss's latest exploration into the questions that propel humanity would have to wait. The strike imposed a pencils-and-laptops-down mandate on WGA members, and he had to stop all work on *Dollhouse*. Instead of using it as an opportunity to take a break and relax, Joss poured his energy into a collaborative project of another sort: becoming a voice for the striking WGA writers.

//////////

The first day of the strike, Joss was ready to spend the day on the picket line. His body, however, had other plans. "I came out and I was lying down on the grass with my picket sign," Joss recalls. "Aly [Hannigan] and Alexis [Denisof] were like, 'You have to go back home.'" The next day, he was too ill to leave the house, and two days after that, he could barely get out of bed.

He and Kai both were sick and getting sicker, and their symptoms could not be written off as the inevitable result of having two kids in preschool. Eventually they learned that they were having a reaction to mold in their home, which was concentrated in their bedroom. Until Joss could recover and show his support on the picket line, he took to Whedonesque.com to share his favorite strike movies (*Matewan, Newsies, Norma Rae, Day of the Dead, Billy Elliot*) and otherwise "vent his spleen for the cause":

> November 7, 2007
>
> . . . The easiest tactic is for people to paint writers as namby pamby arty scarfy posers, because it's what most people think even when we're not striking. Writing is largely not considered work. Art in general is not considered work. Work is a thing you physically labor at, or at the very least, hate. Art is fun. (And Hollywood writers are overpaid, scarf-wearing dainties.) It's an easy argument to make. And a hard one to dispute. . . .
>
> And as work? Well, in the first place, it IS fun. When it's going well, it's the most fun I can imagine having. . . . Writing is enjoyable and ephemeral. And it's hard work.
>
> It's always hard . . . the ACT of writing is hard. When Buffy was flowing at its flowingest, David Greenwalt used to turn to me at some point during every torturous story-breaking session and say "Why is it still hard? When do we just get to be good at it?" I'll only bore you with one theory: because every good story needs to be completely personal (so there are no guidelines) and completely universal (so it's all been done). It's just never simple. . . .

December 6, 2007

. . . Marti Noxon has tried to HIJACK this entire site for some "cause." She forwarded this letter she wanted me to print:

"We think it would be unbelievably amazing if Joss were able to tell whomever might be reading his blog for info on the Friday picket that . . . the WGA is doing a Holiday Harvest Food drive for local food banks (that have reached an all-time low in donations, recently) and we're asking everyone who can to bring jars of peanut butter, cans of tuna, and tons of powdered milk. In this way, besides just making a statement in solidarity and support of the WGA strike, we can also be re-stocking the shelves of the local food banks and feeding the poor and hungry of our community."

Like I'd print something so depressing! This event is about one thing: my famousnessness. First everyone's all about "the strike," now it's "helping people" . . . let's not lose sight of the point, people! You can't spell M.E. without, well, me.

Like screenwriting itself, championing the writers' strike was a role Joss was born and bred to play. "I was a '70s Upper West Side, proto-socialist radical lefty, so it was kind of nice to be able to flex that again," Joss says. "My dad said that I was named for Joe Hill [labor activist and songwriter]—I don't know if it's true—but I did have a real feeling about that stuff. So it's nice to be able to fight the good fight on any level." Joss even penned a Hill-esque protest song for Whedonesque:

> CBS and Fox they think they got us,
> Do they got us? NO!
> Even though we all wear scarves and glasses,
> We're a union, just by sayin' so . . .

//////////

Joss was back on the picket lines in time for Mutant Enemy Day, held on Friday, December 7, at the picket on the 20th Century Fox lot. It kicked off with a delivery of one thousand donuts from Sarah Michelle Gellar to the Whedon writers, actors, and fans—some had flown in for support—who had come out. The actors that came spanned the entire Mutant Enemy oeuvre: Nicholas Brendon, Eliza Dushku, Juliet Landau, and Harry Groener from *Buffy*; J. August Richards and Amy Acker from *Angel*; Nathan Fillion, Morena Baccarin, Summer Glau, and Alan Tudyk from *Firefly*. And of course the writers, to whom the strike meant the most: Tim Minear, Marti Noxon, Jane Espenson, David Fury, Drew Goddard, and several others.

Joss announced later that he'd brought four Sharpies, prepared to sign autographs for the fans who came out to support them. But he never had to take a single marker from his pocket—fans were certainly happy to see and talk with the writers and stars, but they had no time for autographs. They were focused on marching, waving at motorists, and encouraging drivers to honk in solidarity.

"The fans from day one have understood what this is about," Joss enthused. "There's never been any 'Where's our shows? Why are you guys doing this?' They understand that we're reacting to an impossible situation. They also understand that making a show or a film is collaboration between the artists and the fans. They come out and support not just with us but with each other and the whole concept of an artistic community."

Whedon fan support was not limited to special Mutant Enemy strike days. Fans came by to support the writers at other times, and even delivered pizzas to Jane Espenson's group at Universal. The pizza drive was organized by Whedonesque (Kai later told Joss that "these people are going to be running the world"), and it surprised strikers who didn't quite understand what was going on. "The writers . . . were very appreciative. They were kind of confused though," one of the organizers reported. " 'Joss Whedon sent us pizza?' 'No, his *fans*.' I don't think most of them were familiar with the idea of TV and film writers having fans."

///////////

The strike went into the new year, and Joss kept penning missives. Some of the pieces he wrote were so angry that the Writers Guild didn't use them—yet when the strike looked like it was coming to a sudden close, the group suddenly wanted to get his words in the press. On February 6, 2008, a day after the WGA leadership scheduled a meeting with active members to get feedback on a proposed contract, a letter from Joss was sent to guild members:

Dear Writers,

I have good news. I have lots of good news. In fact, I have **way too much** good news.

The strike is almost over. . . . The Oscars seem to be the point of focus for a lot of this speculation. That either they must be preserved, or that the studios feel they must be preserved, and therefore this terrible struggle will end. There is an argument to be made for wanting the show to go on: it showcases the artists with whom we are bonded (there's no award for Best Hiding of Net Profits), and it provides employment and revenue for thousands in the community that has been hit so hard by this action. Having said that, it's a f%$#ing awards show. It's a vanity fair. It's a blip. We're fighting (**fighting**, remember?) for the future of our union, our profession, our art. If that fight carries us through the Holy Night when Oscar was born, that's just too bad. . . .

I ask you all to remember: the studios caused an industry-wide shutdown. They made a childishly amateurish show of pretending to negotiate, then retreated into their lairs (yes, they have lairs) to starve us out. They emerged just before Christmas to raise our hopes, then left in a premeditated huff. . . .

This is not over. Nor is it close. Until the moment it is over, it can never **be** close. Because if we see the finish line we will flag and they are absolutely counting on us to do that. In the room, reason. On the streets, on the net, I say reason is for the "moderates." Remember what they've done. Remember what they're trying to take from us. FIGHT. FIGHT. FIGHT.

I have been mugged an embarrassing number of times, even for a New Yorker. I've been yelled at and chased, beaten down and kicked, threatened with a gun and the only mugger who still hurts my gut is the one who made me shake his hand. Until there is a deal—the right deal . . . let's keep our hands in our pockets or on our signs. Let's not be victims. Let's never.

In solidarity,

Joss Whedon

It had been six years since Malcolm Reynolds left the small screen, but Joss was still revving up his inner Browncoat. "That's the reason I write that guy," he explains. "Because I write about helplessness, and in the face of a massive corporation or Rupert Murdoch, what else could you ever feel . . . but helpless. In general, the strike was depressing because there is a systematic destruction of the middle class in this country that is intentional and successful. It's a constant thing—it is corporate greed and calumny, those things stick. Bullies are bullies— they must not be tolerated."

On February 9, the WGA and the AMPTP reached a tentative deal. Three days later, WGA president Patric Verrone announced that the guild membership had voted to end the strike, and on February 26, a new three-year contract was overwhelmingly approved. The 2008 Minimum Basic Agreement gave the WGA new rights for creating new-media content. Writers would also receive better residuals for "the reuse of movies and television programs on the Internet and in new media."

Joss was not thrilled with the final deal; "He thought it was a bad idea," Kai says. He felt that the WGA had been beaten down and had given in without adequately considering the artists' livelihood. He wanted to find a new way of doing things completely outside the system represented by the AMPTP. It was time for Joss Whedon to rewrite the rules yet again.

DR. HORRIBLE, I PRESUME

Without the writers' strike, Joss Whedon's next groundbreaking project might never have come to pass, at least not in the same ambitious form. He'd been thinking prior to the strike of self-producing an audio podcast, but he'd only gotten as far as coming up with a title and a basic concept: *Dr. Horrible's Sing-Along Blog*, a musical about a would-be supervillain who details his exploits on his blog and tries to win over the girl of his dreams. "I wanted to write songs," Joss said. "I really liked and related to this character and thought, I could just put up some songs as a fun side project."

Then the WGA went on strike, and with Joss's studio work on hold, his side project became a major focus of his attention. He decided to expand it from a podcast to a visual web series, and to bring in other people who would act and sing different parts. Still, he wanted to keep it low-budget, something he could produce himself without any involvement from the studio system he and the WGA were currently battling on the picket lines. With *Dr. Horrible*, he would be the "studio"—he would make the decisions instead of waiting for the green light from someone else. "Freedom is glorious," Joss said. "The fact is, I've had very good relationships with studios, and I've worked with a lot of smart executives. But there is a difference when you can just go ahead and do something."

////////////

The first thing he did was to enlist some producing partners. Joss had seen a YouTube video in support of the writers' strike that was written and produced by his brothers Zack and Jed Whedon and Jed's fiancée, Maurissa Tancharoen. *WGA vs. AMPTP* was a witty, tongue-in-cheek piece that illustrated the huge divide between the two camps. Joss loved it, and on December 20, 2007, he promoted the video on Whedonesque—ending his post with a vague promise that he was "scheming schemes" to make new stories and asking his fans to stay tuned. It's easy to surmise that the scheme in question was *Dr. Horrible*. He asked the trio behind the video to join him on his new project.

This would not be the first film project that Joss and Jed had worked on together, since young Joss had directed his little brother in his short film *Stupidman* when Jed turned eight. "The embarrassing thing about that," Joss said, "is that it was a group of eight year olds and I did stand in the next room pacing back and forth going, 'they're not laughing, they're not laughing,' like it was a Broadway opening." Joss needn't have worried. After the kids watched the fifteen-minute movie, they immediately requested repeat screenings.

Joss had already written one song for the web series, "Freeze Ray," and he played it for everyone on his keyboard at the collaborators' first official creative meeting. "All of a sudden the world of Dr Horrible started to come clear to us," Tancharoen said. "It all evolved from there." Tancharoen and Jed felt that the musical should start with "Freeze Ray," because it was such a disarming introduction to a supervillain out to take over the world: Dr. Horrible's alter-ego Billy is an awkward boy with the aching desire to talk to Penny, a girl he sees in the Laundromat.

> With my Freeze Ray, I will stop
> The world
>
> With my Freeze Ray, I will find the time to
> Find the words to
>
> Tell you how
> How you make
> Make me feel

With "Freeze Ray" setting the tone for the script, Tancharoen and the Whedon brothers began to flesh out the characters. Dr. Horrible is an aspiring evil mastermind who longs to be welcomed into Bad Horse's Evil League of Evil but has yet to make more than a whimper in the villainous world. Where he sees the world as utter chaos and wants to take over, his crush Penny is an idealist who volunteers at a homeless shelter as one of her ways to make the world a better place. Threatening both his villainous and his romantic aspirations is Captain Hammer, a jocky, self-centered oaf of a superhero who dates Penny as a way of lording it over his nemesis.

Joss wanted to make the web series in three parts, corresponding to the three acts of the story, but without network commercial breaks and time constraints to worry about, those parts could be of any length. He and his collaborators decided that they would just fit in everything that served the story. They aimed for the full story to be thirty minutes, and the final product would clock in at forty-two minutes—an epic by the standards of original online media at the time.

By 2008, there had been several web series that had their own small followings—*lonelygirl15* aired on YouTube from 2006 to 2008, *Quarterlife* aired on MySpace in early 2008, and *The Guild* premiered on YouTube in 2007. Episodes tended to be only a few minutes each, and almost none were over ten minutes. Most series were very low-fi, shot with a reality television aesthetic. A high-production-value series broken into three episodes, each nearly fifteen minutes long, was a daunting, daring task.

///////////

Initially, their plans for the series were more modest; they thought they'd shoot the whole thing on a webcam and play all the parts themselves. But as they wrote more songs, the scope of the project kept expanding, and by the time they'd finished about half of the script, Joss began reaching out to his actor friends.

Neil Patrick Harris, who had previously missed out on the role of Simon Tam in *Firefly*, was approached to play the titular Dr. Horrible. Joss only got as far as telling him that he was doing a web musical before Harris said yes. "Then he got mad and said 'Wait a second, let me pitch first,'" Harris explained. "Then he told me the name of it, the idea behind it, and the reasoning behind it and I said 'Hell, yes.'"

For the role of Captain Hammer, Joss turned to a Whedonverse stalwart. Nathan Fillion says that Joss called him with the news that he and his brothers were working on a project. "'Hey, so, we have this thing and we're thinking about putting it together, and the writers' strike—,' and I said, 'I'm in.' He said, 'It's a musical.' My heart went [*exalted sigh*]. Because, you know, to be recorded singing, that's another thing altogether." Fillion had been incredibly impressed with "Once More, with

Feeling," and he longed to add a musical to the projects he did with Joss. "Then he told me Neil Patrick Harris was gonna be in it. Now, to be recorded singing is one thing. To be recorded singing next to Neil Patrick Harris, that's another thing altogether."

Apparently learning his lesson from two interrupted pitches by phone, Joss e-mailed Felicia Day to ask if she could sing, hoping she could take on the part of Penny. The actress had been a friend since she played one of the Potentials on the seventh season of *Buffy*, and she was the creator and star of the web series *The Guild*. That series, a comedy about a group of online gamers, had been an inspiration for *Dr. Horrible*. "The thing about Joss is that he definitely attracts the most talented people in all areas," Day said. "When he wants to do an Internet musical starring a supervillain, everybody's saying 'Yes, please.'"

Harris had done a number of musicals, including *Sweeney Todd* and a Broadway run of *Assassins*, both by Joss's beloved Sondheim. Fillion had done musicals in high school and college and had worked his way through college as a karaoke host. With a cast of this caliber, it quickly became obvious that *Dr. Horrible* would no longer be a webcam video. With improved production values, the budget climbed to roughly $200,000—still limited for the scope they had in mind, but far higher than that of the average Internet project.

Raising the necessary funds was the biggest challenge of the project. To quote Dr. Horrible himself, "It's not about making money, it's about *taking* money. Destroying the status quo." In this case, the money that Joss initially took was from himself. Joss and Kai approached their accountant, who was resistant to the idea of them using their own money to bankroll *Dr. Horrible*, but the Whedons were insistent. They also worked together to reach out to others who might be interested in funding the project. The couple found enough people who wanted to be a part of Joss's labor of love that they were able to raise the $200,000 they needed.

The budget would have been roughly double that amount if not for the fact that most of the participants agreed to work for free, in exchange for a share of future profits. "[Joss] said that obviously none of us will be paid," Harris explained, "but if it catches on like he hoped it would, we would all be paid handsomely at the tail end of it all. That really wasn't even a concern for me. I would have done it for zero dollars."

When it came to working out the details of everyone's profit participation, Joss was willing to be generous—drawing a contrast with the way the AMPTP was treating the WGA. He was very vocal about the fact that his passion for *Dr. Horrible* came out of his feelings regarding the writers' strike. He saw the Internet as a medium in which he could set the rules—because, as he puts it, the "guilds haven't been beaten down yet." Since there were no established pay scales for actors and crew working on scripted Internet content, "I got to invent them," Joss said. "I got to make the writers and stars profit participants on gross level." They used the WGA and Screen Actors Guild general rates for a series-related webisode as their initial model, and worked with the guilds to finalize the compensation agreements.

"There's no reason why there can't be a business model that is completely inclusive in profit participation," Joss said. "I'm the studio. I still get way more than everybody else, after I make back my production costs and everything's paid out. When we're into pure profit . . . I win. So—and this was the whole thing during the strike—why try to offer us nothing, when all we're asking for is a percentage?"

"The concept was so pure and kind of amazingly moral," Harris said. "Joss wanted not just to walk the picket lines but actually do something about it."

///////////

To keep *Dr. Horrible* on budget, the project needed to run as smoothly and efficiently as possible. Michael Boretz, Joss's assistant in the later *Buffy* years, was brought in as a producer, and his first task was enlisting key crew who knew how Joss worked and could quickly get them into production. Lisa Lassek, editor on *Buffy*, *Angel*, and *Firefly*, came in, as did Shawna Trpcic, costume designer for *Angel* and *Firefly*. Ryan Green, *Serenity* camera operator, jumped in as director of photography. "It was helpful having those years of experience to know the people," Boretz said, and "then once they were hired, to be able to communicate effectively with them to relay Joss' vision and help facilitate getting us into production quickly."

Boretz credited Joss with inspiring such loyalty and eagerness among his collaborators. Aside from his writing and storytelling talents, Boretz said, Joss is very warm and inviting. "He creates that kind of environment on the set as well. And that's why people like to come back and continue to work for him and are willing to do favors." Whedon studies scholar Rhonda V. Wilcox agrees. "One of the things that makes him a really strong television creator is that he is good at collaboration. He's good at drawing the best out of other folks because if you're going to do good television, you normally have got to have other people to help you write it. Joss gets people who are glad to work with him. They know they're going to do interesting work and so they're willing to do stuff like *Dr. Horrible*."

Simon Helberg, who played supporting character Moist, marveled at Joss's ability to call in favors. Helberg had produced his own comedy web series, *Derek & Simon: The Show*, so he had quite a bit of experience with online content budgets and the need to rely on others' goodwill. "When I pull a favor, it's like, 'Can we use your TV room for this party scene?' When Joss does it, you're talking about [using] a [Universal Studios] back lot and [getting] a horse." He adds, "Everybody there was his crew and his team, and it's rare. I think there are probably a lot of directors and filmmakers out there who don't have a solid company of people they work with consistently—but a lot of the great ones do. It seems like Joss definitely had that, so when he said, 'I'm gonna take a camera and take some money of mine and make this little thing, and can I get some of you guys to help?' they all jumped on the bandwagon. That speaks volumes for what he's like to work with."

By the time the producers had finished writing and had the cast and crew locked, the writers' strike was over and everyone had to get back to their "regular jobs." That meant they had virtually no rehearsal time before the shoot. The vocals for all the songs were recorded in Joss's loft from March 1 to March 5, 2008, and they found a window of an additional six days in March to get everything shot. Yet despite such a quick turnaround, production seemed to go smoothly, due in large part to Joss's direction. "Joss knows what he wants and sort of how to get there," Helberg says. "I think Joss and I had strong visions of [Moist]. They were slightly different, I think, and we came to a place that we were both really happy with. Working with Joss is to work with somebody with such a creative voice and a very specific vision and where every detail of it is chosen with care and a point of view."

There was lots of scurrying around and shooting on the fly. Joss empowered the very bare-bones crew to do whatever was needed to get each shot. Harris says that it was "all kinds of guerilla filmmaking, but with great passion and love, not anger that it wasn't going differently."

Dr. Horrible became a community project, where "everybody was like a family," Kai says. Nathan Fillion agrees. "More than any project I've done, *Dr. Horrible* had the feeling of, 'Hey, I got a box of costumes and old clothes we could use, and there's an old barn we can use for a stage,' and everybody pulling together and saying, 'I've got some old lights we could use.'" It was like a bunch of friends having fun and putting on a show, and if someone new came in, "an hour later you know their name and you know what they're like, and you have a good time with them. It felt the least like a job."

///////////

Joss's experiment with a new model of filmmaking was succeeding, but the old ways were just as frustrating as ever. The end of the strike meant that production on his studio projects could continue, but at Universal Pictures, circumstances conspired to keep *Goners* in limbo. On March 13, *Variety* announced that Mary Parent was leaving the studio to chair MGM's Worldwide Motion Picture Group. Without Parent to shepherd the project through the Universal preproduction maze, the future of the film was in question. Joss told MTV in July that it had "gotten backburnered," and four years later he'd explain that the change in management resulted in his story being orphaned. "Everything was in place. And the new people just completely shit-canned it," he said. "And I wasn't ready for that."

Parent's move to MGM may have orphaned *Goners*, but it found a home for another Whedonverse project. The first film she greenlit in her new position was Joss and Drew Goddard's horror tale *The Cabin in the Woods*. When the studio announced the purchase on July 8, it also laid out two brand-new paths for the writers: *Cabin* would be the first feature film produced by Joss, and the first feature directed by Goddard.

The two writers had decided on this division of labor while they were working on the script, but Goddard wasn't convinced that it would actually come to pass. "I kept waiting for the other shoe to drop. I had a feeling at some point Joss was going to say, 'You know what? I think I want to direct this one.' Which he did," he laughs. It was disappointing, but to him it meant that they had something special in the script. And if he wasn't going to direct *The Cabin in the Woods*, Goddard could "ask for no better director than Joss Whedon to take over." Fortunately, Joss changed his mind, and Goddard ended up in the director's chair.

///////////

With *The Cabin in the Woods* and his Fox series *Dollhouse* yet to go
into production, Joss concentrated his energies on launching *Dr. Horrible*. He and the producers had meetings about how to roll out and promote the show with a few companies, including Creative Artists Agency,
where his agent, Chris Harbert, had moved several years earlier. Since
web series were such a new venture, no one knew quite how to proceed.
So *Dr. Horrible* star Felicia Day took charge, drawing on her experience
distributing *The Guild* online. She explained how streaming worked and
warned that certain potential hosting sites would not have the bandwidth to support the demand for the show. "She was so on top of it," Joss
said. "The rest of us were like, 'Yeah, what she said.' It was like a *Buffy*
moment—the cute little girl in the room blows everybody out of the
water." They decided to distribute the show themselves, with help from
the online video service Hulu.

The next hurdle was possibly the most important: publicizing the
show and attracting viewers. This is where most original Internet content
failed, because unlike a television network with an established audience
of millions of viewers, few online sites at the time had the ability to reach
a wide audience. But with Joss's very loyal and very web-savvy fan base,
it ended up being one of the easiest things to deliver. Joss needed only to
post a message on Whedonesque. He told fans that the episodes would
initially be available to stream for free, and after that brief window passed
the series could be purchased for download on iTunes. The grassroots
publicity engine of Whedon fans that had faithfully forwarded his pro-
WGA messages throughout the writers' strike was now laser-focused on
Dr. Horrible. Fans even managed to track down and watch the trailer
before Joss and company were ready to release it. But that was a small
price to pay for so much free publicity.

Midnight on July 15, episode one of *Dr. Horrible's Sing-Along Blog*
was released to the world. Until everything crashed shortly thereafter.
The streaming servers were not prepared for the onslaught of viewers.
"We like to say we broke the Internet," Joss said, "because 'we were too
cheap to pay for more bandwidth' doesn't have the same ring to it." Jed
Whedon explained that they were hoping the audience would build over
time; they didn't expect everybody to try to see it all at once. But they
did—to the tune of about a thousand viewers a second. "We broke other

things they had streaming nearby and all ancillary sites, like Whedon-esque and Felicia's site for *The Guild*, they all went down." Joss added. "There was this domino effect, people either looking for it or some con-nection, and that made us feel pretty awesome. We didn't feel bright, but we felt cool." By the time the next day rolled around, the sites stayed up and the views kept coming.

"Releasing it for free was a brilliant idea," Neil Patrick Harris says. The fact that it was available to stream for only a limited time gave the fans a sense of urgency and excitement. "It was very, very enjoyable for me and the rest of the cast and crew and writers to sit and watch the com-ments right after episode one was released—to see what people thought of it," Harris says. They watched fans speculate on what was to come next as they waited for subsequent episodes to be released. Harris likens it to the way that Stephen King published his 1996 serial novel *The Green Mile*: "The paperback books came out once a month for [six] months, and I had that same feeling when the new paperback dropped. I would go out to the bookstore and buy it first thing [and] read it, devour it." *Dr. Horrible* proved that people will come, and keep coming back, for online content that they're interested in.

//////////

Fans also turned out in droves for the *Dr. Horrible* panel at San Diego Comic-Con on July 25, 2008. Joss was surprisingly nervous to face the four thousand attendees, Simon Helberg recalls. "Backstage, he was even redder than he normally is, then he goes up and destroys, and you feel like, 'How could you be this nervous? You're such an amazing writer, and every question that somebody asks you, you have the most hilarious, articulate answer.' He was amazing."

It was Helberg's first year at Comic-Con, and it gave him a glimpse at the differences between Joss Whedon fandom and the fans of his hit CBS television series *The Big Bang Theory*. While the two groups had huge overlap, *Dr. Horrible* fans tended to be consistently younger. "[*Big Bang*] has an array of people, whereas *Dr. Horrible*, those Joss fans, are all the geeky hipsters or just pure geeky people," he says. "I think it's definitely that quality that Joss has that I don't know how to even really describe, but that sort of self-reflective, kind of intellectual, self-deprecating geek pop culture kind of thing. It's so tasteful and specific. I think that appeals to a lot of younger [fans]—and by younger, I just mean not seventy. I don't mean, like, twelve."

Helberg was utterly unprepared for the event and surprised to discover that excited *Dr. Horrible* fans had even infiltrated his *Big Bang* panels. "I didn't know that this kind of thing existed," he says. "I thought you do a television show, and if you're popular maybe some people will come up to you during the day or you hang out and there's press there, and that's as intense as it gets." The fact that Comic-Con was a place where thousands of people sleep out and wait to listen to actors and producers share anecdotes was overwhelming. "That was a crazy day, and I just realized at that point, 'OK, there's something in the zeitgeist here that hasn't been fully recognized by me.'"

That night, there was a scheduled *Dr. Horrible* screening. Fans were ready in homemade Dr. Horrible and Captain Hammer costumes. Early on, the line of people waiting had already well exceeded the capacity of the space. One of the producers was running around trying to find another copy of the musical and an additional room in which to screen it. Ultimately, they were able to set up several theaters to play *Dr. Horrible* all at the same time. The cast snuck into the back of one of the rooms and watched along. It was the first time that they all got to watch it with an audience, who were already singing along and shouting back at the screen. "It was very surreal," Harris says. "We had clearly succeeded in our core goal, which was to create something that would amuse. And it was amusing. There was great ferocity that night.

"It was just very out-of-body to watch," he adds. "A lot of people laughing so actively, and deeply into the experience. I hadn't really experienced that before. Joss has a hardcore adoration that follows him around, and when people laugh at Joss Whedon's jokes, it's a big-ass belly laugh, and that was kind of crazy to witness."

//////////

Critically, the series was a hit as well, praised for its witty writing and musical numbers. Ironically, the weakest part of *Dr. Horrible* was the one thing that Joss had been lauded for through most of his career: his female characters. Penny is a disappointment, a one-note "nice girl" who serves as little more than a prize for which Dr. Horrible and Captain Hammer compete. She comes across as naive and bland, especially when compared to her vibrant and over-the-top suitors. At the very end of the series, Dr. Horrible accidentally kills her with a death ray meant for Captain Hammer. Her last words are "Captain Hammer will save us," and her death gives Horrible the villainous cred he needs to be accepted by the Evil League of Evil. Thus, Penny plays an important role in the main character's emotional arc, but she fails as a well-developed, independent character.

Where *Dr. Horrible* fares better is in a realm that Joss doesn't often do well. For a person who has developed and nurtured such a large group of friends, Joss has a surprisingly soft track record when it comes to depicting male friendships. Most of the men in Joss's stories have prickly or begrudgingly respectful relationships with one another, and they almost never unabashedly express their love—in opposition to the believable and inspiring female friendships (Buffy/Willow, Inara/Kaylee) and male/female friendships (Malcolm/Zoe, Cordelia/Angel). Dr. Horrible and Moist are an example of one of the few easy and plausible male friendships in the Whedonverse.

Joss showed the finished series to one of the most important men in his own life: his father, Tom. As a musicals fanatic who'd written lyrics for off-Broadway shows, Tom was thrilled. "But what he loved more than anything," Joss said, was "when the credits came up at the end and he just saw so many Whedons. I watched him just tearing up with joy that so many of us were involved in it. He just cares that he had so much fun and that it was such a family endeavor."

Once *Dr. Horrible* moved to iTunes, it remained the number-one download for five weeks. Joss's skeptical accountant changed his tune and asked if a *Dr. Horrible 2* was in the works. "It's not like a huge moneymaker, but it's something everyone believed in and everyone trusted and everyone put their egos aside," Kai says. "That could be the future, you know. That could be how we make movies."

There was no denying that the Whedons had found an innovative way to both engage viewers and make some money in an untested medium. Even the Hollywood trade papers took notice: *Variety* published a piece on how writers were creating series for the web, featuring Joss and the story of *Dr. Horrible*'s development—both financial and creative—and its ultimate success. Joss was gratified by the headline: SCRIBES STRIKE BACK. "There was a picture of Dr. Horrible, a picture of me with a picket sign, and nothing else on the front page. Just that article," he recalled. "All of a sudden the politics came back into play, in a good way. People started going, 'Okay, we did accomplish something, we didn't do it during the strike, but we did it and now it means something.' Because it went from this is a political action to this is us making jokes about a horse, to this is a political action again. That was very gratifying."

///////////

The next step was to release *Dr. Horrible* on DVD. Joss and his collaborators decided that it should be a special experience, like the Internet release had been. Joss suggested that in addition to the standard DVD commentary in which the cast and crew talk about what is happening on screen, they could record an extra commentary track in which scripted versions of the writers and actors *sing* their thoughts about the project. And so *Commentary! The Musical* was born. It serves as a bonus soundtrack to the series, if not an entirely new musical on its own. "I'll probably regret [that idea] forever . . . or at least Jed will, because he had to produce everything," Joss said. "It took us about twice as long to write and produce as the actual film. It has to contain about twice as much music, because you can't just sort of have people talking in a musical commentary because then it just sounds like a commentary."

Commentary! has been called "ambitious and funny while still being cleverly lyrical." It adds an entirely new level to Dr. Horrible and the idea of going "behind the scenes." "Those songs are as equally entertaining to me as the songs from *Dr. Horrible* itself," Harris says. "It never really felt like, 'Great, we did it, now let's sell out and make money back.' If they're going to whore themselves out, it's going to be a fantastic—where do prostitutes live? Bordello. It's going to be a fantastic bordello."

Joss performed "Heart (Broken)," a song about having to do DVD commentary as a writer and producer (something he'd done many times by this point, over a total of thirteen DVD sets for *Buffy*, *Angel*, and *Firefly*). "I always want to get behind or inside everything I'm doing," Joss said. "I want to dig underneath it and say, what's the point of this, of this medium, of this experience? Why did you sit down with me for an hour? Why did you do it? Why did I do it? Why did I write this?"

> Homer's Odyssey was swell.
> A bunch of guys that went through hell.
> He told the tale, but didn't tell

The audience why.
He didn't say, here's what it means.
And here's a few deleted scenes.
Charybdis tested well with teens. . . .

But now we pick, pick, pick, pick, pick it apart.
Open it up to find the tick, tick, tick of a heart.

Over the next year, the critical accolades and awards continued to roll in. *Dr. Horrible* ranked number fifteen in *Time* magazine's list of the top fifty inventions of 2008. It took home the 2009 Hugo Award for Best Dramatic Presentation, Short Form, beating out the smash hit *Lost* and Hugo favorites *Doctor Who* and *Battlestar Galactica*. In September 2009, *Dr. Horrible* scored Joss his first Emmy win, for Outstanding Special Class—Short-Format Live-Action Entertainment Programs.

30

DOLLHOUSE

As the writers' strike ended and *Dr. Horrible* went into postproduction, Joss also went back to work on his upcoming series for Eliza Dushku. Although Fox had already committed to seven episodes of *Dollhouse*, network executives still wanted to see a pilot. So Joss began writing the introductory episode "Echo," fleshing out his noirish tale of the mysterious lab where "dolls," or Actives, having been stripped of their original memories and personalities, are temporarily implanted with new personal backgrounds and skills, to be hired out for particular jobs—most often committing crimes or fulfilling customers' sexual fantasies. As the series begins, Dushku's character, the Active codenamed Echo, starts to recover pieces of her native personality, forcing her to deal with the questions of who she really is and what her identity means to herself and the world around her. Meanwhile, the FBI has gotten wind of the Dollhouse's very illegal operations and is investigating the facility and its owner, the Rossum Corporation.

Next, Joss assembled the supporting cast. The writer with the passionate fan following became a fanboy himself when Tahmoh Penikett of *Battlestar Galactica* was cast as Paul Ballard, the FBI agent making trouble for the Dollhouse. Joss was a very vocal fan of the Sci Fi Channel remake and had done his best not to be "too embarrassing" when chatting up series creator Ron Moore on the WGA picket lines. "Joss and I found common ground with *Battlestar*," Penikett says. "Initially, that was the main thing that really brought us together. We would talk and talk about the show, talk about specific episodes—telling stories about the actors and the episodes. He had the opportunity to meet a lot of them, and if the show went on, you would have had seen a lot of *Battlestar* actors on *Dollhouse*."

311

In the role of Adelle, the ruthless and cold head of the Dollhouse, Joss cast British actress Olivia Williams. Like Anthony Stewart Head, Williams was impressed by Joss's ability to write for an English accent. Lesser attempts can often result in "painfully convoluted sentences and ridiculous circumlocution," she says. "In order to make sense of badly executed English baddie-speak it is necessary to put a rod up your arse, and nobody likes to work in those conditions." The best British villains, on the other hand, "have a kind of cool and succinct way of speaking" that Joss completely nailed.

Fran Kranz was cast as Topher, the snarky and morally challenged programmer who is in charge of implanting the dolls' temporary personalities. *Angel*'s Amy Acker returned to the Whedonverse as Dr. Saunders, who tends to the physical health of the dolls, while Harry Lennix assumed the role of Boyd, Echo's newbie handler, who looks after her when she goes on missions. Young actors Dichen Lachman, Enver Gjokaj, and Miracle Laurie would play Echo's fellow Actives Sierra, Victor, and November.

//////////

With a premise that centered on attractive young people being programmed to serve a corporation's paying customers, Joss anticipated some uneasy public reactions: "Did human trafficking just get pretty?" He knew that the concept was very edgy, even dangerous—one hair out of place and it could be untenable. He went so far as to pitch *Dollhouse* to the staff members of Equality Now in New York. "Some of them said, 'I get it, that's cool, that's something to explore,' and some of them were like, 'You better be very careful!'" Joss says. "And then that rug kind of got pulled out from under us."

Even though the series had been greenlit without a pilot, and Fox had recently upped their order from seven episodes to thirteen, once Joss filmed "Echo" and presented it to Fox, the network requested some changes. "The Network and I had different ideas about what the tone of the show would be," Joss wrote on Whedonesque. "They bought something somewhat different than what I was selling them, which is not that uncommon in this business. Their desires were not surprising: up the stakes, make the episodes more stand-alone, stop talking about relationships and cut to the chase."

It was feeling like *Firefly* all over again, when the network demanded a more action-oriented premiere episode to replace Joss's dark and moody pilot. But whereas Fox made a good call on the *Firefly* premiere, it missed the mark on reworking "Echo." As originally written and shot, the pilot provides a cohesive introduction to the concept of the Dollhouse and the FBI's investigation of it. It succeeds in making the Actives seem empowered and in control as they carry out their programmed assignments, something that is often lacking in the finished episodes. Subsequent episodes would also lose the pilot's noirish commentary on sex trafficking, which was lightened up at Fox's request.

After several rounds of rewriting and editing, this time it was Joss who decided to scrap the pilot script and write a new premiere episode, "Ghost." The new story begins with a strung-out young woman—Echo's former self—agreeing to join the Dollhouse. It then quickly segues into Echo out on a job: a whirlwind date filled with such chemistry that anyone would believe that she and her gentleman friend are a real couple. When that's over, she's programmed to be a hostage negotiator to save a little girl from kidnappers.

Much of the nuance and humor of "Echo" is missing here, and several plot points, like the return of Echo's memories and the Dollhouse's awareness of Ballard's investigation, are removed or stripped way down. Ballard, the confident and competent FBI agent who had met and ended up in a gun-battle standoff with Echo in his apartment in the original pilot, is a now a wild-card loner obsessively pursuing a conspiracy theory about an evil corporation. The character was one of several that had to be significantly rewritten to accommodate the network-mandated changes—which meant that Tahmoh Penikett and a few of his costars needed to relearn their places in the series as well.

Penikett was reassured by something that his mentor and *Battlestar Galactica* costar Edward James Olmos had said: "It takes a long time to find the music of a show, the music of a character." His *Dollhouse* costar Harry Lennix told him something similar, that "every show has its own music and its own tone. It takes you a while to figure that out, but once you do, you really get the rhythm of your character and what's going on." The problem was that *Dollhouse* had found its music in the pilot, but like an old vinyl record, it had been scratched and warped by all of the changes that Fox requested. Joss would have to find a new tone, a new rhythm—and that would take time.

"A good deal of *Dollhouse* had to do with sex. Sexuality and perversion and our sexual and relationship needs and how they define us and what's different about us, what's similar," Joss explains. "[Fox said] 'This show's great! The sex is not so good. We can't have that. It seems like prostitution. So don't do that.' So in the premise, we had to sort of gloss over it or joke about it, and it became kind of offensive."

//////////

Fox approved "Ghost" to kick off the series, but on September 10, 2008, after four scripts had been completed, Fox shut down production. The network wanted tweaks to the fourth episode, and the two-week shooting break would give Joss and his writing staff time to get ahead on scripts. Joss was getting deep into producing duties for *The Cabin in the Woods*, so he'd brought back some major Mutant Enemy players to help him with *Dollhouse*. Tim Minear and David Solomon returned as executive producers; Jane Espenson and Steve DeKnight also came in to pen scripts. And Joss made this project another family affair with the addition of writers Jed Whedon and Maurissa Tancharoen.

Dollhouse was initially announced as a midseason series that would be paired with Fox's hit series *24* on Monday nights. But in November, Fox announced that it had been moved to Friday night, along with former Monday-night series *Terminator: The Sarah Connor Chronicles*, which had suffered from a ratings drop in its second season. Joss's fans, many of whom were still mourning *Firefly*'s demise, were greatly concerned that the move to the Friday-night death slot again showed a lack of support from Fox. When *Dollhouse* premiered on Friday, February 13, 2009, it pulled in 4.72 million Nielsen viewers, comparable to *Firefly*'s bow. In the seven years in between premieres, DVRs had become more commonplace and live viewing numbers had taken a hit, so *Dollhouse*'s ratings, while not stellar, weren't considered as much of a disappointment as *Firefly*'s had been. *Dollhouse* was also the night's second-most-viewed series in the important eighteen-to-forty-nine-year-old demographic and did particularly well with male viewers.

Excitement was high for Joss's return to television after five years, but the reviews were mixed. At a time when so much on TV was generic, this was anything but. But that uniqueness shook up what fans had come to expect from the Whedonverse. Despite Fox's adjustments, *Dollhouse* was distinctly darker than Joss's other series. And maybe because of those adjustments, it became possibly the hardest of his series to connect with as a viewer. Even in the darkest episodes of *Buffy*, viewers felt incredibly attached to the characters and their struggles. *Dollhouse*, on the other hand, was filled with characters who were either unlikeable or deliberately undefined. It was difficult to care about a main character whose personality was going to change dramatically from week to week depending on her assignment.

Joss could see all too clearly that the changes to the show had diluted his original premise of an objectified woman breaking free of her programming. This, in turn, was making it more and more difficult to find the "Echo of it" in each episode. "*Dollhouse* was the one time I looked around and said, 'I don't know what show I'm making.' It had sort of been eaten away from the center," he said. "It was the only time I felt like, 'Am I steering this ship? Our ship? Are we the iceberg?'"

Reviews improved as the season went on and the series, like *Angel* before it, shifted its focus from the main character and her mission of the week to become a larger ensemble piece grounded in the characters and their complex relationships. Alan Tudyk made several appearances as Alpha, a psychotic former Active who's obsessed with Echo.

While shooting an episode, Tudyk noticed a change in Joss since their *Firefly* days. During rehearsal, the actor improvised a line at the end of a scene. Tudyk was shocked when he was told to keep it in the final scene. "I said, 'Whoa, no way! Are you serious? I cannot believe I'm getting my own line in a Joss Whedon thing.' Joss was there, and he goes, 'Really? Oh. I've relaxed,'" Tudyk said. "And he meant it like he was surprised to hear me say that." Joss may have been more open to the occasional ad-lib, but his own words remained of paramount importance to him—something costar Olivia Williams has said she realized in her earliest conversations with him. Tahmoh Penikett agrees, saying, "There's no mediation for the way he's written—he's such a specific writer. For some shows, an actor can change this word or do this a little differently. You can't do that with Joss's material. You have to deliver it the way it's written. Which, he has every right [to demand], because there's specific timing that has to be honored or else it won't work. It'll flop."

Unfortunately, by the time *Dollhouse* started to find a new focus, many viewers had moved on; viewership bounced between 4.3 and

2.75 million for the rest of the thirteen episodes. Fran Kranz says that they were always just waiting to get canceled, so it made the cast very close. "Maybe with a different creator, director, guy at the top, it might have made us all hate each other and want to get home that much faster each day. Instead, on *Dollhouse*, we loved each other that much more. Each day we were grateful to be working, and we kind of felt like we were in our own little pocket of the Fox lot, doing weird little things. It brought us closer together, knowing that at any moment it could all be over."

//////////

When comedian-actor Patton Oswalt guest-starred in the sixth episode of *Dollhouse*, he and Joss bonded over the frustration of becoming a fan of a series that only exists for a brief time and then is gone. Oswalt, a fellow comic book and sci-fi nerd, brought up the *Firefly* universe, which he'd followed from series to movie to comics. After the 2005 *Serenity* tie-in comic *Those Left Behind* became the bestselling Dark Horse title up to that point, more volumes had followed, and Oswalt told Joss that these comics had made him want to learn more about the *Firefly* characters. Joss said to let him know if he had any ideas for other stories in that world.

Oswalt, who would later improvise an eight-minute rant detailing an epic crossover between *Star Wars* and *The Avengers* for a 2013 episode of *Parks and Recreation*, did some thinking and pitched Joss three *Firefly* ideas. The first was about the cannibalistic Reavers and what their society might look like; the second focused on troubled psychic River Tam and what it would be like to get impressions of the future but not necessarily understand what they mean. Finally, Oswalt suggested a story exploring the history of pilot Wash and the impact of his death, which occurred at the end of *Serenity*. This last idea hit a nerve for Joss, and he enlisted Oswalt to write it as a comic, *Float Out*, which Dark Horse would release in 2010.

"It's kind of an elegy for the character of Wash," Oswalt told *Time*. "It's three of his friends, who haven't met before, old friends from before he was piloting the *Firefly*, and they've bought a new boat and they're christening it *Jetwash*, and they're telling stories about him before they christen it and float it out."

//////////

In April, a minor controversy flared regarding the thirteenth episode of *Dollhouse*, "Epitaph One." Felicia Day, who had played Penny in *Dr. Horrible* and was guest-starring in the episode, told fans that it wouldn't air on Fox, which caused many to think that the network had again canceled one of Joss's shows. Tim Minear allayed their concerns on Whedonesque, explaining that the episode was shot to fulfill contractual obligations to 20th Century Fox Television to deliver thirteen episodes for international sales and the DVD release. But it was not to be part of the Fox network's thirteen-episode order, which was already covered with the scrapped "Echo" episode.

On May 8, 2009, Fox aired the twelfth episode as the season finale. It pulled in the fewest viewers of the entire season—about half as many as the premiere. But mere days later, the network picked up *Dollhouse* for a second season—albeit with a reduced budget. "Epitaph One" never aired in the United States, but in July, Joss screened it at San Diego Comic-Con, and later that month it was included on the *Dollhouse* DVD set.

The unaired episode is a departure for the series, set ten years in the future. Los Angeles has become a postapocalyptic ruin, and a new group of characters breaks into the Dollhouse for refuge and finds videos of the Dollhouse team. Flashbacks reveal what became of the dolls and their overseers in the Rossum Corporation. Joss explained that the second season would continue with the flash-forward device and that several characters who first appeared in "Epitaph One" would have recurring roles in the series.

The flash-forward technique was in the zeitgeist at the time, as ABC's *Lost*, famous for its flashback scenes, had changed up its formula in its 2007–08 season to show the bleak futures of its rescued castaways. And perhaps the dual-world concept was in Joss's consciousness as he readied for production on his latest movie, a fractured take on the beloved tropes of the horror genre.

31

THE CABIN IN THE WOODS

After being acquired by MGM, *The Cabin in the Woods* moved to its subsidiary United Artists for further development. At the time, United Artists was being partly overseen by Tom Cruise, who gave script and story notes to Joss and Goddard. "That was definitely one of those surreal experiences," says Goddard. "It was wonderful. . . . I've never met a more enthusiastic, creative, and supportive person [than Tom Cruise]. He has that energy, and to feel that energy directed toward you, *about* you, it's like a drug. It's wonderful. He was so excited about the script and so complimentary and really just pointed out scenes in the movie that he felt we should bring out more. And he was totally right."

At its core, however, the final version of the screenplay remained pretty close to the draft they'd hammered out during their three-day hotel stay back in 2007. Five college students are lured to the titular cabin, where they become the latest victims of a family of zombie sadists. Unbeknownst to the unfortunate visitors, however, the entire scenario is in fact a high-tech setup. Though at first it seems to resemble some sort of twisted lab experiment, it's ultimately revealed to be an elaborate ritual to appease a group of malevolent gods who would otherwise destroy the world. The scenario's creators force each of their victims to conform to one of five predetermined roles before offering his or her life to the Ancient Ones. With the deaths of the Athlete, the Whore, the Scholar, and the Fool (the Virgin's death is optional, as long as she suffers greatly), the gods will be sated and all of humanity can go living another day, none the wiser.

It was important to Joss and Goddard that the technicians who engineer the ritual be believable and realistic characters. They're certainly the villains of the film, but they're villains with an understandable belief

system. They think that causing the deaths of five young people is a ratio-
nal and proper action if it saves the rest of the human race from anni-
hilation—even if they do take a kind of pride in watching the results of
their handiwork. Goddard based them on people he knew growing up
in Los Alamos, New Mexico, the men and women who developed and
built atomic weapons. "They're wonderful, decent people and yet their
job is to create weapons of mass destruction," he said. "They're all just
people. They believe what they believe for a reason, and their reason is
not ridiculous."

Joss mined his own childhood memories to further develop the technician characters, once again calling on the perspective of an educator's
son who knew better than most how his teachers saw the school and the
kids. When the *Cabin in the Woods* techs aren't knee-deep in manipulation,
they're grumbling about other departments in the compound failing to do
their part to ensure a successful slaughter. "This is basically the same thing,"
Joss said. "They're in the faculty lounge complaining about the kids."

//////////

While writing the script, Joss and Goddard had one actor in mind for the
role of lead technician Gary Sitterson. They thought that Richard Jenkins (*Six Feet Under*) had the gravitas the role required and the fearlessness to jump into such an unconventional project. Joss, however, warned
Goddard against getting his hopes up, because at the time Jenkins was
in contention for an Oscar for his turn in *The Visitor* (2008). "Here's an
example of me really showing what a great producer I am—I told Drew,
'Don't even try, it's not worth it. . . . We don't have a chance," Joss said.
"Good call, pretty proud of that."

But Jenkins was their dream choice, and they decided that it couldn't
hurt to send the script to his agent. That was on a Friday night. She read
it, and even though she knew her client was skeptical about appearing in
a horror project, she insisted that Jenkins check it out. Once he finished
the script, it took him two seconds to decide to sign on. He was won over
by the "very good, funny and smart" writing of a story concept that he'd
never come across before. Monday morning, Jenkins called and said that
he was in.

On their first try, Joss and Goddard had scored big. Not only did
they get their ideal actor for the role, but they also got the enhanced

cachet that came with having an Oscar-nominated actor signed to their project. People started to take the film more seriously than a run-of-the-mill slasher film, and it attracted a higher caliber of talent. Bradley Whitford (*The West Wing*) came aboard as Sitterson's partner, Hadley.

Joss and Goddard next set about casting the roles of the techs' five sacrificial lambs. Since the idea was to show multifaceted young people who are forced into stock horror roles for the sake of the ritual, the actors needed to both fit into and work against stereotypes. For the part of the Fool, the stoner Marty, Joss suggested they look close to home—on the set of *Dollhouse*. Goddard had come to the set to look over different cabin locations that the location scouts had suggested to Joss. Actor Fran Kranz started to geek out over horror films with them, excitedly explaining that he had held a *Friday the 13th* marathon in college. Goddard pointed out that one of the locations they were considering was the original Crystal Lake, where that film's Jason Voorhees does his stalking and killing.

Neither Joss nor Goddard said anything more to Kranz about *Cabin*, so he didn't know what to think when he got an audition toward the end of *Dollhouse*'s first season. He wasn't given the actual script but rather some fake scenes in which the police interrogate his character after a multi-clawed monster rips his friends' heads off. Kranz took on a defiant slacker attitude that would play well into Marty. After the audition, he heard nothing until he had pretty much forgotten about it. Eventually Joss approached him on set and said that he was really good in his audition tape, but the testing process went on. Although Joss and Goddard were happy with Kranz as Marty, the studio took a while to sign off on him.

The waiting did lead to several tense moments on set. "It was awkward," Kranz said. "We had a good working relationship so I felt comfortable talking to him about mostly anything. But there was this big elephant in the room, at least for me. I would be on pins and needles whenever he walked by. At one point . . . Eliza Dushku asked him how *Cabin in the Woods* was coming and he said, 'We're just putting together a really second-rate cast.' It was a joke but I was so insecure I was like, 'Oh, s——, what's happening?' It totally freaked me out. Of course, he's screwing around."

When Kranz was finally told that he got the part, he found out that his initial meeting with Goddard was not as random as he'd initially thought. "Joss [said that he'd] been seeing me in this role for a while, and that he brought Drew to set to check out this dude for Marty,"

Kranz recalls. "So that whole day that I just happened to be geeking out with Drew, I probably could not have done better [than] just sitting around being a fan of horror films and just being myself. Luckily, Drew right then was like, 'Yeah, let's definitely read him,' and one thing led to another and I got the part."

Two more roles were cast with television actors: Jesse Williams (*Grey's Anatomy*) would play the Scholar, grounded new guy Holden, and Kristen Connolly (*As the World Turns*) would be Dana, the essential horror-flick "virgin." The final two were far harder to cast—the Athlete, Curt the jock, and the Whore, blonde party girl Jules. New Zealand actress Anna Hutchison auditioned for Jules from where she was working in Australia, and locked the role mere days before they were set to shoot.

Goddard found his Jock in another actor from Down Under: the relatively unknown Chris Hemsworth. The Australian actor had filmed a brief but pivotal sequence for J. J. Abrams's upcoming reboot of *Star Trek*, playing James T. Kirk's father. "We probably saw over 100 people for [the role of Curt]," Goddard said. "I was looking for actors that can break your heart. These people need to be real, because we go to such unreal places. He just had that. As soon as he walked out of the room I said, 'That guy's got the job.'"

//////////

With the cast announced on March 10, 2009, production could begin. The original plan was to shoot in California so that Joss and Goddard wouldn't be far from their families for the several months of production. But right before they planned to shoot, the Canadian dollar dropped; combined with British Columbia's tax incentives, the production could save a few million dollars by shooting in Vancouver instead. It was too much of a difference to ignore, so they packed up and headed north to the Canadian woods.

Goddard settled into his position as director, with Joss serving as lead producer and second unit director. They both bounded into their new roles with a naïveté that both helped and hindered the production. The first day of principal photography, they were scheduled to do a scene in which our intrepid college students make a stop at an old-fashioned gas station on their way to the cabin. But when the crew arrived at the location, the set was covered in snow—not ideal for a film set in the summer.

It was the first significant moment when Joss and Goddard realized that it was up to them to figure out what to do. They lost half a day out of their schedule resolving the problem, which they kept chasing to get back for the rest of the shoot.

Initially, Joss thought that he'd spend more time on set as the producer, but he quickly realized that it was better for him to stick around Los Angeles to handle the bigger questions and manage day-to-day operations so that Goddard could concentrate on directing. Joss also accepted that while he'd had his moments of wanting to direct the film, it was much better off in Goddard's bloodied hands. "Drew is a horror aficionado in a way that I am not. If you look at *Buffy*, it's the least frightening horror show in the history of time and space. I have a problem with dismembering people," Joss said. "Drew was ready to commit to it in a way that I wasn't, and was ready to buy the most amount of blood you can purchase in Canada."

And there was a lot of blood—particularly during the final battle, in which surviving heroes Marty and Dana, having discovered the secret installation beneath the cabin, turn the tables on their tormentors by uncaging the facility's vast menagerie of monsters. During the shooting of the ultragory battle scenes, the room had to be squeegeed, mopped, scrubbed, and bleached and still needed a couple of days before it was ready again. Just as impressive as the gore is the diversity of the creatures causing it; Joss, Goddard, and their crew developed numerous distinctive monster types: a werewolf, clowns, scarecrows, a dragonbat, a merman, "dismemberment goblins"—and Joss's favorite, a ballerina whose entire face consists of lamprey-like rings of teeth.

There was great excitement when a new performer arrived on set to take part in the final sequence of the film. In it, Marty and Dana confront the Director, the head of the facility, who explains the purpose of the ritual and the reason why Marty must play the part of the Fool and die to complete it—because otherwise humanity is doomed. Joss and Goddard wrote the part of the Director without specifying the character's gender, which made it a perfect fit for the actress who had brought so much to another gender-unspecified role, iconic badass Lt. Ripley in *Alien*.

Sigourney Weaver had the strength and authority to convince the audience that even if they still were rooting for Marty and Dana to make it through to the end alive, the Director's decision to kill the five young people was the proper choice to make. Joss and Goddard discussed many other people for the role, but ultimately felt that, as Joss put it, "there's nobody else who should be coming up those stairs."

Joss knew Weaver from working with her on *Alien: Resurrection*, but Goddard was intimidated by the prospect of working with the legendary actress—until they talked. The first thing she did was to ask him when the werewolf arrived, because she was so excited to work with a werewolf. She told him that they should make sure that the werewolf had someone to sit with at lunch. By the time the cast and crew were shooting the final confrontation, everyone else was burned out by the intensity of the production. When Weaver came in with her bubbly and enthusiastic attitude, it reenergized the set. "A person that has done the things that she has done is still excited about the fun of moviemaking," Goddard recalled. "There's something that's so inspiring about that."

//////////

Filming wrapped in May 2009, and Joss left it to Goddard to oversee the film's postproduction stage. He'd already found that he was able to let go of his perfectionist tendencies, his need to control all aspects of the production. His more limited role on the film had also given him some flexibility in his schedule, which allowed him, in April at age forty-four, to accept the 2009 Outstanding Lifetime Achievement Award in Cultural Humanism from Harvard's Humanist Chaplaincy and the Secular Society. It was the third time the two groups had bestowed the award, this time given for how Joss's works consistently deliver the message that to be a good person one need not believe in God but may instead "believe in yourself and in each other." (The award was inscribed with a quote recommended by Kai: "However you live, / There's a part of you always standing by, / Mapping out the sky" from Sondheim's *Sunday in the Park with George*.)

Joss talked about his moment of geeker joy when Barack Obama acknowledged atheists in his 2009 inaugural speech. He compared his feeling of worthiness in that moment to those of gay fans who'd thanked him for his stories that gave them the courage to come out. He discussed how he sees religion as a tool that humanity created, and how religious people have laughed at him and his atheism, thinking that because he doesn't have a "belief system that they can understand, it means that he doesn't have a system of belief." He ended his speech with a plea for people to embrace education—not because all educated people will come out as nonbelievers, but because they all will learn to question and examine the religious and political rhetoric with which they've been indoctrinated.

"The enemy of humanism is not faith," he said. "The enemy of humanism is hate, is fear, is ignorance, is the darker part of man that is in every humanist, every person in the world. That is what we have to fight. Faith is something we have to embrace. Faith in God means believing absolutely in something with no proof whatsoever. Faith in humanity means believing absolutely in something with a huge amount of proof to the contrary. We are the true believers."

His speechifying was not done; he headed back to Wesleyan to be the keynote speaker at the 2009 Shasha Seminar for Human Concerns. The seminar's focus was almost custom made for Joss: "Defining American Culture: How Movies and TV Get Made." He spoke to students looking to break into the television industry, telling them that they shouldn't feel prohibited by the cost of production, because they would have increasing access to high-quality, low-cost equipment. Instead, he felt that their real hurdle would be finding an audience. Joss proposed the idea for a website where writers and producers could collaborate on projects that could be later viewed on the site. He encouraged them to tell their own stories in new ways, like he had with *Dr. Horrible*.

///////////

In July, Joss returned to *Dollhouse* with a challenge ahead of him. He knew that the first season had been uneven and he needed to figure out how to right the ship. "About two hours after starting to talk to the writers about story," he later recalled, "I was back with such a vengeance, and so energized and so pumped because we really understand the show now. We understand what works, and what didn't work so well or what we weren't so thrilled about. We don't have the onus of trying to be a big hit sitting on our shoulders. We can just be ourselves. And so the stories we're breaking are pure, and exciting, and everybody's on-board in the room, and it's never flowed better."

In its second season, *Dollhouse* moved even further away from realist procedural storylines, embracing an overarching conspiracy narrative with a slightly dystopian bent—an idea closer to Joss's original pilot. The Big Bad of the series shifts from Alan Tudyk's Alpha to the Rossum

Corporation itself. Other familiar faces pop up: *Angel*'s Alexis Denisof plays a US senator whom Rossum kidnaps and turns into an Active so as to have a high-ranking government official under its control, and *Firefly*'s Summer Glau is programmer Topher's counterpart in Rossum's DC Dollhouse facility, with whom Topher indulges in a bit of hero worship.

The second-season episode "Belonging" also serves as a strong return to the sex trafficking themes that Joss had originally hoped to explore. The episode centers on the Active Sierra, played by Dichen Lachman. It reveals that before she came to the Dollhouse, Sierra was Priya, an artist who was being pursued by a wealthy doctor named Nolan Kinnard. When Priya rejects his advances, Nolan has her committed to his psychiatric hospital and then admitted into the Dollhouse under false pretenses. Once Topher has reprogrammed Priya to become Sierra, Nolan continually enlists her services as a sex worker now that her free will is gone.

"'Belonging' is (in a very unpedantic way) a genuinely radical feminist plotline," Emily Nussbaum wrote for *New York* magazine. Nussbaum called the episode "a truly unsettling metaphor about 'false consciousness,' the social condition that results when someone is convinced to crave something they don't in fact want at all. The moment one *Dollhouse* character shifts from one type of slavery to another is almost too hard to take." It directly addresses rape from all sides: Sierra the victim, Nolan the attacker, and Topher the enabler—at first unknowingly complicit and then dealing with his guilt over his involvement in Nolan's ongoing attacks.

Dollhouse's second season premiered on September 25, 2009. The viewership was far more consistent each week, but it was roughly half of what the show had garnered during its first year. The series was officially canceled on November 11, while Joss and company were in production on the eleventh episode of its thirteen-episode order. Fox had learned its lesson from *Firefly*—regarding its relationship with both Joss and his fans—and with the announcement the network confirmed that all of the remaining episodes would air to provide Joss "the opportunity to end [the series] in a significant way." The final episodes ran through January 2010.

Miracle Laurie found the announcement to be bittersweet. While she was losing her job, Joss planned to give her a badass death scene to close out her storyline. "Every actor wants at least one great death scene in his or her career and I got a beautiful one. It was perfect for [the character] and my last gift from Joss during our little adventure in the Dollhouse," she says. "Joss was with us that night on set, which meant a lot to me. That scene was not only my last scene of the series but the last scene I ever shot on *Dollhouse*, the last shot of the night, and the last shot of the episode. I guess you could say for a sad ending, it was a pretty happy one."

//////////

Dollhouse may not have been Joss's most successful project, but it marks an interesting point in his evolution as a writer. "When Joss made *Buffy* and especially the early [seasons] of *Buffy*, it was very much about feminism in its bare form, about teaching girls their power," Emily Nussbaum says. "But the longer he went on, the more his shows become not about individualist things [or] female power but about corporations and corporate control, about the United States, and about politics."

Angel starts out as the story of one man's struggle to "help the helpless," but by its final season it has became a show about an evil law firm and the ethics of working for an organization that is actually in control of the world. *Firefly* shows Joss's issues with a government that claims to be doing what is best for its citizens but in reality does many questionable things in the name of peace and security. And finally *Dollhouse*, created in the shadow of the WGA strike and Joss's autonomous production of *Dr. Horrible*, explores the concept of signing up for a group and expecting to be taken care of, only to find out that you're being used in dehumanizing ways.

As Nussbaum puts it, "It just feels that the longer he's gone on the more his stuff has been not about sexual false consciousness but about political anger and people's gullibility."

"I've had people come up to me who are big *Dollhouse* fans [who told me,] 'That show really helped me,' Joss says. "That is really interesting to me, because that is what it was designed to do, like all my shows. Echo is the most helpless person that I ever invented. I was so excited to tell the story of her building—not only discovering or becoming self-aware, but building a personality. Creating a self from a place of complete self-lessness or being unhappy. To me that was, you know, a beautiful statement—somebody who gets to say, 'I am. I actually exist.' Not just 'Help, help! I'm being oppressed!' as they say in the *Holy Grail*, but starting from nothing and becoming aware of your own existence."

//////////

Though Joss had turned some of his attention away from *The Cabin in the Woods*, he played a decisive role in one major postproduction battle. MGM wanted the filmmakers to cut a particular sequence from the movie: before Dana and Marty discover the truth about the secret facility, their tormentors believe that the latter has been killed, so they gather to celebrate the successful completion of the sacrifice. The studio had issues with the idea that Sitterson, Hadley, and their colleagues would throw a big, alcohol-fueled party as Dana continued to struggle against their monsters on the monitors around the room.

To Drew Goddard, that juxtaposition told the story of *The Cabin in the Woods*. It also set up the third act, in which Dana is saved by a still-living Marty, the two find their way into the facility, and they enact revenge on those who made their life a living hell. Joss, as Goddard's producer, went back and forth with MGM over the issue, until he conceded that it was a battle they had lost. Sitting in the editing room, Goddard started to cry, because it was a battle that he didn't want to lose.

Joss stared at Goddard, then turned and picked up the phone to call the studio head. He simply told them that they were not cutting the sequence from the film. Goddard exhaled. "Oh, thank God."

Throughout the production, Joss questioned what he should and should not be concerned with in his role of producer. He'd had years of experience producing television, but this was an entirely new medium in which he no longer had final say. As his cowriter put it, "You have to fight these battles and sometimes you don't quite know. But when it's important you know."

FANBOY DREAMS COME TRUE: *THE AVENGERS*

32

On January 21, 2010, the Producers Guild of America presented Joss Whedon with a somewhat belated honor. The Vanguard Award, given for achievement in new media and technology, had been bestowed on George Lucas, John Lasseter, and James Cameron, and now they presented it to Joss, for his work on 2008's *Dr. Horrible*. By now, the web series was not only available on DVD but had spawned two soundtrack albums (for the series itself and *Commentary! The Musical*), several high school and college performances, and its own "Once More, with Feeling"–inspired sing-along events.

Joss was preparing to dive into another new technology at the time as MGM, excited by the early buzz for *The Cabin in the Woods*, announced that the film's release would be delayed from February 2010 to January 2011 so that it could be converted into three dimensions. Hollywood was in the midst of a burgeoning 3-D trend that encompassed not only blockbusters like *Avatar* and *Up* but also horror films such as *My Bloody Valentine*, *Saw 3D*, and *The Final Destination*.

However, in June, MGM announced that due to the studio's financial difficulties, it was shelving *Cabin* indefinitely. Joss and Goddard pressed for details, but they were slow in coming. "It was very gradual, because with billion-dollar bankruptcies, no one wants to tell you anything," Goddard says. Once they realized that the studio was going bankrupt, they knew that the January 2011 date was dead; it would take well over a year to get everything figured out. "When we saw things like *The Hobbit* and James Bond getting delayed, we knew we were in trouble," he says. "Because if those heavy hitters are getting delayed, it's gonna take us a while to come out." Yet knowing that they were in the company of Peter Jackson's highly anticipated *Hobbit* adaptation gave them a small sense of peace. "When *The Hobbit* is getting delayed, there's not a lot you can do," Goddard laughs. " 'Cause every movie studio in the city would rush to get it into production."

With *Cabin* postponed and his only television project canceled, Joss was susceptible to a new attempt to woo him back into a familiar universe. By 2010, Marvel Comics had developed its film licensing arm into a full-fledged studio capable of financing its own movie projects. Marvel Studios quickly set out to create a franchise of interconnected superhero films, finding success with *Iron Man* (2008), *The Incredible Hulk* (2008), and *Iron Man 2* (2010). Up next were *Thor* (2011) and *Captain America: The First Avenger* (2011)—but the capstone of the project would be to bring all these characters together as Marvel's ultimate superhero team in *The Avengers*. But who would direct?

"We needed somebody who wasn't going to reinvent the wheel, because the die was cast and the cast was cast," said Kevin Feige, president of production at Marvel Studios. "And yet we wanted somebody with a unique voice, because this had to feel like a part one, not *Iron Man 3* or *Thor 2*." Marvel also needed someone who could both handle action and juggle the multiple storylines required in an ensemble piece.

Feige was well aware that Joss Whedon was a strong contender. "I've known Joss for many, many years," he says, "going back to almost ten years ago when we had a project set up at New Line back before Marvel was our own studio. We would license our properties [Spider-Man, the Fantastic Four] out to other studies to produce the films, and New Line had a movie that we were sort of interested in Joss directing. We went to lunch with him, and we brought him into New Line. As a very strange aside, the first meeting we were going to have with him we had to reschedule because it was September 11, 2001. And the project that we were talking about having Joss direct at New Line: *Iron Man*."

According to Feige, Joss remained on Marvel's radar for the next decade. He wrote a treatment for *Iron Man* that was approved, but with *Buffy* and *Angel* on the air and *Firefly* in development, he had to back out. There were also brief discussions with him to direct *X-Men* and *X2* (both of which were ultimately helmed by Bryan Singer). More recently, he'd put in a good word with *Thor* director Kenneth Branagh when his *Cabin in the Woods* star Chris Hemsworth was auditioning for the title role. "I was about to go back for the audition for Ken and Joss called him just, you know, without me even knowing and just said, 'Hey, look. I really like this guy' and 'He's talented and fights for the right things,'" Hemsworth says. "Ken really respected his opinion, and I'm sure that helped me get the job." (Joss and Drew Goddard also prepped the actor with a slew of *Thor* comic books.)

Joss, says Feige, "was always somebody that I was a very, very big fan of and I always sort of hoped that our paths would cross, but frankly, he's got the Whedonverse, right? He's got his own empire. But when I started making calls about *The Avengers*, his agent mentioned his name. And I said, 'Of course.'"

Joss agreed to the meeting because he was a fan of the Avengers, but he didn't necessarily want to take on the project. First, *Dr. Horrible* had proved that he could have great success on a project that he fully controlled. He and Kai were already set to meet with their accountant to do another self-funded project. Second, would he even be the right person to write for the Avengers? In 2005, he told *In Focus* magazine that the X-Men universe was the only Marvel property he felt comfortable in. "The thing about the X-Men is they have a coherent core. The Avengers to me is tough. I wouldn't approach The Avengers, I wouldn't approach the Fantastic Four," he said. "The X-Men are all born of pain, and pain is where I hang my hat." Third, he'd already struggled in *Serenity* to tell a cohesive story about a diverse group of people with extensive backstories that would be accessible to both devoted fans and complete newbies. And last, he'd been burned in his past three attempts to make a comic book movie, the perpetually delayed *Wonder Woman* project being the latest and most frustrating failure.

He went into the meeting with a single intention: to have a discussion about the current version of the script, by Zak Penn, the screenwriter for *The Incredible Hulk*. That is not what happened. Between the end of filming on *Thor* and the start of filming for *Captain America*, Joss and Feige got together, and the production chief explained the *Avengers* script and laid out how each movie related to the next.

"I don't think you have anything," Joss told Feige. "You need to pretend this draft never happened." Then he went home and wrote five pages of material explaining how he would tell the story of the Avengers. "In the process of writing it, I got that bug," Joss said. "I realized, oh, yeah, this would be so much fun."

Joss's document, according to Feige, was incredibly well written and articulate, was full of great ideas, and ended with the motto "The Avengers: Some Assembly Required." "What a great way to kick off this project!" says Feige. He loved the phrase so much that when they added an *Avengers* teaser to the end of *Captain America* in July 2011, they used it as a tagline. "That's where 'Some Assembly Required' came from—I remembered it from Joss's original memo."

It was the underlying concept of family that spoke to Joss. "He's got a great quote," Feige says, remembering Joss's line about *The Avengers* being a group of people who have no business being in the same room together, and yet they are forced to work together. "Isn't that the perfect definition of a family?"

Marvel liked Joss's ideas and gave him an offer to write and direct, with several stipulations, including a ninety-two-day shoot and a quick turnaround for postproduction, even the substantial special effects sequences. The studio specified that the villain must be Loki, brother of the fallen Norse god Thor, who turns against his sibling in the superhero's solo film. Also, it wanted a big fight among the Avengers in the middle of the film that leaves the team shattered, and an epic battle at the end. "I was like, great, you just gave me your three acts," Joss said. "Now all I have to do is justify getting to those places and beyond them." Or as he put it at another point, "I have enough signposts to build from, all I had to do was try to make it matter and try to have reasons for the conflicts."

The Avengers was already set for release in May 2012, which gave Joss confidence that, unlike *Wonder Woman*, this film was really going to happen. He was all in.

"I kept telling my mom that reading comic books would pay off," Joss joked. His stepfather, Stephen, had jokingly taunted him for years with the question "When are you going to make a real, grown-up picture, without the vampires and the rocket ships?" Each time, Joss would reply with the same answer: "Never. It's never gonna happen." Now he was about to board the biggest rocket ship of his career.

//////////

In fan circles, rumors abounded over who would take the helm of *The Avengers*. Early buzz focused on *Iron Man* and *Iron Man 2* director Jon Favreau, but he declared himself out of the running. Other rumors pointed to *The Incredible Hulk* director Louis Leterrier, who reportedly had expressed interest in the project. But fans really started to get fired up with the news that Joss Whedon was in the mix.

Oddly, the possibility was first raised on April 1, 2010, via the now-defunct website IESB. The fact that the story was posted on April Fool's Day caused many to question its validity. The *Los Angeles Times*' Hero Complex website did some digging and reported on April 3, 2010, that "insiders at Marvel Studios say no director has been signed yet but that Whedon was on the short-list and conversations took place. This could be promising, Whedonites."

By April 13, 2010, *Deadline Hollywood* was reporting it as all but a done deal, yet official confirmation actually wouldn't come for another three months. At San Diego Comic-Con, Joss himself confirmed the story, during *Entertainment Weekly*'s Visionaries panel on July 22, 2010. Sharing the stage with his former WB neighbor J. J. Abrams, Joss told the crowd that "that is not an official thing, because I think Marvel couldn't afford a press release, so can I just make that an official thing? I'm directing *The Avengers*." Two days later, it became *extremely* official when franchise stars Robert Downey Jr. and Samuel L. Jackson took to the Comic-Con stage to officially introduce the full cast and director of *The Avengers*.

On the surface, Joss might have seemed a risky choice to oversee the culmination of a half-dozen blockbuster motion pictures. Marvel had tapped other non-blockbuster directors like Favreau and Branagh, but those filmmakers had a roster of previous films under their belt. Up to this point, Joss had directed just one feature film, *Serenity*, which starred largely box office unknowns with whom he had already worked on *Firefly*. But fans were confident in Marvel's pick. "Oftentimes in the Marvel fan community, there's a lot of second guessing," Feige says. "There's a lot of 'OK, let's see—how are you gonna screw it up?' The more movies we make, the more benefit of the doubt I think they give us. But in the case of the Joss choice, it was unanimously positive for the decision, and I think that extended across the Marvel universe and the Whedon universe equally."

//////////

One of Joss's first tasks was to get the script in order. He retained some story elements from previous drafts, sharing "story by" credit with Zak

Penn, but Joss would ultimately receive the sole screenplay credit. Nevertheless, the writing of *The Avengers* was a collaborative process, much like Joss's work on *Toy Story* with Pixar. He popped into Marvel headquarters fairly regularly to talk about the essentials of the *The Avengers* script: structure, narrative, and characters—generally, how exactly to build this blockbuster. The members of the studio's team were all exceptionally well versed in comic book lore; they and Joss shared the same reference points, which immediately put everyone on the same page. Feige was taken with Joss's love for the characters in particular. "There's been much made of superheroes being the myths of our time," he says. "Joss looks at these characters, as we do, not just as comic book characters but as great literary characters. And he is so well read that he pulls on all of those examples to put them together. He'll often go to great composers. He always has music running in his office and it's often film music, often classical music."

Joss also contributed a dialogue polish to the *Captain America* screenplay. It gave him a stronger foundation with the character of Captain America / Steve Rogers, who he felt would be the audience's connection to world of *The Avengers*. "I did spend a lot of time with the character, which for me was important, because Steve's perspective in this world is very much, as much as anybody's if not more, the audience's," Joss said. As a supersoldier from the 1940s who awakens in the modern world at the end of *Captain America*, Steve Rogers "is looking at this world with fresh eyes and he is not impressed. His feeling of disconnection is something that's going to be laced throughout [*The Avengers*]. It's a film about lonely people, because I'm making it, and my pony only does one trick. . . . He's a classic man out of time in the very literal sense and so to have worked on his '40s incarnation, even a little bit, was a nice introduction to this and kept me grounded in his perspective."

In addition, Joss consulted with Kenneth Branagh, who was in the middle of postproduction on *Thor*. He asked Branagh if he could see a rough cut of the film that laid out the full narrative for villain Loki, because he wanted to know where both he and Thor ended up in the film so he could take off in the right direction in *The Avengers*. After viewing it, Joss asked the actor playing Loki, Tom Hiddleston, to meet up for a cup of tea and just talk about the character. Hiddleston recalls the e-mail, which, among other things, said, "The motherfucker lives in you, and I want to know it all."

Hiddleston had actually met the writer years earlier, when Joss saw him in a production of *Othello* in his native London. Chiwetel Ejiofor, who played the stoic and menacing Operative in *Serenity*, starred as the titular Moor, and Hiddleston was his lieutenant, Michael Cassio. As Joss caught up with his friend Ejiofor, he spoke with Hiddleston and was "very sweet" in his appraisal of his performance. They met again in L.A. in 2009 to discuss a possible role in *The Cabin in the Woods*, but in the end, Joss told him that he'd love to find something for them to do together but he didn't think there was a part for him in the film. "I was like, 'Dude, totally fine,'" Hiddleston laughs. "We then disappeared from each other's lives for a period of 365 days, and the next time I meet him, he had signed on to write and direct *The Avengers*."

They met in Santa Monica, and Hiddleston ran through what he'd done to prepare for and play the character of Loki. He listed the wide variety of research material he'd consulted: all of the Stan Lee and Jack Kirby comics, *The Ultimates*, comics by J. Michael Straczynski, the Norse myths themselves, the works of Wagner. He discussed how he approached the role of the damaged brother, mentioning several Shakespearean influences: Edmund in *King Lear* and Cassius in *Julius Caesar*. "I literally plugged in some kind of USB into his hard drive, and downloaded all of the Loki information—metaphorically," Hiddleston laughs.

Joss completely understood where he was coming from. They shared the same references, and the love of villains both classic and pop cultural. "Alan Rickman as Hans Gruber in *Die Hard* was a landmark moment in my conception of bad guys in the movies. He's magnetic," Hiddleston says. "We used to talk a lot about Peter O'Toole, and James Mason. Joss is a huge, huge fan of James Mason and his work. And how long before my time, before Alan Rickman's time and any of the current crop of British bad guys, the great godfather of British actors playing the roles in Hollywood movies was James Mason. That was such a touchstone for us."

After ingesting all there was from Hiddleston's dissertation on Loki, Joss said, "I want to dive off the deep end. . . . Because of the way that you've established the spiritual origin of the character, I now want to create the Lord of Misrule, the God of Mischief," Hiddleston remembers. "And in *The Avengers*, I need you to be more menacing, more feral—and above all enjoy yourself."

//////////

Hiddleston, of course, wasn't the only actor to reprise his role from Marvel's previous superhero films. *The Avengers* would also feature the return of Robert Downey Jr. as Tony Stark / Iron Man, Chris Evans as Captain America, and Chris Hemsworth as Thor. (After Joss cast him in *The Cabin in the Woods* and then recommended him for *Thor*, Hemsworth says, "it was funny to come full circle and now be working with him again.") Scarlett Johansson and Jeremy Renner would reprise their supporting roles as Black Widow from *Iron Man 2* and Hawkeye from *Thor*, respectively, while Samuel L. Jackson and Clark Gregg would continue their string of appearances as Nick Fury and Phil Coulson of the shadowy defense organization S.H.I.E.L.D.

But one major role would need to be recast. Edward Norton, who played the title character in *The Incredible Hulk*, had met with Joss to discuss his participation in the film—a meeting that, according to Norton's agent, went well. But contract negotiations stalled, and in July 2010, Kevin Feige released a statement confirming that Ed Norton would be replaced with a new actor in the role of the Hulk / Bruce Banner. Fan reaction was mixed; many liked Norton's take on Banner and looked forward to seeing how his character worked in an ensemble piece, while others were soured by his involvement in the media-hyped drama behind the scenes of *The Incredible Hulk*, in which the actor and the studio clashed over the tone of the film and issues of creative control.

Joss already knew who he wanted for the new Hulk: indie actor Mark Ruffalo. "Mark was my dream choice and I had my heart set on him," Joss explained. "I wanted a completely fresh take on the character so I went to Marvel very early on and said, 'I know the guy who would be a great Bruce Banner' and they said, 'Unless it's Mark Ruffalo, we really don't know.' And I was like 'What?!' I just froze and said, 'You've got to be kidding. You did not just say that,' and I showed them my list that I had in my wallet with his name at the top and they were completely on board."

The news that he was on Joss's list came as something of a surprise to Ruffalo. (Not that it should have—Louis Leterrier had originally wanted him for the lead in *The Incredible Hulk*, but he and Marvel went with the more well-known Norton instead.) "Joss said, 'I'm excited by what I think you'll do with it, and I think you'll bring a humility and a sense of humor,'" Ruffalo remembers. He'd wanted to play the character since Ang Lee was casting the earlier adaptation *Hulk* (2003), and he was disappointed when Eric Bana won the part instead.

The Avengers was different, however, as Banner would be not the lead character but rather a member of an entire team of larger-than-life heroes—and a reluctant member at that. "For me, it's a tough part, because you're trying to watch a guy that doesn't want to be there in the movie scenario; that could be deadly, you know. It's a tough nut to crack, to watch a movie about a guy who doesn't want to be there." Before agreeing to the role, Ruffalo reached out to his good friend Norton to ask for his blessing. "The way I see it is that Ed has bequeathed this part to me," he said. "I look at it as my generation's Hamlet."

Joss also helped pave the way for his friend Cobie Smulders to join the cast as S.H.I.E.L.D. agent Maria Hill, a character from the comic books making her cinematic debut. When Smulders was considering whether to audition, the role was still somewhat vague; "It was like 'Female Agent #12,'" she says. "But it was a significant amount of dialogue where it wasn't just reading lines about protocol. There was an emotional arc within the scene. I knew this person has a story in this ginormous action movie instead of just giving information to the audience," she says. "So I went in. And I did it. Joss wanted to see me."

But she was in New York, and Joss wanted to see her the next day in L.A. Smulders offered to make an audition tape and send it to him. That won her a screen test with Samuel L. Jackson. "Sam Jackson's there, sitting in the corner dressed as Nick Fury. I've screen tested for many shows. But it just has the feeling of such a big project. Like, what could this mean for me? And it's like you're at that level," she explains. "We did it three or four times. And Joss, every time, came up with great notes and great advice. I left not knowing if it was good or not."

Apparently, it was: Joss called her forty-five minutes later to deliver the good news. "I said, 'Thank you so much for thinking of me and giving me this opportunity. And I hope I don't let you down. And I'm going to work really hard,'" Smulders says. "And he was like, 'You know, I don't do favors. So you should know that. I'm not doing this because we're friends. It's because you were the best.' It's so cool for him to say."

//////////

The complexity of the casting, particularly coordinating the schedules of so much high-level talent, necessitated some changes throughout the writing process. "I wrote an entire draft with a new character [Wasp] because we thought we weren't going to have [Scarlett Johansson]," Joss explains. "And then that didn't happen, so then I had to go back and write another draft with that person back in it. That was a bit of a rigamarole. . . . But, you know, it all comes out in the wash."

After several drafts that were nixed by Marvel, Joss finally had one that was ready to send to the cast. Even with five previous films in the Marvel Cinematic Universe to build on, Joss had approached the story as the first part of an Avengers narrative rather than a continuation of all the storylines from the earlier movies. After all, Marvel had plans to make *The Avengers* into its own movie franchise, so it needed to work independently of any previous projects. Joss felt strongly that it also needed to work independently of any *future* projects; he thought that too many studios tried to kick off franchises with stories that were all setup and no conclusion. "Even though *The Empire Strikes Back* is better, in innumerable ways, than *Star Wars*," he said, "*Star Wars* wins because you can't end a movie with Han frozen in Carbonite. That's not a movie, it's an episode."

As a standalone origin story, Joss's script had to introduce each character as if he or she is brand new to the viewer. It does so via S.H.I.E.L.D. head Nick Fury, who must assemble a group of heroes to save the world. The threat harks back to Stan Lee and Jack Kirby's first *Avengers* comic book from 1963: resentful god Loki comes to Earth to obtain the Tesseract, a powerful energy source that he can use to obtain an extraterrestrial army, conquer and rule the Earth, and take revenge on his brother Thor. When Loki attacks the research facility holding the Tesseract, Fury reactivates the "Avengers Initiative" to head off the catastrophic battle he sees coming. Black Widow goes to Calcutta, India, in order to recruit Dr. Bruce Banner, Agent Coulson enlists Tony Stark, and Fury seeks out the first Avenger, Captain America. Thor later joins them after first fighting with Iron Man over the custody of the captured Loki—who makes his escape from S.H.I.E.L.D.'s Helicarrier when the group is manipulated into fighting one another. The Avengers must get past their egos and assemble into a proper team to defeat Loki and his alien army.

Clark Gregg describes the cast's reaction to the first distributed draft: "[The script] was funny and still tongue-in-cheek and really got the tone, the Tony Stark tone of the Marvel universe, and still furthered and explored each one of those characters and those relationships. I found out later from other people involved that had the same reaction—like, oh, wow. Oh, wow. Everybody gets to play. Everybody gets to play, and it's going to be better than anything we reasonably hoped for." He adds, "To me, Joss seemed like the perfect guy for *The Avengers*, because he had perhaps the deepest, most comprehensive grasp and history with the various characters in *The Avengers*. He seems like he grew up steeped in the Marvel comic book universe."

Tom Hiddleston was so incredibly moved by the first draft of the script he saw that he shot off an e-mail to Joss as soon as he was able to process the storyline he'd been given:

Joss,
I am so excited I can hardly speak.

The first time I read it I grabbed at it like Charlie Bucket snatching for a golden ticket somewhere behind the chocolate in the wrapper of a Wonka Bar. I didn't know where to start. Like a classic actor I jumped in looking for LOKI on every page, jumping back and forth, reading words in no particular order, utterances imprinting themselves like flash-cuts of newspaper headlines in my mind: "real menace"; "field of obeisance"; "discontented, nothing is enough"; "his smile is nothing but *a glimpse of his skull*"; "Puny god" . . .

. . . Thank you for writing me my Hans Gruber. But a Hans Gruber with super-magic powers. As played by James Mason. . . . It's high operatic villainy alongside detached throwaway tongue-in-cheek; plus the "real menace" and his closely guarded suitcase of pain. It's grand and epic and majestic and poetic and lyrical and wicked and rich and badass and might possibly be the most gloriously fun part I've ever stared down the barrel of playing. It is just so *juicy*.

I love how throughout you continue to put Loki on some kind of pedestal of regal magnificence and then consistently tear him down. He gets battered, punched, blasted, side-swiped, roared at, sent tumbling on his back, and every time he gets up smiling, wickedly, never for a second losing his eloquence, style, wit, self-aggrandisement or grandeur, and you never send him up or deny him his real intelligence. . . . That he loves to make an entrance; that he has a taste for the grand gesture, the big speech, the spectacle. I might be biased, but I do feel as though you have written me the coolest part.

. . . But really I'm just sending you a transatlantic shout-out and fist-bump, things that traditionally British actors probably don't do. It's epic.

Joss responded in kind:

Tom, this is one of those emails you keep forever. Thanks so much. It's more articulate (and possibly longer) than the script. I couldn't be more pleased at your reaction, but I'll also tell you I'm still working on it. . . . Thank you again. I'm so glad you're pleased. Absurd fun to ensue.

Best, (including uncharacteristic fist bump), joss.

Despite the grand scale of the film, Joss was able to bring past experiences to bear on the project. "You know, ironically, I said this last week—doing a super-giant budget movie is more like doing an Internet musical than anything else," he explained in May 2011. "Having everything and having nothing are very similar. I've had no rehearsal time with my actors. I had none on *Dr. Horrible* because we were so under the gun. I have none now because they're all so famous and they're all busy making movies."

BUFFY LIVES, AGAIN?

While Joss was working on the *Avengers* script, another big announcement rocked the Whedonverse. In November 2010, Warner Bros. Pictures and Atlas Entertainment announced plans to reboot the *Buffy the Vampire Slayer* franchise with a new feature film. The *Buffy* reboot would not be written, directed, or produced by Joss Whedon. In fact, it would have no involvement from any of the behind-the-scenes or on-camera talent previously affiliated with the television series.

The project had originated a year earlier, when Fran and Kaz Kuzui decided to capitalize on the vampire craze that was in full swing thanks to the success of *Twilight*. As the director and producer of the 1992 *Buffy* movie, the Kuzuis retained the film rights to the property, so they partnered with Roy Lee and Doug Davison of Vertigo Entertainment to develop a new version of *Buffy* for the big screen, in the hopes of creating a new blockbuster franchise. Joss was actually offered a role in the project, but with so much else on his plate, he declined. So did 20th Century Fox, the studio that produced the first film and the television series—most likely because they were not interested in reworking one of their biggest cult hits without its creator, with whom they'd had a long relationship.

Without Joss or Fox on board, the new film would have very few if any connections with the *Buffy* TV series. The Kuzuis owned only the rights to the original film's characters and story. They'd licensed those rights to Fox for the television series, which meant that Fox held the rights for anything new created for the show. Gone would be Willow, Xander, Giles, and Sunnydale, replaced with new characters and settings.

Whit Anderson, a writer with no feature writing credits—much like Joss when he created the original film—signed on to tell the story. She had grown up watching the *Buffy* series in its original run, passing each

high school benchmark the same year the Slayer did. She wanted to balance her reinvention of the mythology with what she found so compelling about Buffy's emotional arc, "the deep struggle she had with duty
and destiny, that tug between what you're supposed to be doing and what
you *want* to be doing," Anderson told the *Los Angeles Times*. "The fate of
the world is on her shoulders, but some days she wakes up, and she just
doesn't want to do it. And are we doomed and destined to love someone?
That conflict was very interesting to me."

Her pitch won over the Vertigo producers, and with Warner Bros.
signed on, the press release went out on November 22, 2010. The response
from fans and media critics was immediate, intense outrage.

Genre reboots are nothing new. Batman, Spider-Man, and Superman
have all been reimagined numerous times for both the big and the small
screen, generally with little input from previous producers. But the prospect of rebooting a television series that had averaged only 4.5 million
viewers over its seven-year run on two small, often-struggling networks, a
series that itself was a reboot of a poorly received film, was widely considered unthinkable. The uproar was covered by mainstream media outlets
that wouldn't have bothered with *Buffy* when it premiered on the WB in
1997. That reaction was a testament to the passionate following that Joss
Whedon had cultivated over the past thirteen years.

Fans doubted that a newcomer with no connection to Joss would be
able to capture the spirit that had defined the *Buffy* universe. Even Tim
Minear, who earned Joss's utmost trust in writing his characters, had
felt uncomfortable when faced with writing Buffy Summers herself.

Reaction from the *Buffy* actors was unanimously negative. Back
when the first reboot rumors trickled out in 2009, Alyson Hannigan had
said it was a very big mistake, that without Joss, it was just a story that
shared the same title. After the official announcement, Anthony Stewart
Head called the reboot "a hideous idea," while David Boreanaz posted
his reaction to the news on Twitter: a picture of himself pouting. Charisma Carpenter felt that it was an "opportunity to take something that
was loved and cherished and lucrative and franchise it—and make more
money from it."

"There's no public outcry for a remake of *Buffy*, there's only the
opportunity in pop culture where vampires are very popular," Seth Green
said. "If Joss came out and said, 'I want to make a new Buffy movie,' even
if he said, 'I want to do it like the reboot of Spider-Man. I want to put

Buffy back in high school and I want to tell a different story with this character,' I think people would go with that. But the fact that people who are not connected to it and were not connected to the show or any of the mythology that was created going back to the movie—which everyone kind of agreed wasn't a perfect version of its potential—you know, I think that really confuses people. It confuses the audience. They're like, 'How am I supposed to feel about this?'"

Like Green, Sarah Michelle Gellar was not opposed to the idea that the series might one day be reimagined with a different actress in the title role. "I love the Buffy that I played and I'll always be protective of her," she says, "but if somebody else does it later on then it's an honor to the character." Still, she calls the proposed reboot "the stupidest idea I've ever heard. *Buffy* is Joss." She adds, "I hate to say this but it was a movie and it didn't totally work and there was a reason why it didn't work. You don't relate with a story of a Valley girl Buffy in two hours. You have to get to know her. And by the way, as Joss says, I'm one of the lone fans of the movie—I love the movie."

As soon as the press release went out, Joss himself provided a more measured response:

> This is a sad, sad reflection on our times, when people must feed off the carcasses of beloved stories from their youths—just because they can't think of an original idea of their own, like I did with my Avengers idea that I made up myself. Obviously I have strong, mixed emotions about something like this. . . . I always hoped that Buffy would live on even after my death. But, you know, AFTER.

////////////

In a frustrating turn of events, *Buffy* was getting an unnecessary reboot while *The Cabin in the Woods* remained on the shelf with no hope of making it to theaters any time soon. MGM's financial situation continued to get worse, and Mary Parent left the studio as it spiraled down. As with *Goners* when Parent left Universal, Joss had lost his film's champion, and things were looking very bleak for the horror tale.

At least MGM's issues came after shooting was done and the film was in good shape. Goddard and Joss were frustrated, but they found a little consolation in the idea that if *Cabin* never saw the light of day through proper channels, they could always leak it. "OK, if worse comes to worst, we can just let this out to our fan base. We'll get it out," Goddard laughs. "There was a lot of quoting of *Serenity* around that time: 'You can't stop the signal.'"

///////////

A year later, the *Los Angeles Times*' Hero Complex would break the news that Whit Anderson's script for the *Buffy* reboot had been rejected and the project was on hold until they found a new writer. "If you're going to bring it back, you have to do it right," one individual involved in the project said. "[Anderson] came in with some great ideas and she had reinvented some of the lore and it was pretty cool but in the end there just wasn't enough on the page."

This announcement provoked far less of a response than the original press release. Perhaps fans still hoped that the whole thing would be abandoned. In any event, there was no doubt that if a new non-Whedonverse writer stepped up to take Anderson's place, he or she would face another barrage of attacks.

Marti Noxon told MTV that she couldn't see anyone but Joss having success bringing Buffy back to the big screen. "I wouldn't want to be the person trying to write it. And I worked on the show, but I would not want to be that [person] because the fans are very loyal. They're *excruciatingly* loyal."

"Unless they hate you," she added, "in which case they're excruciating about that too." Joss agreed: "The people who feel the most strongly about something will turn on you the most vociferously if they feel you've let them down. . . . You don't get the big praise without getting the big criticism. Because people care. So. Much."

34

AVENGERS ASSEMBLE

Although Joss's screenplay for *The Avengers* was in good enough shape to distribute to his main cast, that didn't mean his screenwriting work on the project was at an end. He asked all the actors for their notes on the script and their characters so he could continue to refine things. "At the beginning I'm an open book," Joss said. "So, 'Tell me what it is that you don't want to repeat or you feel like you didn't explore.'"

Scarlett Johansson felt the initial draft was a little confusing, because the storylines seemed "cobbled together." On the other hand, Robert Downey Jr., quite notorious for taking command in his films and doing his own rewrites, was content once the storyline was agreed upon. "It wasn't broke, so it's not like we had to fix things," he said. "With some of the *Iron Man* movies, I feel like more of a producer . . . but with this, it is a bit of a relief—it's nice when the car drives all by itself."

Samuel L. Jackson, who'd been donning the mantle of Nick Fury since 2008's *Iron Man*, found Joss's outreach to be a new and welcome experience. "It was the first chance I had to actually be a part of the process in terms of being Nick Fury, understanding what the director was trying to do, what the story was about," he says. "A lot of times I don't even know what the films are about; I just kind of show up and be the connector. But in this instance, Joss and I talked before the film started. He told me what his concept was, what he wanted Nick Fury to do, how he perceived him."

The director, in turn, called Jackson's reaction to his call for feedback "my favorite response." Joss recalled, "I was like, 'Is there anything you're particularly looking for. . . . Anything you're looking for or anything you particularly want to avoid?' [Jackson] was like, 'Hell no. Thank you for asking. I don't want to run. Don't make me run a lot.'

Then on set he pointed to the page, 'It says "Fury runs." ' 'I know, it's just this one time.' "

Although limited by his A-list cast's other commitments, Joss also brought the actors together in smaller groups prior to the start of filming. One such meeting involved Joss, Mark Ruffalo, Robert Downey Jr., and Jeremy Renner.

Renner knew Joss from his guest role on *Angel* back in 2000. Back then, Renner saw him as a Godfather-like character—lurking in the back, making sure that every detail was locked down, under his thumb. "But then I got it. He was such a funny, kind of awkward dude that I got along with right away," he says. "It's such a weird connection. Being a generous guy, he kept bringing me in for things always, and he liked me a lot more than I feel like I deserved."

The actor was also impressed by Joss's ability to take in the diverse opinions of his actors without judgment. "Even the craziness of all the different sort of walks of life. It was like *The Magnificent Seven*—we all kind of just stand and hold our ground," Renner says. "Joss is able to [be] an observer. Not like in a creepy way."

As a new arrival to the franchise, Mark Ruffalo was grateful to Joss for helping him get a handle on the character of the Hulk / Bruce Banner. "We spent a long time talking about the script and where we find Banner, how we find him, what state of mind is he in when we find him, what his journey ultimately becomes—you know, the fifteen minutes of screen time that he'll have," Ruffalo explains. "I talked a lot about how Joss would shoot it, and how he really wasn't interested in doing it unless he kind of could do his own take on it, you know, and that was kind of my feeling too—what could we possibly do that hasn't already been done with it?"

//////////

Joss began shooting *The Avengers* on April 25, 2011, with Seamus McGarvey as his director of photography. Marvel had suggested another DP, an experienced action-movie cinematographer who had worked on one of Michael Bay's *Transformers* films but was supposed to be "really mean." "What part of that sentence was supposed to sell me?" Joss asked. He went with "nice Irishman" McGarvey instead. "It's very important to have people around you who are in the spirit of the thing. And besides being ridiculously talented, Seamus is also quite fast, which is something else that I require on the set."

McGarvey's previous films were smaller, more personal fare like *High Fidelity* (2000), *The Hours* (2002), and *Atonement* (2007), but Joss found his films beautiful and thought his aesthetic worked with his own plans for the film. "Joss and I were keen on having a very visceral and naturalistic quality to the image," McGarvey said. "We wanted this to feel immersive and did not want a 'comic book look' that might distance an audience with the engagement of the film. We moved the camera a lot on Steadicam, cranes and on dollies to create kinetic images; and we chose angles that were dramatic, like low angles for heroic imagery."

The initial plan was to shoot in 3-D, which was the format Joss used when he directed a postcredits scene for *Thor* that teases the *Avengers* storyline. But after the equipment caused frustrating delays on that shoot, he decided not to use it for the movie itself. Instead, *The Avengers* would be converted into 3-D in postproduction.

Like Nick Fury, Clark Gregg's Agent Coulson had appeared in most of the previous films in the Marvel Cinematic Universe, so Gregg was in an ideal position to compare Joss's directorial work to that of two other directors in the franchise, Jon Favreau and Kenneth Branagh. Favreau had directed both *Iron Man* and *Iron Man 2*, and yet to Gregg those films felt very different from each other. "I feel like Jon and Robert [Downey Jr.]'s creative process was one that required a certain amount of evolution and improvisation every day," he says. "They would take the words that were there and evolve them, and out of that chaos Tony Stark and the Iron Man universe came into being."

Thor director Kenneth Branagh had a lot of qualities that Favreau had—he was very funny and he loved to work with actors. Yet while he was open to whatever changes and interpretations developed on the day of shooting, Gregg says, "they were very much sticking to the script that was there and trying to be true to a kind of Shakespearian element of Thor's world and yet keep them tethered to the same kind of version of Earth that was represented in *Iron Man* and *Iron Man 2*."

To Gregg, Joss compared favorably to his predecessors; he was "hilariously funny, loves actors, and loves what they do and gets what they do." Gregg adds, "It was interesting to me that he gets what they do in a way just as profoundly as Kenneth and Jon, who are both amazing professional actors." (Unsurprisingly, Joss might have been even more of a stickler about performing the script as written than Branagh; Samuel L. Jackson calls him a "line policeman.")

Mark Ruffalo was also impressed by how well Joss understood the actor's craft. "Joss came to my rescue on many occasions to get me in the right spot. It's surprising how giddy he is with actors, considering people write off that genre as just fluff, as just pure entertainment. But he takes his actors through the paces, and he knows how to talk to an actor," he says. "A lot of directors don't; they can give you ideas, and they explain it to you, but that doesn't necessarily mean that what they're telling you is actable, and a lot of times you've got to translate what the director's saying into making that actable. That's your job, you know; that's what we get paid for. But Joss knows how to do it—he mainlines it, he always knew exactly what to say to me to get me to where I needed to be, and I appreciated that. That's not common.

"I love Banner's introduction. It's one of my favorite scenes, and he knew how to play that. Joss had a great bit where there was just a baby cradle there, and Banner says, 'I don't always get what I want.' Joss suggested that maybe he goes to that cradle and he rocks it. It's just a light thing, but it sort of says a lot. And I just thought that was a really great choice. I was pissed because I didn't come up with it myself."

Cobie Smulders appreciated that Joss "was so protective over me, and he was so protective over Maria Hill. She's in comic books, but she's relatively new in the movies. So it was really important for him to give her a voice."

As usual, Joss continued to rewrite his script as they were filming. The actors were surprised how quickly he could come up with dialogue that immediately made the scene better. Downey recalled a moment toward the end that brought Thor, Captain America, and Iron Man together. "It needed to say a lot and it needed to also not just be one line but it couldn't be two pages, so he said, 'Give me a second' . . . It wound up being four lines which included all of us, and he gave us, I think, three pages of options," he said. "The guy is really just kind of a machine, but it feels organic."

Chris Evans agreed. "That's a great way to put it. He's just so good as a writer—he's amazing. The banter is so witty . . . his set-up lines are seamless, they work, they're right, so when this great exchange happens, you are like, 'Man, that is so clever.' If, for whatever reason, it doesn't work, he can come up with a new exchange just like that."

//////////

While Nick Fury and Agent Coulson serve as a through line that unites the various films in the Marvel Cinematic Universe, there was a more important constant on the set of *The Avengers*. Production spanned the country, from Albuquerque, New Mexico, to locations around Ohio to New York City, and actors came and went as the film's sprawling ensemble format required, but Joss was always there at the center of it all.

"Nobody was doing it every day, eighteen hours a day, except Joss," explains Gregg. "People would come in and work for a couple of weeks. They'd do their combat stuff, their training, their listening, and we got to hang out a couple of times at night, which, I guess, that was the most fun, maybe. They were happy to be there. They had great stuff to do thanks to Joss. It's a very different experience if the script isn't that good or if the director has a kind of megalomaniac power streak, which just isn't Joss's MO. He runs the ship kind of—to me he was the unseen Avenger. He was part of the gang."

Renner noticed Joss's good-natured dedication as well. "All of us would just pass the baton and come in and do our little bit and get the heck out, while he was there just trudging away every day," he says. "Every once in a while, I'd pop in and do one of my bits, and I could see, like, oh yeah, it's starting to wear on him a little bit. But really he never lets it affect anybody else—his professionalism is always right on."

"It was grueling, as big shoots are," says Marvel Studios' Kevin Feige, "but Joss is able to get an atmosphere where everyone's productive, everyone is pleasant, everyone is about the work," Feige says. "He's a self-deprecating guy. It's fun to sit behind the monitor with him and hear him tear apart his own words or tear apart a shot."

//////////

Joss even found a way to relax amid his nonstop work—though he might sometimes have tried to resist it. Much of the crew had been with the shoot for the first three months in Albuquerque and the following six weeks in Ohio. As production was nearing a close in Cleveland and moving on to a much smaller shoot with a smaller crew for three days in New York, Tom Hiddleston realized that there wouldn't be a wrap party with everyone before they left. He wanted to find a way to thank the crew, whom he felt not only had been extremely kind to him, a Brit on foreign shores, but were the unsung heroes of this huge blockbuster.

Hiddleston decided to throw an all-night party at the House of Blues (they had been doing night shoots, so everyone's body clock was set to stay up all night). But the night of the party was right before they were scheduled to film a big scene, in which Loki crashes a party at an art gallery and flips a man over and takes out his eyeball. Joss sent Hiddleston a note to let him know that he was exhausted and didn't know if he could make it: "I'll try and come for half an hour. Salute you, then head back and keep writing, and keep cutting, and keep thinking."

"Yeah, he came to the party," Hiddleston laughs. "And then he was the first person on the dance floor and the last person to leave."

It was not the only time during the shoot that Joss used dancing to unwind. He would spend weekend downtime going to dance clubs with the cast. And Joss, Gregg, Renner, and Hiddleston confirmed that there was "some *Avengers* affinity" for the video game *Dance Dance Revolution*.

But Joss had always loved to dance. After all, it's how he impressed Kai the first time they met. Sister-in-law and *Dr. Horrible* collaborator Maurissa Tancharoen confirms that Joss "is not just a big dancer. He is a dancing machine. A dancing fiend. Whenever there is music playing, he does not care where he is, he will start dancing. And soon enough, a circle forms around him, and everyone is dancing. Seriously. Anywhere. If he could dance twenty-four seven, he would."

Joe Quesada, editor in chief of Marvel Comics, calls Joss "the most enthusiastic white boy dancing fool that I have ever seen in my entire life. He's that kind of dancer that I wish I could be, which is 'Hey there's nobody dancing on the dance floor—I'll change that!' He'll just go out there, and then everybody's dancing."

The most distinctive description came from Eliza Dushku. "He has this crazy-legs dance, and that's what I lovingly, affectionately call him. His knees are double jointed or something and they pop out to the sides, and nobody can replicate his dance. His crazy-legs dance is a genius creation that only he can demonstrate." (It sounds remarkably like the "Dance of Joy," which Joss performed in a cameo as the demon Numfar in the *Angel* episode "Through the Looking Glass.") Dushku once joined Joss at a super-trendy club to go dancing. He was decked out in khakis, a button-down shirt, and Reebok sneakers. "Boy just had such swagger, and we danced for like four or five hours. Some people came in and joined our circle, but he was the star of the room."

"He's a grown-ass man, and he takes care of business," says Clark Gregg, "but like a lot of great creative people, he's still really deeply in touch with this kind of fantastical, energetic childlike qualities that we really love to play. You really see the joy—that joyous side that a lot of grown-ups lose track of, a kind of Peter Pan side that comes out in his desire to go get bacchanalian at night." Gregg found a kinship working with Joss and a new inspiration on the dance floor. When his wife asked what he wanted to do for his birthday, Gregg responded, "I think I want to go Joss style. I just want a fantastic party and I just want to dance until I can't move anymore."

//////////

Back on the *Avengers* set, Joss the dancing fiend became Joss the perfectionist. He insisted on being involved in even the seemingly minor details of production. "From my own experience, because he wrote it, he did a part of everything," Cobie Smulders says. "How my hair is, how I look in my wardrobe, how's the strap. 'What about this light here, can we move that?' 'I think you need to be a bit tighter here, switch this up a little bit.' 'I think this line needs to be dripping a little bit.' He's so hands-on, and it's basically because he cares about the characters."

His exactness even carried over to his daily drink orders, which had to be made precisely to his specifications, a combination of distilled water, lemon juice, agave, and cayenne pepper. He would drink eight bottles a day on set. He gave one to Smulders, who found it gave her quite the rush. "I thanked him for it," she laughs. But she understood the need for both the extra energy and the routine. "That's the only routine you can have on the set of a crazy movie. That's the only thing you can hold on to."

Jeremy Renner marveled at Joss's ability to keep so many facets of such a huge production moving. "I don't know who else could have done *The Avengers*, by the way. Pulled all those people together," he says. "In my experience on *The Avengers*, there's so many people to appease and to make feel good or to wrangle in, and he tracks everything. He's just on it, and you just know you're in good hands when he's there."

"When you're doing a movie like *The Avengers*," explains Kevin Feige, "it basically means you have six A-list stars who are used to starring in their own movies. Every one of our characters and every one of the actors has carried their own films. And people have asked, 'Well, [is it hard to deal with] all those egos on set?' And the truth of the matter is, all of the actors we have are as excited as we are about this movie and about putting this together. So if they have egos they certainly have kept them in check. But I do think that Joss led by example in that regard. Joss does not have a giant ego, does not go around beating his chest."

Robert Downey Jr. prided himself on his cantankerous attitude while filming movies, often starting each day "refusing to do what [he'd] signed on to do." He "happily" brought that attitude along to *The Avengers*. "I just thought 'How are you gonna put all of us clowns together? He's wearing a suit, he's all jacked up, he's so and so and poor Mark Ruffalo, he's gonna out do us,'" he said six weeks into production. "And I have to say Joss Whedon is nailing it. He's so smart and so good. And it's gonna be great. I can't believe I just said it, I never could've believed this but it's gonna be great."

Chris Evans, who'd previously starred not only in *Captain America* but also in two Fantastic Four films as the Human Torch, enthused, "Personally, just the stuff I have been able to do on this movie, to date, this has been the most geeked out that I have felt on a movie set. I literally come sometimes and get truly, truly excited about coming to work, and that's a good feeling." Reports from the set echoed Evans's sentiments. The pressure on Joss and the cast to deliver a film that would satisfy the expectations of comic book fans and a blockbuster-hungry studio was balanced with the determination to have fun.

Joss and Hiddleston, for instance, got to indulge their fanboy love of *Die Hard*. For every Loki speech, Joss would explain what kind of performance he wanted Hiddleston to give him: vulnerable, complete megalomania, absolutely terrifying—or the Alan Rickman. "When I actually did the Alan Rickman for the first time, the crew didn't know what was going on," he laughs. "They burst out laughing—they just loved it."

Joss also gave into the absurdity of the moment from time to time. Hiddleston describes one instance while they were shooting the scene at the end of the film in which Loki gets Hulk-smashed. Ruffalo had already taped his motion capture performance for the CGI Hulk at the

Industrial Light & Magic studios, so Hiddleston was the only performer on set, throwing himself into the six-foot-by-two-foot trenches that the art department had carved into the floor of Stark Tower. "[I was] literally jumping into the air and hurling myself to the floor," he says. "Joss had written this wonderful moment where Loki essentially looks like he's being stunned almost to death—apart from emitting a very quiet, high-pitched squeal."

With two cameras on him, Hiddleston was lying in the trench and trying to produce the highest pitch at the quietest volume imaginable without moving. It was a challenge to stay so still and also deliver this very specific squeal—all the while holding a look of inconceivable shock and terror. And behind the camera, Joss got the giggles.

"I could hear him chuckling by the monitor—he has a laugh that is not loud, but it's not quiet," Hiddleston says. "I could see his shoulders shaking. As soon as I realized that he was laughing, I started laughing, and then it's one of those things where I couldn't get it back. We were both gone.

"I remember that moment really fondly. Because we're shooting this incredible, enormously expensive superhero film—there is so much pressure on both of our shoulders, and both of us are in fits of hysterics," he says. "And possibly unable to complete the day because we're having so much fun."

Kevin Feige credits Joss with encouraging "this collaborative spirit across the whole cast and the whole crew that kept everything running very smoothly. Frankly, on days in which some of the cast weren't shooting they would come just to watch. Mark Ruffalo would bring his ten-year-old son just to watch Evans and Downey do a scene as Cap and Iron Man. You don't see that all the time, and that's a testament to Joss and to the way he ran that set."

//////////

Principal photography wrapped in September 2011, with a two-day shoot for the final battle in New York City. By then, no one would have faulted the cast and director for being exhausted or even a little sick of the film. But the Big Apple brought a new energy to the set, as citygoers gathered all around them, excited to see the Avengers. Parents brought their children, pie-eyed and awed, to meet their favorite superheroes.

A photo of Loki giving a piggyback ride to a five-year-old boy with a Captain America shield became a viral phenomenon. The story behind it is even more charming: The boy, Edison, had seen *Captain America* for the second time in the theater the day before. When he and his mom happened upon the set, he was excited to see Nick Fury's car, and it was Hiddleston who asked if he could put Edison on his shoulders. Later, Chris Evans's mom beckoned an uncostumed Captain America over so he could meet him, and the two discussed proper techniques for shield handling and enemy fighting. Then Joss interrupted the two because they had a shot to get. He turned to Edison and, fully understanding the moment, said, "Sorry, little buddy, I need Captain America for a minute."

Another youngster had the experience of a lifetime: Mark Ruffalo's son, Keen, who was about the same age Joss was when he fell in love with superheroes. Keen came to set often, and it was as if everything he saw was the most incredibly awesome thing that anyone could ever have conceived of. Especially Hiddleston as Loki. After every take, the boy would gush over the actor.

"Like, 'Tom, that was so awesome, you have no idea!'" Hiddleston says, emphatically reenacting the boy's reaction. "And then he would tell me exactly what had happened in the scene as if I didn't know," he laughs. "'And then you said this, and then Hulk comes in and he does this, and then what happens . . .' He was just reliving it in his own mind, it was so wonderful.

"I remember so clearly, like it was yesterday, the excitement of watching Christopher Reeve as Superman, the feeling of watching *Indiana Jones* films." Hiddleston pauses. "He just was extraordinary, young Keen Ruffalo. He reminded me why I was doing it in a way—not that I needed reminding, 'cause the kid in me is alive and well. He was so honest, and so pure, and it was so inspiring to have that response. It made me feel so warm and fuzzy to be at work."

//////////

Kai visited Joss in New York as he finished his last week of shooting. He had a break coming up between the end of principal photography and an intense postproduction phase. And still more work lay ahead: in July, Lionsgate had announced that it had obtained the worldwide distribution rights to *The Cabin in the Woods*, slating it for an April 2012 release. That would put it out just weeks before *The Avengers* was set to bow in May.

So it made sense for Joss to take a moment to breathe while he could. One idea was to head over to Venice, Italy. ("Not for a month like it says on the Internet—yeah, that's a dream. I have children," Kai cracks.) Joss also discussed hosting another Shakespeare reading; Kai suggested that he film it, as they had discussed in the past. For years, they had wanted to do a Sundays with Shakespeare series—they could film readings in their home, then distribute the videos to high schools to help inspire more students' interest in the Bard.

From there, suddenly, the idea evolved into producing a full Shakespeare movie. It was Kai's contention that Joss didn't need to get away physically so much as mentally. "He told me all he remembers is me saying, like, 'Why don't we do it instead of going to Venice? Venice isn't sinking that fast,'" Kai says.

After shooting a multimillion-dollar blockbuster and spending months away from their loved ones, most people would take a break to decompress—maybe run away for some decadent vacation. Most people wouldn't decide to fund and shoot an independent film in their home in about thirty days. Joss Whedon isn't most people.

35

SOMETHING PERSONAL:
MUCH ADO ABOUT NOTHING

The incredible success of *Dr. Horrible's Sing-Along Blog* had inspired Joss and Kai to seriously pursue the possibility of establishing a small-scale "digital studio" that would allow them to make what they wanted, how they wanted, with their own money. But the very week they were to begin consulting with their financial manager on the logistics of opening such a studio, Joss signed on to direct *The Avengers*. Still, the endeavor continued; while Joss was away directing the blockbuster, Kai was working on producing another one of his scripts, *In Your Eyes*. They planned for it to be the first film from Bellwether Pictures, named for Lee's unpublished novel.

Now, however, with principal photography on *The Avengers* completed, another small-scale project began to take precedence. When he returned home, Joss reached out to his friend and fellow Shakespeare buff Alexis Denisof. "I think he was mourning for a passion project, so by the time he got to my house having said he wanted to chat about something, he had already decided that he wanted to do a full-blown movie shoot," Denisof says. "He proposed to me that we shoot *Much Ado About Nothing* at his house on a super-low budget. The lines would be memorized and he'd make a lot of cuts [to Shakespeare's text], and he had his own ideas about the style of it. We talked about the style, the interpretation, and we got extremely excited about it, and it just went from there."

After more than a decade, Joss's unofficial repertory company was still mounting its private Shakespeare readings, although in recent years, they'd been a bit fewer and further between, due to everyone's family and other commitments. *A Midsummer Night's Dream* was a hot commodity in the later years. In one performance, Fran Kranz played Francis Flute and Alan Tudyk was Bottom. "[Within that,] we had to go up and perform *Pyramus and Thisbe*," Kranz recalls. "I was Thisbe, [Alan] was my Pyramus, and Alexis Denisof was the wall [that the two characters speak through]—it was hilarious."

Amy Acker had played Helena, one of the young lovers, in one of their readings of the play, and *Dollhouse*'s Olivia Williams assumed the same role in another. "I begged to play Helena, as I am now too old to play her on stage and I wanted to play it before I die," she says. Williams's performance in a reading of *Hamlet* may even have had an influence on her *Dollhouse* character. "I have always believed that Gertrude [Hamlet's mother] has a drink problem, so I played her drunk at his house, aided by a rather fine bottle of Grgich Hills [wine], and in the following [*Dollhouse*] episode it emerged that Adelle was no stranger to the gin."

Colbie Smulders, however, learned the hard way that Joss was very serious about these readings. Joss told her about an upcoming reading that was scheduled to start at two o'clock, and she said she might not be able to make it until six. "I never heard back from him," she laughs. "I was so jealous when Alexis and Alyson [Hannigan] would go or tell me about it. Alexis trained at LAMDA (London Academy of Music and Dramatic Art), and I went to LAMDA for a summer semester, so I like to think that I would be able to hold [my own, but] I'd probably totally embarrass myself."

///////////

Joss and Kai had to move extremely quickly from talking about a *Much Ado About Nothing* film to taking it seriously to coming up with a team to make it happen, and the process was never without doubt. After all, Joss only had a short window of time to write, cast, and shoot before he needed to dive into editing for *The Avengers*.

"I said to her, 'There's no way I can adapt the text and prep the movie and get a cast together in one month,'" Joss remembered. "And she was like, 'Really? Because November doesn't work for us.'" But what concerned him more than the time crunch was that he didn't have a personal take on the play. "A production, let alone a movie, without a point of view is inevitably soggy," he said.

Much Ado About Nothing had long been a favorite of Joss's and his cast of merry players, ever since the performance one Sunday with Alexis Denisof as Benedick and Amy Acker as Beatrice. It is a play about the power of wordsmithery, how it can be used for anything from the bickering that covers up mutual desire to the false rumors that can break spirits and ruin reputations. Yet while Joss loved the text, it was not one of the many plays he'd studied in depth at Winchester, and he didn't feel as strong a pull toward it as he had toward some of Shakespeare's other works. Plus, he had enjoyed Kenneth Branagh's 1993 version and didn't know what else he had to say "about a movie where half of the title says 'About Nothing,' since I tend to like things that are about something."

His vision of the story was also colored by the first live performance he'd seen of the play, which was broadly comedic. While living in England, Joss had gone to a performance at Regent's Park Open Air Theatre and returned two more times because he was "floored" by the absurd and "over the top" hilarity. It was difficult for him to embrace the idea that this play could be more than just a comedy.

"I was interested in a slightly darker vision of it," Joss says, "noir in the sense that these people are basically espionage agents or spies, and they spend all of their time just making up schemes—some of them are hilarious, some of them are disastrous—and tricking each other, and not understanding each other, and lying to each other, and lying to themselves. There's so much manipulation and there's so much of taking what we assume to be romantic behavior for granted or turning it on its head and saying this is actually not in the least bit romantic." That's when Joss suddenly realized that he didn't feel the play was about nothing—that the love the squabbling Beatrice and Benedick finally discover for one another is arrived at through "the process of maturing past all of our ideas about how we're supposed to behave when we're in love."

He explains: "Every movie about love, to paraphrase Preston Sturges in *Unfaithfully Yours*, questions the necessity of marriage for the first eight reels and then it just happens in the ninth. It just gets to the point where they have to just go, 'Oh, but you are in love now.' And any question they may have asked about being in love sort of just falls by the wayside so they can end the movie. As we all know, a lot of what people consider to be romantic comedy behaviors are usually the kind of thing that would land you in jail—or at least the neighbors would be like,

'Please stop holding that boom box of Peter Gabriel up over your head and waking us all up. Just stop.'"

But with *Much Ado*, he could explore "the idea that love is for grown-ups and that romantic love as we know it is kind of a construct. That the more mature, married love—basically marriage—is an escape from the sort of whirligig of what we consider to be love. That it is actually a much deeper, more adult, and more interesting kind of love."

It was an idea very much in keeping with his favorite subjects as a writer—from his long-standing interest in how people treat one another to his more recent fascination with institutional control. Joss had moved beyond the idealized teenage romance of his early work on *Buffy*, replacing the notion of inevitable soulmates with the messier, more authentic idea that love is something two people must deliberately choose to work at despite all obstacles. And those obstacles often include the expectations of their friends and family, as well as of the lovers themselves. "I deal with a lot of societal manipulation or secret government manipulation—how certain things are expected of us in the ways we behave," Joss says. "This deals with that on a more personal level. It's a very cynical view that blossoms into something very romantic."

Joss's new take on *Much Ado* would also allow him to give equal weight to every character in the play. Other interpretations often focus solely on Beatrice and Benedick, while the play's other main couple, Hero and Claudio, are considered important only inasmuch as they serve Beatrice and Benedick's journey. "To me, who Claudio is and who Hero is and what Leonato's going through and Don Pedro and Margaret . . . everybody, particularly Borachio, has a part of what this movie is about," Joss said. "When you give yourself up to them and invest equal weight in all of these characters, you really have something that's more than the sum of its parts, something that's dark, something that's not necessarily as charming as it appears to be, but is ultimately very romantic."

In adapting the four-hundred-year-old play, Joss also had to decide how to handle a decidedly misogynistic plot point. When Hero is accused of sleeping with another man the night before her wedding, she is attacked by both her intended, Claudio, and her father, Leonato; by no longer being a virgin, she has shamed them and is thus unworthy of marriage. Joss chose to focus on the "night before" aspect of Claudio's accusation rather than the alleged deflowering. "The story there . . . isn't that Claudio thinks she's not a virgin, it's that he thinks she's cheating on him. It's jealousy, which is universal and very modern—it's not about propriety," Joss said. "When Claudio turns on her at the wedding, it's because he thinks she's making a fool of him." He reinterpreted Leonato's reaction as well, noting that Hero's mother is nowhere to be found in the play and postulating that this tight family unit of father and daughter has been shattered by an assumption of betrayal. "There was his humiliation in front of all of his peers, and his betrayal by the most important person in his life," Joss said. "For her to be lying to him is heartbreaking to him."

Joss would dedicate the project to the memory of his own late mother, as well as stepfather Stephen Stearns, who passed away in January 2011. Ten months after his death, Joss was ready to do the thing he'd told his stepfather he would never do—make a "grown-up" movie.

//////////

While working on *In Your Eyes*, Kai had met with their friend Michael Roiff, a producer whose credits included *Waitress* (which costarred Nathan Fillion), and writer David Rothenberg; together they readied Bellwether Pictures so that everything would be set to go once Joss finished with postproduction on *The Avengers*. The team didn't expect to sneak in *Much Ado* before *In Your Eyes*, but they managed to do so by repurposing resources—they cut the preproduction timeline by using some line producers, crew members, and caterers who had just wrapped up on a movie Roiff had produced, which allowed for more time to figure out who would shoot and star in *Much Ado*. (*In Your Eyes* would shoot in 2012, with Joss's script entrusted to director Brin Hill. In April 2014, after the movie's world premiere at the Tribeca Film Festival, Joss made a video announcement that it would immediately be released via streaming video.)

Joss knew he wanted Amy Acker and Alexis Denisof to reprise their roles as Beatrice and Benedick. "I talked to them before I even started to try to do the thing. They were available and on board, so that was good," he says. But he was deliberately furtive when reaching out to other potential cast members. Under the guise of a coming-home celebration of sorts, Joss had a party shortly after getting back from shooting *The Avengers*. He wanted to feel out his potential cast—the actors he brought in would need to be able to handle the intense shooting schedule of "eight pages a day of Elizabethan dialogue with very few stage directions. Your actors have to be splendid and very on point, because we made this for one-tenth the cost of an episode of television," he said.

"There were a lot of people at the party that I was like, 'So, what are you doing in October? Which days exactly?' without saying why, because I wanted to shake it out, make sure [I had] the right bunch," he recalls. "I was very cagy with everybody for a while, and then I just dove in."

Fran Kranz got an e-mail from Joss that simply said he was thinking about doing another Shakespeare reading and this time he might film it—would he be around and what did he think? "Just like that. A real short e-mail. At the time, I was doing a little workshop for a play in New York, and I always want to be there for Joss and I love doing those Shakespeare readings," Kranz says. "I didn't want to miss out. I said, 'I'm in New York and I've got these couple things going on, but I'll be there.'" Joss got back to him a few days later and asked if he'd be interested in playing Claudio. "'I'd love to see him as a temperamental jock and not the whelp he's usually played as'—those were his words. I was super excited about this cool role, configurative of what I had done before," Kranz adds. "Basically I was just saying, yes, yes, yes to everything and I'll deal with it later. But, again, I didn't know what I was walking into. This is probably naive, but I honestly thought we were just going to be reading the play like we normally do outside and in this little theater, and he might be holding a little handheld camera, like a camcorder, and just filming."

It wasn't until he was contacted for costume fittings and his Social Security number that he realized it was much bigger than he'd expected. "I literally wrote back, 'Wait, am I being paid for this? What is going on?'" They responded that yes, he was being paid—not much, but it was a paid role. Finally, he realized that Joss was taking this project pretty seriously. "It all was so bizarre—I really believed it was just the most casual thing. I always imaged [they would perform it] script in hand, but then Joss was sending e-mails and he was saying, 'Know your lines, we're going to be moving really fast.'"

Amy Acker was also surprised once things got under way. "When we showed up for the first day of filming, everyone was like, 'Oh, a real movie.' We weren't sure if it was Joss with a Flip camera," she explained. "And when we got there, there was a crew and craft service and trucks and lights, so it was for real. Luckily, he only gave us about two weeks' notice and he didn't give us enough time to panic and realize, oh, we're playing these majorly important and great parts. We just had to learn the lines and do it."

Alexis Denisof noted the many differences between their informal Shakespeare readings and shooting an actual film. The latter would require a completely different approach to the acting process and a greater sense of commitment—and provoke a higher level of anxiety. "The readings afforded anyone who participated the opportunity to really play and do whatever they wanted in a no-fail situation, because there were no stakes," Denisof explains. But with *Much Ado*, the actors went from sitting around Joss's house with scripts in their laps, enjoying cocktails and cheese as they read their dialogue, to rehearsing, learning their lines quickly, and committing their portrayal to film with the idea it would eventually be shown to a larger audience. "On the one hand, it has the excitement of being pressed and relatively unrehearsed," Denisof says. "But on the other hand, it also has the challenges of being fresh and unrehearsed."

Anthony Stewart Head, who had last worked with Joss as Giles on *Buffy*, was originally set to play Leonato, Hero's father. His schedule couldn't be worked out, however, so to replace him Joss reached out to Clark Gregg, who also just got done shooting *The Avengers*. He explained that he wanted to make a movie version of *Much Ado* at his house— yes, before he finished the *Avengers* edit. Gregg thought Joss was kidding when he explained that the movie would be shot during his vacation from the film; unfortunately, the actor was already booked for another film, but a week later that project was moved.

"I got another call from him saying, 'Are you available now?' I said, 'It's funny you called. Absolutely, from about three hours ago I am available,'" Gregg recalls. Joss explained there was a part for him but an awful lot of lines for him to learn—and filming started the next day. "The next thing I know, I spent the next ten days completely steeped in trying to learn and act this role in his adaptation of *Much Ado*."

Fortunately, Gregg was already a great fan of the play. It was the first of Shakespeare's works he'd ever performed in—he played Benedick in a college production. "Joss's version was very stripped down, and his interpretation of it wasn't reverential," he says. "My first line was walking in with an iPad—I see the message that Don Pedro of Aragon comes this night to Messina, and I'm reading it off an iPad, and I thought, 'OK, I'm in. I like this.'"

Nathan Fillion was a bit less eager to take on the role of the constable Dogberry. He had taken part in Shakespeare readings at Joss's house, but he had never "done Shakespeare" in a professional capacity. So in the week before he was supposed to shoot, he called Joss and tried to back out.

"I was tense. I was trying to work fourteen-, fifteen-, sixteen-hour days at [my television series] *Castle*, and trying to memorize Shakespeare on the side. I was not having an easy time with it, and I was getting very nervous and very tense. I hadn't been challenged in a long time," Fillion says. "Acting is great and fun, and it's fulfilling, but television is a machine. You've got to pump 'em out—you gotta make it happen. Time is a luxury you don't have, so there's not a lot to challenge. This was an incredible challenge for me, and I tried to chicken out—Joss would not let me. And I'm so glad."

Once Fillion got into filming, the experience reminded him of *Dr. Horrible*—once again, it felt like they were just doing a fun project with a bunch of friends. And the new faces quickly became new friends. "Amy Acker was there, Alexis Denisof was there. Some of his kids from *Dollhouse* were there. There's a fellow from *The Avengers* there," Fillion says. "When I first moved out to Los Angeles, when they didn't get a job people would say, 'Well, it's not what you know, it's who you know.' And it sounded so dirty and nepotistic and I didn't like the sound of it." But his view shifted thanks to projects like *Dr. Horrible* and *Much Ado*: "If you work with people and you know what they're capable of, and you know what they're like to work with, what they're going to bring, and you have them in mind when you're building a project, why wouldn't you want to work with someone you knew?" He adds, "When I dream about projects, I don't find myself saying, 'Oh, I'd love for this star I've never met to be in it.' I dream of myself saying, 'Let's do a project with me and Alan Tudyk, and Sean Maher, Ron Glass. I always dream about people I've already worked with."

Gregg had a similar epiphany when he got to the set. "I walked on and looked around and went, 'Hey, I know who these people are. These are all the people who have worked in his other stuff—these are his family.' I've always felt like there's a certain kind of creative person who keeps talented people they've worked with in the past close to them."

Firefly's Sean Maher would play the villainous Don John, and the rest of the cast was rounded out with a few people whom Joss greatly admired, like comic actors Brian McElhaney, Nick Kocher, and Riki Lindhome. Joss also tapped Jillian Morgese, an extra in an *Avengers* scene, to play Hero. "I had a feeling about her that she ought to play the cousin of Amy," Joss says. "I feel that I was right."

///////////

To fill the position of director of photography, Jed Whedon suggested Jay Hunter. Joss and Hunter already had a good working relationship—the cinematographer had been the second unit DP on *Dollhouse*, and second unit was almost always directed by Joss. Hunter was invited to meet with Joss at his house; all he was told prior to the meeting was that Joss had a movie. Was he interested? Hunter was surprised, and he needed to take the pitch in for a minute before he answered: "Of course."

When he arrived at the Whedon home, he says, "it was, like, six in the morning and I walk in and I was like, 'Hey, how's it goin', haven't seen you, like, in forever.' Joss made me some tea and then he said, 'OK, *Much Ado About Nothing*. I want to shoot it in black and white and hand-held. How do you feel about that?'"

Hunter was excited by the idea—he couldn't think of another example of a Shakespeare film with a black-and-white, handheld approach, but he thought it was a fittingly contemporary way to approach the material, because *Much Ado* felt like a very modern play. "The humor, the issues. I mean, slap some modern dialogue in it and it feels like it's happening right now," he says. "Joss and I jelled on this idea that we've seen Shakespeare done many times in this very kind of classical, almost cliché at this point, manner, where there's lots of beautiful dolly shots and lots of long lenses, and people shoot it almost as if it's a play happening in front of them." Hunter adds, "I'm sure a lot of the justification in that is it lets us see the actors act. It ends up feeling very theatrical, and I always wonder when I'm watching it, why am I watching this as a film? If I want to see this kind of interpretation, I should just go to the theater—to the actual, live theater—and see it."

Joss's concept was to strip down and simplify the visuals. Shooting it in black and white puts the story—and the audience—in another world, one lacking the distraction of color. "It's supposed to be invisible photography that's supposed to immerse the audience into the scene rather than them watching from fifty feet away," Hunter explains. "You're actually in there. The actors are moving around the camera; the camera is very close to the actors and shifting around within their space."

On the first day of shooting, a cable snapped off a camera and hit Hunter right above his eye. "We have pictures of him walking around with this huge bloody gauze," Kai says. "He probably should have gotten stitches, but he didn't. He was like, 'No, let's just keep going.' [The shoot] had really a great feel to it, like everyone just—like a family, like, let's do it, let's make it."

"Kai knew better than I did how much I needed it," Joss said. "On the first day of filming, she said, 'So, are you happy?' And I smiled so hard that my face broke. My lips just split because I was smiling so hard."

///////////

Part of Joss's delight came from the fact that he was shooting in his own home. He had always wanted to film there, and after being away for so long shooting *The Avengers*, he got the chance to settle into a place that he loved, and to share that love. When Kai was first renovating the 1920s, Mediterranean-style house, they'd modeled it on the feeling of Lee's farm in the Catskills—an "eclectic, artistic space" where people could connect and create.

They'd unknowingly had a trial run for the film a few years earlier, when Jane Espenson was looking for a space to rehearse and perform a stage show. "At the last minute we had no place to perform it. Joss opened his house to me and my little troupe of actors for about a month," Espenson says. "I had a key to the house and we moved his furniture around and the actors were shouting and singing at all hours. We broke a glass and a picture frame and once we left a window open—we were like bison, and Joss and Kai were cool with it! Kai even stapled fabric to their sofa for us. Their children provided us with our only rehearsal audience. I can never repay that whole family for their kindness."

Joss was overjoyed that Arden and Squire were exposed to the very intimate and all-encompassing expression of art, as he had been in his mother's house. "We wanted to encourage people to come in and just do artistic [endeavors]—we wanted our kids to be around as much art and life [as possible]," he said. "This was something both of us were very committed to." And so their spacious home, with features like the stone amphitheater Kai had built for his Shakespeare readings and the small dance studio that could double for a police interrogation room, was the perfect setting for the film.

"It's almost like Kai designed the house for this movie to be shot in," Jay Hunter says. "I don't think anybody who watches the movie is going to think this is Joss's house unless they've heard that. Because it feels like the location was chosen for the movie—it feels very appropriate. But when you first hear, 'Oh, we shot the movie in my house,' it sounds like it was just a matter of convenience. It was, but then also it fit it so well. It was a perfect location."

It was also the most practical choice, because there was no way that they could have gotten a location and permits to shoot in the short amount of time Joss had away from *The Avengers*. Plus, Kai said, "It was also a great way to finally get me to clean the basement. I had been putting that off for a year and we used it for Dogberry and Verges' interrogation room."

The Whedons opened up nearly their entire house for the film, both to the cast and crew and to the viewers who would ultimately see it immortalized on screen. It was a whole new level of intimacy even for a man who had been deeply connected to his fans for years. "We struggled with that a little bit, especially when hiring extras," Joss says. "But, at the end of the day, love the space, and it remains in its own way anonymous. It's performing a part; it's slightly in disguise. [The movie] isn't a tour of the house—it is sort of nether space, and the fact that it's black and white too takes it apart from our day-to-day life."

Being in Joss's home also changed the tone of shooting slightly. "If we had been shooting this in some other location, I'm sure more things would have been broken or something, or more holes would have been hit through the wall by mistake," Hunter explains. "Everyone knew that 'Hey, this is the man's house. Let's walk on eggshells and be very delicate.'"

Yet the home wasn't in a bubble, and real life kept intruding. At times it was charming, like seeing Arden and Squire come down for their breakfast at 6 AM as everyone else was arriving for the day's shoot. More often it came with stress, like when demolition started on the house next door the day before shooting began. That sent Joss into a state of panic, but Kai simply went into producer mode and convinced the workers to take a break when they were shooting. That same day, the sewer went out and the toilets backed up, and the entire sewer line needed to be redone. Then the people across the street decided to sand their floors. And suddenly Kai became aware that her home, which had seemed like the quietest place, was under the flight path of a number of airplanes and helicopters every day.

Kai had checked with the police and found out that she didn't need a permit to shoot on her own property, but she later found out when an officer showed up that the streets were city property and people couldn't park there. He had actually come by to respond to a neighbor's complaint, and he shut down their production when he learned that they didn't have any permits. Joss suggested that they take a break as Kai quickly headed off to recheck the permit situation, but Clark Gregg pushed him to continue shooting. They had been filming the wedding scene, in which Claudio announces that Hero slept with someone the night before and Leonato, shamed, verbally attacks his daughter. When Joss called "action," Gregg started "yelling at his daughter [even louder] than he had before," the director recalled. "And I, of course, was filled with terror that this was going to get us all thrown in the Big House. . . . We made Shakespeare against the law. We fought Johnny Law for art."

//////////

Strangely, working on a blockbuster film with A-list actors who had strong opinions about their characters set Joss up well to shoot a low-budget film in a short time frame. His infamous determination to have everything how he wanted it—from costumes to line readings—had to give way to a necessary flexibility when logistics didn't match up with desire.

One scene, in particular, posed a huge obstacle: Joss and Hunter had discussed the setting of a scene with Beatrice and Benedick, one that Joss felt should be shot in late afternoon. He had many stills of the actors that he'd taken in rehearsals, when the light was hitting the staircase and his courtyard in such a beautiful way. He wanted to capture that look in the scene; it was the first thing about the film for which he declared, "This is how I want it to be."

With about five days left before production ended, Hunter had spent an entire day observing light patterns at the house, determining how they shifted and changed throughout the day. They would use his observations to inform the shooting order of scenes—to ensure that, among other things, they had the ideal natural lighting for the scene in question. So of course on the day they shot it, the sky was completely overcast. With such a small budget, there was no big lighting crew to simulate the sun. Nor did they have enough money and time to save the scene for another day. They had no choice but to just roll with the visual hand they were dealt.

Instead of the "backlit, golden sunlight kind of elements" they had planned, "this fog rolled in as the scene progressed, and it was kind of creating the opposite mood of what we had originally intended," Hunter recalls. By the end of that shot, Joss realized that Hero's funeral procession, which was to follow this Beatrice and Benedick scene, had been shot a couple of days earlier and then, too, there had been a crazy amount of fog. So Joss ultimately shifted the order of the scenes, setting a melancholy tone as the fog rolls in and around the marchers, then gradually lightening the mood as Benedick scripts a sonnet for Beatrice while on her staircase and the fog seems to recede.

"It's like a wild, magical moment," Hunter explains. "Some directors and DPs would probably have lost their minds, because if you have this [image] set and then the film gods give you something different, it can be devastating. But Joss decided to just roll with it, and the film gods ended up giving us this huge gift."

Joss easily guided his actors into the emotions and actions he wanted, but found that he had certain limitations. "Apart from a basic understanding of what people were saying, I didn't research the text," he said. When it came to explaining exactly what Shakespeare meant by a line, he'd summon Denisof over. In addition to studying the Bard at the London Academy of Music and Dramatic Art, Denisof had worked with the Royal Shakespeare Company, so he slipped easily into the role of Shakespeare interpreter.

The entire film was shot secretly in twelve days, over one week and three weekends. Joss took one short break to support sister-in-law Maurissa Tancharoen with her "Club Mo" team at the 2011 Walk for Lupus Now in Los Angeles. Along with Felicia Day, Joss helped the team raise over $70,000 for the charity.

Tancharoen had been diagnosed with lupus as a teenager, and she was dealing with the side effects of the chemotherapy she was on to fight the disease. She wasn't sure if she'd be physically able to attend the walk, but Joss showed up extra early, arriving only after her two friends who organized the group. "I was worried I wouldn't get a T-shirt," he said; Jed had told him that he wasn't getting one of the limited-edition custom shirts made by *Firefly* costume designer Shawna Trpcic, because younger brother Zack had raised more money than him. Like showing up on his first day of *Roseanne* with a hundred no. 2 pencils, he knew it was probably a joke but he wasn't taking any chances.

/////////

Much Ado remained a closely guarded secret until after principal photography had wrapped. On October 24, 2011, Nathan Fillion was the
first to announce it by tweeting out a photo of himself, Sean Maher, and
Joss with the message "Hey, guys! Let's make a movie!" Immediately,
Whedon fans were abuzz with excitement.

Fillion also tweeted the link to a website, MuchAdoTheMovie.com.
The site was simple, with a photo of Kranz clad in scuba gear and holding
a cocktail, standing in an infinity pool. Internet speculation about the
project was wild—was it a film, another Web series, something entirely
different? Soon a press release was added to the site, explaining that Joss
had just wrapped on a film adaptation of Shakespeare's play. "Filmed in
just 12 days entirely on location in exotic Santa Monica, the film features
a stellar cast of beloved (or soon to be beloved) actors . . . all dedicated
to the idea that . . . the joy of working on a passion project surrounded
by dear friends, admired colleagues and an atmosphere of unabashed
rapture far outweighs their hilariously miniature paychecks." The press
release also officially announced the establishment of Bellwether Pictures
as a micro-studio for "the production of small, independent narratives for
all media, embracing a DIY ethos and newer technologies."

Joss jumped back into editing *The Avengers* with a renewed spirit,
which he credited to *Much Ado*. "Making *The Avengers* was very important to me, but it was also extremely arduous," he said. "I missed my
friends and I missed my home, so I decided to throw them all on camera
which is the only way I seem to know to relate to people." Emotionally and mentally renewed, he was able to take a fresh look at the initial
assembly of *Avengers* footage that he'd put together before his sabbatical.
It had been running way too long for a feature film, but he'd been having
a difficult time finding a way for the story to address everything that it
needed to in just over two hours. "When I came back from *Much Ado*,"
he said, "without any rancor or confusion, I was able to cut the film down
to length and readily focus on the things that mattered. I think I would
have come to that one way or another, but *Much Ado* sped it up."

36

THE YEAR OF JOSS WHEDON

As 2012 approached, it was quickly shaping up to be the year of Joss Whedon films. *The Avengers* was coming out in the spring, *Much Ado About Nothing* was in postproduction, and *The Cabin in the Woods* finally had a release date that wasn't threatened by financial problems or studio tinkering. It was an exciting time for Joss, but also a daunting one—particularly where the Marvel film was concerned.

The May 4 premiere of *The Avengers* was set in stone, but much postproduction work remained. In addition to finalizing the edit, Joss also had to oversee the film's conversion to 3-D, as well as the completion of the thousands of special effects shots, which artists had been working on since even before filming began. That included all the scenes involving the Hulk, many of Iron Man's flight and battle scenes, and many aspects of the S.H.I.E.L.D. Helicarrier. He had help from editor Lisa Lassek, who, like Joss, had developed her skills and keen storytelling sense through more than a decade with the Whedonverse. After starting as an assistant editor on *Angel* and working on *Buffy* and *Firefly*, she'd moved up with Joss on *Serenity* and *The Cabin in the Woods* before taking on *The Avengers* alongside *Captain America* editor Jeffrey Ford. (Her rise was no doubt an inspiration to Joss's current assistant and *Much Ado* coproducer Daniel Kaminsky, who edited *Much Ado* on his laptop in Joss's office while the blockbuster was being shaped.)

Publicity for the film had also begun in earnest. The same month that Joss was filming *Much Ado*, a New York Comic Con panel wooed fans with *Avengers* footage. When the first full-length trailer was released on iTunes on October 11, it garnered over ten million downloads in the first twenty-four hours, a new record for trailers on the service.

It was a lot of hype for Joss to live up to—especially considering he'd never helmed a high-budget blockbuster before—but he still managed to get the job done. "This was a movie that came in on time and under budget in our production period, which is very impressive for a director who hadn't tackled anything of this scale," Kevin Feige says. "I think it is, in large part, due to his experience on his own—producing his own shows. And it was great to see him able to manage that while at the same time getting the performances."

/////////

The Cabin in the Woods, of course, had proceeded less smoothly from script to screen. When Lionsgate bought the film in July 2011, Joss and Drew Goddard had felt battered from being in limbo for so long; they no longer had the energy to protect their film. And ironically, the movie they had written as a critique of modern horror tales was being released by the same studio as the *Saw* series. But they discovered that Lionsgate truly cared about *Cabin*, which in turn helped them believe in it again, and reignited the vision and enthusiasm they'd been drained of.

They also realized that there was a positive side to the film's delay when *Cabin* headlined the South by Southwest festival in Austin, Texas, in March 2012. So far removed from the struggles of production, SXSW felt like one giant four-day party, where they were just so excited to be out and have people finally see this film they had loved so much. "Usually, by the time you get to the film release, it all feels like business. You have to do these promotional things, and it feels like work," Goddard says. "Whereas with *Cabin*, it was sort of like seeing an old friend again that you hadn't seen in a while. It was like, 'Oh, let's just celebrate.'" Their excitement was returned tenfold by the fans, who had been waiting to see it for years and were rewarded for their patience with an engaging new spin on the horror genre.

The festival audience loved it, and when *Cabin* was released a month later, on April 13, many critics agreed. *Rolling Stone*'s Peter Travers wrote that "by turning splatter formula on its empty head, *Cabin* shows you can unleash a fire-breathing horror film without leaving your brain or your heart on the killing floor." Roger Ebert praised Joss and Goddard for constructing *Cabin* "almost as a puzzle for horror fans to solve. Which conventions are being toyed with? Which authors and films are being referred to? Is the film itself an act of criticism?"

Not every reviewer felt that the film's deconstruction of horror conventions made for a compelling example of the genre. Some thought that Joss and Goddard had fallen short of horror's traditional thrills by being too enamored of their own gags. The *Hollywood Reporter* called *Cabin* "a hollow exercise in self-reflexive cleverness that's not nearly as ingenious as it seems to think," and the *L.A. Times* felt that it was one big "inside joke."

But word of mouth about the film was strong, drawing more than just Whedon devotees into movie theaters. In its opening weekend, *Cabin* grossed $14.7 million domestically, and it would pull in $66 million worldwide by the end of its run. People immediately started asking about Joss and Goddard's next project—as if *The Avengers* weren't taking up enough of Joss's time. *Variety* suggested that the two take on *Catching Fire*, the upcoming sequel to *The Hunger Games*, an idea that was embraced online by excited fans of that series and the Whedonverse.

"It's the nature of it," Goddard says. "Those games are fun to play, when people ask, 'What are you doing next?' But the nice thing I've learned from working with Joss is that he always said, 'Look, I've never taken a job for money. I've never taken a job just because it pays well. I only take jobs because they speak to me, and I feel like there's something interesting emotionally to relate to in these jobs.' And if you just stick to that rule, it ends up guiding your career. And so it sounds so simple, yet it's difficult to maintain sometimes. Especially when you're getting offered nice things, like the *Hunger Games* of the world. But if you just write what speaks to you, it all tends to work out."

///////////

The Avengers had a splashy Hollywood premiere on April 11, 2012, and the positive buzz kept growing as the film went into wide release a month later. It was hailed as a colossal summer blockbuster with heart—with precisely the kind of emotional touchstones that tend to be lost when comic book lore is translated to the big screen. The story resonated with adults who understood the nuances of the character development, and the children who loved the thrilling superheroics. "I have kids running up to me all the time saying, 'I'm always angry,'" Mark Ruffalo laughs, quoting Bruce Banner's signature line before Hulking out.

"As human beings we want to be superhuman but we know that we're fallible, and Joss allows us to see ourselves in these superhumans—that's our touch point to the fantastic," Ruffalo says. "It's no different than the stories of the saints and the gods—it's our modern version. We want to put our stories in context, and he really tapped into that in a way that's astounding."

And it's quite fitting that many fans connected most strongly to Scarlett Johansson's turn as Black Widow—a complex, powerful female character. Her role in the film is not a lighthearted one, nor is it a story of redemption, which is why Joss was so drawn to her. "She doesn't live in a hero's world; she lives in a very noir/duplicitous world . . . and there's a darkness to her and her past," he explained. Black Widow is, as Hawkeye says, a spy, not a soldier, yet she readily joins the fight. At no point is she the "token" female of the group; from the moment we meet her—tied to a chair clad in a tight black dress, allowing herself to be interrogated by Russian mobsters while she's actually pumping *them* for information— she is clearly in control. Throughout the film, her "superpower" is the way she manipulates people—quite often making them believe that she is weak and easily broken. It's only when she's being chased through the bowels of the Helicarrier by the Hulk, the one person she cannot reason with, that she is truly shaken.

The way that the Hulk overpowers her can be read as Joss's latest retelling of his childhood terror at the world around him. For many women watching the scene, it's also a reminder of the lessons life has taught them—that they must be constantly vigilant, because even the "nice guys" can turn into monsters. Black Widow runs for her life, dodging Hulk's attacks, until he catches up and throws her against a wall. She's cowed, letting the others take charge in taking the green monster down, and shortly thereafter it takes a moment for her to answer Nick Fury's summons to the next battle. In writing this scene, Joss imbued her with the spirit of Buffy—empowered to kick ass but aware that defeat is a possibility in every battle. It's always about getting back up, no matter how slowly one does it.

The prominence of Black Widow also sparked conversation about the lack of female superheroes in feature films. In the past thirty years, an average of only two superhero movies per decade have centered on a female superhero: *Supergirl* (1984) and *Red Sonja* (1985); *Tank Girl* (1995) and *Barb Wire* (1996); *Catwoman* (2004) and *Elektra* (2005). The disappointing box office receipts of *Catwoman*, *Elektra*, and *Supergirl* in particular are held up in the industry as irrefutable evidence that a female superhero film will never be successful—never mind that those films were just not very good. Joss never found such arguments persuasive. "Toymakers will tell you they won't sell enough, and movie people will point to the two terrible superheroine movies that were made and say, You see? It can't be done. It's stupid," he said.

"It's frustrating to me that I don't see anybody developing one of these movies," he added. "It actually pisses me off. My daughter watched *The Avengers* and was like, 'My favorite characters were the Black Widow and Maria Hill,' and I thought, Yeah, of course they were. I read a beautiful thing Junot Diaz wrote: 'If you want to make a human being into a monster, deny them, at the cultural level, any reflection of themselves.' " But perhaps Joss's film would inspire a change for the better: in February 2014, Kevin Feige announced that Johansson would have an expanded role in several upcoming films in the Marvel Cinematic Universe, and that Marvel had begun development on a Black Widow solo film. Still, with just one female superhero story in the earliest stages of development, the studio and the industry have a long way left to go.

Four days after *The Avengers* opened, as the massive international media blitz was reaching its peak, Joss made a very personal post on Whedonesque. It had the typical wit and self-effacing humor of a Joss screed ("People have told me that this matters, that my life is about to change. I am sure that is true. . . . I think—not to jinx it—that I may finally be recognized at Comic-Con. Imagine!"), yet in the middle he dropped the quips to pen an incredibly direct message of gratitude to those who had supported him long before he had the world's biggest superheroes doing his bidding:

> What doesn't change is anything that matters. What doesn't change is that I've had the smartest, most loyal, most passionate, most articulate group of—I'm not even gonna say fans. I'm going with "peeps"—that any cult oddity such as my bad self could have dreamt of. When almost no one was watching, when people probably should have STOPPED watching, I've had three constants: my family and friends, my collaborators (often the same), and y'all. A lot of stories have come out about my "dark years," and how I'm "unrecognized" . . . I love these stories, because they make me seem super-important, but I have never felt the darkness (and I'm ALL about my darkness) that they described. Because I have so much.

I have people, in my life, on this site, in places I've yet to discover, that always made me feel the truth of success: an artist and an audience communicating. Communicating to the point of collaborating. I've thought, "maybe I'm over; maybe I've said my piece." But never with fear. Never with rancor. Because of y'all. Because you knew me when. If you think topping a box office record compares with someone telling you your work helped them through a rough time, you're probably new here. . . . So this is me, saying thank you. All of you. You've taken as much guff for loving my work as I have for over-writing it, and you deserve, in this our time of streaming into the main, to crow. To glow. To crow and go "I told you so," to those Joe Blows not in the know.

//////////

The Avengers was an instant smash, earning more than $1 billion in just nineteen days. It would go on to become the third-highest-grossing film in history—both domestically and worldwide (among numerous other records, including best opening weekend and opening week for any film). And Joss had delivered it on schedule and under budget. So the fact that the studio asked him to sign on for an *Avengers* sequel was hardly unexpected. What was a little less certain was whether he would accept.

While the business details were being worked out on both sides, Joss knew that he wouldn't make the deal if he didn't have another story to tell about this dysfunctional family. A few days after *The Avengers* premiered, Joss told the *L.A. Times* that he wasn't sure if he wanted to dive back so quickly into that universe. "I'm very torn," Joss said. "It's an enormous amount of work telling what is ultimately somebody else's story, even though I feel like I did get to put myself into it. But at the same time, I have a bunch of ideas, and they all seem really cool."

When Joss gave himself a tiny break in a London pub to think about those ideas, he realized that he couldn't leave the Avengers behind so easily. Within forty minutes, fueled by fish and chips and a pint, he'd filled a notebook with his ideas for the future of the superhero team. He texted agent Chris Harbert and told him to make the deal.

"I'm so in love with that universe and the characters and the way they were played and I have so much more I want to do with them," Joss said. "I know I can't match the success of the first one but I can try to make a better film and that's what I'm excited about, that's the new room of fear I'm entering now."

//////////

In July, Joss returned to San Diego Comic-Con, the place where he had reconnected with the Marvel world through Joe Quesada in 2003 and announced that he was indeed writing and directing *The Avengers* in 2010. Comic book conventions had been a part of his blood since he was ten years old, and young Joss could never have imagined the fan response he'd get at them almost forty years later.

"I don't know how he does it, really. He'll wait until the end and sign everything," Kai says. "He never complains about the attention he gets. The only thing that he actually sort of laments is not being able to geek out on other people. He can't go to the tables and see the stuff that he wants to see. But it's his job and he really loves it and he loves the fans and he appreciates what he's got. [There are] other people who complain about it and whine about it, but he's like, 'No, this is why we're here. Without them, we wouldn't have anything.'"

Not that Joss always got recognized at the big geek love-in. Just a year earlier, he'd showed up at one of the San Diego Comic-Con parties with the cast of *Dollhouse* and Drew Goddard. The doorman didn't recognize him and refused them all entry. "I'm standing there," Goddard remembers. "I'm like, 'Do you guys understand? This is . . . everyone in that party was . . .'" He laughs.

Joss didn't play the "Don't you know who I am?" card. He turned to his group and said, "OK, well, we'll just go make our own party."

"I feel like that summarizes Joss better than anything I've ever seen," Goddard says. "There was no anger at not getting into the party. It was just, 'You know what? Let's just go make our own party. It'll be fun.' And it was. It was way more fun than I'm sure that party was. But I will never forget being at Comic-Con and being like, 'Oh, you didn't hear? People are still not letting him in.'"

There was no question that Joss would be allowed into the party this year, but the biggest and most emotional moment was the *Firefly* reunion panel. Ten years after the series was canceled, over four thousand fans packed the hall, many of whom had slept in line the night before to ensure they'd get a seat. In the middle of the night, Joss went out to the line to thank them. Later that day, the panel moderator asked Joss what the fans meant to him. Joss broke down and wept, speechless. The audience of four thousand Browncoats stood up and roared.

//////////

A month later, Marvel announced that they were expanding their relationship with Joss. He would again write and direct his family of superheroes in the *Avengers* sequel, which reunites the superhero team after a two-year string of other Marvel projects: *Iron Man 3* (2013), *Thor: The Dark World* (2013), *Captain America: The Winter Soldier* (2014), and *Guardians of the Galaxy* (2014). And he'd be overseeing Marvel's venture into prime-time television. First they'd worked together on comics, then films, and next up Joss was developing a series for ABC that would give the secret agents of S.H.I.E.L.D. a chance to be more than superhero support staff.

The S.H.I.E.L.D. project was not something new; Marvel and ABC had been working on it for some time (along with a proposed reboot of *The Incredible Hulk*). When the studio talked to Joss about it, he was initially wary that they were jumping into it because they had a deal with Disney, which owned both Marvel and ABC. "A good opportunity to make a show is not a good reason to make a show," he explained. And he was a little thrown by their requirement that the series feature Agent Coulson—especially since Joss had killed him off, at Marvel's request, in the movie. Yet it was the presence of Coulson that convinced him the series could work. In *The Avengers*, Coulson is the "little guy" among superheroes, and Joss loved the idea of him being "the common man in an uncommon world." "He's an enthusiast," Joss said. "And he loves this world as well as wanting to protect the people in it." That's a rather apt description of Joss as well.

Joss wanted to extend that same "little guy" feel to the series as a whole. After all, without the main Avengers, what would be the draw of a series filled with people who had been mostly supporting characters and extras in the films? "Well, what does S.H.I.E.L.D. have that the other superheroes don't?" Joss asked. "And that, to me, is that they're not superheroes. But they live in that universe. Even though they're a big organization, that [lack of powers] makes them underdogs, and that's interesting to me."

Joss pitched his ideas for the series to Marvel Television—which was headed by Jeph Loeb, his former collaborator on the *Buffy* animated series. Loeb was on board, so Joss was set to direct the pilot. He brought along *Dr. Horrible* coconspirators Jed Whedon and Maurissa Tancharoen to write and produce, along with *Angel* executive producer Jeffrey Bell.

The biggest draw for fans, aside from Joss himself, was the return of Clark Gregg as Agent Phil Coulson. "We all love Clark Gregg, there's no doubt about that," Joss said in a taped announcement at the Marvel TV panel at 2012 New York Comic Con. "From before we made *The Avengers*, we discussed whether there was a way for him to be a part of the Marvel Universe, perhaps a part of a TV show even after his death." The casting announcement was met with an outpouring of cheers.

//////////

As the *S.H.I.E.L.D.* pilot went into development, the public got its first look at Joss's passion project. *Much Ado About Nothing* premiered at the Toronto International Film Festival in September 2012. The response from festival-goers was intense and incredibly positive. When the cast came to the stage after the movie ended, Joss was overcome with emotion from all the support for his "little" personal movie.

"You make a strong man cry," he told the crowd.

He and Kai had gone into their production of *Much Ado* eager to do something of their own, together and quickly. They hadn't really planned what to do with it once it was done. When they finally discussed bringing the film to the festival circuit with those far more familiar with the traditional indie route, they were asked what their expectations for marketing and distribution were. "We didn't think about that," Kai says. "It was about the process of getting it done, making the movie with our own little studio. Let's just make this stuff. Don't worry about the end—what we're going to do with it, who our audience is. Just make the thing, make it great, and it will find a home."

Joss had taken the film to Toronto in the hopes of finding theatrical distribution, and he found it in a familiar place. Lionsgate, in partnership with Roadside Attractions, picked up *Much Ado* just as it had *The Cabin in the Woods*. The Shakespeare adaptation would have a far shorter wait to hit theaters, though, as it was set to premiere in select cities eight months later, in June 2013.

But the rest of 2012 was all about *The Avengers*. Marvel gave the blockbuster film a blockbuster marketing campaign, and with it, Joss Whedon was thrust into the spotlight of the mainstream press. In addition to all his superheroes landing on magazine covers across newsstands, *Wired* and *GQ* did big features on him, and *Entertainment Weekly* named him one of its Entertainers of the Year. This was going to be a difficult year to top.

37

THE YEAR OF JOSS WHEDON, AGAIN (REALLY)

As the new year began, Joss was well into preproduction on the *Agents of S.H.I.E.L.D.* pilot. He cowrote the script with Jed Whedon and Maurissa Tancharoen, creating all-new characters for the regular cast aside from Clark Gregg's Agent Coulson. Once shooting began, directing duties were all on Joss, but there were other familiar faces on set to help ease the hectic schedule. Guest stars included Cobie Smulders as Agent Maria Hill, Ron Glass (*Firefly*) as Dr. Streiten, and J. August Richards (*Angel*) as Mike Peterson, the first superhero with whom S.H.I.E.L.D. works on the series. The main cast included Ming-Na Wen as Agent Melinda May, whom Gregg said "seems very Whedonverse to me, but I guess she hadn't worked with him before." The rest of the regulars, he said, "are young actors I didn't know well, and then as soon as I got to act with them a little bit, I said, 'Oh, Joss really knows what he's doing. New members of the Whedonverse!' "

Production on the *S.H.I.E.L.D.* pilot wrapped on February 12, announced via Twitter by Tancharoen. As the series headed into editing, Joss needed to tend to *Much Ado About Nothing*. Lionsgate and Roadside Attractions did not have the same marketing budget as a studio like Marvel, so Joss headed up the promotions juggernaut on his own. This brought about Joss's first foray into social media, as up until now he'd only posted on sites devoted to him or his series. He tweeted under the film's account, @MuchAdoFilm; in May, he'd officially join under his own name.

On March 7, 2013, the cast headed to the film's US premiere at the South by Southwest festival—many by bus. In a publicity stunt dubbed Bus Ado About Nothing, Joss and much of his young cast made the twenty-four-hour trip from Los Angeles to Austin in a tour bus with only one toilet, documenting their journey via Twitter, Instagram, and Vine videos. The adventure had been conceived when some of the cast were discussing how they'd get to the festival for the March 9 premiere. "I knew people wanted to go and they couldn't get rooms and they couldn't get flights. Some of them couldn't afford them," Joss said. So he decided to hire the bus. When Lionsgate found out, the studio picked up the tab.

"I can't believe Joss took two days out of his time to do that with us. It's a little insane," *Much Ado* cast member Tom Lenk said. "Does Michael Bay get on a party bus with his cast? Probably not—they're robots. He drives inside of them!" The rest of the cast—including Amy Acker, Alexis Denisof, Nathan Fillion, and Clark Gregg—met them in Texas for a discussion panel and screening.

A week after the bus took off, another beloved set of collaborators announced an even bigger venture in the world of DIY-ish filmmaking. Taking a cue from Joss's long history of fan outreach, Rob Thomas and Kristen Bell announced a Kickstarter campaign asking fans to help fund a *Veronica Mars* movie. The plan was to raise $2 million to prove to Warner Bros. that the series, which had gone off the air six years prior, was a viable prospect for a relaunch. If they could raise the money, Thomas, Bell, and much of the original cast would return for a feature film continuation of the cult hit, to be shot later that year. The news immediately went viral, and on March 13, excited fans met the goal in less than ten hours. (Ultimately, the campaign would raise $5.7 million from more than 97,000 devoted fans.) By the next day, news outlets were already reaching out to Joss to see if he'd consider using the crowdfunding method to relaunch *Firefly* yet again.

Joss knew the question was coming as soon as he heard about Thomas's campaign, which tempered his own excitement as a *Veronica Mars* fan with a feeling of dread. He pronounced his love for *Firefly* at every turn, often saying how much he'd love to do another film with the cast. "I did have a moment of just, *Oh my god! I'm in trouble now,*" he said. He worried about matching the level of quality fans had come to expect from the series. "*What if it's not that good?* I can do something that's not that good—that's fine. But if I do *that* and it's not that good, I'm going to feel really stupid." Ultimately, it was a hypothetical concern; he cited his busy Marvel schedule and his gestating plans for a *Dr. Horrible* sequel as the reasons why he didn't currently have time to pursue a fan-funded *Firefly* film.

/////////

On May 14, ABC announced that *Agents of S.H.I.E.L.D.* would be joining its schedule for the 2013–14 season. With his commitment to the *Avengers* sequel, Joss said that the series would be in the hands of show-runners Jed Whedon and Maurissa Tancharoen. Still, it would bring Whedon storytelling back to television three years after *Dollhouse* was canceled, and on a brand-new network.

Two weeks later, Joss was back at Wesleyan to receive an honorary degree and deliver the commencement address at the school's 181st graduation ceremony. "He came for our breakfast for seniors and alumni—and he knew what that meant. He stood on his feet for four hours, and he never stiffed anyone," Jeanine Basinger says. "Joss talked to every student, he talked to every parent—he was the last person out the door, because he didn't leave before anybody who wanted to talk to him had left."

These one-on-one interactions were much less stressful for Joss than the task that lay just ahead; he was quite nervous about giving his commencement speech, which he opened by telling the graduates that they were all going to die. After that uplifting message, he went on to explain that we all live with the duality of wanting to experience and create everything while at the same time we're bound to the limitations of our physical selves and our limited life spans. And that we're all torn, as well, between the two metaphorical roads that Robert Frost wrote about. In making a choice to take one road, one job, one relationship, other options will be closed—yet instead of the dread young Joss felt when listening to Sondheim's "The Road You Didn't Take," this older, possibly wiser one asserted that it's not the roads we take that will bring us to happiness but the determination to keep searching, questioning, and learning.

"If you think that happiness means total peace, you will never be happy. Peace comes from the acceptance of the part of you that can never be at peace. It will always be in conflict. If you accept that, everything gets a lot better," he said. "To accept duality is to earn identity. And identity is something that you are constantly earning. It is not just who you are. It is a process that you must be active in. It's not just parroting your parents or the thoughts of your learned teachers. It is now more than ever about understanding yourself so you can become yourself."

///////////

After the weekend at his alma mater, Joss dove back into selling people on the project that he said made him the happiest—the one that he got to do how he wanted, with whom he wanted. *Much Ado About Nothing* is the film that he'd earned through over twenty years in Hollywood— learning how to direct, saving the money, and most important, collecting the people he wanted close and forming a little family with them. The film opened in the United States on June 7 and in the United Kingdom on June 14. Joss, Alexis Denisof, and Amy Acker spent several weeks in a hard publicity push. Even Kai was pulled into the media blitz to discuss her role as producer and the extensive renovations she'd made to the house that served as the film's setting.

Joss, in particular, did interviews across all media—online, in print, and on television, including two PBS appearances that would have pleased his public television–loving mother. In the United Kingdom, the highly respected national newspaper the *Guardian* did a major feature on Joss, and *Much Ado* was covered in depth on arts shows like Radio 4's *Front Row*. The publicity schedule was exhausting for Joss, who was in the spotlight just as much as the film itself was. *The Avengers* had been covered from multiple angles—the A-list stars, the new superhero story, and the blockbuster hype. For *Much Ado*, a well-known tale played by lesser-known actors, the press primarily covered Joss and his approach to Shakespeare's beloved play.

And for the most part, critics and audiences praised *Much Ado About Nothing* for making the centuries-old comedic play (with some questionable commentary on women's sexual expression) seem accessible and contemporary. Mark Kermode of BBC Radio 5 Live said that it made "all the dialogue and the language completely comprehensible," which helped audiences connect with the story. "Any twelve-year-old could follow everything that was going on," he added. The *Guardian* called it "the first great contemporary Shakespeare since Baz Luhrmann's *Romeo and Juliet*."

The Whedon repertory players also drew fine notices. Amy Acker's portrayal of Beatrice was often called out as a highlight, as were Nathan Fillion and Tom Lenk's dry, *Law & Order*–esque take on hapless constables Dogberry and Verges, more traditionally portrayed as broadly buffoonish. Joss's fans delighted in the Whedonverse Easter eggs throughout: Maurissa Tancharoen sings at the party (showing off her skills as former member of the 1990s teen pop group Pretty in Pink), and Drew Goddard and Kai are prominent wedding guests. (Kai also shows up in the party scene, lying across the piano as Maurissa sings.)

Boston's *Patriot Ledger* drew witty connections between Joss's latest films: "OK, Marvel fan boys. I reluctantly sat through 'The Avengers,' now it's your turn to reciprocate by seeing a more erudite offering from your sainted Joss Whedon—by way of Shakespeare. It's called 'Much Ado About Nothing,' and like 'The Avengers,' it has an effete villain in Don John, a ball-breaking Black Widow babe in Beatrice and a smooth-talking charmer in the smug, Iron Man-ish Benedick. They, along with various cohorts, are involved in all natures of treachery and mayhem, as various factions do battle over a key ingredient in maintaining homeland security: Love. And, boy, does it get ruthless."

In the United States, *Much Ado* was first released in five theaters across New York City, Los Angeles, and San Francisco, with a wider release following on June 21. That weekend brought the box office to over $1.2 million, and by September 15 it had taken in over $5 million worldwide. Hardly an *Avengers*-size haul, but for a low-budget art film screening in far fewer theaters, it was an impressive showing, even setting house records at the Film Society of Lincoln Center.

//////////

During a small break from promoting *Much Ado*, Joss returned to San Diego Comic-Con, speaking to a capacity crowd of almost five thousand after a screening of the *Agents of S.H.I.E.L.D.* pilot. He was clearly exhausted, sipping tea to soothe his throat, but never hesitating to connect with his fans at his solo Q&A session. *S.H.I.E.L.D.* premiered on ABC on September 24, to mixed reviews but strong enough ratings that the network would quickly pick up the series for a full twenty-two-episode season.

On November 4, Joss was again honored by Equality Now. However, his acceptance speech at the Make Equality Reality event had a distinctly different tone from his oft-quoted 2006 speech in which he asserted that he wrote for strong female characters "because you're still asking me that question." This time, Joss chose to attack the word *feminist*. He argued that it was polarizing to those who assumed being a feminist meant hating men, and claimed that labeling people who believed in gender equality implied that such beliefs were "not a natural state." (A notion we as a society were "done with," Joss proclaimed—despite all the evidence to the contrary.) He proposed that we instead label those who *fail* to acknowledge equality between the sexes; they should be called *genderist*, as those who declare all races to be unequal are racist.

The impetus for his treatise came from the number of celebrities—Joss called out pop star Katy Perry specifically—who directly stated that they were not feminists, following up with an explanation along the lines of "I don't think women are better than men. We're all equal!" But it seemed strange that a man who had for years proudly proclaimed himself to be a feminist was now deliberately creating a divide and attempting to prescribe the words that women should use to refer to themselves. It was almost as if he was still the naive college student who was shocked by the fact that the world in 1983 wasn't a direct reflection of his mother's household and who didn't understand why women still had to push to be accepted in all fields.

A far smaller event offered a more intimate and endearing reflection on Joss's past. In September, Wesleyan University premiered "Joss Whedon: From Buffy to the Bard," a small yet memorable exhibit that told Joss's story through rarely seen artifacts from his series and films over the years. These included Buffy's Slayer scythe, Hawkeye's quiver from *The Avengers*, and several pieces provided by the man himself: the poster for his student film premiere, notebooks in which he'd scrawled early ideas for the *Buffy* series, and an original sketch he'd made of Buffy garbed in a torn dress and motorcycle jacket below BUFFY in bubble letters.

The very first piece in the exhibit was a photo of Joss and Jeanine Basinger taken when she was given an honorary degree from the American Film Institute Conservatory in 2006. There is clearly much joy between the two as they share easy smiles in their traditional academic gowns. Basinger could have chosen anyone to introduce her on that day, and she asked Joss. And as someone who has had such a deep connection with Joss for almost thirty years, she is drawn to him and his work with the same reverence as fans donning JOSS WHEDON IS MY MASTER NOW T-shirts.

As for what comes next—whether it's the long-promised *Dr. Horrible* sequel, the ballet he's often mentioned, or an adaptation of his favorite novel, Frances Hodgson Burnett's *A Little Princess*—no matter the medium, no matter the approach, what Joss Whedon does will always revolve around the story he is telling.

"I think about the old days, ancient days, where there were men who were created as storytellers, designated storytellers," Basinger says. "They wandered the Earth, and they told stories. They had friends, they had companions—probably they had families. But mostly, they were alive just to be there to tell stories, to bring the stories because we need stories, we must have stories. Those of us who can't write them, create them, tell them, our job is to consume them. And we die if we don't have them. And he feeds us. It's a kind of sacrifice to be the storyteller. And Joss is the modern version of that character. You know? He really is—he's the storyteller. He will never run out of stories."

// ACKNOWLEDGMENTS //

"Would you be interested in writing a Joss Whedon biography?" The question seemed so innocuous when I read the e-mail in late December 2010. "Of course," I said, thinking that it would be for an in-depth magazine article.

I had been a fan of Joss's work since his teen Slayer hit the big screen in 1992, but it was during the summer of 1998 that I quickly became obsessed with this witty series that filled the space in my heart left by *My So-Called Life*'s cancellation. (Awkward but smart Willow was my girl.) I was a year out of college, lonely and lost, so I sought out people online with whom I could discuss the show. I found the Bronze, and the fact that Joss and the writers would take part in the conversation was exciting. I have always loved television in a way that the stories were as real and important as my own life. (One of my first memories is at three years old, sitting at my kitchen table and watching *Snoopy, Come Home*, hysterically sobbing and yelling at the TV, "Snoopy, go home! Charlie Brown loves you! He loves you!") So to have that direct connection to those who wrote those stories, who created those characters, was both thrilling and inspiring. To me, knowing that Joss was reading my words somehow bestowed upon me a sense of legitimacy as a fan, and a writer. Six months later, I flew out to Los Angeles to meet my fellow Bronzers at our party. I met Joss very briefly on that trip, but I had no idea of how much he would change my life.

When I say that Joss Whedon changed my life, I'm not being hyperbolic. If anything, it seems inadequate to say that he changed it only once. Through the Bronze, I found a community of friends that I have to this day, and through Joss's characters, I found a strength and confidence in myself that I would have never thought possible that summer. And on a more superficial level, my daily conversations are peppered with Whedonverse quotes and my vocabulary is filled with Slayer slang.

So first, of course, I must thank Joss Whedon for being so generous with both his time and the personal stories he shared with me. Kai Cole was equally wonderful, and I quickly understood why their friends adore her so much. Joss and Kai have truly cultivated an artistic community around them and, mirroring much of his work, created an extended family from their friends.

I am so grateful for every person who trusted me with their stories about Joss: Tim Minear, David Greenwalt, David Solomon, Anthony Stewart Head, Sarah Michelle Gellar, Tom Hiddleston, Mark Ruffalo, Clark Gregg, Chris Hemsworth,

Cobie Smulders, Jeremy Renner, Samuel L. Jackson, Kevin Feige, Joe Quesada, Jeph Loeb, Eric Wight, Scott Allie, Alexis Denisof, Drew Goddard, Marti Noxon, Jane Espenson, Jed Whedon, Maurissa Tancharoen, Jorge Saralegui, Andrew Stanton, Howard Gordon, Chris Boal, Chris Buchanan, Eliza Dushku, Julie Benz, Fran Kranz, Neil Patrick Harris, Simon Helberg, Morena Baccarin, Jewel Staite, Adam Baldwin, Amy Acker, Jay Hunter, Olivia Williams, Miracle Laurie, Tahmoh Penikett, Nicholas Brendon, Ryan Penagos, Mike Marts, Nick Lowe, Patton Oswalt, Paul Reubens, Rob Thomas, Diego Gutierrez, Dean Batali, David Fury, Shawn Ryan, Danny Strong, Amy Britt, Jessica Neuwirth, Christian Kane, Marc Blucas, and Tom Lenk. They have been so open with their personal memories that I wish that this book could be twice the size to get everything in.

A very special and enormous thank you to Nathan Fillion. I was so enthralled during our conversation, especially when he explained why he felt Joss's work is so relevant and relatable. Much of his impromptu musing became the foreword, and I'm moved every time I read it.

Huge thanks to Daniel Kaminsky, who has been incredibly patient and helpful with all my requests, and to Chris Harbert for his kindness and for taking the time to open a lot of doors for me.

Jeanine Basinger does indeed make you wish that you'd studied film at Wesleyan—but more than that, she makes you wish that human cloning existed so that we could each have our personal Jeanine mentor. The second time we spoke, I was finally nearing the end of writing and rapidly approaching complete burnout. I was taken again by her brilliance and warmth, and reenergized by her encouragement. I taped note cards with quotes from our conversation on my wall to get me through the final weeks.

Also at Wesleyan, Lea Carlson, Joan Miller, and Andrea McCarty invited me into the intimate exhibit on Joss's life and career they had so superbly curated, and Suzy Taraba helped me navigate the library archives to find Joss's yearbook photos. The utterly wonderful Suzanne Foster at Winchester College was incredibly instrumental in uncovering Joss's life in England for me, and also connected me with the late Mr. Dick Massen and his wife, Jane, who shared their remarkable and vivid memories of Joss. I have such tremendous gratitude for them all.

I had such fun and fascinating conversations about Joss and his work with Emily Nussbaum, Gail Collins, and Rhonda Wilcox. I've known for years that Joss's fans are amazing, and I am always in awe of their remarkable dedication to cataloging all things relating to his work for almost twenty years. I'm forever indebted to the Wayback Machine at www.archive.org for saving all of the sparkly, purple-text-on-black-screen pages of magnificence, and to Whedonesque for both providing a place for Joss to "vent his spleen" for any number of causes and being an amazing guide to the timeline of Joss's career. Thank you to Caroline van Oosten de Boer, Simon Fraser, Jennifer Riem, and Damon

Schmidt, and also to the One True b!X for his site documenting *Goners'* currently thwarted path to the big screen.

Much thanks, and many drinks owed, to my agent, Brandi Bowles, who was my cheerleader when I needed it the most. And also to her husband, Matt Sears, who sent me that seemingly innocent e-mail that sent me on the most amazing and difficult adventure of my life. Jacqueline Day was a great support and editor in the early drafts, Sam Harrison at Aurum Press gave me such thoughtful and important feedback, and Devon Freeny at Chicago Review Press shaped my words into a coherent narrative.

"When you can't run, you crawl, and when you can't crawl—when you can't do that. . . ." "You find someone to carry you." I have such magnificent friends who have kept me propped up both metaphorically and literally as I've worked on this book. The magnificent ladies Fionna Boyle, Elizabeth Spencer, Carlie Todoro-Rickus, Sharon and Vicki Weyser, April H, Melanie Morris, and Celi Clark have all carried me with such love and support, especially at the times where I could barely think of crawling. And I've had the best battalion of brilliant and witty warriors to charge into the Hellmouth with: Matthew Nolan, Laura Smith, Melynee Weber, Asim Ali, Suzanne Galle, Sarah N. Gatson, Paula Carlson, Stephanie Tuszynski, Cori Killian, Sharlene Mousfar, Michelle Lehman, Lisa Cronin, Katharine Beutner, Irene Adsuar, Matt McDonough, Jessica Brearton, Nezka Pfeifer, Angela Cheng, Lance Nealy, Jen Mercer, Lauren Epstein, Lu Chekowsky, Joe Ortiz, Jesse Loyd, Tami Katzoff, and Patricia Nash.

Finally, thank you to my family: my mother, Kathleen, who loves stories as much as I do, and taught me from an early age that the ones that move us can come from any and all kinds of media; my father, Joe, who has filled my life with fascinating pieces of trivia, noting important facts about family and places and showing me that the smallest thing can have an incredible impact; my brother, Joe, who could never understand my love for Buffy but equaled my fanaticism in his own for the Chicago Bears, which always reminds me how important having a passion is—especially when that passion connects you to a bigger community; my sister-in-law, Neha, who secured a special place in my heart once she explained that if a TV series had aliens, she was in; and my nephew, Gavin, who is barely a year old and I'm already excited about introducing him to Vampire Slayers, renegade space travelers, comic book heroes, and the idea that family is filled with people we choose, and that "if nothing we do matters, then all that matters is what we do."

My deepest apologies to anyone I've missed. I am forever grateful to everyone who has supported me, from those who put up with my madness for three straight years to those who came in and did one small thing at the exact time I needed it. Every kindness is remembered, and means far more than you know.

// NOTES //

Introduction

"There is a tiny story that I want to tell you" . . . Whedon, interview by the author.

"And I will always write about yearning" . . . Whedon, interview by the author.

"Helplessness was what I realized . . ." Ibid.

an American television show interviewed Russians . . . "Behind the Iron Closet," *The Daily Show.*

people who "should not even be in the same room . . ." Whedon, Visionaries panel.

"If Joss Whedon had had one good day in high school . . ." Greenwalt, quoted in Springer, "High School Hell."

1. A Family of Storytellers

"the perfect comic-book movie" . . . Leitch, "The Perfect Comic-Book Movie."

"vivid, realistic image of wartime small-town America" . . . McLeod, "The Great Gildersleeve."

"When I was a child, my father wrote at home" . . . Tom Whedon, quoted in Rosen, "Family Tradition."

When one of them implicated a writer . . . Rosen, "Family Tradition."

"Lee Jeffries and Thomas Whedon were the stalwarts of the cast . . ." Langguth, "Great to Be Back!"

"My mother . . . was extremely intelligent . . ." Whedon, quoted in BAFTA, *Joss Whedon: A Life in Pictures.*

"You're gonna be a writer" . . . Tom Whedon, quoted in Rosen, "Family Tradition."

"Italian Renaissance-palazzo-style building" . . . StreetEasy, "895 West End Avenue," http://streeteasy.com/nyc/building/895-west-end-avenue-new_york.

"We were living in a Westside apartment . . ." Tom Whedon, quoted in Rosen, "Family Tradition."

"Was I the weak person who got pounded on? . . ." Whedon, interview by the author.

"charming, but merciless" . . . Whedon, quoted in Said, "Interview with Joss Whedon."

"Some fathers can't really talk to their sons . . ." Joss Whedon, quoted in Rosen, "Family Tradition."

"extremely outspoken, strong and loving" . . . Whedon, interview by the author.

"She was very smart . . ." Whedon, quoted in Nussbaum, "Must-See Metaphysics."

"lured back" to children's television . . . Tom Whedon, quoted in Rosen, "Family Tradition."

"There were always eight . . ." Stone, quoted in Davis, *Street Gang,* 157.

"While I really enjoyed all of the funny things . . ." Whedon, quoted in Longworth, "Joss Whedon, Feminist," 199.

"There were times when I didn't feel . . ." Whedon, quoted in Havens, *Joss Whedon,* 5.

Joss worked through his feelings . . . Schiff, "Joss Whedon: Absolute Admiration for Sondheim."

"The notion that every choice you make . . ." Whedon, quoted in Schiff, "Joss Whedon: Absolute Admiration for Sondheim."

"*Sondheim wasn't someone you would go to . . .*" Ibid.

"*He was always the funniest kid . . .*" Boal, interview by the author.

"*I was like nine . . .*" Whedon, quoted in Ridley, "Three Writers."

"*We kicked it full '70s*" . . . Whedon, interview by the author.

"*walking up and down . . .*" Whedon, quoted in Hibberd, "Joss Whedon: The Definitive EW Interview."

"*He looks like an easy mark*" . . . Cole, interview by the author.

"*I duck under them . . .*" Whedon, quoted in Hibberd, "Joss Whedon: The Definitive EW Interview."

"*You just hold onto that*" . . . Cole, interview by the author.

"*We were super upset . . .*" Boal, interview by the author.

"*It was the first horror movie I'd seen . . .*" Whedon, quoted in Syfy UK, "Joss Whedon— Favourite Horror."

"*I wanted to be a part of a group . . .*" Whedon, quoted in Ken P., "An Interview with Joss Whedon."

"*We'd walk down the street . . .*" Boal, interview by the author.

"*I gave myself this little mantra . . .*" Whedon, quoted in Tavi, "Yay, Geometry."

2. "Being British" in the Land of Shakespeare (and Giles)

"*Winchester is timelessly beautiful . . .*" Whedon, "Higher Learning."

"*I was lonely*" . . . Whedon, quoted in Ken P., "An Interview with Joss Whedon."

"*I was very dark and miserable . . .*" Whedon, quoted in BAFTA, *Joss Whedon: A Life in Pictures*.

"*I'm alone out here . . .*" Whedon, "Joss Whedon: From Buffy to Dr Horrible," Sydney Opera House.

"*ice cold room*" . . . Whedon, "Higher Learning."

"*When there was a lull . . .*" Ibid.

"*somebody makes these [films] . . .*" Whedon, interview in *Joss Whedon: The Master at Play*, DVD.

the "*reality of being human*" . . . Whedon, quoted in Kappala-Ramsamy, "Joss Whedon."

"*[I] came out of the theater with an understanding . . .*" Whedon, Lifetime Achievement Award acceptance speech.

"*extraordinary epiphany of the nature . . .*" Ibid.

"*Oh! Other people have gone through this!*" . . . Whedon, quoted in Kappala-Ramsamy, "Joss Whedon."

"*I saw them in the front row . . .*" Whedon, interview by the author.

"*difficult to teach*" . . . Dick Massen, quoted in Jane Massen, interview by the author.

"*American, and sometimes rather dubious . . .*" "Fencing Report 1981," *Wykehamist*.

"*And if you believe that, you'll believe anything*" . . . Whedon, quoted in Jane Massen, interview by the author.

"*It could have been absolutely ghastly*" . . . Jane Massen, interview by the author.

"*We'd have class for an hour and twenty minutes . . .*" Whedon, quoted in Ken P., "An Interview with Joss Whedon."

"*clearly surrogate [Joss] as a grown-up . . .*" Whedon, interview in *The Write Environment*, DVD.

"*a person of a great deal of originality*" . . . Jane Massen, interview by the author.

"*no grades . . . [and] a lot of reports . . .*" Whedon, quoted in Ken P., "An Interview with Joss Whedon."

"*It was only when I got to college . . .*" Whedon, quoted in Gilbey, "Joss Whedon."

"*I was very aware that my interest . . .*" Whedon, interview by the author.

"*You can't write from a political agenda . . .*" Ibid.

"*It was the year that Superman [III] came out . . .*" Tom Whedon, quoted in Rosen, "Family Tradition."

"*Sometimes people are flexible . . .*" Basinger, interview by the author.

"*I've had two great teachers in my life*" . . . Whedon, quoted in Stafford, "Slayage Conference."

"*The way everyone in the film department . . .*" Cole, interview by the author.

"*[There were] people who understand theory . . .*" Whedon, quoted in Ken P., "An Interview with Joss Whedon."

He wrote a paper on Alfred Hitchcock's The Birds . . . Stafford, "Slayage Conference."

"*His papers seemed so natural . . .*" Basinger, interview by the author.

"*where the simplicity is . . .*" Whedon, quoted in Ken P., "An Interview with Joss Whedon."

Basinger explained that her students felt . . . Stafford, "Slayage Conference."

"*I was terrified*" . . . Whedon, interview by the author.

"*When somebody didn't get it . . .*" Basinger, interview by the author.

"*I had an old photograph . . .*" Whedon, interview by the author.

"*Pretty much what I had learned . . .*" Whedon, interview by the author.

"*They both showed great talent . . .*" Basinger, interview by the author.

"*ward off the evil spirits*" . . . Whedon, interview by the author.

3. Crash Course in Television

"*That freaked me out a little bit*" . . . Whedon, interview in *Making It with Riki Lindhome* podcast.

"*young, hip, and cool*" . . . Ibid.

"*It was the most terrifying experience . . .*" Ibid.

"*We didn't ever shoot it . . .*" Ibid.

"*I had no idea how huge . . .*" Whedon, interview in *The Write Environment*, DVD.

"*It came down to about the middle . . .*" Whedon, interview by the author.

"*Very '80s, slick, like frat boy*" . . . Whedon, interview in *Making It with Riki Lindhome* podcast.

"*something creepy happened . . .*" Whedon, interview in *The Write Environment*, DVD.

Barr "*changed the landscape . . .*" Whedon, quoted in Ken P., "An Interview with Joss Whedon."

"*had a feminist agenda . . .*" Ibid.

"*I know he meant that . . .*" Whedon, "Joss Whedon: From Buffy to Dr Horrible," Sydney Opera House.

"*total chaos*" . . . Whedon, quoted in Ken P., "An Interview with Joss Whedon."

"*It's us against the world . . .*" Ibid.

It was a plot twist . . . Whedon, quoted in Hibberd, "Joss Whedon: The Definitive EW Interview."

"*It made me realize . . .*" Whedon, quoted in Ken P., "An Interview with Joss Whedon."

"*Because they just . . . they had nobody . . .*" Ibid.

"*It's totally the same . . .*" Whedon, interview in *Making It with Riki Lindhome* podcast.

"*That was the first script of mine . . .*" Whedon, interview by the author.

"*It was quite extraordinary*" . . . Whedon, quoted in Ken P., "An Interview with Joss Whedon."

"*If you met my mom . . .*" Whedon, quoted in Benedictus, "The Ladies' Man."

"*It was about Michael Jordan*" . . . Whedon, interview by the author.

at least $3,000 a week . . . Klaus, "The War of the Roseanne."

"*The idea . . . came from seeing . . .*" Whedon, quoted in Havens, *Joss Whedon*, 21.

"*more power than was imaginable*" . . . Whedon, quoted in Ken P., "An Interview with Joss Whedon."

"There is no way you could hear the name . . ." Ibid.

"jolly fun" . . . Whedon, interview in *The Write Environment*, DVD.

"I just wanted to be able . . ." Whedon, quoted in Ken P., "An Interview with Joss Whedon."

"It was a very talented ensemble . . ." Whedon, interview by the author.

"This is terrible" . . . King, quoted in ibid.

"He was far across the room . . ." Cole, interview by the author.

"I like your boots" . . . Whedon, quoted in ibid.

"the fact that we were at a gay bar . . ." Whedon, interview by the author.

"We sort of celebrate . . ." Cole, interview by the author.

"My husband and I were both here . . ." Basinger, interview by the author.

"Oh, God no. I'm trying to fix it!" . . . Cole, quoted in Whedon, interview by the author.

"It was very important" . . . Whedon, interview by the author.

4. The Blonde in the Alley Fights Back

"When we're kids . . ." Fran Kuzui, quoted in Tracy, *The Girl's Got Bite*, 3.

"The original script of 'Buffy' . . ." Fran Kuzui, quoted in Miller, "From Box Office Hit to Serenity of Temples."

"That theatrical, neo-surf speak" . . . Saralegui, interview by the author.

"Buffy's the one who's . . ." Perry, quoted in Tracy, *The Girl's Got Bite*, 4.

Buffy "isn't a vampire movie . . ." Fran Kuzui, quoted in ibid., 6.

"Fran Kuzui came in . . ." Whedon, quoted in Ken P., "An Interview with Joss Whedon."

"Kristy Swanson [said] . . ." Ibid.

"He had a very bad attitude . . ." Whedon, quoted in Robinson, "Joss Whedon" (interview), September 5. 2001.

"You can't sit down at your desk . . ." Whedon, interview by the author.

"They thought the movie was very serious . . ." Kaz Kazui, quoted in Tracy, *The Girl's Got Bite*, 7.

"OK, that made me feel a bit better . . ." Whedon, interview by the author.

"I didn't know that you people existed!" . . . Ibid.

"Paul's adjustment was about spinning . . ." Ibid.

"a comedy, but also a satire . . ." Swanson, quoted in Diamond, "'Buffy the Vampire Slayer.'"

"this is not going to be a critically acclaimed movie . . ." Perry, quoted in ibid.

5. The World Upends

"At this time a lot of people turn to . . ." Whedon, director's commentary, "The Body."

"no solution, catharsis, or anything else . . ." Ibid.

"I wanted to be very specific . . ." Ibid.

"Ha ha ha, you little naive fool . . ." Whedon, interview by the author.

"His very simple advice . . ." Ibid.

"I would go upstairs and start writing . . ." Whedon, quoted in Legel, "COMIC CON."

"If you look carefully at The Getaway" . . . Whedon, quoted in Robinson, "Joss Whedon" (interview), September 5. 2001.

"That's a movie that goes genuinely insane . . ." Whedon, quoted in Bailey, "12 Things We Learned from Joss Whedon's SXSW Talk."

a "dog movie . . ." Whedon, interview in *Making It with Riki Lindhome* podcast.

"Don't option it . . ." Saralegui, quoted in Whedon, interview in *Making It with Riki Lindhome* podcast.

"when he hooks up with other policemen . . ." Whedon, quoted in Havens, *Joss Whedon*, 128.

"I wanted a baby for that spot" . . . Whedon, undated *Suspension* draft, 41.

"*It's one of those scripts . . .*" Saralegui, interview by the author.

"*I knew it sucked*" . . . Ibid.

"*I turned him into a likeable . . .*" Whedon, interview in *Fresh Air*, May 9, 2000.

"*What if he's just the polite guy . . .*" Whedon, quoted in Kozac, "Serenity NOW!"

"*It's all about finding . . .*" Whedon, interview by the author.

"*Films like Speed belong . . .*" Ebert, review of *Speed*.

"*If it weren't for the smart-funny twist . . .*" Hinson, review of *Speed*.

"*The arbitration was a great sticking point . . .*" Whedon, quoted in Kozac, "Serenity NOW!"

Joss "*deserved credit*" . . . Saralegui, interview by the author.

"*wrote 98.9 percent of the dialogue*" . . . Yost, quoted in O'Hare, "The 'Bus Guy' Triumphs on 'Boomtown.'"

"*When I read his draft . . .*" Yost, quoted in Bierly, " 'Justified' EP Graham Yost."

"*Graham Yost has always been . . .*" Whedon, quoted in Kozac, "Serenity NOW!"

6. To Infinity and Beyond: *Toy Story* and *Alien: Resurrection*

a rough draft of the picture . . . Price, *The Pixar Touch*, 130.

Katzenberg "*would always . . . be pushing . . .*" Schumacher, quoted in Iwerks, *Pixar Story*, documentary.

"*It was fascinating to read . . .*" Stanton, interview by the author.

"*I often say to people . . .*" Cole, interview by the author.

"*a perfect structure with a ghastly script . . .*" Whedon, interview by the author.

"*Everything can be negotiated except Kai*" . . . Basinger, interview by the author.

"*One day, we were reading . . .*" Cole, interview by the author.

"*Many of you are going to be laid off . . .*" Whedon, quoted in Kozac, "Serenity NOW!"

"*Oh! We already know how . . .*" Ibid.

"*It would have been a really bad musical . . .*" Whedon, quoted in " 'Toy Story': The Inside Buzz," *Entertainment Weekly*.

"*He would wear his musical interests . . .*" Stanton, interview by the author.

"*They were so sweet . . .*" Whedon, interview by the author.

"*We're all animators . . .*" Stanton, interview by the author.

"*She's [Terminator 2's] Sarah Connor . . .*" Whedon, quoted in " 'Toy Story': The Inside Buzz," *Entertainment Weekly*.

"*We decided we could either be PC . . .*" Stanton, quoted in ibid.

Joss "*wrote a lot of great lines . . .*" Stanton, interview by the author.

"*Joss helped set the tone . . .*" Ibid.

"*utterly brilliant anthropomorphism*" . . . Maslin, review of *Toy Story*.

"*I can hardly imagine . . .*" Gleiberman, review of *Toy Story*.

"*For once, reality lives up to hype . . .*" McManus, "Toy Story: A Treasure."

"*[It is] gratifying to me . . .*" Whedon, quoted in Kozac, "Serenity NOW!"

"*When they said . . .*" Whedon, interview by the author.

"*I was there for seven weeks*" . . . Whedon, quoted in Robinson, "Joss Whedon" (interview), September 5. 2001.

"*I can't see the water*" . . . Whedon, interview by the author.

"*Of course it got thrown out*" . . . Ibid.

"*He puts together these unbelievable bits . . .*" Cole, interview by the author.

"*absolutely the part in The Remains of the Day . . .*" Whedon, interview by the author.

"*Every once in a while . . .*" Cole, interview by the author.

"*I put it on, and he just . . .*" Ibid.

"*I wasn't supposed to meet my wife . . .*" Whedon, interview by the author.

"*Sigourney Weaver is the centerpiece . . .*" Roth, quoted in Kaplan, "Last in Space."

a "*wooden planet*" . . . Jolin, "Alien 3: The Lost Tale of the Wooden Planet."

"a slap in the face" . . . Cameron, director's commentary, *Aliens*.
"the fans were robbed . . ." Whedon, quoted in Havens, *Joss Whedon*, 27.
"Scary like Alien . . ." Whedon, featurette commentary in "From the Ashes."
"a total identification" . . . Whedon, interview in *Joss Whedon: The Master at Play*, DVD.
"It's very important to me . . ." Whedon, quoted in Havens, *Joss Whedon*, 28.
"What if I'm even stranger? . . ." Weaver, quoted in Whedon, featurette commentary in "From the Ashes."
"She created an extraordinary character" . . . Whedon, featurette commentary in "From the Ashes."
"When Call, who was played by Winona Ryder . . ." Whedon, interview in *Joss Whedon: The Master at Play*, DVD.
"An android and a clone . . ." Saralegui, interview by the author.
"Then I put on a brave face . . ." Whedon, interview by the author.
"The first one was in the forest . . ." Whedon, quoted in Kozac, "Serenity NOW!"
"It was mostly a matter of doing everything wrong . . ." Whedon, quoted in Harris, "Joss for a Minute."
"I don't remember writing . . ." Whedon, quoted in Kozac, "Serenity NOW!"
"Listen, I don't want to be a jerk . . ." Whedon, quoted in Saralegui, interview by the author.
"I think the biggest problem . . ." Saralegui, interview by the author.
"It was the final crappy humiliation . . ." Whedon, quoted in Havens, *Joss Whedon*, 29.

7. *Buffy:* Resurrection

"a brilliant show . . ." Whedon, director's commentary, "Innocence."
"no show on TV has ever come close . . ." Whedon, printed insert, *My So-Called Life*, DVD.
"I'd been waiting and waiting . . ." Whedon, interview by the author.
"big movie projects" . . . Berman, quoted in Sepinwall, *The Revolution Was Televised*, 194.
"A couple of weeks later" . . . Ibid, 194.
"When I pitched Buffy The Vampire Slayer . . ." Whedon, printed insert, *My So-Called Life*, DVD.
"beautiful images" to demonstrate . . . Daniels, *Season Finale*, 118.
"sketched . . . out in Dickensian detail . . ." Ibid, 119.
looking for a female teen superhero series . . . Daniels, interview in "Front Row Special on Buffy the Vampire Slayer."
"slight bias" against the project . . . Daniels, quoted in Sepinwall, *The Revolution Was Televised*, 195.
"was such a fresh and improved take . . ." Ibid.
"overall vision that Joss pitched . . ." Daniels, *Season Finale*, 120.
"It's amazing that they're really letting . . ." Whedon, interview by the author.
"the great square hole . . ." Whedon, Visionaries panel.
Joss called this "reset television" . . . Whedon, interview in *The Write Environment*, DVD.
"TV is a question . . ." Whedon, interview in *Joss Whedon: The Master at Play*, DVD.
"Buffy was always intended . . ." Whedon, comments in 20th Century Fox Television, *Buffy the Vampire Slayer* international press kit.
"They said to me . . ." Gellar, interview by the author.
"You tell them not to leave . . ." Carpenter, quoted in "How Charisma Nearly Missed the Buffy Audition," BBC.
a "loud, abusive Scot" . . . Whedon, handwritten notes, in "Joss Whedon: From Buffy to the Bard" exhibit.
"What he is not . . ." Ibid.
"I'd read the scripts in a restaurant . . ." Head, interview by the author.

"I was looking for a guy whose life . . ." Whedon, interview by the author.

"This is completely different . . ." Head, interview by the author.

"It has nothing to do . . ." Whedon, quoted in Head, interview by the author.

"shy, clumsy, sensible . . ." Whedon, handwritten notes, in "Joss Whedon: From Buffy to the Bard" exhibit.

her *"own sort of shy quirkiness"* . . . Whedon, director's commentary, "Welcome to the Hellmouth."

"charming, decent looking . . ." Whedon, handwritten notes, in "Joss Whedon: From Buffy to the Bard" exhibit.

a *"friendly but pointed" conversation* . . . Daniels, *Season Finale*, 123.

"They had absolutely no time . . ." Head, interview by the author.

a *"nightmare, [with] the worst crew . . ."* Whedon, interview by the author.

"But the suits don't get it . . ." Head, interview by the author.

"it would be like if somebody . . ." Solomon, interview by the author.

"I don't read the notes" . . . Ibid.

"Hey, if this thing goes to series . . ." Whedon, quoted in Solomon, interview by the author.

"They all just kind of fit . . ." Solomon, interview by the author.

"I thought that he had captured . . ." Daniels, quoted in Sepinwall, *The Revolution Was Televised*.

"The pilot was not great" . . . Ancier, quoted in Sepinwall, *The Revolution Was Televised*.

"I think Buffy will do for The WB . . ." Daniels, quoted in Jacobs, "Interview with a Vampire Chronicler."

"part of the reason . . ." Regan, quoted in Whedon, interview in *Making It with Riki Lindhome* podcast.

Regan *"came into the room . . ."* Whedon, interview in *Making It with Riki Lindhome* podcast.

"OK, so she's talking about how guys . . ." Hannigan, quoted in Perenson, "Leather on Willow."

"Willow is a good role model" . . . Hannigan, comments in 20th Century Fox Television, *Buffy the Vampire Slayer* international press kit.

"I'm no more Buffy . . ." Gellar, interview by the author.

8. *Buffy* Premieres

"could go down as the creepiest show . . ." Everett, review of *Profit*.

"It's got feeling . . ." Greenwalt, interview by the author.

"David was more responsible . . ." Whedon, interview by the author.

"Joss remembered one line . . ." Batali, interview by the author.

"Tell me your favorite horror movie . . ." Whedon, interview in "Joss Whedon on Buffy's Legacy."

"controlling parents as Stepford . . ." Whedon, handwritten notes, in "Joss Whedon: From Buffy to the Bard" exhibit.

"Oh! This show's gonna be . . ." Whedon, interview by the author.

"I like my stuff to have an edge . . ." Ibid.

"We learned early on . . ." Greenwalt, interview by the author.

"He knows what he wants when he sees it . . ." Espenson, interview by the author.

"The question then becomes . . ." Batali, interview by the author.

"Joss reverse engineered . . ." Gordon, interview by the author.

"When we'd break stories" . . . Greenwalt, interview by the author.

"We spent four or five hours . . ." Batali, interview by the author.

"Well, here's what it should look like" . . . Whedon, quoted in Batali, interview by the author.

"The first year, it was like . . ." Whedon, quoted in Ken P., "An Interview with Joss Whedon."
"I did not cook at all . . ." Cole, interview by the author.
"One of them is funny . . ." Whedon, quoted in "'Avengers' Director Joss Whedon," CBS News.
Joss had wanted to preface the story . . . Holder, *Buffy: The Making of a Slayer*, 21.
"For each generation, there is only one slayer" . . . Buffy the Vampire Slayer premiere trailer, WB.
"The following two-hour world premiere . . ." Ibid.
"You know, we had our television tropes" . . . Whedon, interview by the author.
"He's atheist, but never seemed . . ." Batali, interview by the author.
"We didn't write that . . ." Ibid.
"I'll never forget . . ." Greenwalt, interview by the author.

9. The Bronze

"We were not a wealthy or respected show . . ." Solomon, interview by the author.
"Part of Joss's genius . . ." Head, interview by the author.
"People who never watched Buffy . . ." Greenwalt, interview by the author.
"These are really, really smart people . . ." Cole, interview by the author.
"So many of the people . . ." Buchanan, interview by the author.
"It's a place where, in order to really fit in . . ." Nielsen, quoted in Rachel Hyland, "The Bronze Age."
"I remember him frequently talking . . ." Batali, interview by the author.
"I'd rather make a show . . ." Whedon, featurette commentary in *"Buffy the Vampire Slayer*: TV with Bite."
"Well, you have to go on . . ." Hannigan, quoted in Head, interview by the author.
"And so I did" . . . Head, interview by the author.
"Some Bronzers hated everything . . ." Noxon, interview by the author.
"Am interested in showing dreams . . ." Whedon, Buffy.com post, circa February 2, 1998.
"It was always such a BIG DEAL . . ." Morris, interview by the author.
"It was special that [Joss] . . ." Solomon, quoted in Tuszynski, "IRL (In Real Life): Breaking Down the Binary of Online Versus Offline Social Interaction."
"It was always lovely . . ." Noxon, interview by the author.
"I don't think people realize . . ." Cole, interview by the author.

10. The *Buffy* Way

"It is a show . . ." Greenwalt, interview by the author.
"distinctive voices who can blend . . ." Whedon, interview in *Joss Whedon: The Master at Play*, DVD.
"the person behind the words . . ." Ibid.
"I got offered a job . . ." Noxon, interview by the author.
"a director doesn't have to . . ." Whedon, quoted in Ken P., "An Interview with Joss Whedon."
"I don't have to write . . ." Ibid.
"The thing about fantasy . . ." Whedon, interview by the author.
"possibly the best" scene . . . Whedon, director's commentary, "Innocence."
"harder edged" and "uglier" . . . Ibid.
"You have to make sure . . ." Whedon, interview by the author.
"Not only were we making a movie . . ." Ibid.
"This one's a French farce! . . ." Ibid.
"Joss's shows are really . . ." Espenson, interview by the author.
"There was almost never a day . . ." Ibid.

"Once, I'd worked a long time . . ." Ryan, interview by the author.
"Behind all of the intelligence . . ." Gordon, interview by the author.
"He would pace around the room . . ." Espenson, interview by the author.
"delightful, funny people . . ." Noxon, interview by the author.
"Sofas, easy chairs, etc. . . ." Fury, interview by the author.
"We had lots of toys . . ." Espenson, interview by the author.
"there were little magnetized ball bearings . . ." Ibid.
"If he lies down on a table . . ." Greenwalt, interview by the author.
"But he wanted us to look . . ." Noxon, interview by the author.
"I think that is the great privilege . . ." Gordon, interview by the author.
"Marti, we've read your script . . ." Whedon, quoted in Noxon, interview by the author.
Joss said "Leprechauns" . . . Ibid.
"I have never lived the leprechauns down . . ." Noxon, interview by the author.
"I go for the comic ones . . ." Whedon, interview in *The Write Environment*, DVD.
"I had just come off . . ." Espenson, interview by the author.
"That's dumb" . . . Whedon, quoted in Gutierrez, interview by the author.
"Joss was definitely . . ." Gutierrez, interview by the author.
"Muji made a wonderful notebook . . ." Whedon, interview by the author.
"If I'm writing by pacing . . ." Ibid.
"By the time he sits down . . ." Greenwalt, interview by the author.
"He basically taps his thumb . . ." Gutierrez, interview by the author.
"Oh my God, he would do this thing . . ." Noxon, interview by the author.
"He hates to rewrite" . . . Greenwalt, interview by the author.
"You could always tell . . ." Head, interview by the author.
"I would get up at five . . ." Greenwalt, interview by the author.
"Can we make him smile . . ." Batali, interview by the author.
"The Dear Leader of that cult . . ." Espenson, quoted in Bridges, "SerenityStuff Welcomes Jane Espenson."
"He sent us all out . . ." Ibid.

11. Front-Page News

"My first impression wasn't . . ." Espenson, quoted in Vary, "Life Inside the Whedonverse."
"There was a lot of tension" . . . Whedon, quoted in Ken P., "An Interview with Joss Whedon."
"You just had to encourage actors . . ." Britt, interview by the author.
"two kids who suspect . . ." Whedon, quoted in Hontz and Petrikin, "Whedon, Fox Vamping."
a comedy about someone who is kidnapped . . . Hontz and Petrikin, "Whedon, Fox Vamping."
"none of us turn out exactly . . ." Whedon, interview in *Joss Whedon: The Master at Play*, DVD.
"It's hard to ignore the idea . . ." Whedon, Buffy.com post, December 15, 1998.
"On the inevitable subject . . ." Whedon, Buffy.com post, May 13, 1999.
"if anything [violent] had happened . . ." Turell, quoted in "Buffy Breaks Out," *Entertainment Weekly*.
"Even Elvis Costello riffed . . ." "Buffy Breaks Out," *Entertainment Weekly*.
"OK, I'm having a Grateful Dead moment . . ." Whedon, quoted in Johnson, "Fans Sink Teeth into Bootlegged 'Buffy.'"
"hot water" with the WB . . . Whedon, Buffy.com post, June 19, 1999.
"We are the people . . ." JenKatz, "Bootlegging Buffy."
"Joss had an old black Toyota . . ." Brendon, interview by the author.

12. Growing Up: *Angel*

"When Joss [brought up the idea] . . ." Greenwalt, interview by the author.

"David was a great guy . . ." Ibid.

Joss was *"blown away"* . . . Whedon, interview in *Joss Whedon: The Master at Play*, DVD.

"I frankly didn't think . . ." Minear, interview by the author.

"Marti Noxon, Jane Espenson . . ." Gordon, interview by the author.

"Trust me. I don't sing . . ." Ibid.

"There were the freshmen" . . . Minear, interview by the author.

"We wanted a much darker show . . ." Whedon, quoted in Havens, *Joss Whedon*, 101.

"One time, Angel arrives too late . . ." Greenwalt, interview by the author.

"Buffy is always the underdog . . ." Whedon, quoted in Havens, *Joss Whedon*, 102.

"Touched by an Equalizer" . . . Whedon, interview in *Joss Whedon: The Master at Play*, DVD.

"turned it into another ensemble . . ." Ibid.

"terrific, but troubled . . ." Greenwalt, interview by the author.

"weird uncomfortableness" . . . Minear, interview by the author.

"Well, when you wipe your ass . . ." Ibid.

"There was sort of a high school . . ." Ibid.

"I quit" . . . Ibid.

"We've been here for months! . . ." Ibid.

"Great" . . . Ibid.

"That's a really big show . . ." Greenwalt, quoted in Minear, interview by the author.

"Because I wasn't happy" . . . Minear, interview by the author.

"I don't even think . . ." Whedon, interview by the author.

"I had already fallen in love . . ." Denisof, interview by the author.

"We just couldn't figure it out . . ." Britt, interview by the author.

"I ran into David Boreanaz . . ." Benz, interview by the author.

"If you're available . . ." Ibid.

"Angel got very dark . . ." Minear, interview by the author.

"When he talked about a story . . ." Ibid.

"I had always had the belief . . ." Ryan, interview by the author.

"Look, I've been lucky enough . . ." Minear, interview by the author.

"I definitely want to get credit . . ." Whedon, quoted in Minear, interview by the author.

"Let's be honest . . ." Minear, interview by the author.

"At the beginning of season one . . ." Ibid.

"Absolutely, you should . . ." Whedon, quoted in Minear, interview by the author.

he called Minear a *"genius writer"* . . . Whedon, quoted in Adalian, " 'Angel' Writer Gets Fox Wings."

"That's the thing . . ." Minear, interview by the author.

13. A New Challenge: Silence

"just get his coverage . . ." Whedon, interview by the author.

"remind people of what scared them . . ." Whedon, director's commentary, "Hush."

"The Globolinks came . . ." Whedon, quoted in "Joss Whedon's Plan to Monetize Internet Content," Knowledge@Wharton.

"genuinely disturbing imagery" . . . Murray, review of "Hush."

"a true tour de force . . ." Bianculli, TV Tonight, March 21, 2000.

"in a medium in which producers . . ." Bianco, Critic's Corner, December 14, 1999.

" 'Hush' . . . redefined what an episode . . ." Espenson, featurette commentary in " 'Hush' Featurette."

conservative church groups told members . . . Tuszynski, "IRL (In Real Life): Breaking Down the Binary of Online Versus Offline Social Interaction."

the fans *"heard from other people . . ."* Paula "Polgara" Carlson, quoted in ibid.

"LESBIAN TOASTER . . ." Whedon, Buffy.com posts, August 1, 2000.

"Somewhere along the line" . . . "Missi," quoted in Tuszynski, "IRL (In Real Life): Breaking Down the Binary of Online Versus Offline Social Interaction."

as the organizers established partnerships . . . Gatson and Zweerink, "Choosing Community: Rejecting Anonymity in Cyberspace."

"you could see the stars of the show . . ." "Leather Jacket," quoted in Tuszynski, "IRL (In Real Life): Breaking Down the Binary of Online Versus Offline Social Interaction."

"I read the Parable . . ." Whedon and Fury, Buffy.com posts. May 17, 2000.

"Joss came on . . ." Hein, quoted in Tuszynski, "IRL (In Real Life): Breaking Down the Binary of Online Versus Offline Social Interaction."

"There's no other word . . ." Gellar, quoted in Pond, "Sarah Michelle Gellar's New World Order."

"He was very upset . . ." Pruitt, interview in the Hellmouth, June 21, 2000.

14. Shakespeare Fanboy

"You can't get upset . . ." Whedon, quoted in Minear, interview by the author.

"What we decided to do . . ." Minear, quoted in Gross, "ANGEL: Writer-Producer on directing 'Darla.'"

"You know what we should do? . . ." Whedon, interview by the author.

"It's hilarious . . ." Whedon, quoted in Ken P., "An Interview with Joss Whedon."

"I think Shakespeare works . . ." Ibid.

"No one cares. Just come . . ." Whedon, quoted in Head, interview by the author.

"James had always had a real thing . . ." Head, interview by the author.

"I waited, waited" . . . Whedon, interview by the author.

"He found nuances in it . . ." Head, interview by the author.

"When you're in a couple . . ." Cole, interview by the author.

"a happy one" . . . Ibid.

"He knows I love it . . ." Denisof, interview by the author.

"It's not always the part . . ." Ibid.

"He called me . . ." Benz, interview by the author.

"If you're working with him . . ." Acker, interview by the author.

"We had amazing, amazing readings" . . . Whedon, interview by the author.

"Suddenly you saw a whole different side . . ." Head, interview by the author.

"I told him 'I can't talk . . .'" Cole, interview by the author.

"I was 'nonspecific duke . . .'" Denisof, interview by the author.

"It's just the fun of hearing . . ." Ibid.

"It made me want to eat . . ." Harris, interview by the author.

"It's crazy! . . ." Espenson, interview by the author.

"It was that that got him thinking . . ." Denisof, interview by the author.

Joss describes it as Vietnam in the morning . . . Whedon, interview by the author.

"I just pictured it in my head . . ." Cole, interview by the author.

"He loves it so much" . . . Ibid.

15. Buffy Goes Back to High School

"have a really important, intense emotional relationship . . ." Whedon, quoted in Miller, "The Man Behind the Slayer."

"She was all cranky . . ." Whedon, quoted in Havens, *Joss Whedon,* 19.

portraying Buffy's grief "was probably the most awful . . ." Gellar, quoted in Jensen, "To Hell & Back."

"It's my own fault . . ." Whedon, quoted in Jensen, "To Hell & Back."

"Buffy had cut a swath . . ." Loeb, interview by the author.

"I'm not sure if he's asking . . ." Ibid.

"One wanted to star Giles . . ." Ibid.

"funny, clever, had twists . . ." Whedon, interview in *Joss Whedon: The Master at Play*, DVD.

"Unlike the series . . ." Whedon, quoted in Robinson, "Joss Whedon—Web Exclusive" (interview).

"That's a tall order . . ." Loeb, interview by the author.

his new series and his previous one "were very similar . . ." Wight, interview by the author.

a demonic driver's ed instructor . . . Loeb, quoted in Cairns, "An Animated Guy."

"It's a very silly show" . . . Whedon, quoted in Robinson, "Joss Whedon—Web Exclusive" (interview).

"the scripts were like fine pastries . . ." Loeb, interview by the author.

"We were met . . ." Buchanan, interview by the author.

"It was like getting ready . . ." Loeb, interview by the author.

"because of the sale . . ." Buchanan, interview by the author.

"Essentially what that means . . ." Ibid.

"I've always said . . ." Loeb, interview by the author.

"The first time we move . . ." Grushow, quoted in Hontz, "Bloody 'Buffy' Spectre."

16. Once More, with Feeling

"We will take all the revenue . . ." Kellner, quoted in Schneider and Adalian, " 'Buffy' a Toughie for WB."

"They don't have wheelbarrows . . ." Grushow, quoted in ibid.

"The WB has been so supportive . . ." Gellar, quoted in Grossberg, "Gellar: I'm Gone if Buffy Leaves WB."

"Nobody wanted the show" . . . Kellner, quoted in in Rice, "Slayer It Ain't So."

"26 to 29 years old in year 2 . . ." Whedon, quoted in ibid.

"Other networks reach more people . . ." Ibid.

"The studio did everything it could . . ." Armstrong, "Vampire Smackdown."

"The whole thing made me so angry . . ." Whedon, quoted in Jensen, "To Hell & Back."

their "contractual right to exclusively promote . . ." Schneider and Adalian, "WB Bans 'Buffy' Adieu."

"The STORY is in charge . . ." Whedon, Buffy.com post, May 23, 2001.

"The community . . ." Cole, interview by the author.

it didn't seem as if the WB "realized . . ." Quoted in Jensen, "To Hell & Back."

"They were actually really excited" . . . Whedon, quoted in Owen, "Is Buffy Dead?"

"The college years can be . . ." Noxon, interview by the author.

"reading new writers . . ." Ibid.

"Sarah Michelle piped up . . ." Head, interview by the author.

"He's a huge musical theater aficionado . . ." Batali, interview by the author.

"That's really almost kind of like music . . ." Saralegui, interview by the author.

"No, it doesn't feel right" . . . Whedon, quoted in Head, interview by the author.

"I was doing this jump backwards . . ." Strong, interview by the author.

"I was basically his slave" . . . Cole, interview by the author.

"We listened to that over and over . . ." Ibid.

"I started to listen . . ." Head, interview by the author.

"It's obvious now that they were good . . ." Marsters, quoted in Norton, "411mania Interviews: James Marsters."

"At that point the cast knuckled down . . ." Ibid.

"I basically started to cry . . ." Gellar, quoted in Schilling "Vamping It Up."

"It took something like 19 hours . . ." Ibid.

"an incredible experience" . . . Gellar, quoted in McCabe, "Buffy Hits a High Note."

"I was rather sad . . ." Head, interview by the author.

"*He has exquisite taste . . .*" Minear, interview by the author.

"*It wasn't Hello Kitty*" . . . Whedon, interview by the author.

"*At that point we were overjoyed . . .*" Marsters, quoted in Norton, "411mania Interviews: James Marsters."

"*Being able to navigate the swing . . .*" Noxon, interview by the author.

"*the songs were only half-memorable . . .*" Zacharek, "The Hills Are Alive."

"*There are websites devoted to . . .*" Noxon, interview by the author.

"*It wasn't who Buffy was . . .*" Gellar, quoted in Jensen, "The Goodbye Girl."

"*I really thought that was out of character . . .*" Ibid.

"*That's where having feedback . . .*" Noxon, interview by the author.

"*The truth is the writers on Buffy . . .*" Marsters, quoted in Norton, "411mania Interviews: James Marsters."

"*Spike's a villain*" . . . Noxon, interview by the author.

"*I realized, just the other day . . .*" Whedon, quoted in Utichi, "A Buffy-Style Kicking."

"*If you heard her talking . . .*" Gutierrez, interview by the author.

"*Let's end it in the asylum . . .*" Whedon, quoted in Gutierrez, interview by the author.

"*Joss never undermined . . .*" Gutierrez, interview by the author.

17. We Aim to Misbehave: *Firefly*

"*a gritty realism . . .*" Whedon, quoted in Russell, "The CulturePulp Q&A: Joss Whedon."

"*particularly the '70s westerns . . .*" Whedon, interview by the author.

"*I wanted to play with that classic notion . . .*" Whedon, quoted in Nussbaum, "Must-See Metaphysics."

"*Never watched any British sci-fi*" . . . Whedon, interview by the author.

"*how politics affect people . . .*" Whedon, quoted in Russell, "The CulturePulp Q&A: Joss Whedon."

"*Buck, the serio-comic driver . . .*" Erisman, "Stagecoach in Space."

"*about Joe Schmo . . .*" Whedon, quoted in Miller, "The Man Behind the Slayer."

"*It was nice to have a show that was about . . .*" Ibid.

Captain Reynolds "*is a man who . . .*" Whedon, quoted in Nussbaum, "Must-See Metaphysics."

A "*guy who looks into the void . . .*" Ibid.

"*Of course the captain was . . .*" Whedon, quoted in Miller, "The Man Behind the Slayer."

"*Wash is an absolute contrast . . .*" Whedon, *Serenity: The Official Visual Companion*, 11.

"*The last thing that Fox said was . . .*" Ibid, 11.

"*I walked into an office*" . . . Fillion, interview by the author.

"*This'll be great*" . . . Whedon, quoted in Fillion, interview by the author.

"*Which I am*" . . . Fillion, interview by the author.

"*He would describe something in the universe . . .*" Ibid.

"*I've had a lot of meetings . . .*" Ibid.

"*After that, it was up to me . . .*" Torres, quoted in Whedon, *Firefly: A Celebration*, 48.

"*You wouldn't want to cross him . . .*" Baldwin, interview by the author.

"*I was petrified*" . . . Staite, interview by the author.

Neil Patrick Harris was in contention . . . Harris, interview by the author.

"*This whole moment in the pilot . . .*" Maher, quoted in Vary, "Life Inside the Whedonverse."

"*He immediately started joking . . .*" Baccarin, interview by the author.

"*I put on my coat . . .*" Fillion, interview by the author.

"*I had trouble in the early going . . .*" Baldwin, interview by the author.

"*It does make perfect sense*" . . . Kozac, "Serenity NOW!"

"*You can say something that's paragraphs long . . .*" Ibid.

"When Joss directs . . ." Fillion, interview by the author.
"If you don't have a second-in-command . . ." Whedon, *Firefly: A Celebration*, 16.
he *"could not find anybody even remotely of the caliber . . ."* Ibid.
"I want to give you a spaceship" . . . Whedon, quoted in Minear, interview by the author.
"Oh, for God's sake . . ." Minear, interview by the author.
David Greenwalt *"did not take it lightly . . ."* Whedon, *Firefly: A Celebration*, 16.
"When Angel came around . . ." Whedon, interview by the author.
"when three shows came on . . ." Ibid.
"He's done his thing" . . . Buchanan, quoted in Adalian, "Whedon Widens Mutant's Reach."
"OK, you did your time" . . . Cole, quoted in Whedon, interview by the author.
"I didn't feel a daily pressure . . ." Fillion, interview by the author.
"Because I've had experience . . ." Whedon, quoted in Baldwin, interview by the author.

18. Curse Your Sudden but Inevitable Cancellation

"My marching orders . . ." Buchanan, interview by the author.
"hugely depressing" . . . Whedon, quoted in Vineyard, " 'Buffy the Vampire Slayer' Sing-Alongs Killed."
"That's what we do in our homes . . ." Whedon, interview in *Joss Whedon: The Master at Play*, DVD.
"This is something that was problematic" . . . Whedon, interview by the author.
"It was very dark" . . . Minear, comments in *Firefly 10th Anniversary: Browncoats Unite*.
"the most twisted new show . . ." *Firefly* promos, Fox network.
"We knew we were in real trouble . . ." Buchanan, interview by the author.
"we got the best people . . ." Fillion, interview by the author.
"I never worked with an ensemble . . ." Whedon, interview in *The Write Environment*, DVD.
"I've always pulled . . ." Fillion, interview by the author.
"seeing this beautiful woman . . ." Minear, comments in *Firefly 10th Anniversary: Browncoats Unite*.
"I went to Fox very early . . ." Buchanan, interview by the author.
"Without Whedonesque . . ." Cole, interview by the author.
"I'm only posty for a moment . . ." Whedon, Buffistas.org post, December 12, 2002.
"We were on the bridge . . ." Minear, interview by the author.
"I've never seen him so mad" . . . Baldwin, interview by the author.
"It was right before . . ." Staite, interview by the author.
"We've just been canceled . . ." Minear, interview by the author.
"We would screw things up . . ." Baccarin, interview by the author.
"I understood how that scene . . ." Ibid.
"It's Friday. The show is finished . . ." Minear, interview by the author.
"God bless them . . ." Fillion, interview by the author.
"I promised these [actors] . . ." Whedon, interview in *The Write Environment*, DVD.
"I went crazy . . ." Whedon, interview in *Making It with Riki Lindhome* podcast.
"Joss was so dedicated . . ." Baldwin, interview by the author.
"I love him" . . . Baccarin, interview by the author.

19. End of (*Buffy's*) Days

"Every set has its own sort of tenor . . ." Whedon, quoted in News of the Week, Sci Fi Wire, November 25, 2002.
"We both kind of felt . . ." Gellar, quoted in Jensen, "The Goodbye Girl."
"A lot of people were ready . . ." Ibid.

"A lot of people owe Sarah . . ." Prinze, quoted in O'Hare, "End of 'Buffy' Only Makes Gellar Stronger."

"Not everybody was best of friends . . ." Whedon, quoted in Ken P., "An Interview with Joss Whedon."

"There was a whole thing about it . . ." Whedon, quoted in Faraci, "Exclusive Interview."

"Villains don't think . . ." Fillion, interview by the author.

"Honestly, gentle viewers" . . . Andrew in "Storyteller," Buffy the Vampire Slayer.

"Buffy also became a little bit . . ." Whedon, quoted in "10 Questions," New York Times.

"It would have been Faith . . ." Minear, quoted in "Kung Fu Faith," BBC.

"Honestly, if I had a strong answer . . ." Whedon, quoted in "10 Questions," New York Times.

"I realized that there was a scene . . ." Whedon, interview by the author.

"We had taken that story . . ." Whedon, quoted in Ausiello, "Angel Mystery."

"My relationship with Joss . . ." Carpenter, panel comments, Dragon Con.

"The character lost its thrill . . ." Kartheiser, quoted in "The Man in the Light Gray Flannel Suit," Giant.

"spent most of this year trapped . . ." Gunn in "Players," Angel.

20. An Astonishing Return to His Roots

"Hey, Mr. Whedon . . ." Quesada, interview by the author.

"Can I take a day or two . . ." Whedon, quoted in ibid.

"I wish Joss Whedon . . ." Quesada, interview by the author.

"What Joss is popular for . . ." Marts, interview by the author.

"If there's a bigger influence . . ." Whedon, quoted in Edwards, "Whedon, Ink."

"We started talking . . ." Marts, interview by the author.

Claremont's stories "played a pivotal role . . ." Levitz, quoted in Reid, "X-Men Writer Chris Claremont Donates Archive."

"It was fun to see these guys . . ." Marts, interview by the author.

"When Joss's scripts came in . . ." Ibid.

"The craziest thing . . ." Lowe, interview by the author.

"More than the plots . . ." Marts, interview by the author.

"Joss's run was a pitch-perfect mix . . ." Lowe, interview by the author.

"best X-Men title published . . ." George, Review of Astonishing X-Men HC vol. 1.

21. Not Fade Away

"She would come in . . ." Buchanan, interview by the author.

"So, [Levin] canceled . . ." Whedon, quoted in Acker, interview by the author.

"Unlike early Buffy seasons . . ." Fury, quoted in Jozic, "David Fury Interview."

"I started bawling . . ." Carpenter, panel comments, Dragon Con.

"It's such a big part of my life . . ." Carpenter, quoted in Goldman, "IGN Interview: Charisma Carpenter."

"I heard it . . ." Carpenter, panel comments, Dragon Con.

"Move on the surface . . ." Adalian, "Frog Net's Drama 'Angel' Folds Wings."

"Joss did not want . . ." Fury, Whedonesque post, December 15, 2005.

"This isn't about the WB bailing . . ." Levin, quoted in Adalian, "Frog Net's Drama 'Angel' Folds Wings."

"Yes, my heart is breaking . . ." Whedon, BronzeBeta.com post, February 14, 2004.

"I miss those days . . ." Goddard, interview by the author.

"I thought Muppets were cool . . ." Whedon, quoted in Partney, "The Puppet Summit."

"That was great, entertaining television . . ." Fury, quoted in ibid.

"I've been in Hollywood . . ." Buchanan, interview by the author.

"I was in the car . . ." Staite, interview by the author.

"*There had been rumors . . .*" Baldwin, interview by the author.
"*It was one of the happiest days . . .*" Baccarin, interview by the author.
"*I don't wanna sound . . .*" Borenaz, quoted in Malcom, "Boreanaz Bids Angel Adieu."
"*They had pushed for an early decision . . .*" Ancier, quoted in "WB Wants Angel Movie," Sci Fi Wire.
"*I want to end the show . . .*" Whedon, quoted in Hiatt, "No 'Angel.'"
"*The original goal . . .*" Whedon, quoted in "One Last Stake in Heart as 'Angel' Bites It," *Alameda Times-Star*.
"*We knew [season six] . . .*" Fury, quoted in Jozic, "David Fury Interview."
"*The last thing you will see . . .*" Whedon, quoted in Jensen, "The X Factor."

22. Grant Me the Serenity

He also found it difficult . . . Whedon, *Serenity: The Official Visual Companion*, 25.
"*he brings such depth . . .*" Whedon, director's commentary, *Serenity*.
"*comedians, because they have the chops . . .*" Whedon, interview in *Joss Whedon: The Master at Play*, DVD.
"*I'll always remember . . .*" Baldwin, interview by the author.
"*We didn't have to worry . . .*" Staite, interview by the author.
"*There was a scene where I had . . .*" Ibid.
"*I thought I was going to . . .*" Fillion, interview by the author.
"*say something that Mal would say*" . . . Whedon, director's commentary, *Serenity*.
"*You're basically teaching people . . .*" Whedon, *Serenity: The Official Visual Companion*.
"*That was very humbling and very difficult . . .*" Ibid.

23. Election 2004

"*regarded with more contempt . . .*" Whedon, quoted in Doux, "High Stakes 2004."
"*If you're for Bush . . .*" Whedon, Whedonesque post, October 21, 2004.
"*A svelte and mysterious Jewel Thief . . .*" Whedon, Whedonesque profile.
High Stakes 2004 . . . Doux, "High Stakes 2004."
"*Q: You mentioned in . . .*" Whedon, quoted in ibid.
"*always been motivated by altruism . . .*" Ibid.
"*I spent a lot of time . . .*" Whedon, quoted in in Schneider, "Joss Whedon Wants Out of TV."
"*Even if you're worried . . .*" Doux, "High Stakes 2004."
"*Joss didn't really know . . .*" Cole, interview by the author.
"*My study was filled with crap . . .*" Whedon, interview in *Nerdist Podcast*.
"*extraordinary heroism*" . . . "Valor Awards for John Whedon Steele," *Military Times*.
"*gathered up a force of stragglers . . .*" Ibid.
"*No wonder [my parents] got divorced*" . . . Whedon, interview by the author.

24. I Wrote My Thesis on You

"*a not-soon-to-be-exhausted . . .*" "About Slayage," Slayage Online.
"*Twilight Zone or Star Trek had wonderful symbolism . . .*" Wilcox, interview by the author.
"*There are many audience members . . .*" Ibid.
"*You have to wait . . .*" Ibid.
"*That was one of the most wonderful experiences . . .*" Ibid.

25. *Serenity* Lands

"*All the work the fans have done . . .*" Whedon, introduction to *Serenity* special screenings.
"*Until Joss Whedon and Serenity . . .*" Fillion, interview by the author.
"*He would take pictures of me . . .*" Ibid.
"*I don't actually have anything . . .*" Whedon, Q&A session on Australian *Serenity* DVD.

26. Strong Female Characters

"crazed Veronica Marsathon" . . . Whedon, Whedonesque post, August 12, 2005.

"Joss Luvs Veronica . . ." Ibid.

"We're both sort of writing . . ." Thomas in Fernandez, "Cult King in Orbit on Mars."

"The most beautiful final episode . . ." Thomas, interview by the author.

"Last year, Veronica Mars' . . ." Whedon, "Ace of Case."

"the world's greatest dad . . ." Ibid.

"Trust me, I cast guest star actors . . ." Thomas, interview by the author.

"Joss is such an intelligent guy . . ." Bell, quoted in Fernandez, "Cult King in Orbit on Mars."

"a face of a series" . . . Thomas, interview by the author.

"Wonder Woman was the first great . . ." Silver, quoted in Warner Bros., "Silver Pictures and Warner Bros. Pictures Sign Joss Whedon."

"It was after I made 'The Matrix' . . ." Silver, quoted in in Douglas, "Exclusive: Joel Silver on Wonder Woman."

"Are you kidding? . . ." Cole, quoted by Whedon, quoted in Kozac, "Serenity NOW!"

"In my version, there was actually . . ." Whedon, quoted in Seijas, "Joss Whedon Talks About His 'Batman' Movie That Never Was."

"It was the key to the whole movie" . . . Whedon, quoted in Hibberd, "Joss Whedon: The Definitive EW Interview."

"I was clearly not on the same wavelength" . . . Whedon, quoted in in Kozac, "Serenity NOW!"

"There are great DC books . . ." Whedon, interview by the author.

"Batman is the only Marvel character . . ." Ibid.

"he's got the greatest rogues gallery . . ." Whedon, quoted in Jensen, "Buffy's Back."

"She doesn't have good villains" . . . Whedon, interview by the author.

"I think she sort of . . ." Whedon, quoted in Carroll, "Joss Whedon Vows He Won't Do Anything Silly with Wonder Woman."

She's "fascinating, very uncompromising . . ." Whedon, quoted in Warner Bros., "Silver Pictures and Warner Bros. Pictures Sign Joss Whedon."

"She comes from a civilization . . ." Whedon, quoted in O'Hara, "His Whedonness Talks Serenity."

Wonder Woman's vulnerability is her "outdatedness" . . . Whedon, interview by the author.

"The fact that she was a goddess . . ." Whedon, quoted in Tavi, "Yay, Geometry."

"If they will allow for you to have . . ." Torres, panel comments, FanExpo Canada.

a "young woman's journey" . . . Whedon, quoted in Fleming, "Whedon's a Goner for U."

"When he was released . . ." Neuwirth, interview by the author.

"full of light . . ." Ibid.

"Indirectly, his work . . ." Ibid.

"I think it's because of my mother . . ." Whedon, Equality Now address, May 15, 2006.

"He's very fond of the songs . . ." Basinger, interview by the author.

"You know, Miss Leslie . . ." Ibid.

"Joss Whedon and his wife" . . . Sondheim, quoted in Cole, interview by the author.

"The people who liked it . . ." Cole, interview by the author.

"Plot-wise, I was like . . ." Whedon, interview by the author.

"I wrote a script . . ." Whedon, quoted in Alt, "Exclusive: 'Dollhouse' Creator Joss Whedon."

"I never wrote my definitive version . . ." Whedon, interview by the author.

"Joss will not be fighting . . ." Whedon, Whedonesque post, February 3, 2007.

"I think that was more of . . ." Smulders, interview by the author.

he "was so ground down . . ." Whedon, quoted in "Bryan Hitch & Joss Whedon," Newsarama.

"I would go back in a heartbeat . . ." Whedon, quoted in Robinson, "Joss Whedon" (interview), August 8, 2007.

"I really kept Goners at bay . . ." Whedon, quoted in Gopalan, "Whedon After 'Wonder'-land."

"was not incredibly well-received" . . . Whedon, quoted in Snierson, "Joss Whedon Taps Eliza Dushku for New Fox Series."

"a real production company" . . . Whedon, quoted in "Joss Whedon Goes into 'Sugar Shock.' "

"I'm tired of not telling stories" . . . Ibid.

27. A New Way of Storytelling

"Karl would give me thumbnails . . ." Whedon, quoted in Bendis, "Brian Bendis Presents . . ."

"His writing chops translate really well . . ." Allie, interview by the author.

"What that tells me . . ." Ibid.

"There were definitely things . . ." Ibid.

"She's . . . more like me . . ." Whedon, quoted in "Joss Whedon Goes into 'Sugar Shock.' "

"I came back on Monday . . ." Lowe, interview by the author.

"The sales were great" . . . Ibid.

28. WGA Writers' Strike

"I've told passionate Whedon fans . . ." Goddard, interview by the author.

"To the MPAA . . ." Whedon, quoted in Soloway, "Remove the Rating for Captivity."

"pretty much all you learn . . ." Whedon, Whedonesque post, May 20, 2007.

"kids we don't care about . . ." Whedon, interview in *Fanboy Radio* podcast.

"It was a crazy three days" . . . Goddard, interview by the author.

"Six minutes later . . ." Whedon and Goddard, *The Cabin in the Woods: The Official Visual Companion*, 17.

The lack of scripted series ushered in . . . Schechner, "This Writers' Strike Feels Like a Rerun."

ABC, CBS, and NBC saw their prime-time ratings . . . Ibid.

"salaries, benefits, pensions . . ." Writers Guild of America East, "Minimum Basic Agreement."

As it stood, writers were only paid . . . "Hollywood Writers Go on Strike," AFP.

"the Internet has to be . . ." Bowman, quoted in in Fernandez, "A Line in the Sand."

"imprinted with personality packages" . . . Snierson, "Joss Whedon Taps Eliza Dushku for New Fox Series."

"We call it . . ." Whedon, quoted in ibid.

her run of "crappy horror movies" . . . Whedon, quoted in Goldman, "Joss Whedon: Inside Dollhouse."

"I said, 'I love you . . .' " Ibid.

"It was a mistake!" . . . Whedon, quoted in Schneider, "Joss Whedon Preps Fox Series."

"He had my back" . . . Dushku, interview by the author.

"I came out and I was . . ." Whedon, interview by the author.

"The easiest tactic . . ." Whedon, Whedonesque post, November 7, 2007.

"Marti Noxon has tried to HIJACK . . ." Whedon, Whedonesque post, December 6, 2007.

"I was a '70s Upper West Side . . ." Whedon, interview by the author.

"CBS and Fox think . . ." Whedon, Whedonesque post November 17, 2007.

"The fans from day one . . ." Whedon, quoted in Goldman, "Joss Whedon, Friends & Fans on the Picket Line."

"These people are going to be . . ." Cole, interview by the author.

"The writers . . . were very appreciative . . ." dreamlogic, Whedonesque post, November 6, 2007.
"Dear Writers . . ." Whedon, "From Joss Whedon: Do Not Adjust Your Mindset."
"That's the reason I write . . ." Whedon, interview by the author.
"the reuse of movies and television programs . . ." Writers Guild of America, West, "Writers Guild Members Overwhelmingly Ratify New Contract."
"He thought it was a bad idea" . . . Cole, interview by the author.

29. Dr. Horrible, I Presume

"I wanted to write songs" . . . Whedon, interview in *Fresh Air*, February 12, 2009.
"Freedom is glorious" . . . Whedon, quoted in Baldwin, "The Web Has Been Wonderful."
he was "scheming schemes" . . . Whedon, Whedonesque post, December 20, 2007.
"The embarrassing thing . . ." Joss Whedon, quoted in Rosen, "Family Tradition."
"All of a sudden the world . . ." Tancharoen, quoted in "Jed Whedon & Maurissa Tancharoen," Dr. Horrible official fan site.
"Then he got mad . . ." Harris, quoted in Vary, "'Dr. Horrible's Sing-Along Blog.'"
"'Hey, so, we have this thing . . .'" Fillion, interview by the author.
"The thing about Joss . . ." Day, quoted in Vary, "'Dr. Horrible's Sing-Along Blog.'"
"[Joss] said that obviously . . ." Harris, quoted in Vary, "'Dr. Horrible's Sing-Along Blog.'"
the "guilds haven't been beaten down . . ." Whedon, interview by the author.
"I got to invent them" . . . Ibid.
"There's no reason . . ." Whedon, quoted in Rosen, "New Media Guru."
"The concept was so pure . . ." Harris, quoted in Vary, "'Dr. Horrible's Sing-Along Blog.'"
"It was helpful having those years . . ." Boretz, quoted in "Producer, Michael Boretz," Dr. Horrible official fan site.
"He creates that kind of environment . . ." Ibid.
"One of the things that makes him . . ." Wilcox, interview by the author.
"When I pull a favor . . ." Helberg, interview by the author.
"Joss knows what he wants . . ." Ibid.
"all kinds of guerilla filmmaking . . ." Harris, interview by the author.
"everybody was like a family" . . . Cole, interview by the author.
"More than any project . . ." Fillion, interview by the author.
it had "gotten backburnered" . . . Whedon, quoted in Vineyard, "Joss Whedon's Hollywood Status Update."
"Everything was in place . . ." Whedon, quoted in Utichi, "A Buffy-Style Kicking."
"I kept waiting for the other shoe. . ." Goddard, interview by the author.
"She was so on top of it" . . . Whedon, quoted in Rosen, "New Media Guru."
"We like to say we broke . . ." Ibid.
"Releasing it for free . . ." Harris, interview by the author.
"Backstage, he was even redder . . ." Helberg, interview by the author.
"It was very surreal" . . . Harris, interview by the author.
"But what he loved . . ." Whedon, interview in *Fresh Air*, February 12, 2009.
"It's not like a huge moneymaker . . ." Cole, interview by the author.
"There was a picture of Dr. Horrible . . ." Whedon, quoted in Rosen, "New Media Guru."
"I'll probably regret [that idea] forever . . ." Whedon, interview in *Fresh Air*, February 12, 2009.
"ambitious and funny while still being . . ." Bianculli, *Fresh Air*, February 12, 2009.
"Those songs are as equally entertaining . . ." Harris, interview by the author.
"I always want to get behind . . ." Whedon, interview in *Fresh Air*, February 12, 2009.
"Homer's Odyssey was swell . . ." Whedon, "Heart (Broken)," in *Commentary!: The Musical*.

30. *Dollhouse*

had done his best not to be "too embarrassing" . . . Whedon, quoted in "Exclusive: Joss Whedon Talks DOLLHOUSE," theTVaddict.com.

"Joss and I found common ground . . ." Penikett, interview by the author.

"painfully convoluted sentences . . ." Williams, interview by the author.

"Did human trafficking just get . . ." Whedon, interview by the author.

"Some of them said . . ." Ibid.

"The Network and I had different ideas . . ." Whedon, Whedonesque post, October 26, 2008.

"It takes a long time to find . . ." Penikett, interview by the author.

"every show has its own music . . ." Lennix, quoted in ibid.

"A good deal of Dollhouse . . ." Whedon, interview by the author.

"Dollhouse was the one time . . ." Whedon, quoted in Hibberd, "Joss Whedon: The Definitive EW Interview."

"I said, 'Whoa, no way! . . .'" Tudyk, quoted in Adams, "Alan Tudyk" (interview).

"There's no mediation . . ." Penikett, interview by the author.

"Maybe with a different creator . . ." Kranz, interview by the author.

"It's kind of an elegy . . ." Oswalt, quoted in Wolk, "Q&A: Patton Oswalt."

31. *The Cabin in the Woods*

"That was definitely one of . . ." Goddard, quoted in Colis, " 'The Cabin in the Woods.' "

"They're wonderful, decent people . . ." Whedon and Goddard, filmmakers' commentary, *The Cabin in the Woods*.

"This is basically the same . . ." Ibid.

"Here's an example . . ." Whedon and Goddard, *The Cabin in the Woods: The Official Visual Companion*, 21.

"very good, funny and smart" . . . Jenkins, quoted in Whedon and Goddard, *The Cabin in the Woods: The Official Visual Companion*, 48.

"It was awkward" . . . Kranz, quoted in Colis, " 'The Cabin in the Woods.' "

"Joss [said that he'd] been seeing me . . ." Kranz, interview by the author.

"We probably saw over 100 people . . ." Goddard, quoted in Colis, " 'The Cabin in the Woods.' "

"Drew is a horror aficionado . . ." Whedon and Goddard, *The Cabin in the Woods: The Official Visual Companion*. 19.

"there was nobody else . . ." Whedon and Goddard, filmmakers' commentary, *The Cabin in the Woods*.

"A person that has done . . ." Ibid.

"believe in yourself . . ." Whedon, Lifetime Achievement Award acceptance speech.

a "belief system that they can understand . . ." Ibid.

"The enemy of humanism is not faith" . . . Ibid.

"About two hours after starting . . ." Whedon, quoted in Bierly "Exclusive: Joss Whedon on 'Dollhouse.' "

" 'Belonging' is (in a very unpedantic way) . . ." Nussbaum, "The Fascinating No-Consent Fantasia of *Dollhouse* and *Mad Men*."

"the opportunity to end . . ." Schneider, " 'Dollhouse,' 'Hank' Get the Ax."

"Every actor wants at least . . ." Laurie, interview by the author.

"When Joss made Buffy . . ." Nussbaum, interview by the author.

"I've had people come up to me . . ." Whedon, interview by the author.

"Oh, thank God" . . . Whedon and Goddard, filmmakers' commentary, *The Cabin in the Woods*.

"You have to fight these battles . . ." Ibid.

32. Fanboy Dreams Come True: *The Avengers*

"It was very gradual . . ." Goddard, interview by the author.

"We needed somebody who wasn't . . ." Feige, quoted in Rogers, "With The Avengers, Joss Whedon Masters the Marvel Universe."

"I've known Joss for many . . ." Feige, interview by the author.

"I was about to go back . . ." Hemsworth, interview by the author.

"was always somebody that I . . ." Feige, interview by the author.

"The thing about the X-Men . . ." Whedon, quoted in Kozac, "Serenity NOW!"

"I don't think you have anything" . . . Whedon, quoted in Rogers, "With The Avengers, Joss Whedon Masters the Marvel Universe."

"What a great way . . ." Feige, interview by the author.

"I was like, great . . ." Whedon, quoted in Rogers, "With The Avengers, Joss Whedon Masters the Marvel Universe."

"I have enough signposts . . ." Whedon, interview in *The Q&A with Jeff Goldsmith* podcast.

"I kept telling my mom . . ." Whedon, quoted in John, "Joss Whedon: 'I Kept Telling My Mum Reading Comics Would Pay Off.'"

"When are you going to make a real . . ." Whedon, interview in *Studio 360.*

Leterrier, who reportedly had expressed interest . . . Beaks, "Louis Leterrier Officially in the Running."

"insiders at Marvel Studios . . ." Phillips, "'Avengers' Talk, Comic Book Signings."

Deadline Hollywood was reporting . . . Fleming, "Whedon to Direct Marvel's 'The Avengers.'"

"that is not an official thing . . ." Whedon, Visionaries panel.

"Oftentimes in the Marvel fan community . . ." Feige, interview by the author.

"There's been much made of superheroes . . ." Ibid.

"Joss looks at these characters . . ." Ibid.

"I did spend a lot of time . . ." Whedon, quoted in Sciretta, "/Film Set Interview: 'The Avengers' Writer/Director Joss Whedon."

Steve Rogers "is looking at this world . . ." Ibid.

"The motherfucker lives in you . . ." Whedon, quoted in Hiddleston, interview by the author.

was "very sweet" in his appraisal . . . Hiddleston, interview by the author.

"I was like, 'Dude . . .'" Ibid.

"I literally plugged in . . ." Ibid.

"I want to dive off the deep end . . ." Whedon, quoted in Hiddleston, interview by the author.

"it was funny to come full circle . . ." Hemsworth, interview by the author.

"Mark was my dream choice . . ." Whedon, quoted in Wilding "Joss Whedon and Mark Ruffalo."

"Joss said, 'I'm excited . . .'" Ruffalo, interview by the author.

"For me, it's a tough part . . ." Ibid.

"The way I see it . . ." Ruffalo, quoted in Jensen, "'Avengers': New Hulk Mark Ruffalo."

"It was like 'Female Agent #12' . . ." Smulders, interview by the author.

"I wrote an entire draft . . ." Whedon, interview by the author.

"Even though The Empire Strikes Back . . ." Whedon, interview in *The Q&A with Jeff Goldsmith* podcast.

"[The script] was funny . . ." Gregg, interview by the author.

"Joss, I am so excited . . ." Hiddleston, e-mail to Whedon, shared with the author by sender.

"Tom, this is one of those emails . . ." Whedon, e-mail to Hiddleston, shared with the author by recipient.

"You know, ironically . . ." Whedon, interview by the author.

33. *Buffy* Lives, Again?

"the deep struggle she had . . ." Anderson, quoted in Boucher, "Joss Who?"

"a hideous idea" . . . Head, quoted in Bricker and Moorhouse, *"Buffy the Vampire Slayer* Star Calls Movie Reboot a 'Hideous Idea.'"

"opportunity to take something . . ." Carpenter, quoted in Hernandez, "Exclusive: Charisma Carpenter on a Possible 'Buffy' Remake."

"There's no public outcry . . ." Green, quoted in Hoevel, "Seth Green Talks 'Robot Chicken.'"

"I love the Buffy that I played . . ." Gellar, interview by the author.

"This is a sad, sad reflection . . ." Whedon, quoted in Dos Santos, "Joss Whedon Reacts to *Buffy* Movie News."

"OK, if worse comes to worst . . ." Goddard, interview by the author.

"If you're going to bring it back . . ." Boucher, "'Buffy the Vampire Slayer' Movie Looking for New Writer."

"I wouldn't want to be . . ." Noxon, quoted in "'I Am Number Four' Writer Marti Noxon," MTV.com.

"The people who feel . . ." Whedon, quoted in Robinson, "Joss Whedon" (interview), September 5, 2001.

34. Avengers Assemble

He asked all the actors for their notes . . . Weintraub, "35 Things to Know About THE AVENGERS."

"At the beginning I'm an open book" . . . Whedon, quoted in Weintraub, "Director Joss Whedon."

the storylines seemed "cobbled together" . . . Weintraub, "35 Things to Know About THE AVENGERS."

"It wasn't broke . . ." Downey, quoted in Weintraub, "Robert Downey Jr. and Chris Evans."

"It was the first chance I had . . ." Jackson, interview by the author.

"my favorite response" . . . Whedon, quoted in Weintraub, "Director Joss Whedon."

"But then I got it . . ." Renner, interview by the author.

"We spent a long time talking . . ." Ruffalo, interview by the author.

"What part of that sentence . . ." Whedon, interview in "Joss Whedon: Why He Chose an Irish Man to Film Avengers."

"It's very important . . ." Ibid.

"Joss and I were keen . . ." McGarvey, quoted in Tran, "Avengers Assemble."

"I feel like Jon and Robert . . ." Gregg, interview by the author.

he was "hilariously funny . . ." Ibid.

"line policeman" . . . Jackson, interview by the author.

"Joss came to my rescue . . ." Ruffalo, interview by the author.

Joss "was so protective . . ." Smulders, interview by the author.

"It needed to say a lot . . ." Downey, quoted in Weintraub, "Robert Downey Jr. and Chris Evans."

"That's a great way to put it . . ." Evans, quoted in ibid.

"Nobody was doing it every day . . ." Gregg, interview by the author.

"All of us would just pass . . ." Renner, interview by the author.

"It was grueling . . ." Feige, interview by the author.

"I'll try and come . . ." Whedon, quoted in Hiddleston, interview by the author.

"Yeah, he came to the party" . . . Hiddleston, interview by the author.

there was "some Avengers affinity" . . . Gregg in Radish, "Jeremy Renner, Tom Hiddleston, Clark Gregg, Cobie Smulders and Joss Whedon."

Joss "is not just a big dancer . . ." Tanchoeren, interview by the author.

"the most enthusiastic white boy . . ." Quesada, interview by the author.
"He has this crazy-legs dance . . ." Dushku, interview by the author.
"Boy just had such swagger . . ." Ibid.
"He's a grown-ass man . . ." Gregg, interview by the author.
"From my own experience . . ." Smulders, interview by the author.
"I don't know who else . . ." Renner, interview by the author.
"When you're doing a movie . . ." Feige, interview by the author.
starting each day "refusing to do . . ." Downey, quoted in Lussier, "Robert Downey Jr. and Jon Favreau."
"Personally, just the stuff I have been able . . ." Evans, quoted in Weintraub, "Robert Downey Jr. and Chris Evans."
"When I actually did the Alan Rickman . . ." Hiddleston, interview by the author.
"[I was] literally jumping . . ." Ibid.
"this collaborative spirit . . ." Feige, interview by the author.
"Sorry, little buddy . . ." Whedon, quoted in Gould, "Story of a Five Year Old Avenger."
"Like, 'Tom, that was so awesome . . .'" Keen Ruffalo, quoted in Hiddleston, interview by the author.
"And then he would tell me . . ." Hiddleston, interview by the author.
"Not for a month . . ." Cole, interview by the author.
"He told me all he remembers . . ." Ibid.

35. Something Personal: *Much Ado About Nothing*

"I think he was mourning . . ." Denisof, interview by the author.
"[Within that,] we had to go up . . ." Kranz, interview by the author.
"I begged to play Helena . . ." Williams, interview by the author.
"I have always believed that Gertrude . . ." Ibid.
"I never heard back . . ." Smulders, interview by the author.
"I said to her, 'There's no way . . .'" Whedon, quoted in Buchanan, "Joss Whedon on How *Much Ado About Nothing* Made Him a Better Filmmaker."
"A production, let alone a movie . . ." Whedon, *Much Ado About Nothing*," 16.
"about a movie where half of the title . . ." Whedon, quoted in Buchanan, "Joss Whedon on How *Much Ado About Nothing* Made Him a Better Filmmaker."
"floored" by the absurd . . . Whedon, *Much Ado About Nothing*, 14.
"I was interested in a slightly darker . . ." Whedon, interview by the author.
"the process of maturing . . ." Ibid.
"the idea that love is for grown-ups . . ." Ibid.
"I deal with a lot of societal . . ." Ibid.
"To me, who Claudio is . . ." Whedon, *Much Ado About Nothing*, 14.
"The story there . . ." Ibid., 18.
"There was his humiliation . . ." Ibid., 19.
"I talked to them before . . ." Whedon, interview by the author.
"eight pages a day . . ." Whedon, quoted in Buchanan, "Joss Whedon on How *Much Ado About Nothing* Made Him a Better Filmmaker."
"There were a lot of people . . ." Whedon, interview by the author.
"Just like that . . ." Kranz, interview by the author.
"'I'd love to see him as . . .'" Whedon, quoted in ibid.
"I literally wrote back . . ." Kranz, interview by the author.
"When we showed up . . ." Acker, quoted in Germain, "'Much Ado About Nothing."
"The readings afforded anyone . . ." Denisof, interview by the author.
"I got another call . . ." Gregg, interview by the author.
"I was tense . . ." Fillion, interview by the author.
"I walked on . . ." Gregg, interview by the author.

"I had a feeling . . ." Whedon, interview by the author.

"Of course" . . . Hunter, interview by the author.

"We have pictures . . ." Cole, interview by the author.

"Kai knew better . . ." Whedon, quoted in Buchanan, "Joss Whedon on How *Much Ado About Nothing* Made Him a Better Filmmaker."

an "eclectic, artistic space" . . . Whedon, *Much Ado About Nothing*, 16.

"At the last minute we had no place . . ." Espenson, interview by the author.

"We wanted to encourage people . . ." Whedon, *Much Ado About Nothing*, 15.

"It's almost like Kai . . ." Hunter, interview by the author.

"It was also a great way . . ." Cole, quoted in Cadenas, "Interview with Kai Cole."

"We struggled with that . . ." Whedon, interview by the author.

"If we had been shooting this . . ." Hunter, interview by the author.

"yelling at his daughter . . ." Whedon, *Much Ado About Nothing*, 26.

"This is how I want . . ." Whedon, quoted in Hunter, interview by the author.

"backlit, golden sunlight . . ." Hunter, interview by the author.

"Apart from a basic understanding . . ." Whedon, *Much Ado About Nothing*, 23.

" 'I was worried I wouldn't . . ." Whedon, quoted in Boerner, "Warrior Princess."

"Hey, guys! . . ." Fillion, Twitter post, October 24, 2011.

"Filmed in just 12 days . . ." Bellwether Pictures, *Much Ado About Nothing* press release.

"Making The Avengers was very important . . ." Whedon, quoted in Yamato, "Joss Whedon Q&A."

"When I came back . . ." Ibid.

36. The Year of Joss Whedon

"This was a movie that came in . . ." Feige, interview by the author.

"Usually, by the time . . ." Goddard, interview by the author.

"by turning splatter formula . . ." Travers, review of *The Cabin in the Woods*.

"almost as a puzzle . . ." Ebert, review of *The Cabin in the Woods*.

"a hollow exercise . . ." Rooney, review of *The Cabin in the Woods*.

one big "inside joke" . . . Sharkey, " 'The Cabin in the Woods' Is Joss Whedon's Inside Joke."

"It's the nature of it" . . . Goddard, interview by the author.

"I have kids running up . . ." Ruffalo, interview by the author.

"She doesn't live . . ." Whedon, quoted in Warner, " 'Avengers' Director Joss Whedon."

"Toymakers will tell you . . ." Whedon, quoted in Stern, "Joss Whedon's Passion Project."

"It's frustrating to me . . ." Ibid.

"People have told me . . ." Whedon, Whedonesque post, May 9, 2012.

"What doesn't change . . ." Ibid.

earning more than $1 billion . . . Downey, " 'The Avengers' Rules at Box Office."

"I'm very torn" . . . Whedon, quoted in Clark, " 'Avengers': Joss Whedon Talks Sequel."

"I'm so in love . . ." Whedon, quoted in Ramos, "Why You Need a Creative Shift."

"I don't know how . . ." Cole, interview by the author.

"I'm standing there" . . . Goddard, interview by the author.

"OK, well . . ." Whedon, quoted in Goddard, interview by the author.

"I feel like that summarizes . . ." Goddard, interview by the author.

"A good opportunity . . ." Whedon, quoted in Poniewozik, "Joss Whedon Talks SHIELD."

"He's an enthusiast" . . . Ibid.

"Well, what does S.H.I.E.L.D have . . ." Whedon, quoted in Wigler "Joss Whedon Says 'S.H.I.E.L.D.' TV Series Will Star 'New Characters.' "

"We all love Clark Gregg . . ." Whedon, *Agents of S.H.I.E.L.D.* announcement.

"You make a strong man cry". . . Whedon, quoted in Ramos, "Why You Need a Creative
    Shift."
"We didn't think . . ." Cole, interview by the author.

37. The Year of Joss Whedon, Again (Really)

"seems very Whedonverse . . ." Gregg in Vary, "Life Inside the Whedonverse."
"I knew people wanted to go . . ." Whedon, quoted in ibid.
"I can't believe Joss . . ." Lenk, quoted in ibid.
"I did have a moment of just . . ." Whedon, quoted in Vary, "Joss Whedon on Kickstarter."
"He came for our breakfast . . ." Basinger, interview by the author.
"If you think that happiness . . ." Whedon, 181st Wesleyan commencement speech.
"all the dialogue and the language . . ." Kermode, *Much Ado About Nothing* review.
"the first great contemporary Shakespeare . . ." Shoard, *Much Ado About Nothing* review.
"OK, Marvel fan boys . . ." Alexander, "Shakespeare Would Approve of This 'Much
    Ado.'"
such beliefs were "not a natural state" . . . Whedon, Equality Now address, November
    6, 2013.
"I think about the old days . . ." Basinger, interview by the author.

// BIBLIOGRAPHY //

Books

Abbot, Stacey, ed. *Reading Angel: The TV Spin-Off with a Soul*. London: I. B. Tauris, 2005.

Adams, Michael. *Slayer Slang: A Buffy the Vampire Slayer Lexicon*. Oxford: Oxford University Press, 2003.

Castlemon, Harry, and Walter J. Podrazik. *Watching TV: Six Decades of American Television*. Syracuse, NY: Syracuse University Press, 2010.

Daniels, Susanne. *Season Finale: The Unexpected Rise and Fall of the WB and UPN*. New York: Harper, 2007.

Davis, Michael. *Street Gang: The Complete History of Sesame Street*. New York: Penguin, 2008.

Early, Frances, and Kathleen Kennedy. *Athena's Daughters: Television's New Women Warriors*. Syracuse, NY: Syracuse University Press, 2003.

Espenson, Jane, ed. *Finding Serenity: Anti-heroes, Lost Shepherds and Space Hookers in Joss Whedon's Firefly*. Dallas: Smart Pop, 2005.

———. *Inside Joss' Dollhouse: From Alpha to Rossum*. Smart Pop, 2010.

Havens, Candace. *Joss Whedon: The Genius Behind Buffy*. Dallas, TX: BenBella Books, 2003.

Holder, Nancy. *Buffy: The Making of a Slayer*. 47North, 2012.

Kaveney, Roz. *Reading the Vampire Slayer: The Complete, Unofficial Guide to 'Buffy' and 'Angel.'* London: Tauris Parke, 2004.

Leonard, Kendra Preston, ed. *Buffy, Ballads, and Bad Guys Who Sing: Music in the Worlds of Joss Whedon*. Lanham, MD: Scarecrow Press, 2010.

Levine, Elana, and Lisa Parks, eds. *Undead TV: Essays on Buffy the Vampire Slayer*. Durham, NC: Duke University Press, 2007.

Longworth, James, Jr. "Joss Whedon, Feminist." In *TV Creators: Conversations with America's Top Producers of Television Drama*. Vol. 2. Syracuse University Press, 2002.

Lotz, Amanda D. *Redesigning Women: Television After the Network Era*. Urbana, IL: University of Illinois Press, 2006.

McCloud, Scott. *Understanding Comics: The Invisible Art*. New York: William Morrow, 1994.

PopMatters. *Joss Whedon: The Complete Companion; The TV Series, the Movies, the Comic Books and More—The Essential Guide to the Whedonverse*. London: Titan Books, 2012.

Price, David A. *The Pixar Touch*. New York: Knopf, 2008.

Sepinwall, Alan. *The Revolution Was Televised: The Cops, Crooks, Slingers and Slayers Who Changed TV Drama Forever*. New York: Touchstone, 2013.

Stafford, Nikki. *Bite Me!: Sarah Michelle Gellar and Buffy the Vampire Slayer*. Toronto: ECW Press, 1998.

Stevenson, Gregory. *Televised Morality: The Case of Buffy the Vampire Slayer*. Lanham, MD: Hamilton Books, 2004.

Stuller, Jennifer K. *Ink-Stained Amazons and Cinematic Warriors: Superwomen in Modern Mythology*. London: I. B. Tauris, 2010.

Tracy, Kathleen. *The Girl's Got Bite: The Original Unauthorized Guide to Buffy's World*. Completely rev. and updated ed. New York: St. Martin's Griffin, 2003.

Whedon, Joss. *Dr Horrible's Sing-Along Blog Book*. London: Titan Books, 2011.

———. *Firefly: A Celebration*. Deluxe anniversary ed. London: Titan Books, 2012.

———. *Firefly: The Official Visual Companion*. Vol. 1. London: Titan Books, 2006.

———. *Much Ado About Nothing: A Film By Joss Whedon*. London: Titan Books, 2013.

———. *Serenity: The Official Visual Companion*. London: Titan Books, 2005.

Whedon, Joss, and John Cassady. *Astonishing X-Men Ultimate Collection*. Vol. 1. New York: Marvel, 2012.

Whedon, Joss, and Drew Goddard. *The Cabin in the Woods: The Official Visual Companion*. London: Titan Books, 2012.

Whedon, Joss, Karl Moline, and Andy Owens. *Fray*. Milwaukie, OR: Dark Horse, 2003.

Whedon, Joss, and Michael Ryan. *Runaways, Vol. 8: Dead End Kids*. New York: Marvel, 2008.

Whedon, Zack, Joss Whedon, and Chris Samnee. *Serenity: The Shepherd's Tale*. Milwaukie, OR: Dark Horse, 2010.

Wilcox, Rhonda V. *Why Buffy Matters: The Art of Buffy the Vampire Slayer*. London: I. B. Tauris, 2005.

Wilcox, Rhonda V., and Tanya R. Cochran, eds. *Investigating Firefly and Serenity: Science Fiction on the Frontier*. London: I. B. Tauris, 2008.

Wilcox, Rhonda V., and David Lavery, eds. *Fighting the Forces: What's at Stake in Buffy the Vampire Slayer*. Lanham, MD: Rowman & Littlefield, 2002.

Yeffeth, Glenn, ed. *Five Seasons of Angel: Science Fiction and Fantasy Authors Discuss Their Favorite Vampire*. Dallas: Smart Pop, 2004.

———. *Seven Seasons of Buffy: Science Fiction and Fantasy Authors Discuss Their Favorite Television Show*. Dallas: Smart Pop, 2003.

Articles

Adalian, Josef. "'Angel' Writer Gets Fox Wings." *Variety*, August 1, 2001.

———. "Frog Net's Drama 'Angel' Folds Wings." *Variety*, February 16, 2004.

———. "Whedon Widens Mutant's Reach." *Variety*, March 31, 2006.

Adams, Sam. "Alan Tudyk" (interview). *AV Club*, September 30, 2011. www.avclub.com/articles/alan-tudyk,62557/.

AFP. "Hollywood Writers Go on Strike over New-Media Pay." November 5, 2007.

Alameda Times-Star. "One Last Stake in Heart as 'Angel' Bites It." May 19, 2004.

Alexander, Al. "Shakespeare Would Approve of This 'Much Ado.'" *Patriot Ledger*, June 21, 2013. www.patriotledger.com/entertainment/movies/x1213260930/MOVIE-REVIEW-Shakespeare-would-approve-of-this-Much-Ado.

Alt, Eric. "Exclusive: 'Dollhouse' Creator Joss Whedon." Maxim.com, February 12, 2009. Archived at Wayback Machine, https://web.archive.org/web/20090315100340/http://www.maxim.com/joss-whedon-q-and-a/Guy-TV/blogs/4309/48713.aspx.

Armstrong, Mark. "Vampire Smackdown: Buffy to UPN." E! Online, April 20, 2001. www.eonline.com/news/41495/vampire-smackdown-buffy-to-upn.

Ausiello, Michael. "Angel Mystery: Will Cordy Wake Up?" *TV Guide Online*, May 27, 2003. https://web.archive.org/web/20030622090757/http://www.tvguide.com/newsgossip/insider/030527b.asp.

Bailey, Jason. "12 Things We Learned from Joss Whedon's SXSW Talk." *Flavorwire*, March 10, 2012. www.flavorwire.com/268267/12-things-we-learned-from-joss -whedons-sxsw-talk.

Baldwin, Drew. "The Web Has Been Wonderful for 'Horrible.'" Tubefilter, July 14, 2008. www.tubefilter.com/2008/07/14/joss-whedon-interview-the-web-has-been -wonderful-for-horrible-2/.

BBC. "How Charisma Nearly Missed the Buffy Audition." www.bbc.co.uk/cult/buffy /angel/interviews/carpenter/page5.shtml.

———. "Kung Fu Faith." April 14, 2003. Archived at Wayback Machine, http:// web.archive.org/web/20030611190643/http://www.bbc.co.uk/cult/news /buffy/2003/04/14/3812.shtml.

Beaks. "Louis Leterrier Officially in the Running to Assemble THE AVENGERS!" *Ain't It Cool News*, March 20, 2010. www.aintitcool.com/node/44352.

Bellwether Pictures. *Much Ado About Nothing* press release, October 24, 2011. Archived at Wayback Machine, https://web.archive.org/web/20111026221318/http://www .muchadothemovie.com/documents/MuchAdoPressRelease.pdf.

Bendis, Brian. "Brian Bendis Presents . . ." *Wizard*, June 12, 2006. Archived at Way-back Machine, https://web.archive.org/web/20060715080845/http://www.wizard universe.com/magazine/wizard/000495675.cfm.

Benedictus, Luke. "The Ladies' Man." *Age*, September 25, 2005.

Bianco, Robert. Critic's Corner. *USA Today*, December 14, 1999.

Bianculli, David. TV Tonight. *New York Daily News*, March 21, 2000. www.nydaily news.com/archives/entertainment/tv-tonight-article-1.861429.

Bierly, Mandi. "Exclusive: Joss Whedon on 'Dollhouse'—'Back with Such a Vengeance.'" *Entertainment Weekly*, June 12, 2009. http://popwatch.ew.com/2009/06/12 /joss-whedon-buffy-dollhouse-1/.

———. "'Justified' EP Graham Yost" *Entertainment Weekly* October 23, 2012.

Boerner, Heather. "Warrior Princess." Lupus Foundation of America official website, March 1, 2012. www.lupus.org/magazine/entry/warrior-princess.

Boucher, Geoff. "'Buffy the Vampire Slayer' Movie Looking for New Writer." *Los Angeles Times*, December 22, 2011. http://herocomplex.latimes.com/movies /buffy-the-vampire-slayer-movie-looking-for-new-writer/.

———."Joss Who? Meet the Writer of the New 'Buffy the Vampire Slayer' Film." *Los Angeles Times*, November 22, 2010. http://herocomplex.latimes.com/movies /joss-who-meet-the-writer-of-the-new-buffy-the-vampire-slayer-film/.

Bricker, Tierney, and Drusilla Moorhouse. "*Buffy the Vampire Slayer* Star Calls Movie Reboot a 'Hideous Idea'" E! Online, August 2, 2011. www.eonline.com /news/255585/buffy-the-vampire-slayer-star-calls-movie-reboot-a-hideous-idea.

Bridges, Chris. "Joss Whedon on 'Dr. Horrible.'" *Daytona Beach News-Journal*, July 14, 2008.

———. "SerenityStuff Welcomes Jane Espenson." SerenityStuff blog, October 24, 2007. http://cabridges.com/2007/10/24/serenitystuff-welcomes-jane-espenson/.

Brodie, John. "Suspension Toll: $1 Mil from Largo." *Variety*, June 23, 1993.

Buchanan, Kyle. "Joss Whedon on How *Much Ado About Nothing* Made Him a Bet-ter Filmmaker." *Vulture*, September 15, 2012. www.vulture.com/2012/09/joss -whedon-much-ado-about-nothing-film.html.

Cadenas, Kerensa. "Interview with Kai Cole—Producer of Much Ado About Noth-ing" IndieWire, June 21, 2013. http://blogs.indiewire.com/womenandhollywood /interview-with-kai-cole-producer-of-much-ado-about-nothing.

Cairns, Bryan. "An Animated Guy." *Cult Times Special* 27 (September 2003).

Carroll, Larry. "Joss Whedon Vows He Won't Do Anything Silly with Wonder Woman." MTV.com, March 22, 2005. www.mtv.com/news/articles/1498869 /joss-whedon-gives-his-take-on-wonder-woman.jhtml.

CBS News. "'Avengers' Director Joss Whedon: Yes, He's a Geek." April 29, 2012. www.cbsnews.com/8301-3445_162-57423797/avengers-director-joss-whedon -yes-hes-a-geek/.

Ciepley, Michael, and Brooks Barnes. "Writers Say Strike to Start Monday." *New York Times*, November 2, 2007.

Clark, Noelene. "'Avengers': Joss Whedon Talks Sequel, 'Buffy' and 'X-Men' Parallels." *Los Angeles Times*, May 15, 2012. http://herocomplex.latimes.com/movies /avengers-joss-whedon-talks-sequel-buffy-and-x-men-parallels/.

Colis, Clark. "'The Cabin in the Woods': How Joss Whedon and Drew Goddard's 'Insane Frolic' Became the Year's Most Buzzed-About Fright Flick" *Entertainment Weekly*, April 12, 2012. http://insidemovies.ew.com/2012/04/12/the -cabin-in-the-woods-joss-whedon/.

Diamond, Jamie. "'Buffy the Vampire Slayer': How It Came to Be." *Entertainment Weekly*, August 14, 1992.

Dos Santos, Kristen. "Joss Whedon Reacts to *Buffy* Movie News." E! Online, November 22, 2010. www.eonline.com/news/212644/joss-whedon-reacts -to-buffy-movie-news-i-have-strong-mixed-emotions.

Douglas, Edward. "Exclusive: Joel Silver on Wonder Woman." ComingSoon .net, July 22, 2006. Archived at Wayback Machine, https://web.archive.org /web/20081209053504/http://www.superherohype.com/news/featuresnews .php?id=4543.

Doux, Bonnie. "High Stakes 2004: Whedon Fans for Kerry." Doux Reviews, October 2004. www.douxreviews.com/2004/11/high-stakes-2004-whedon-fans-for-kerry .html.

Downey, Ryan J. "'The Avengers' Rules at Box Office, Joins $1 Billion Club." MTV .com, May 14, 2012. www.mtv.com/news/articles/1685006/avengers-box-office -billion-dollars.jhtml.

Dr. Horrible official fan site. "Jed Whedon & Maurissa Tancharoen." July 19, 2008. http://doctorhorrible.net/exclusive-jed-whedon-maurissa-tancharoen/151/.

———. "Producer, Michael Boretz." October 18, 2008. http://doctorhorrible.net /exclusive-interview-producer-michael-boretz/438/.

Ebert, Roger. Review of *The Cabin in the Woods*. *Chicago Sun-Times*, April 11, 2012. www.rogerebert.com/reviews/the-cabin-in-the-woods-2012.

———. Review of *Speed*. *Chicago Sun-Times*, June 10, 1994.

Edwards, Gavin. "Whedon, Ink." *New York*, June 7, 2004. www.nymag.com/nymetro /arts/9218/.

Entertainment Weekly. "Buffy Breaks Out." June 18, 1999. www.ew.com/ew/article /0,,273808,00.html.

———. "'Toy Story': The Inside Buzz." December 8, 1995, www.ew.com/ew/article /0,,299897,00.html.

Everett, Todd. Review of *Profit*. *Variety*, April 8, 1996. http://variety.com/1996/film /reviews/profit-1200445655/.

Faraci, Devin. "Exclusive Interview: Joss Whedon—Part 2." CHUD.com, September 22, 2005. www.chud.com/4435/exclusive-interview-joss-whedon-part-2/.

Fernandez, Maria Elena. "Cult King in Orbit on Mars." *Los Angeles Times*, November 9, 2005. http://articles.latimes.com/2005/nov/09/entertainment/et-mars9.

———. "A Line in the Sand." *Los Angeles Times*, November 1, 2007. http://latimes blogs.latimes.com/showtracker/2007/11/their-entire-st.html.

———. "Q & A with Joss Whedon, Writer, Producer and Director." *Los Angeles Times*, May 15, 2008.

Fleming, Michael. "Whedon's a Goner for U." *Variety*, September 22, 2005. http:// variety.com/2005/film/news/whedon-s-a-goner-for-u-1117929558/.

———. "Whedon to Direct Marvel's 'The Avengers'" *Deadline Hollywood*, April 13, 2010. www.deadline.com/2010/04/marvel-close-to-whedon-hire-on-the-avengers/.

George, Richard. Review of *Astonishing X-Men* HC vol. 1. IGN.com, May 17, 2006. www.ign.com/articles/2006/05/17/astonishing-x-men-hc-vol-1-review.

Germain, David. " 'Much Ado About Nothing': Joss Whedon's Film Picked Up by Lions-gate" *Huffington Post*, September 11, 2012. www.huffingtonpost.com/2012/09/12 /much-ado-about-nothing-joss-whedon_n_1876682.html.

Giant. "The Man in the Light Gray Flannel Suit." September 5, 2007.

Gilbey, Ryan. "Joss Whedon: Hollywood's Golden Boy." *Guardian*, April 21, 2012.

Gleiberman, Owen. Review of *Toy Story*. *Entertainment Weekly*, November 23, 1995.

Goldman, Eric. "IGN Interview: Charisma Carpenter." IGN.com, August 31, 2006. www.ign.com/articles/2006/08/31/ign-interview-charisma-carpenter.

———. "Joss Whedon, Friends & Fans on the Picket Line." IGN.com December 10, 2007. www.ign.com/articles/2007/12/11/joss-whedon-friends-fans-on-the-picket-line.

———. "Joss Whedon: Inside Dollhouse." IGN.com, May 27, 2008. http://www.ign .com/articles/2008/05/27/joss-whedon-inside-dollhouse.

Gopalan, Nisha. "Whedon After 'Wonder'-land." *Entertainment Weekly*, August 2, 2007. www.ew.com/ew/article/0,,20399642_20049318,00.html.

Gould, Erin. "Story of a Five Year Old Avenger, Meeting the Avengers." g33kWatch, May 14, 2012. www.g33kwatch.com/movies/story-of-a-five-year-old-avenger-meeting-the -avengers/.

Gross, Edward. "Angel: Writer-Producer on directing 'Darla.'" Mania.com, November 13, 2000. www.mania.com/angel-writerproducer-tim-minear-directing-darla_article _25787.html.

Grossberg, Josh. "Gellar: I'm Gone if Buffy Leaves WB." E! Online, January 22, 2001. www.eonline.com/news/41051/gellar-i-m-gone-if-buffy-leaves-wb.

Harrington, Richard. "Unsung 'Buffy': Props for a Magical Musical Moment." *Washington Post*, July 2, 2002.

Harris, Will. "Joss for a Minute." Bullz-Eye.com, November 29, 2005. www.bullz-eye .com/mguide/interviews/2005/joss_whedon.htm.

Hernandez, Lee. "Exclusive: Charisma Carpenter on a Possible 'Buffy' Remake." Latina.com, July 25, 2011. www.latina.com/entertainment/tv/exclusive-charisma -carpenter-possible-buffy-remake-personally-i-think-it-stinks.

Hiatt, Brian. "No 'Angel.'" *Entertainment Weekly*, March 25, 2004. www.ew.com/ew /article/0,,604905,00.html.

Hibberd, James. "Joss Whedon: The Definitive EW Interview." *Entertainment Weekly*, August 30, 2013. http://insidetv.ew.com/2013/09/24/joss-whedon-interview/.

Hinman, Michael. "Buffy Season 8 Not Ruled Out." Airlock Alpha, June 20, 2002. www.airlockalpha.com/node/919/node/2375/helpless-pest-control-5-best-bug -horror-flicks.html.

Hinson, Hal. Review of *Speed*. *Washington Post*, June 10, 1994.

Hoevel, Ann. "Seth Green Talks 'Robot Chicken,' Lucas and 'Buffy.'" CNN.com, January 11, 2011. www.cnn.com/2011/SHOWBIZ/TV/01/07/robot.chicken/index .html.

Hollywood.com. "Joss Whedon Goes into 'Sugar Shock.'" August 6, 2007. www.hollywood .com/static/comic-con-07s-fantatsic-filmmakers-joss-whedon-goes-into-sugar -shock.

Hontz, Jenny. "Bloody 'Buffy' Spectre Eyed by Studios, Webs." *Variety*, January 13, 1999.

Hontz, Jenny, and Chris Petrikin. "Whedon, Fox Vamping." *Variety*, June 5, 1998. http://variety.com/1998/film/news/whedon-fox-vamping-1117471584/.

Hyland, Rachel. "The Bronze Age." *11th Hour*, July/August 2000. Archived at Wayback Machine, https://web.archive.org/web/20070712150602/http://www.the11thhour.com/archives/072000/features/bronzeage2.html.

Jacobs, A. J. "Interview with a Vampire Chronicler." *Entertainment Weekly*, April 25, 1997. www.ew.com/ew/article/0,,287570,00.html.

JenKatz. "Bootlegging Buffy." *Slashdot*, June 7, 1999. http://news.slashdot.org/story/99/06/07/2217210/bootlegging-buffy.

Jensen, Jeff. "'Avengers': New Hulk Mark Ruffalo on Replacing Edward Norton, plus Oscar Buzz for 'The Kids Are All Right.'" *Entertainment Weekly*, July 29, 2010. http://popwatch.ew.com/2010/07/29/avengers-new-hulk-mark-ruffalo/.

———. "Buffy's Back." *Entertainment Weekly*, January 4, 2007. www.ew.com/ew/article/0,,1562057,00.html.

———. "The Goodbye Girl." *Entertainment Weekly*, March 3, 2003. www.ew.com/ew/article/0,,422783,00.html.

———. "To Hell & Back." *Entertainment Weekly*, September 7, 2001. www.ew.com/ew/article/0,,254961,00.html.

———. "The X Factor." *Entertainment Weekly*, May 21, 2004.

John, Emma. "Joss Whedon: 'I Kept Telling My Mum Reading Comics Would Pay Off.'" *Observer*, June 1, 2013. www.theguardian.com/culture/2013/jun/02/joss-whedon-reading-comics-pay-off.

Johnson, Kevin V. "Fans Sink Teeth into Bootlegged 'Buffy.'" *USA Today*, June 3, 1999.

Jolin, Dan. "Alien 3: The Lost Tale of the Wooden Planet." *Empire*. www.empireonline.com/features/alien-3-tale-of-the-wooden-planet/5.asp.

Jozic, Mike. "David Fury Interview." MikeJozic.com, December 10, 2005. Archived at Wayback Machine, http://web.archive.org/web/20051211085159/http://www.mikejozic.com/buffyweek6.html.

Kaplan, James. "Last in Space." *Entertainment Weekly*, May 29, 1992.

Kappala-Ramsamy, Gemma. "Joss Whedon: The Film That Changed My Life." *Guardian*, April 14, 2012.

Keegan, Rebecca. "'Much Ado About Nothing': A DIY Film Project at Joss Whedon's Home." *Los Angeles Times*, May 31, 2013.

Ken P. "An Interview with Joss Whedon." IGN, June 23, 2003. www.ign.com/articles/2003/06/23/an-interview-with-joss-whedon.

Klaus, Barbara. "The War of the Roseanne." *New York*, October 22, 1990.

Knowledge@Wharton. "Joss Whedon's Plan to Monetize Internet Content (Watch Out, Hollywood)." February 4, 2009. http://knowledge.wharton.upenn.edu/article.cfm?articleid=2152.

Kozac, Jim. "Serenity NOW!" *In Focus*, August 2005.

Langguth, Arthur J. "Great to Be Back!" *Harvard Crimson*, April 22, 1955. www.thecrimson.com/article/1955/4/15/great-to-be-back-pit-was/.

Legel, Laremy. "COMIC CON: Exclusive Interview with Joss Whedon." Rope of Silicon, August 3, 2007. www.ropeofsilicon.com/comic_con_exclusive_interview_with_joss_whedon.

Leitch, Will. "The Perfect Comic-Book Movie. *The Avengers*, Reviewed." *Deadspin*, May 4, 2004. http://deadspin.com/5907618/the-perfect-comic+book-movie-the-avengers-reviewed.

Lussier, Germain. "Robert Downey Jr. and Jon Favreau Talk 'Iron Man 3' Difficulties, Plus 'The Avengers.'" /Film, June 12, 2011. www.slashfilm.com/robert-downey-jr-jon-favreau-talk-iron-man-3-difficulties-the-avengers/.

Malcom, Shawna. "Boreanaz Bids Angel Adieu." TV Guide Online, May 12, 2004. www.tvguide.com/news/boreanaz-angel-buffy-36927.aspx.

Maslin, Janet. Review of Toy Story. New York Times, November 22, 1995. www.nytimes.com/movie/review?res=9905EEDA1339F931A15752C1A963958260.

McCabe, Kathy. "Buffy Hits a High Note," Sunday Mail (Queensland, Australia), April 14, 2002.

McLeod, Elizabeth. "The Great Gildersleeve: Character Counts." RadioSpirits.com. www.radiospirits.com/email/gildersleeve_article0811.asp.

McManus, Kevin. "Toy Story: A Treasure." Washington Post, November 24, 1995. www.washingtonpost.com/wp-srv/style/longterm/movies/videos/toystory.htm.

Miller, Karryn. "From Box Office Hit to Serenity of Temples." Japan Times, March 21, 2009.

Miller, Laura. "The Man Behind the Slayer." Salon, May 20, 2003. www.salon.com/2003/05/20/whedon/.

MTV.com. "'I Am Number Four' Writer Marti Nixon Talks 'Buffy' and 'Fright Night' Reboots." February 18. 2011. http://moviesblog.mtv.com/2011/02/18/i-am-number-four-buffy-fright-night/.

Murray, Noel. Review of Buffy the Vampire Slayer, "Hush." AV Club, August 14, 2009. www.avclub.com/articles/hush-etc,31725/.

New York Times. "10 Questions for Joss Whedon." May 16, 2003. www.nytimes.com/2003/05/16/readersopinions/16WHED.html.

Newsarama. "Bryan Hitch & Joss Whedon—One-On-One," pt. 2. May 21, 2007. Archived at Wayback Machine, https://web.archive.org/web/20070523094129/http://www.newsarama.com/marvelnew/Ultimate/hitch_whedon_2.html.

Norton, Al. "411mania Interviews: James Marsters (Buffy the Vampire Slayer, Angel)." 411mania.com, March 10, 2012. www.411mania.com/movies/columns/228484/411mania-Interviews:-James-Marsters-(Buffy-the-Vampire-Slayer,-Angel).htm.

Nussbaum, Emily. "A DVD Face-Off: The Official vs. the Homemade." New York Times, December 21, 2003.

———. "The Fascinating No-Consent Fantasia of Dollhouse and Mad Men." New York, October 22, 2009. http://nymag.com/daily/tv/2009/10/a_weird_meditation_on_dollhous.html.

———. "Must-See Metaphysics." New York Times Magazine, September 22, 2002. www.nytimes.com/2002/09/22/magazine/must-see-metaphysics.html.

O'Hara, Helen. "His Whedonness Talks Serenity." Empire, March 2006. www.empireonline.com/interviews/interview.asp?IID=459.

O'Hare, Kate. "The 'Bus Guy' Triumphs on 'Boomtown.'" Zap2It, May 24, 2003. Archived at Whedon.info, www.whedon.info/The-Bus-Guy-Triumphs-in-Boomtown.html.

———. "End of 'Buffy' Only Makes Gellar Stronger." Zap2It, April 17, 2003. Archived at Buffy-Boards, www.buffy-boards.com/archive/index.php/t-4882.html.

Owen, Rob. "Is Buffy Dead?" Pittsburgh Post-Gazette, May 24, 2001. http://old.post-gazette.com/tv/20010524owen5.asp.

Partney, Matt. "The Puppet Summit." Angel (Titan Magazines), 2004 yearbook.

Perenson, Melissa J., "Leather on Willow." Cult Times, April 1999.

Phillips, Jevon. "'Avengers' Talk, Comic Book Signings: It's Whedon Weekend (Actually, When Is It Not?)." Los Angeles Times, April 3, 2010. http://herocomplex.latimes.com/2010/04/03/its-whedon-weekend-actually-when-is-it-not/.

Pond, Steve. "Sarah Michelle Gellar's New World Order." *Premiere Magazine*, October 2000. Archived at Wayback Machine, http://web.archive.org/web/20010617052753 /http://www.premiere.com/Premiere/Features/1000/buffy1.html.

Poniewozik, James. "Joss Whedon Talks SHIELD, Superheroes, and Secrets." Time .com, September 12, 2013. http://entertainment.time.com/2013/09/12/joss -whedon-talks-shield-superheroes-and-secrets-i-guess-im-just-not-very-good-at -reality/.

Pruitt, Jeff. Interview in the Hellmouth, June 21, 2000. Archived at Wayback Machine, http://web.archive.org/web/20010218021556/http://www.thehellmouth.fsnet .co.uk/Features/jeff_sophia.htm.

Radish, Christina. "Jeremy Renner, Tom Hiddleston, Clark Gregg, Cobie Smulders and Joss Whedon Talk THE AVENGERS." Collider.com, April 26, 2012. http:// collider.com/joss-whedon-the-avengers-cast-interview/.

Ramos, Steve. "Why You Need a Creative Shift Instead of a Vacation, as Explained by Joss Whedon." *Fast Company*, September 18, 2012. www.fastcocreate.com/1681608 /why-you-need-a-creative-shift-instead-of-a-vacation-as-explained-by-joss-whedon.

Reid, Calvin. "X-Men Writer Chris Claremont Donates Archive to Columbia University." PublishersWeekly.com, November 14, 2011. www.publishersweekly.com /pw/by-topic/industry-news/comics/article/49499-x-men-writer-chris-claremont -donates-archive-to-columbia-university.html.

Rice, Lynette. "Slayer It Ain't So." *Entertainment Weekly*, March 21, 2001. www.ew.com /ew/article/0,,92414,00.html.

Ridley, John. "Three Writers Are Drawn by the Allure of Comics." *NPR Morning Edition*, March 25, 2008. www.npr.org/templates/transcript/transcript .php?storyId=87867518.

Robinson, Tasha. "Joss Whedon" (interview). *AV Club*, September 5, 2001. www .avclub.com/article/joss-whedon-13730.

———. "Joss Whedon" (interview). *AV Club*, August 8, 2007. www.avclub.com /article/joss-whedon-14136.

———. "Joss Whedon—Web Exclusive" (interview). *AV Club*, September 5, 2001. www.avclub.com/article/joss-whedon-web-exclusive-13729.

Rogers, Adam. "With The Avengers, Joss Whedon Masters the Marvel Universe." *Wired*, April 30, 2012. www.wired.com/underwire/2012/04/ff_whedon/all/1.

Rooney, David. Review of *The Cabin in the Woods*. *Hollywood Reporter*, March 9, 2012. www.hollywoodreporter.com/movie/cabin-woods/review/298129.

Rosen, Lisa. "Family Tradition." *Written By*, May 2007.

———. "New Media Guru." *Written By*, January 2009

Russell, Mike. "The CulturePulp Q&A: Joss Whedon." *CulturePulp* blog, September 24, 2005. Archived at Wayback Machine, http://web.archive.org/web/20051001005104 /http://homepage.mac.com/merussell/iblog/B835531044/C1592678312/E200 50916182427/index.html.

Said, S.F. "Interview with Joss Whedon." Shebytches.com, May 24, 2006. http://web .archive.org/web/20100512141258/http://www.shebytches.com/SFSaidgb.html.

Schechner, Sam. "This Writers' Strike Feels Like a Rerun from 1988." *Wall Street Journal*. November 12, 2007. http://online.wsj.com/news/articles /SB119482950368089597.

Schiff, Len. "Joss Whedon: Absolute Admiration for Sondheim." *Sondheim Review*, Summer 2005. www.sondheimreview.com/v11n4.htm#sample.

Schilling, Mary Kaye. "Vamping it Up." *Entertainment Weekly*, November 9, 2001. www.ew.com/ew/article/0,,253579,00.html.

Schneider, Michael. "'Dollhouse,' 'Hank' Get the Ax." *Variety*, November 11, 2009. http://variety.com/2009/tv/news/dollhouse-hank-get-the-ax-1118011179/.

————. "Joss Whedon Preps Fox Series." *Variety*, October 31, 2007. http://variety
.com/2007/scene/news/joss-whedon-preps-fox-series-1117975136/.

————. "Joss Whedon Wants Out of TV." Yahoo.com, October 25, 2004. Archived at
Whedon.info, www.whedon.info/Joss-Whedon-wants-out-of-TV.html.

Schneider, Michael, and Josef Adalian. "Buffy a Toughie for WB." *Variety*, January 8,
2001. http://variety.com/2001/tv/news/buffy-a-toughie-for-wb-1117791443/.

————. "WB Bans 'Buffy' Adieu." *Variety*, May 2, 2001. http://variety.com/2001/tv
/news/wb-bans-buffy-adieu-1117798447/.

Sci Fi Wire. News of the Week, November 25, 2002. Archived at Wayback Machine,
https://web.archive.org/web/20030207184704/http://www.scifi.com/sfw
/issue292/news.html.

————. "WB Wants Angel Movie," July 15, 2004. Archived at Wayback Machine,
http://web.archive.org/web/20041208060321/http://www.scifi.com/scifiwire/art
-tv.html?2004-07/15/12.10.tv.

Sciretta, Peter. "/Film Set Interview: 'The Avengers' Writer/Director Joss Whedon"
/Film, April 2, 2012. www.slashfilm.com/film-set-interview-the-avengers-writer
director-joss-whedon/.

Seijas, Casey. "Joss Whedon Talks About His 'Batman' Movie That Never Was."
MTV.com, August 11, 2008. http://splashpage.mtv.com/2008/08/11/joss-whedon
-talks-about-his-batman-movie-that-never-was/.

Sharkey, Betsy. "'The Cabin in the Woods' Is Joss Whedon's Inside Joke." *Los Angeles Times*, April 13, 2012. http://articles.latimes.com/2012/apr/13/entertainment
/la-et-cabin-in-the-woods-20120413.

Shoard, Catherine. *Much Ado About Nothing* review *Guardian*, September 13, 2012.
www.theguardian.com/film/2012/sep/13/much-ado-about-nothing-review.

Snierson, Dan. "Joss Whedon Taps Eliza Dushku for New Fox Series." *Entertainment
Weekly*, November 1, 2007. http://insidetv.ew.com/2007/11/01/whedon-returns/.

Soloway, Jill. "Remove the Rating for Captivity." *Huffington Post*, March 27, 2007.
www.huffingtonpost.com/jill-soloway/remove-the-rating-for-cap_b_44404.html.

Springer, Matt. "High School Hell." *Buffy the Vampire Slayer Official Magazine*,
December 1999.

Stern, Marlow. "Joss Whedon's Passion Project." *Newsweek*, June 5, 2012. http://mag
.newsweek.com/2013/06/05/joss-whedon-on-shakespeare-female-superheroes
-and-feminism.html.

Tavi. "Yay, Geometry: An Interview with Joss Whedon." *Rookie*, November 7, 2011.
www.rookiemag.com/2011/11/yay-geometry-an-interview-with-joss-whedon/.

theTVaddict.com. "Exclusive: Joss Whedon Talks DOLLHOUSE and His Love
Affair with BATTLESTAR GALACTICA." July 16, 2008. www.thetvaddict
.com/2008/07/16/exclusive-joss-whedon-talks-dollhouse-and-his-love-affair-with
-battlestar-galactica/.

Tran, An. "Avengers Assemble." ARRI Group official website, April 26, 2012. www
.arri.com/camera/alexa/news/avengers-assemble/.

Travers, Peter. Review of *The Cabin in the Woods*. *Rolling Stone*, April 12, 2012. www
.rollingstone.com/movies/reviews/the-cabin-in-the-woods-20120412.

Utichi, Joe. "A Buffy-Style Kicking for Torture Porn." *Sunday Times*, April 15, 2012.
www.thesundaytimes.co.uk/sto/culture/film_and_tv/film/article1014088.ece.

Vary, Adam B. "'Dr. Horrible's Sing-Along Blog': An Oral History." *Entertainment
Weekly*, July 25, 2008. www.ew.com/ew/article/0,,20214910,00.html.

————."Joss Whedon on Kickstarter and 'Firefly.'" *BuzzFeed*, March 14, 2013. www
.buzzfeed.com/adambvary/joss-whedon-on-kickstarter-and-firefly.

————. "Life Inside the Whedonverse." *BuzzFeed*, June 5, 2013. www.buzzfeed.com
/adambvary/what-its-like-to-live-in-the-whedonverse.

Vineyard, Jennifer. "'Buffy the Vampire Slayer' Sing-Alongs Killed . . . but Can They Be Resurrected?" MTV.com, October 15, 2007. www.mtv.com/news/articles /1571966/buffy-vampire-slayer-sing-alongs-get-killed.jhtml.

———. "Joss Whedon's Hollywood Status Update: Horror Fantasy 'Goners,' 'Cabin in the Woods' and More" MTV.com, July 7, 2008. http://moviesblog.mtv .com/2008/07/07/joss-whedons-hollywood-status-update-horror-fantasy-goners -cabin-in-the-woods-and-more/.

Warner, Kara. "'Avengers' Director Joss Whedon Loves the 'Duplicitous' Black Widow." MTV.com, April 16, 2012. www.mtv.com/news/articles/1683208/avengers-scarlett -johansson-black-widow.jhtml.

Warner Bros. Pictures. "Silver Pictures and Warner Bros. Pictures Sign Joss Whedon to Write & Direct DC Comics' Wonder Woman" Press release, March 17, 2005. www .timewarner.com/newsroom/press-releases/2005/03/17/silver-pictures-and-warner -bros-pictures-sign-joss-whedon-to.

Weintraub, Steve. "Director Joss Whedon THE AVENGERS Set Visit Interview." Collider.com, April 2, 2012. http://collider.com/joss-whedon-the-avengers-interview/.

———. "Robert Downey Jr. and Chris Evans THE AVENGERS Set Visit Interview." Collider.com, April 5, 2012. http://collider.com/the-avengers-robert-downey -jr-chris-evans-interview/.

———. "35 Things to Know About THE AVENGERS from Our Set Visit." Collider. com, April 4, 2012. http://collider.com/the-avengers-set-visit/.

Whedon, Joss. "Ace of Case" Entertainment Weekly, October 7, 2005. www.ew.com/ew /article/0,,1114734,00.html.

———. "From Joss Whedon: Do Not Adjust Your Mindset." United Hollywood blog, February 6, 2008. http://unitedhollywood.blogspot.com/2008/02/from-joss -whedon-do-not-adjust-your.html.

———. "Higher Learning." Rookie Mag, September 2011.

Wigler, Josh. "Joss Whedon Says 'S.H.I.E.L.D.' TV Series Will Star 'New Charac- ters'" MTV.com, September 12, 2012. http://splashpage.mtv.com/2012/09/12 /joss-whedon-shield-new-cast/.

Wilding, Josh. "Joss Whedon and Mark Ruffalo on Introducing a New Bruce Banner in THE AVENGERS." ComicBookMovie.com, April 1, 2012. www.comicbook movie.com/fansites/JoshWildingNewsAndReviews/news/?a=57269.

Wolk, Douglas. "Q&A: Patton Oswalt on His 'Serenity' Comic Book." Time.com, March 9, 2010. http://techland.time.com/2010/03/09/qa-patton-oswalt-on-his -serenity-comic-book/.

Writers Guild of America East. "Minimum Basic Agreement: An Overview." WGAE official website. www.wgaeast.org/index.php?id=162.

Writers Guild of America, West. "Writers Guild Members Overwhelmingly Ratify New Contract." Press release, February 26, 2008. www.wga.org/subpage_newsevents .aspx?id=2780.

Wykehamist. Fencing Report 1981." December 4, 1981.

Yamato, Jen. "Joss Whedon Q&A on Eve of SXSW." Deadline Hollywood, March 7, 2013. www.deadline.com/2013/03/sxsw-interview-joss-whedon-avengers-marvel -much-ado-about-nothin/.

Zacharek, Stephanie. "The Hills Are Alive with the Sound of . . . Vampire Slaying!" Salon, November 7, 2001. www.salon.com/2001/11/07/buffy_musical/.

Media

BAFTA. Joss Whedon: A Life in Pictures. June 14, 2013. www.bafta.org/film/features /joss-whedon-a-life-in-pictures,3816,BA.html.

Bianculli, David. Fresh Air. NPR, February 12, 2009.

Cameron, James. Director's commentary, *Aliens*. In *Alien Quadrilogy*, DVD. 20th Century Fox, 2003.

Carpenter, Charisma. Panel comments. Dragon Con, Atlanta, GA, September 4, 2009.

Commentary!: The Musical. In *Dr. Horrible's Sing-Along Blog*, DVD. Mutant Enemy, 2008.

Daily Show, The. "Behind the Iron Closet." Comedy Central, February 12, 2014. http://thedailyshow.cc.com/videos/wxwuti/jason-jones-live-from-sochi-ish ---behind-the-iron-closet.

Daniels, Susanne. Interview in "Front Row Special on Buffy the Vampire Slayer." *Front Row Daily*, BBC Radio, December 26, 2013. www.bbc.co.uk/programmes /b03m7zmq.

Espenson, Jane. Featurette commentary in "'Hush' Featurette." In *Buffy the Vampire Slayer: The Complete Fourth Season*. 20th Century Fox, 2003.

Firefly 10th Anniversary: Browncoats Unite. Science Channel, November 11, 2012.

Fox network. *Firefly* promos. Summer/fall 2002.

Iwerks, Leslie. *The Pixar Story*. Documentary. Disney/Pixar, 2007.

Kermode, Mark. *Much Ado About Nothing* review. In *Kermode and Mayo's Film Review*, BBC Radio 5 Live, June 14, 2013.

Paley Center for Media. *2008 PaleyFest: Buffy the Vampire Slayer Reunion*. DVD. CreateSpace, 2009.

Syfy UK. "Joss Whedon—Favourite Horror." April 2, 2012. www.syfy.co.uk/videos /joss-whedon-favourite-horror.

Torres, Gina. Panel comments. FanExpo Canada, August 24, 2013. Archived at YouTube, www.youtube.com/watch?v=9lf9aZZDKU8.

20th Century Fox Television. *Buffy the Vampire Slayer* international press kit, November 1998. www.youtube.com/watch?v=355AMVyCyIg.

WB. *Buffy the Vampire Slayer* premiere trailer, March 10, 1997. Archived at Television Obscurities, www.tvobscurities.com/2008/06/buffy-the-vampire-slayer-premiere -trailer/.

Whedon, Joss. *Agents of S.H.I.E.L.D.* announcement. New York Comic Con, October 13, 2012.

———. Director's commentary, *The Avengers*. In DVD release. Marvel Studios, 2012.

———. Director's commentary, "The Body." In *Buffy the Vampire Slayer: The Complete Fifth Season*, DVD. 20th Century Fox, 2008.

———. Director's commentary, "Hush." In *Buffy the Vampire Slayer: The Complete Fourth Season*. 20th Century Fox, 2003.

———. Director's commentary, "Innocence." In *Buffy the Vampire Slayer Season Two*, DVD. 20th Century Fox, 2002.

———. Director's commentary, *Serenity*. In DVD release. Universal Pictures, 2005.

———. Director's commentary, "Welcome to the Hellmouth." In *Buffy the Vampire Slayer Season One*, DVD. 20th Century Fox, 2002.

———. Equality Now address, May 15, 2006.

———. Equality Now address, November 6, 2013.

———. Featurette commentary in "*Buffy the Vampire Slayer*: TV with Bite." In *Buffy the Vampire Slayer Season Six*, DVD. 20th Century Fox, 2004.

———. Featurette commentary in "From the Ashes: Reviving the Story." In *Alien Quadrilogy*, DVD. 20th Century Fox, 2003.

———. Interview in *Fanboy Radio* podcast, November 26, 2006. www.fanboyradio .com/fanboy-radio-352-joss-whedon-live/.

———. Interview in *Fresh Air*, NPR, May 9, 2000.

———. Interview in *Fresh Air*, NPR, February 12, 2009. www.npr.org/templates /story/story.php?storyId=100601869.

————. Interview in "Front Row Special on Buffy the Vampire Slayer." *Front Row Daily*, BBC Radio, December 26, 2013. www.bbc.co.uk/programmes/b03m7zmq.

————. Interview in *Joss Whedon: The Master at Play*. DVD. Creative Screenwriting Magazine, 2005.

————. Interview in "Joss Whedon: Why He Chose an Irish Man to Film Avengers." RTÉ, June 11, 2013. www.youtube.com/watch?v=TRRIuk1M_vc.

————. Interview in *Making It with Riki Lindhome* podcast, December 19, 2011. www.nerdist.com/2011/12/making-it-23-joss-whedon/.

————. Interview in *Nerdist Podcast*, July 22, 2013. www.nerdist.com/2013/07/nerdist-podcast-joss-whedon/.

————. Interview in *The Q&A with Jeff Goldsmith* podcast, December 23, 2012. www.theqandapodcast.com/2012/12/joss-whedon-avengers-q.html.

————. Interview in *Studio 360*, PRI, June 14, 2013. www.studio360.org/story/297764-joss-whedon-hollywood-slayer/.

————. Interview in *The Write Environment*. DVD. RDRR Productions, 2008.

————. Introduction to *Serenity* special screenings. In DVD release. Universal Pictures, 2005.

————. "Joss Whedon: From Buffy to Dr Horrible, Infinity & Beyond." Sydney Opera House, August 29, 2010.

————. Lifetime Achievement Award in Cultural Humanism acceptance speech. Harvard Humanist Society, April 10, 2009.

————. 181st Wesleyan commencement speech. Wesleyan University, May 26, 2013.

————. Printed insert. *My So-Called Life: The Complete Series*, DVD. Shout! Factory, 2007.

————. Q&A session on Australian *Serenity* DVD. Transcribed in "Joss Whedon on Religion." *Incarnational Iconoclast* blog, July 4, 2008. http://incarnationaliconoclast.blogspot.com.au/2008/07/joss-whedon-on-religion.html.

————. Visionaries panel. San Diego Comic Con, July 23, 2010.

Whedon, Joss, and Drew Goddard. Filmmakers' commentary, *The Cabin in the Woods*. In DVD release. Lionsgate, 2012.

Internet Posts

dreamlogic, Whedonesque post, November 6, 2007. http://whedonesque.com/comments/14629#195348.

Fillion, Nathan. Twitter post, October 24, 2011. https://twitter.com/NathanFillion/status/128597808973488128.

Fury, David. Whedonesque post, December 15, 2005. http://whedonesque.com/comments/8936#100028.

Simone, Gail. Women in Refrigerators website. March 1999. Archived at Beau Yarbrough personal website, http://lby3.com/wir/.

Slayage Online. "About Slayage." http://slayageonline.com/pages/Slayage/About_Slayage.htm.

Stafford, Nikki. "Slayage Conference: Jeanine Basinger." *Nik at Nite* blog, June 12, 2008. http://nikkistafford.blogspot.com/2008/06/slayage-conference-jeanine-basinger.html.

Whedon, Joss. BronzeBeta.com post, February 14, 2004. Archived at Bronze VIP Archive, www.cise.ufl.edu/~hsiao/media/tv/buffy/bronze/20040214.html.

————. Buffistas.org post, December 12, 2002. www.buffistas.org/archives/threads/PXFirefly01.zip.

————. Buffy.com post, circa February 2, 1998. Archived at the Cult of Joss, https://web.archive.org/web/20000126180200/http://moonlight.dreamhost.com/coj/gospels/gospel3.html.

———. Buffy.com post, December 15, 1998. Archived at Bronze VIP Archive, www
.cise.ufl.edu/cgi-bin/cgiwrap/hsiao/buffy/get-archive?date=19981215.

———. Buffy.com post, May 13, 1999. Archived at Bronze VIP Archive, www.cise.ufl
.edu/cgi-bin/cgiwrap/hsiao/buffy/get-archive?date=19990513.

———. Buffy.com post, June 19, 1999. Archived at Bronze VIP Archive, www.cise.ufl
.edu/cgi-bin/cgiwrap/hsiao/buffy/get-archive?date=19990619.

———. Buffy.com posts, August 1, 2000. Archived at Bronze VIP Archive, www.cise
.ufl.edu/cgi-bin/cgiwrap/hsiao/buffy/get-archive?date=20000801.

———. Buffy.com post, May 23, 2001. Archived at Bronze VIP Archive, www.cise
.ufl.edu/cgi-bin/cgiwrap/hsiao/buffy/get-archive?date=20010523.

———. Whedonesque post, October 21, 2004. http://whedonesque.com/comments
/5133#38839.

———. Whedonesque post, August 12, 2005. http://whedonesque.com/comments
/7502.

———. Whedonesque post, February 3, 2007. http://whedonesque.com/comments
/12385.

———. Whedonesque post, May 20, 2007, http://whedonesque.com/comments/13271.

———. Whedonesque post, November 7, 2007. http://whedonesque.com/comments
/14650.

———. Whedonesque post, November 17, 2007. http://whedonesque.com/comments
/14772.

———. Whedonesque post, December 6, 2007. http://whedonesque.com/comments
/14910.

———. Whedonesque post, December 20, 2007, http://whedonesque.com/comments
/15023.

———. Whedonesque post, October 26, 2008. http://whedonesque.com/comments
/17945.

———. Whedonesque post, May 9, 2012. http://whedonesque.com/comments/28797.

———. Whedonesque profile. http://whedonesque.com/user/13.

Whedon, Joss, and David Fury. Buffy.com posts, May 17, 2000. Archived at Bronze VIP
Archive, www.cise.ufl.edu/cgi-bin/cgiwrap/hsiao/buffy/get-archive?date=20000517.

Academic Writings

Albright, Richard. "'[B]reakaway Pop Hit or . . . Book Number?': 'Once More, with
Feeling' and Genre." *Slayage* 5, no. 1 (June 2005).

Ali, Asim. "Community, Language, and Postmodernism at the Mouth of Hell." In
Buffy and Angel Conquer the Internet: Essays on Online Fandom, ed. Mary Kirby-
Diaz. Jefferson, NC: McFarland, 2009.

———. "'In the World, but Not of It': An Ethnographic Analysis of an Online *Buffy
the Vampire Slayer* Fan Community." In ibid.

Erisman, Fred. "Stagecoach in Space: The Legacy of Firefly." *Extrapolation*, June 22,
2006. www.thefreelibrary.com/Stagecoach+in+space%3A+the+legacy+of+Firefly
.-a0154392855.

Gatson, Sarah N., and Amanda Zweerink. "Choosing Community: Rejecting Anonymity in Cyberspace." *Research in Community Sociology* 10 (August 2000): 105–37.

———. "www.buffy.com: Cliques, Boundaries, and Hierarchies in an Internet Community." In *Fighting the Forces: What's at Stake in Buffy the Vampire Slayer*. Lanham, MD: Rowman & Littlefield, 2002, 239–50.

Hill, Annette, and Ian Calcutt. "Vampire Hunters: The Scheduling and Reception of
Buffy the Vampire Slayer and *Angel* in the UK." *Intensities: The Journal of Cult
Media* 1 (Spring/Summer 2001).

Military Times. "Valor Awards for John Whedon Steele." http://projects.militarytimes
.com/citations-medals-awards/recipient.php?recipientid=2035.

Tuszynski, Stephanie. "IRL (In Real Life): Breaking Down the Binary of Online Versus
Offline Social Interaction." PhD diss., Bowling Green State University, 2006.

Whedon, Joss. Handwritten notes. In "Joss Whedon: From Buffy to the Bard" exhibit.
Nicita Gallery, Wesleyan University, 2013.

Original Interviews

Acker, Amy. October 2011.

Allie, Scott. May 2011.

Baccarin, Morena. June 2011.

Baldwin, Adam. May 2011.

Basinger, Jeanine. June 2011, August
2013.

Batali, Dean. August 2011.

Benz, Julie. May 2011.

Blucas, Marc. June 2011.

Boal, Chris. April 2012.

Brendon, Nicholas. July 2011.

Britt, Amy. July 2011.

Buchanan, Christopher. October 2011.

Cole, Kai. July and November 2011.

Collins, Gail. June 2011.

Denisof, Alexis. May 2011, January 2012.

Dushku, Eliza. October 2011.

Espenson, Jane. July 2011.

Feige, Kevin. October 2011.

Fillion, Nathan. April 2012.

Fury, David. August 2011.

Gellar, Sarah Michelle. July 2011.

Goddard, Drew. September 2012.

Gordon, Howard. August 2011.

Greenwalt, David. June 2011.

Gregg, Clark. February 2012.

Gutierrez, Diego. June 2011.

Harris, Neil Patrick. July 2011.

Head, Anthony Stewart. June 2011.

Helberg, Simon. June 2011.

Hemsworth, Chris. June 2011.

Hiddleston, Tom. May 2012.

Hunter, Jay. November 2011.

Jackson, Samuel L. November 2011.

Kane, Christian. June 2011.

Kranz, Fran. June 2011, November 2011.

Laurie, Miracle. April 2011.

Lenk, Tom. June 2011.

Loeb, Jeph. July 2012.

Lowe, Nick. September 2011.

Marts, Mike. November 2011.

Massen, Jane. April 2012.

Minear, Tim. June 2011.

Morris, Melanie. September 2011.

Neuwirth, Jessica. July 2012.

Noxon, Marti. June 2012.

Nussbaum, Emily. June 2011.

Oswalt, Patton. June 2011.

Penikett, Tahmoh. April 2011.

Quesada, Joe. August 2011.

Renner, Jeremy. October 2011.

Reubens, Paul. January 2012.

Ruffalo, Mark. August 2012.

Ryan, Shawn. September 2011.

Saralegui, Jorge. July 2011.

Smulders, Cobie. July 2011.

Solomon, David. July 2011.

Staite, Jewel. June 2011.

Stanton, Andrew. June 2012.

Strong, Danny. May 2011.

Tancharoen, Maurissa. July 2011.

Thomas, Rob. March 2011.

Whedon, Jed. July 2011.

Whedon, Joss. May, June, and November 2011.

Wight, Eric. May 2012.

Wilcox, Rhonda V. October 2011.

Williams, Olivia. June 2011.

// INDEX //

ABC, 87, 289, 378, 383
Abrams, J. J., 285
Academy Awards, 77
Acker, Amy, 169, 238, 252, 294, 312, 358, 382
  in *Much Ado About Nothing*, 170, 361,
    362–363, 384
Ad Man Out, 12
Adams, Michael, 258
Adelle DeWitt (*Dollhouse* character), 312,
  358
Adventures of Pete & Pete, The, 105
Afterlife (script), 63–64
Agents of S.H.I.E.L.D., 6, 378–379, 381, 383,
  385
Ain't It Cool News, 251
Alias, 285
Alice in Wonderland (play), 12
Alien (1979), 21, 79
Alien 3 (1992), 80–81
Alien: Resurrection (1997), 81–85
Alienated (script), 138
Aliens (1986), 80
Alliance of Motion Picture and Television Pro-
    ducers (AMPTP), 289–290, 296, 301
Allie, Scott, 279, 280–282
Ally McBeal, 212
aloneness, 21–22
Alpha (*Dollhouse* character), 315
Alphona, Adrian, 283
"Amends" (*Buffy* episode), 139, 225
American Academy of Dramatic Arts, 13
American Film Institute (AFI), 32, 37, 386
American Pie (1999), 135–136
Amnesty International, 57, 272
AMPTP. *See* Alliance of Motion Pictures and
    Television Producers
Ancier, Garth, 99, 245
Anderson, Gillian, 88, 121
Anderson, Whit, 341–342, 344
Angel (series), 4, 327
  cancellation of, 238, 240–242, 245–246
  cast changes on, 150, 152–153, 228–229
  development of, 138, 145–146
  final seasons of, 228–230, 238–239,
    245–246
  premiere of, 148–149
  storytelling adjustments on, 149, 154, 230
  writing staff tensions on, 150–152, 155–156,
    208

Angel/Angelus (*Buffy/Angel* character), 3, 99,
    111–112, 124–125, 138–139, 145, 148–
    149, 239–240, 242–243
Angell, Louise Carroll (grandmother), 10, 11
Anya (*Buffy* character), 158, 191, 198
Arnold, Tom, 43
Astonishing X-Men, 232–236, 279
Aswad, Du'a Khalil, 287
atheism, 28, 263, 324–325
Atlantis: The Lost Empire (2001), 71
Atlas Entertainment, 341
Attanasio, Paul, 64
Avengers, The (2012), 1, 178, 371, 373
  box office, 6, 376
  casting of, 334–337
  hiring of Joss for, 330–333
  Joss's meetings with cast prior to filming,
    345–346
  postproduction of, 370–371
  production of, 349, 351–353
  sequel to, 376–377, 378
  wrap party for, 349–350
  writing of, 333–334, 337–340

B movies, 45
Baccarin, Morena, 205–206, 220, 222, 244,
  294
Bad and the Beautiful, The (1952), 33
"Bad Eggs" (*Buffy* episode), 129–130
Baldwin, Adam, 205, 206–207, 210, 219, 221,
  244, 249
Bana, Eric, 336
Barb Wire (1996), 374
Barbie (proposed *Toy Story* character), 75
Barnstable County Fair, 1–2
Barr, Roseanne, 40, 41, 43, 46
Basinger, Jeanine, 32–35, 48, 72, 108, 123,
    247, 275, 383, 386–387
Batali, Dean, 105, 107, 112, 118, 122, 133, 186
Batman, film concept for, 269–270
Batman Beyond (animated series), 176–177
Batman: The Animated Series, 177
Battlestar Galactica, 311
Bay, Michael, 35–36
Beck, Christophe, 118, 158
"Becoming, Part 2" (*Buffy* episode), 3, 5
Bell, Jeffrey, 238–239, 379
Bell, Kristen, 265, 267, 382
Bellwether (Stearns and Rosenberg), 57

Bellwether Pictures, 357, 361, 370
"Belonging" (*Dollhouse* episode), 326
"Benediction" (*Angel* episode), 208
Benson, Amber, 159, 162, 167, 196, 252
Benz, Julie, 154, 168–169
Berman, Gail, 51, 88–90, 97, 99, 203, 213
Better Days, 29
Beverly Hills, 90210, 87, 88, 90
Bianco, Robert, 158
Bianculli, David, 158
Big Bad concept, 110, 125, 145, 225, 325
Big Bang Theory, The, 305
Birds, The (1963), 33, 34–35
Black Widow (*Avengers* character), 338, 374, 375
blacklisting, 11
Blair, Selma, 93, 135
"Blood, Text and Fears: Reading Around *Buffy the Vampire Slayer*," 259
Blossom, 88
Blucas, Marc, 158, 161
Boal, Chris, 17–18, 20–22, 25, 57
"Body, The" (*Buffy* episode), 58, 59, 174
Book, Shepherd (*Firefly* character), 200, 202, 205, 248
Boreanaz, David, 95, 99, 120, 125, 138, 145–146, 153–154, 245, 342
Boretz, Michael, 301
Bowman, John, 290
Boyd Langton (*Dollhouse* character), 312
Brain Boy (alter ego), 263
"Brain-Dead Poets Society" (*Roseanne* episode), 43–44
Branagh, Kenneth, 330–331, 334, 347–348, 359
Brave Little Toaster, The (Disch), 69
Brendon, Nicholas "Nick," 95, 98, 120, 143, 252, 293
Britt, Amy, 136, 137, 153, 203, 205
Bronze (message board), 116–120, 140–142, 160–163, 184
BronzeBeta.com, 184, 241
Browncoats (*Firefly* fans), 218, 237, 261, 378
Buchanan, Chris, 117, 178–179, 209, 211, 215, 217, 237, 243, 254
Buffistas.org, 218
Buffy Summers (*Buffy* character), 3–4, 5, 35, 51, 58–60, 92, 98, 158
  casting of, 93–94
  characterization of, 93, 191–193, 226–227, 228
  relationship with Angel, 124–125
  relationship with Spike, 191–192, 194–195
Buffy: The Animated Series, 175–179
Buffy the Vampire Slayer (1992), 3, 9, 45–46, 48–49, 51–56, 60
Buffy the Vampire Slayer (proposed movie reboot), 341–344
Buffy the Vampire Slayer (TV series), 3–4, 87, 115, 139, 173, 225, 292, 327
  academic study of, 257–259

casting of, 93–96, 100–103, 136–137
comic book tie-ins for, 279–280 (see also *Buffy the Vampire Slayer Season Eight*)
decision to end, 223–225
development of, 88–93
final season of, 225–228
move to UPN, 184–198
musical episode of, 186–187
online fan community for, 116–120
pilot of, 96–99
premiere of, 109–111
proposed spin-offs of, 227–228
religious themes in, 111–112, 139
second-season changes to, 123–124
staffing of, 103–105, 122
tensions on the set of, 162, 223–225
WB negotiations and cancellation, 137, 179–185
writers' room on, 105–108, 126–128
Buffy the Vampire Slayer Season Eight (Dark Horse Comics), 279–283
Bullock, Sandra, 64, 66, 271
Burnett, Frances Hodgson, 387
Burton, Tim, 147
Bus Ado About Nothing, 381–382
Buscema, John, 20
Bush, George W., 251, 254
Buzz Lightyear (*Toy Story* character), 70, 73, 75

Cabin in the Woods, The (2012)
  box office and reviews, 373
  casting of, 320–322
  Lionsgate distribution of, 354–355, 372
  MGM and, 303, 319, 328, 329, 343–344
  production of, 322–324, 328
  writing of, 288–289
Call (*Alien: Resurrection* character), 82, 83
Cameron, James, 80, 81, 329
Can't Stop the Serenity, 273
Captain America (*Avengers* character), 334, 354
Captain America: The First Avenger (2011), 334
Captain America: The Winter Soldier (2014), 378
Captain Hammer (*Dr. Horrible* character), 299, 306–307
Captain Kangaroo, 13
Captivity (2007), 285–286
Carpenter, Charisma, 94, 145, 153, 228–229, 239–240, 267, 271, 342
Carsey, Marcy, 41
Carter, Chris, 121, 151
Carter, Lynda, 268
Cassaday, John, 234, 235, 236
Castle, 364
Cat in the Hat, The (2003), 243
Catching Fire (2013), 373
Catwoman (2004), 374
Charmed, 281
Cheap Shots (proposed TV series), 138
Chen, Joan, 53

Chernin, Peter, 64
"Chicken Hearts" (*Roseanne* episode), 44
Chinese language, in *Firefly*, 207
"Chosen" (*Buffy* episode), 226–227
chosen family concept, 4, 6, 153, 171, 197, 220
Chronicles of Riddick, The (2004), 243
"City Of" (*Angel* episode), 148–149
Claremont, Chris, 234
Close Encounters of the Third Kind (1977),
    26–27
Cloverfield (2008), 285
Clueless (1995), 88–89
Cohen, Joel, 70
Colantoni, Enrico, 267
Cole, Michelle "Kai" (wife), 20, 32, 60, 108–
    109, 164, 173, 275, 292, 296, 354–355
    early relationship with, 47–49
    helping with *Buffy* musical episode, 187–188
    and *In Your Eyes*, 357
    on Joss's fans, 117, 120, 184–185, 218, 377
    movie montages for, 78
    and *Much Ado About Nothing*, 358–359,
        366–368, 379, 384–385
    pregnancies of, 209–210, 222, 254–255
    on production of *Dr. Horrible*, 307
    proposal to, 78–79
    road trip with, 71–72
    and Shakespeare readings, 168, 169, 170,
        171
collaboration, 4, 72–73, 126, 294, 301–302,
    353, 376
Colloff, Anya, 136
Colossus (Marvel character), 233, 235
Columbine High School, 140
comic book conventions, 20, 377. *See also* New
    York Comic Con; San Diego Comic-Con
comic books, 1, 3, 18, 128–129, 175
commencement speech, 383–384
Commentary! The Musical, 308
Company (play), 275
connecting, Joss on, 41–42
Connections (BBC series), 19
Connolly, Kristen, 322
Connor (*Angel* character), 229
Coolidge, Martha, 129
Coppola, Francis Ford, 52
Cordelia Chase (*Buffy/Angel* character)
    on *Angel*, 145, 153, 229, 230, 239–240
    on *Buffy the Vampire Slayer*, 93, 94
"Corrupt" (*Angel* script), 149
Costner, Kevin, 77
Cousin Oliver Syndrome, 173–174
Crawford, Joan, 34
Crawford, Sophia, 120, 162
Creative Artists Agency, 304
"Crocodile Rock" (song), 18
crowdfunding, 382
Cruel Intentions (1999), 135
Cruise, Tom, 319
Curt (*Cabin in the Woods* character), 322
Cuthbert, Elisha, 286

Dana (*Cabin in the Woods* character), 322, 323
Dance Dance Revolution (video game), 350
dancing, 18, 47, 119, 350–351
Danes, Claire, 87
Daniels, Susanne, 90–91, 99–100, 183
Dark Angel, 212
Dark Horse Comics, 262, 279, 282
Dark Horse Presents, 282
Dark Shadows (2004 TV pilot), 240–241
Darla (*Buffy/Angel* character), 154, 165, 169
"Darla" (*Angel* episode), 165
Dawn Summers (*Buffy* character), 173–174,
    190
Day, Felicia, 300, 304, 317, 369
de Bont, Jan, 64
"Dead End Kids" (*Runaways* arc), 284
"Dead Things" (*Buffy* episode), 192–193
death
    Joss on, 58–59
    use of, in storylines, 195
DeKnight, Steve, 176, 314
Denisof, Alexis, 152–153, 252, 326, 358
    and *Much Ado About Nothing*, 357, 361, 363,
        364, 369, 382, 384
    at Shakespeare readings, 168, 169, 170, 171
Derek & Simon: The Show (web series), 302
Des Hotel, Rob, 105, 112, 122
Devil's Rejects, The (2005), 286
Diaz, Junot, 375
Dick Cavett Show, The, 15
Dickens, Charles, 258, 259
Die Hard (1988), 62, 335, 352
Director, the (*Cabin in the Woods* character),
    323
Disney, 69–72, 75, 178
Doctor Who, 200
Dollhouse, 6, 290–292, 311–317, 325–327
Done the Impossible, 273
Downey, Robert, Jr., 333, 336, 345, 346, 348,
    352
Doyle (*Angel* character), 145, 150
Dr. Horrible (character), 298
Dr. Horrible's Sing-Along Blog, 6, 297–309, 357
Dracula (1992), 52
drug use, 27
Drusilla (*Buffy* character), 123–124
Duchovny, David, 121
Dungeons & Dragons, 30
Dushku, Eliza, 139, 227, 271, 290–291, 293,
    321, 350–351

"Earshot" (*Buffy* episode), 139–142
Ebert, Roger, 65–66, 372
Echo (*Dollhouse* character), 290, 311, 313, 327
"Echo" (*Dollhouse* episode), 311, 312–313
Eclectic Society, 30
Edison (young Avengers fan), 354
Edlund, Ben, 243
Eisner Award, 236, 283
Ejiofor, Chiwetel, 248, 335
Electric Company, The, 16, 18

Elektra (2005), 374
Elizabeth, Queen of England, 29
Ellen, 160
Emma (Austen), 89
Emmy Awards, 12, 159, 191, 309
"Epiphany" (*Angel* espisode), 263
"Epitaph One" (*Dollhouse* episode), 317
Equality Now, 272–273, 312, 385
Equalizer, The, 149
Erisman, Fred, 200
Espenson, Jane, 130, 136, 139, 147, 148, 159,
    194, 366
  and *Buffy: The Animated Series*, 176, 279
  and *Dollhouse*, 314
  on Joss's writing/producing style, 106,
    126–128, 133
  at Mutant Enemy Day, 294
  at Shakespeare readings, 170–171
Evans, Chris, 336, 348, 352
Evelina (Burney), 10
Evil Dead, The (1981), 61

Faith (*Buffy* character), 139, 155, 226, 227,
    279–280
fan base
  activism of, 245, 252–254, 273, 294–295
  for *Buffy the Vampire Slayer*, 116–120
  thank-you from Joss to, 375–376
fantasy, Joss on, 123
Fastlane, 215
Favreau, Jon, 332, 347
Feige, Kevin, 330–336, 349, 352, 353, 372,
    375, 382
female superheroes, 3, 45, 90–91, 129, 201–
    202, 233–234, 268–269, 374–375
feminism, 15, 30–31, 45, 327, 385–386
fight scenes, 42–43
Fighting the Forces (Lavery and Wilcox), 257
Fillion, Nathan, 95–96, 210, 216, 221, 248–
    250, 252, 294
  audition for *Firefly*, 203–204
  as Caleb on *Buffy*, 225–226
  as Captain Hammer, 299–300, 303
  first day on set of *Firefly*, 206
  on Joss as a director, 207
  on leading roles, 262–263
  and *Much Ado About Nothing*, 364, 370,
    384–385
Film Roman, 177
film studies, 32–35
Fincher, David, 80
Firefly, 4, 203, 216, 237–238, 327, 382
  archetypes in, 201
  cancellation of, 219–222
  casting of, 203–206
  comparison to *Stagecoach*, 200–201
  development of, 199–200
  dialogue on, 206–207
  fan campaign for, 218–219
  marketing of, 214–216
  message board for, 217–218

reunion at San Diego Comic-Con, 377–378
  scheduling of, 212–213
"Firefly: Immediate Assistance" campaign,
    218–219
First Evil (*Buffy* character), 225
Float Out (*Serenity* tie-in comic), 316
Follies, 16–17
"Fool for Love" (*Buffy* episode), 166–167
Ford, Jeffrey, 371
Ford, John, 200
Foul Play (1978), 29
Fox Kids, 178
Fox network, 90, 103, 182, 203
  and *Dollhouse*, 291, 311–314, 317
  and *Firefly*, 212–217
Fray, 280
Frazetta, Frank, 20
Freaks and Geeks, 266
"Freeze Ray" (song), 298
Furies, The (1950), 33, 247
Fury, David, 122, 147, 148, 166, 186, 294
  description of *Buffy*'s writers' room, 128
  and "The Parable of the Knight," 162–163
  on plans for sixth season of *Angel*, 246
  and production of *Angel*, 238–240
  on "Smile Time" episode, 243

Gallin, Sandy, 51
Gary Sitterson (*Cabin in the Woods* character),
    320
Gayheart, Rebecca, 205
"Gee, Officer Krupke" (song), 22
Gellar, Sarah Michelle, 5, 93–94, 101, 111,
    125, 140, 163–164, 176, 185
  and "The Body" episode, 174
  bows out of *Buffy*, 223–224
  on changes to *Buffy*, 192–193
  comments on the WB, 181
  in *Cruel Intentions*, 135
  declines *Angel* guest appearance, 245
  in pilot of *Buffy*, 98, 99
  reaction to proposed *Buffy* reboot, 343
  sends donuts to Mutant Enemy Day, 293
  on singing in "Once More, With Feeling,"
    189
Gentlemen, the Queen, 10
Getaway, The (1993), 61
"Ghost" (*Dollhouse* episode), 313, 314
"Gift, The" (*Buffy* episode), 183, 184
"Gifted" (*Astonishing X-Men* arc), 235
Giles (*Buffy* character). *See* Rupert Giles
"Gingerbread" (*Buffy* episode), 130
Gjokaj, Enver, 312
Glass, Ron, 205, 248, 364, 381
Glau, Summer, 205, 294, 326
Gleiberman, Owen, 76
Goddard, Drew, 242, 283, 285, 294, 303, 373,
    377
  and *The Cabin in the Woods*, 288, 319–322,
    329–330, 343–344, 372
"Going Through the Motions" (song), 188

Goners (script), 272, 276, 277–278, 287, 303

Gordon, Howard, 107, 122, 127, 129, 147, 150, 186

Gordon, Lawrence, 63, 77

"Graduation Day, Part 2" (*Buffy* episode), 141–142

Grampire (script), 138

Grateful Dead, 27

Great Gildersleeve, The, 10–11

Great to Be Back! 12

Green, Jack, 248, 262

Green, Ryan, 301

Green, Seth, 120, 124, 342–343

Green Mile, The (King), 305

Greenwalt, David, 6, 112, 116, 121, 128, 155, 165, 185–186, 229, 292
  as co-showrunner on *Buffy*, 103–107
  and development of *Angel*, 138, 145–152
  on Joss's writing idiosyncrasies, 131–133
  leaves *Angel*, 208

Gregg, Clark, 338, 349, 350–351, 368, 381
  on Joss as a director, 347–348
  and *Much Ado About Nothing*, 363, 364, 367
  as Phil Coulson, 336, 347, 379

Groener, Harry, 139, 294

Grushow, Sandy, 137, 179–180, 181, 183

Guardians of the Galaxy (2014), 378

Guild, The (web series), 299, 300

Gutierrez, Diego, 130–131, 196–197

H. Bramston's boarding house, 24

Hadley (*Cabin in the Woods* character), 321

Halloween (1978), 45

Hamlet, 167

Hampton, Elin, 122

Hannigan, Alyson, 118, 120, 224–225, 252
  in *American Pie*, 135–136
  cast in *Veronica Mars*, 267
  reaction to proposed *Buffy* reboot, 342
  at Shakespeare readings, 168, 358
  on Willow, 100–101

Hans Gruber (*Die Hard* character), 335, 339

Harbert, Chris, 39–40, 41, 61, 89, 91, 96, 221, 269, 376

Harris, Jeff, 41, 44

Harris, Neil Patrick, 170, 205, 299–301, 302, 305, 306, 308

Hart, Angie, 170

Harvard Lampoon, 9

Harvard Radcliffe Dramatic Club (HRDC), 12

Harvard University, 9–10, 12–13, 259, 324

"Harvest, The (*Buffy* episode), 109

Hasty Pudding Club, 9, 10, 12

Hauer, Rutger, 53, 55

Hawkeye (*Avengers* character), 336, 374

Hawn, Goldie, 29

Head, Anthony Stewart "Tony," 94–97, 116, 118, 120, 132, 167, 186–188, 189, 342, 363

"Heart (Broken)" (song), 308–309

"Heart of Gold" (*Firefly* episode), 220

Heathers (1988), 266

Heckerling, Amy, 88

Hedren, Tippi, 33, 35

Helberg, Simon, 302, 305–306

Hellmouth, 92

"Hell's Bells" (*Buffy* episode), 198

Help, Help, the Globolinks! (Menotti), 158

helplessness, 3, 295–296

Hemsworth, Chris, 322, 330–331, 336

Henson, Jim, 14, 15. *See also* Muppets

Hercules: The Legendary Journeys (1995–1999), 88

"Hero" (*Angel* episode), 150, 152

Hey Cinderella! (TV special), 14

Hiddleston, Tom, 334–336, 339–340, 349–350, 352–353, 354

high school as horror movie concept, 89, 107, 124, 266

High Stakes 2004, 252–253

Hill, Brin, 361

Hill, Joe, 293

Hitchcock, Alfred, 33, 34–35

Hitchcock, Michael, 248

Hobbit, The (2012), 330

Holden (*Cabin in the Woods* character), 322

Holmes, Katie, 93

"Home" (*Angel* espisode), 230

Hostel (2005), 286

House Un-American Activities Committee (HUAC), 11

Howard the Duck (comic), 18

Hugo Awards, 191, 243, 309

Huguely, Squire (great-great grandfather), 255

Hulk (*Avengers* character), 336–337, 346, 374

Hulu, 304

Humanist Chaplaincy, 324

Hunter, Jay, 365–366, 367, 368–369

Husbands (web series), 133

"Hush" (*Buffy* episode), 157–159

Hutchison, Anna, 322

"I Robot, You Jane" (*Buffy* episode), 111

Idler Club (Radcliffe College), 12

Importance of Being Earnest, The (Wilde), 26

In Your Eyes (2014), 357, 361

Inara Serra (*Firefly* character), 201, 205, 214, 247

Incredible Hulk, The (TV series), 6, 378

Incredible Hulk, The (2008), 336

"Innocence" (*Buffy* episode), 124, 125

Innocent Blood (1992), 53

Internet distribution and marketing, 217, 290, 296, 299–301, 304. *See also* online fan communities

Interview with the Vampire (Rice), 53

IRL (In Real Life) (2007), 118

Iron Man (2008), 209, 330, 347

Iron Man 2 (2010), 330, 347

Iron Man 3 (2013), 378

It's a Living, 38, 39

It's Garry Shandling's Show, 39

iTunes, 304, 307, 371

Jackson, Peter, 330
Jackson, Samuel L., 333, 336, 337, 345–346, 348
Jarella (Marvel character), 21
Jayne Cobb (*Firefly* character), 201, 205
Jeanty, Georges, 283
Jeffries, Ann Lee (mother). *See* Stearns, Lee
Jeffries, Anna Lee Hill (grandmother), 13
Jeffries, James Harvey (grandfather), 13
Jenkins, Richard, 320
Jeunet, Jean-Pierre, 83
Jobs, Steve, 69
Johansson, Scarlett, 336, 338, 345, 375
John, Elton, 18
Johnny Guitar (1954), 34, 247
Jonathan (*Buffy* character), 139–140, 187
"Joss Whedon: From Buffy to the Bard" exhibit, 386
JossWhedon.net, 218
Journey to the Center of the Earth (Verne), 71
Joyce Summers (*Buffy* character), 58, 99, 174
Jules (*Cabin in the Woods* character), 322
Just in Time, 39
Justice League, 268, 270

Kaminsky, Daniel, 371
Kartheiser, Vincent, 229
Katzenberg, Jeffrey, 70
Kaylee Frye (*Firefly* character), 201, 213, 249
Keeshan, Bob, 13
Keith Mars (*Veronica Mars* character), 267
Kellner, Jamie, 99, 137, 179–180, 181–183
Kermode, Mark, 384
Kerry, John, 251, 254
Kickstarter, 382
Kiene, Matt, 105
"Killed by Death" (*Buffy* episode), 108
Killer Angels, The (Shaara), 199
King, David Tyron "Ty," 46–47, 122, 138
King, Stephen, 305
Kirby, Jack, 231, 338
Kitty Pryde (Marvel character), 233–234, 235
Kocher, Nick, 364
Kraft Television Theatre, 12
Kranz, Fran, 312, 316, 321–322, 358, 362, 370
Kubrick, Stanley, 26, 207
Kuzui, Fran Rubel, 51, 52, 54, 89, 341
Kuzui, Kaz, 51, 52, 55, 89, 341

Lachman, Dichen, 312, 326
Landau, Juliet, 123, 293
Landis, John, 53
Largo Entertainment, 63
Lassek, Lisa, 248, 301, 371
Lasseter, John, 69–70, 73, 76–77, 329
Laura (1944), 33
Laurie, Miracle, 312, 326–327
Lavery, David, 257–258
Lawless, Lucy, 88
Leading Artists, 39
Lee, Stan, 18, 231, 338

Leff, Adam, 30
Lenk, Tom, 382, 384–385
Lennix, Harry, 312, 313
Leprechaun (1993), 130
Leslie, Joan, 275
Leterrier, Louis, 333, 336
Levin, Jordan, 238, 240–241
Levitz, Paul, 234
Lindhome, Riki, 364
Lindsey-Nassif, Robert, 71
Lionsgate, 286, 354–355, 372, 379, 381–382
Little Night Music, A (Sondheim), 15
Little Princess, A (Burnett), 387
"Little Sister, The" (*Roseanne* episode), 42–43
Loeb, Jeph, 175–177, 178, 179, 379
Lois & Clark, 146–147
Loki (*Thor*/*Avengers* character), 332, 334, 352–353
London Academy of Music and Dramatic Art (LAMDA), 358
loneliness, 21–22, 25
Loren, Giselle, 176
Los Angeles Film Festival, 212
Lost, 283, 285, 309, 317
Lost Boys, The (1987), 53
Lowe, Nick, 235–236, 283–284
Lucas, George, 329
Luke Cage (Marvel character), 21
Lux Video Theatre, 11

Mackay, Constance D'Arcy, 10
Mackendrick, Alexander, 129
Magnolia (1999), 78
Maher, Sean, 205, 364, 370
Make Equality Reality, 385–386
Make-a-Wish Foundation, 161
Malcolm "Mal" Reynolds (*Firefly* character), 4, 201, 202, 213, 247, 248, 249
Manson, Marilyn, 140
"Marco Polo Meets My Fair Lady" (film project), 71
Marcus Hamilton (*Angel* character), 244
Maria Hill (Marvel character), 337, 348, 381
Marsters, James, 123, 166, 167, 188–189, 190, 194
Marston, William Moulton, 268
"Martha the Immortal Waitress," 45
Marts, Mike, 233–234, 235, 236, 283
Marty (*Cabin in the Woods* character), 321, 323
Marvel Cinematic Universe, 338, 347, 349, 375
Marvel Comics, 178, 231–232, 283–284, 330, 378
Marvel Studios, 330, 332–333, 378
Marvel Television, 379
Mason, James, 335, 339
Massen, Dick, 28, 29
Master, the (*Buffy* character), 110, 112–113, 165
Masterpiece Theatre, 19
Mattel, 75
McCloud, Scott, 128–129, 234

McElhaney, Brian, 364
McGarvey, Seamus, 346–347
McIntosh, Todd, 118, 120
Melinda May (*Agents of S.H.I.E.L.D.* character), 381
Mendel, Barry, 237–238
Menotti, Gian Carlo, 158
Mercer, Johnny, 11
Merchant of Venice, The, 169
Merrick Jamison-Smythe (*Buffy* character), 51, 53
Merry Wives of Windsor, The, 168
"Message, The" (*Firefly* episode), 219, 220, 237
MGM, 303, 328, 329, 343
Midsummer Night's Dream, A, 357
Mignola, Mike, 177
Mike "Deathlok" Peterson (*Agents of S.H.I.E.L.D.* character), 381
Minear, Tim, 58, 186, 214–215, 294, 314, 342
  asks to direct episode of *Angel*, 165–166
  and *Dollhouse*, 314, 317
  and end of *Firefly*, 219–221
  on Joss's backpack, 190
  on "Out of Gas," 217
  and premiere script for *Firefly*, 213–215
  on proposed *Buffy* spin-offs, 227–228
  tapped to lead *Firefly*, 208
  as writer on *Angel*, 146–148, 150–152, 154–156, 230
Minimum Basic Agreement (MBA), 289–290, 296
Moist (*Dr. Horrible* character), 302, 307
mold, illness from, 292
Moline, Karl, 280
Monty Python's Flying Circus, 19, 25
Moon, Fábio, 283
Moore, Ron, 311
Moore, Sam, 10, 11
Morgese, Jillian, 364–365
Morrison, Grant, 232
Motion Picture Association of America, 286
movie montages, 78, 90
MTV Movie Awards, 135
Much Ado About Nothing (play), 170
Much Ado About Nothing (2012), 357–359, 361, 365–366, 371
  announcement of, 370
  box office and reviews, 384–385
  casting of, 361–365
  Joss's take on, 359–361
  marketing of, 381–382, 384
  premiere at Toronto International Film Festival, 379
  production of, 368–369
  set location for, 366–368
Muji notebooks, 131
Muppets, 14, 15–16, 242
Murdoch, Rupert, 296
musicals, 14, 71, 73, 138, 186–187, 300. *See also* Sondheim, Stephen
Mutant Enemy Day (WGA strike), 293–294

Mutant Enemy Productions, 110, 122, 138, 203, 209, 216, 254
My Brother Benjamin (1986), 35
My So-Called Life, 87–88, 90, 266

Nancy Drew books, 72, 266
National Board of Review of Motion Pictures, 32
Nausea (Sartre), 27
NBC, 10, 90, 289
Nebula Awards, 191
Neuwirth, Jessica, 272–273
"Never Kill a Boy on the First Date" (*Buffy* episode), 107, 112
New Line Cinema, 209, 330
"New Moon Rising" (*Buffy* episode), 159–160
"New World, A" (*Angel* episode), 208
New X-Men, 232, 233
New York Comic Con, 371, 379
New Yorker, 10
Newt (*Aliens* character), 80, 81
Nick Fury (*Avengers* character), 336, 345
Night Alone, A (1986), 36
Night of the Comet (1984), 45
Nobody Move (script), 59, 61
"Normal Again" (*Buffy* episode), 196–197
North, Oliver, 38–39
Norton, Edward, 336, 337
"Not Fade Away" (*Angel* episode), 245
Noxon, Marti, 42, 118, 122, 146, 185, 190–191, 208, 293
  attends Los Angeles Film Festival, 212
  on the *Buffy* writers' room, 128–130
  on feedback from fans, 120, 193–194
  on Joss's writing idiosyncrasies, 132
  on proposed *Buffy* reboot, 344
  on Spike, 194
  storyline changes blamed on, 192
Numfar (*Angel* character), 350
Nussbaum, Emily, 326, 327

Oliver! 38
Olmos, Edward James, 313
"On the Road to Equality: Honoring Men on the Front Lines," 272, 274
"Once More, with Feeling" (*Buffy* episode), 187–191, 212
Once More, with Feeling (soundtrack), 211–212
online fan communities, 116–117, 120, 217–218, 242
Operative, the (*Serenity* character), 248
Oswalt, Patton, 316
Othello (play), 169
O'Toole, Peter, 335
"Out of Gas" (*Firefly* episode), 216–217, 222
"Out of Mind, Out of Sight" (*Buffy* episode), 24, 112
Outstanding Lifetime Achievement Award in Cultural Humanism, 324
Owens, Andy, 283

Oz (*Buffy* character), 124, 142, 159
Oz books, 147

"Pack, The" (*Buffy* episode), 111
"Parable of the Knight, The" (Pruitt), 162
Parent, Mary, 237–238, 250, 272, 303, 343
Parent 'Hood, The, 91
Parenthood, 46
Parkes, Walter F., 64–65
Parton, Dolly, 51
Party of Five, 87–88, 90
Paul Ballard (*Dollhouse* character), 311, 313
PBP (Posting Board Party), 119–120, 161
PCU (1994), 30
Peckinpah, Sam, 213
Penikett, Tahmoh, 311, 313, 315
Penn, Zak, 30, 331, 333–334
Penny (*Dr. Horrible* character), 298–299,
    306–307
Perry, Katy, 386
Perry, Luke, 53, 56
Peter Pan (2003), 243
Petrie, Doug, 148, 176, 279
Phil Coulson (*Avengers* character), 338, 347,
    349, 378, 383
Pillay, Navanethem, 272
Pixar Animation Studios, 69–70, 72–76
Posting Board Party (PBP), 119–120, 161
Potentials (*Buffy* characters), 225–227
Preminger, Otto, 34
presidential election of 2004, 251–255
Pretty in Pink (band), 385
Prinze, Freddie, Jr., 224
Producers Guild of America, 329
Profit, 103
"Prophecy Girl" (*Buffy* episode), 112–113
Pruitt, Jeff, 118, 120, 162–164
Pump Up the Volume (1990), 88

Quarterlife (web series), 299
Quesada, Joe, 231–232, 235, 350
Quick and the Dead, The (1995), 61
Quinn, Glenn, 145, 150

"R. Tam Sessions," 262
Radcliffe College, 12
Radomski, Eric, 177
Raimi, Sam, 61
"Rat Saw God" (*Veronica Mars* episode),
    267
Ray, Nicholas, 34
Real Genius (1985), 129
reality television, 241, 289
Rear Window (1954), 35
Reavers (*Firefly/Serenity* characters), 201, 214,
    249–250
rebirth, theme of, 82, 185
recall button, 216, 222
Red Sonja (1985), 374
redemption, themes of
    in *Angel*, 138, 149, 154, 245–246

in *Buffy the Vampire Slayer*, 4, 197, 225
    in *Suspension*, 62
Reed, Joe, 34
Reeves, Keanu, 65
Regan, Riff, 95, 98, 100
Regeneration Through Violence (Slotkin), 36,
    128
Regent's Park Open Air Theatre, 359
Reilly, John C., 78
Reinkemeyer, Joe, 105
religious themes, 111–112, 139, 263, 324–325
Remains of the Day, The (1993), 78
Renner, Jeremy, 153, 336, 346, 349, 350, 351
reset television, 91, 149, 197
Reston, Dana, 105
Reubens, Paul, 53, 55
Rex (*Toy Story* character), 75
Reynolds, Ryan, 95–96
Rice, Anne, 53
Richard III, 167
Richard Wilkins III (*Buffy* character), 139, 141
Richards, J. August, 230, 252, 294, 381
Riley Finn (*Buffy* character), 158
Ripley (*Alien* character), 79–80, 82–83
Ripping Yarns (BBC series), 19
River Tam (*Firefly/Serenity* character), 200–
    201, 247, 248
Riverdale Country School, 14–15, 16, 30–31,
    272
"Road You Didn't Take, The" (song), 17, 383
Roadside Attractions, 379, 381
Röhm, Elisabeth, 149
Roiff, Michael, 361
Romero, George, 36, 45
Roseanne, 3, 40–44, 46
Rosenberg, Nancy, 57
Rosenman, Howard, 51
Rossum Corporation (*Dollhouse*), 64, 311,
    325–326
Roswell, 142, 154
Roth, Joe, 80
Rothenberg, David, 361
Rounder Records, 211
Ruck, Alan, 65
Ruffalo, Keen, 353, 354
Ruffalo, Mark, 336–337, 346, 348, 352–353,
    373–374
Runaways (comic), 283–284
Rupert Giles (*Buffy* character), 22, 35, 58, 93,
    94–95, 98, 175, 227
Ryan, Michael, 284
Ryan, Shawn, 127, 155
Ryder, Winona, 83

Sailor Moon, 52
San Diego Comic-Con, 232, 262, 273, 305–
    306, 317, 333, 377, 385
"Sanctuary" (*Angel* episode), 155
Sandollar Productions, 51
Saralegui, Jorge, 52, 61–63, 64–66, 79, 81, 83,
    85, 186

Sartre, Jean-Paul, 27
Saunders, Dr. (*Dollhouse* character), 312
Scarlet Empress, The (1934), 33
Schumacher, Tom, 70
Sci Fi Channel, the, 262
Scott, Ridley, 79
Screen Actors Guild, 212
Seagull, The (play), 12
Secular Society, 324
"Seeing Red" (*Buffy* episode), 194–195
"Sense and Sensitivity" (*Angel* episode), 151–152
"Serenity" (*Firefly* episode), 213
Serenity (spaceship), 206, 248–249
Serenity (2005), 1, 243–244, 247–248, 261–264, 316
Serenity: Those Left Behind, 262
7th Heaven, 99, 182
sex trafficking themes, 312–313, 326
Shaara, Michael, 199
Shakespeare, William, 28, 259
Shakespeare readings, 14, 109, 166–171, 355, 357–358, 362–363
Shasha Seminar for Human Concerns, 325
Shield, The, 127
Shining, The (1980), 26
showrunners, 38, 103
Shulman, Marcia, 94, 136
Sierra (*Dollhouse* character), 312, 326
Silver, Joel, 268–269, 271, 276
Silver Lining, The (Mackay), 10
Simon Tam (*Firefly* character), 200
Simply Red, 40
Singer, Bryan, 231, 330
Sky's the Limit, The (1943), 275
Slayage Conference, 257, 259
Slayage: The Online Journal of Buffy Studies, 258
Slayer Slang: A Buffy the Vampire Slayer Lexicon (Adams), 258
Slotkin, Richard, 36, 62, 128, 201
Smashmouth, 215
"Smile Time" (*Angel* episode), 242–243
Smulders, Cobie, 277, 337, 348, 351, 358, 381
soap opera genre, 87–88, 92, 230
Sokolow, Alec, 70
Solomon, David, 97, 99, 104–105, 115, 314
"Somnambulist" (*Angel* episode), 153
Sondheim, Stephen, 3, 14, 16–17, 22, 187, 275
Sony, 63
Sorkin, Aaron, 159
South by Southwest (SXSW) festival, 372, 381–382
space western concept, 199–200
spec scripts, 39
Speed (1994), 64–66
Spider-Man, 18, 270
Spidey Super Stories, 18
Spielberg, Steven, 27, 238
Spike (*Buffy* character), 123–124, 166, 191–195, 238
spin-offs, 138, 227–228

Stagecoach (1939), 200
Staite, Jewel, 205, 219, 244, 249
Stand Up for Buffy campaign, 141
Stanton, Andrew, 71, 73, 74–75, 76
Star Wars, 21, 338
Stearns, Lee (mother, née Jeffries), 9, 12–13, 16, 19, 23, 48, 57
    activism of, 15, 30–31, 57, 272–274
    death of, 58–60, 273
    at Riverdale Country School, 14–15, 16, 30–31, 57, 272
Stearns, Lisa (stepsister), 19
Stearns, Stephen Jerold (stepfather), 19, 57, 274–275, 332, 361
Steele, John Whedon (great-great grandfather), 255
Steve Trevor (DC Comics character), 268, 271
Stone, Benjamin, 17
Stone, Jon, 14, 15–16
Straczynski, J. Michael, 335
Strange World, 122, 147, 150
Streep, Meryl, 274
Strong, Danny, 139, 187, 252
Strong Man (alter ego), 263
Stupidman, 32, 298
Sturges, Preston, 359
Sugarshock! 282–283
Summers family (*Buffy* characters). *See* Buffy Summers; Dawn Summers; Joyce Summers
Sunday in the Park with George (Sondheim), 324
Supergirl (1984), 374
Superman (1978), 21
"Surprise" (*Buffy* episode), 124
Suspension (script), 62–63
Sutherland, Donald, 53, 54–55
Swanson, Kristy, 53, 54, 56
Sweeney Todd, 22, 300
Sweet Smell of Success (1957), 129
SXSW (South by Southwest) festival, 372, 381–382
Symphony Space, 15

Tancharoen, Maurissa, 297, 298, 314, 350, 369, 379, 381, 383, 385
Tank Girl (1995), 374
Tara Maclay (*Buffy* character), 59–60, 159, 195–196
Television Academy, 174, 191
Television Critics Association, 181
Terminator, The (1984), 36
Terminator: The Sarah Connor Chronicles, 314
Texas, Lil' Darlin, 11
Thomas, Rob, 266, 267–268, 382
Thompson, Emma, 78
Thor (*Avengers* character), 332
Thor (2011), 334, 336
Thor: The Dark World (2013), 378
Those Left Behind (*Serenity* tie-in comic), 316

3-D, use of, 329, 347, 371
"Through the Looking Glass" (*Angel* episode), 350
Tin Toy (1988), 69–70
"To Shanshu in L.A." (*Angel* episode), 153
toaster, gift of a, 160
Tobias, Jesse, 170
Tokyo Pop (1988), 51
Tombstone (1987), 36
Tony Award, 186
Tony Stark (*Avengers* character), 336, 338, 347
Topher (*Dollhouse* character), 312, 326
Toronto International Film Festival, 379
Torres, Gina, 204–205, 230, 271
torture porn, 286, 287
Touched by an Angel, 149
Toy Story (1995), 69–77
Trachtenberg, Michelle, 173, 177
"Train Job, The" (*Firefly* episode), 213–214
Trant's boarding house, 24
Travers, Peter, 372
Trio, the (*Buffy* characters), 193
Trpcic, Shawna, 301, 369
Tru Calling, 291
Tsunami (Marvel imprint), 283
Tudyk, Alan, 204–205, 222, 248, 294, 315, 358
Turell, Brad, 141
TV Guide, 228
20th Century Fox, 91, 137, 203, 237–238, 243
and *Buffy* movie, 52, 56
and *Buffy* renewal battle with the WB, 179–183
and *Buffy: The Animated Series*, 178
declines *Buffy* reboot, 341
signs four-year overall deal with Joss, 121–122
suspends Joss's contract, 253–254
See also Fox network
Twenty Four Seven (1997), 78
Two Guys, a Girl and a Pizza Place, 96, 203
Twohy, David, 80

Ultimates, The (comic), 335
Understanding Comics (McCloud), 128–129, 234
Unfaithfully Yours (1948), 359
United Artists, 319
Universal Pictures, 237–238, 243–244, 272, 303
Unsolved Mysteries, 289
UPN, 91, 182–185, 223, 241, 245
Usual Suspects, The (1995), 77

Vallée, Rudy, 10
van Oosten de Boer, Caroline, 218
Vanguard Award, 329
Variety, 44, 53, 218, 307
Vassar College, 10
Vaughan, Brian K., 283–284
Vermeulen, Milo, 218

Verne, Jules, 71
Veronica Mars (TV series), 265–268
Veronica Mars (2014), 382
Verrone, Patric, 296
Vertigo (1958), 48
Vertigo Entertainment, 341, 342
Victor (*Dollhouse* character), 312
VR.5, 96

Walk for Lupus Now, 369
"Walkin' on the Sun" (song), 215
Walt Disney Company, 69–72, 75, 178
Walters, Melora, 78
Warner Bros. Pictures, 341
Warren Mears (*Buffy* character), 193, 195
Wash (*Firefly/Serenity* character), 200, 202, 316
Watcher archetype, 33, 35
Waterworld (1995), 77–78
Wayans Bros., The, 91
WB, the
Angel pitch to, 145–146
Buffy negotiations and cancellation, 137, 179–185
and *Buffy* pilot, 90–93, 99–100
cancellation of *Angel* by, 238–241, 245
marketing of *Buffy*, 110, 115–116
scheduling of *Buffy* episodes, 140–142
shuts down second episode of *Angel*, 149
Weaver, Sigourney, 79–80, 81, 82, 323–324
web series, 297–299, 304
Webber, Pamela Merriam, 18
"Welcome to the Hellmouth" (*Buffy* episode), 98–99, 109
Wen, Ming-Na, 381
Wesley Wyndam-Pryce (*Buffy/Angel* character), 152–153
Wesleyan University, 30, 325, 383, 386
West Side Story, 22, 187
West Wing, The, 159
WGA vs. AMPTP (web video), 297–298
Whedon, Ann Lee Jeffries (mother). *See* Stearns, Lee
Whedon, Arden (son), 222, 366
Whedon, Burt Denison (great-grandfather), 9
Whedon, Jed Tucker (brother), 18, 32, 308, 314, 365, 369
and *Agents of S.H.I.E.L.D*, 379, 381, 383
and *Dr. Horrible's Sing-Along Blog*, 297–298, 304
Whedon, John Ogden (grandfather), 9–12
Whedon, Joseph Hill "Joss"
on aloneness and loneliness, 21–22
asked to write for Marvel Comics, 231–236
award nominations received by, 77, 159, 191, 243
awards and honors received by, 309, 324, 329, 380, 383, 385–386
birth of, 14
on cancellation of *Angel*, 241–242
on cancellation of *Firefly*, 221
childhood memories of, 16, 19

440 INDEX

Whedon, Joseph Hill "Joss" (*continued*)
  chooses nickname, 30
  and comic books, 20–21
  as director, 207, 250, 349, 351–353
  early education of, 22
  early employment attempts of, 37–38
  early television writing experiences of, 41–47
  on fantasy, 123
  first awareness of superheroes by, 18
  at High Stakes 2004, 252–253
  on his ensemble casts, 223
  and his understanding of the actors' craft, 346–347
  influence of *Close Encounters of the Third Kind* on, 26–27
  leadership style of, 108, 123, 128, 208–209, 351
  mugging of, 20, 40, 287
  on Muppets, 242
  pens Bible story sketch, 28
  performances of, 22, 169, 267, 308, 350
  on proposed *Buffy* reboot, 343
  rapport with writers, 129–130
  relationship with casts, 136
  relationship with parents, 14, 37, 60–61
  speeches at Wesleyan University, 325, 383–384
  at Wesleyan University, 30–34
  at Winchester College, 23–26, 28, 29
  writing idiosyncrasies of, 131–132
  writing impetus of, 3
Whedon, Matthew Thomas (brother), 13, 17–18
Whedon, Pamela Merriam Webber (stepmother), 18
Whedon, Roger (great uncle), 9
Whedon, Samuel (brother), 13–14, 17–18, 47, 170
Whedon, Squire (daughter), 255, 366
Whedon, Thomas Avery "Tom" (father), 6, 9–16, 18, 32, 37–39, 60–61, 274–275, 307
Whedon, Zachary Webber "Zack" (brother), 18, 297, 369
Whedonesque.com, 218, 287, 292–294, 298, 312, 317
  Joss announces withdrawal from *Wonder Woman* on, 276
  Joss comments on *Veronica Mars* on, 265
  Joss's posting of gratitude to fan base on, 375–376
  Joss's profile on, 252
  publicity for *Dr. Horrible* on, 304–305

Where the Sidewalk Ends (1950), 34
White House Commission on Presidential Scholars, 57
Whitford, Bradley, 321
Whoosh! The Journal of the International Association of Xenoid Studies, 257–258
"Why We Fight" (*Angel* episode), 239
Wight, Eric, 177
Wilcox, Rhonda V., 257–259, 302
Wild Bunch, The (1969), 213
Wilde, Oscar, 26
Will Eisner Award, 236, 283
Williams, Jesse, 322
Williams, Matt, 41
Williams, Olivia, 312, 315, 358
Willow Rosenberg (*Buffy* character), 92, 95, 100–101, 111, 135–136, 158, 159–161, 185, 192, 197–198
Winchester College, 23–24
"Witch" (*Buffy* episode), 105–106
Wolfram & Hart (*Angel*), 145, 154, 230, 238
Wonder Woman (character), 268–271
Wonder Woman (film project), 270–272, 275–277
Wonder Years, The, 40
Wonderfalls, 238
Woo, John, 52
Wood, Joe, 195
Woodward, Jonathan, 219
Woody (*Toy Story* character), 70, 73, 75
Writers Guild of America (WGA), 64, 66, 289–290, 294, 296
writers' rooms, 126–129, 150
writers' strike, 292–296

Xander Harris (*Buffy* character), 92, 95, 98, 100–101, 111, 119, 197–198
Xena (character), 88
Xena: Warrior Princess (TV series), 88, 258
X-Files, The, 88, 104, 121, 146–147, 152, 195, 212
X-Men (characters), 231, 331
X-Men (2000), 231, 330
X-Treme X-Men, 233
X2 (2003), 330

Yost, Graham, 64, 66–67
"You're Welcome" (*Angel* episode), 239–240

Zacharek, Stephanie, 191
Zoe Washburne (*Firefly* character), 201, 202, 204–205, 213